MW00425297

All the Kingdoms of the World

All the Kingdoms of the World

On Radical Religious Alternatives to Liberalism

KEVIN VALLIER

OXFORD
UNIVERSITY PRESS

Oxford University Press is a department of the University of Oxford. It furthers
the University's objective of excellence in research, scholarship, and education
by publishing worldwide. Oxford is a registered trade mark of Oxford University
Press in the UK and certain other countries.

Published in the United States of America by Oxford University Press
198 Madison Avenue, New York, NY 10016, United States of America.

CIP data is on file at the Library of Congress

ISBN 978–0–19–761137–1

DOI: 10.1093/oso/9780197611371.001.0001

Printed by Sheridan Books, Inc., United States of America

To young people considering illiberal ideas.

Again, the devil took [Jesus] to a very high mountain and showed him all the kingdoms of the world and their splendor; and he said to him, "All these I will give you, if you will fall down and worship me."

—Matthew 4:8–9 (NRSV)

CONTENTS

PREFACE

Liberal societies claim to advance human freedom and equality and resist building social life around a single religion. But today, an opposing clan of doctrines is on the rise. Call them *religious anti-liberalisms.* They claim that society should recognize a single religion as correct and they reject liberal order with intensity—and total conviction.

Twentieth-century politics focused more on economic conflict than religious conflict. Many thought that religion had become a private matter and would fade away. Yes, fanatics might sometimes intrude into secularized politics, but free societies would make quick work of these challengers. Sensible people could safely dismiss anti-liberals as theocrats, bigots, and fascists.

No longer. The twenty-first century has witnessed the revival of faith-infused political movements. Consider Russia, India, Poland, Hungary, Turkey, and China. Their anti-liberalisms sometimes arise from liberal imperialism and colonialism, as we see in Islam and Hinduism. Christian anti-liberalisms often appear after communism. Or they develop as a reaction to excessive church-state separation in liberal orders.

My book assesses the truth of these new anti-liberal ideologies. If you want to understand the case for and against them, this book is for you. I can't cover every version of these doctrines. But I show how to assess them without deciding which religion is true, if any. As a Christian, I see the attractions of these orders, but I also think highly of liberal society. Radical alternatives to liberalism have significant weaknesses. So I reject these doctrines, but I do not dismiss them.

Here I focus on the Roman Catholic anti-liberalism known as *integralism.* But I also address similar anti-liberal doctrines within Chinese Confucianism and Sunni Islam. By the book's end, I will offer you a framework for engaging these doctrines as a class.

Many people reject my project because they believe it addresses outlier views with no influence. So let me explain why these doctrines are on the rise, why they may stick around, and why we should engage them.

Introduction

Religion and Politics as Human Universals

Long ago, the great world religions governed the human race. Their power was limited only by one another. Hinduism, Confucianism, Buddhism, Taoism, Zoroastrianism (we mustn't forget the Zoroastrians), Judaism, Christianity, and Islam created great civilizations that infused human lives with sacredness and meaning. The great faiths shaped our laws, our morals, and our cultures. They crafted our art, architecture, and clothes; our homes, our weapons, our food; our language—even our thoughts.

These doctrinal faiths arose from a universal human tendency to religious belief. The great evolutionary psychologist Robin Dunbar writes, "For as long as history has been with us, religion has been a feature of human life. There is no known culture for which we have an ethnographic or an archeological record that does not have some religion."[1] Even in today's secular cultures, many people remain devout. Nations like the United States, which seem to secularize, might instead be in the process of rejecting Christian beliefs for a more eclectic spirituality.

Like religion, politics has been humanity's constant companion. Like religion, every society has it. How, then, should we expect average humans to approach political life? What are their political aspirations and needs, and how do they articulate their political ideas? For the vast majority of human history, religion helped answer these questions, and in many places, religion answered them in full.

Today many see religion as a private affair, but this view is peculiar. If you think your religion is true, it should *of course* shape political order. Consequently, it is more common for religion to be a purely public matter than a strictly private one. The human default is to form societies that interweave the sacred and the

---

[1] Dunbar 2022, p. xi.

All the Kingdoms of the World. Kevin Vallier, Oxford University Press. © Oxford University Press 2023.
DOI: 10.1093/oso/9780197611371.003.0001

secular. Societies that separate faith and politics are the outliers, so where did these societies come from?

Liberalism, Socialism, and Separation: Rise and Decline

The world began to change 250 years ago, first in Western Europe. Christian infighting and the birth of modern science created secular ideologies. The first we call *liberalism*. Liberals defend human freedom, human equality, religious toleration, and the fundamental harmony of human interests. They include left-liberals, who stress economic equality, approach religion in politics with skepticism, and stress the importance of using democracy to control the ills of the free market. But other liberals, whom we can call classical or right-liberals, stress economic freedom and de-emphasize social equality. They welcome religious influences in politics and highlight the self-regulating power of markets and the limitations of democracy with regard to improving economic outcomes. Nonetheless, liberals share the same underlying values, even if they express them differently.

The classical liberal tradition arose first, but liberalism gradually moved left in response to challenges from the next major political ideology: socialism. Socialists also preach liberty and equality, but they view society in more conflictual terms. They cast history as a contest between the oppressed and oppressors. Socialists also come in great variety. Some favor parliamentary democracy, while others insist that parliamentary democracy is a smoke screen for capitalist domination. Some favor change through reform, while others insist on social revolution. Yet they often share hostility toward religion. Consequently, democratic socialists approach religion in politics as liberals do, but Marxist socialists usually seek religion's annihilation.

Liberalism and socialism have fought established churches. Many have sought to privatize religion, and some have attempted to uproot it altogether. Liberals and socialists have often been religious themselves. But overall, they have sought to limit the role of religion in public life.

In the nineteenth century, liberalism and socialism colonized European elites. In the twentieth century, they divided the world between them and crushed the political power of the great world religions. Often socialists hunted religion to extinction. Liberals were gentler: they usually settled for a domesticated faith that prioritizes liberal values.

If religion is a human universal that invariably shapes politics, liberal and socialist victories were, at best, temporary. And this is what we see. Now that socialism has evaporated, the great religions recover their political expression.

Do not let the United States and Western Europe occlude your vision. Take a global perspective. You may know that many in Poland and Hungary trade liberal democracy for illiberal Christian politics. The Soviet Union was once the world's leading atheist federation. Today, Russia returns to Orthodox Christianity.

China contains a plurality of the world's atheists. But Xi Jinping has had to adopt Maoist methods to control popular religion. He has had to supplement flagging Marxism with Confucianism. The twenty-first century has seen a dramatic revival of Confucian thought.

Muslims have fought secularizing forces for decades, often with stunning success. Afghanistan and Iran are striking examples. Western liberal hopes for a "modern" Islam remain unfulfilled. Indeed, some Muslim regimes de-secularize. Turkey illustrates.

India shocks me. Its elite face a robust challenge from the Hindutva, the Hindu nationalist movement. One of the world's most ancient civilizations had adopted a mix of socialism and liberalism. India proved that Western political ideas had universal appeal. But today, it returns to ancient political form.

Human religiosity persists, and the many adherents of the great faiths have renewed their political ambitions. Liberalism alone prevents them from reconquering politics. A central question for twenty-first-century humanity is whether liberalism can succeed. Another question is whether it deserves to.

Liberalism in the Twenty-First Century

Today liberalism has become associated with abstract academic theorizing. Liberals obsess over esoteric debates about sex and gender that make no sense to most humans. The authoritarian leaders of the world have noticed, eagerly pointing out liberal insularity. Consider the bizarre spectacle of Russian president Vladimir Putin complaining that transgender activists have mistreated famed children's book author J. K. Rowling. Why does Putin care? He doesn't. He wants to delegitimize liberal order by drawing attention to its flaws.

The authoritarians of the world are on offense. They smell liberal weakness. But they must grapple with liberalism's historic achievements.

In most places, liberalism was a practical program of reform. Liberals sought to protect human liberty from concentrated and arbitrary power. Liberals promulgated religious toleration, challenged state absolutism, helped abolish slavery, and pioneered the liberation of women. Liberalism defeated fascism *and* communism, created the post–World War II human rights regime, and led late-twentieth-century fights against racism and sexism. Liberals helped lift billions out of grinding poverty by defending the market economy. Today's anti-liberals cannot say one nice thing about liberal order. But liberalism *delivers*.

Of course, we must not whitewash liberal history. Beyond their frequent intolerance of religion, liberals have taken up unjust causes—imperialism, colonialism, eugenics, and an indifference to the unborn. But in the main, liberals have made humans better off. And yet today, liberals no longer inspire. Fewer and fewer people claim their mantle, and many young people abandon liberalism for other doctrines. This situation is dire. If we lose liberalism, we may lose its achievements, and the rapid expansion of freedom, equality, and prosperity may reverse.

Liberals did not anticipate the challenges that followed the demise of socialism. For centuries many liberals have predicted the end of religion. Or they comforted themselves with the belief that religion would become private. Socialism enabled that illusion to endure. But if, as Dunbar argues, religion is a human universal, liberals face a grave global challenge. They must accept the permanence of religious belief and accommodate those who would give political expression to their faiths. And they must do so while preserving liberalism's concrete accomplishments.

To do this, liberals must shed their hostility toward religion. Millions of people of faith mistrust liberalism, viewing it as a covert but aggressive secularizing ideology. Liberals must dispel this suspicion or discredit themselves.

Robert Frost once said, "A liberal is a person who can't take his own side in a quarrel."[2] Nobody says that anymore. But that was the liberal promise: liberal order should be a diverse and open inquiry into better ways of living together. Liberals should reclaim intellectual humility and curiosity. They must engage those eager for liberalism to follow socialism into oblivion.

Why This Book?

This book is an attempt to practice what I preach. I take religious anti-liberalisms seriously. Religious anti-liberals have potent arguments. Their doctrines draw on the accomplishments of great civilizations and retain their capacity to generate intense political passion. While the anti-liberals are wrong, we must honor them anyway.

So I write to take liberals on a tour through these doctrines. But, I also reach out to those skeptical of liberal order. As a Christian and a liberal, I hope I can engage liberalism's religious critics.

We must not dismiss these doctrines as mere impulses or as hatred. Non-Marxist anti-liberalism, New York University law professor Stephen Holmes

---

[2] Quoted in Harvey Shapiro, "Story of the Poem," *New York Times*, January 15, 1961, p. 2.

argues, is "a resilient, diverse, fairly consistent, unbroken . . . intellectual tradition."[3] I deepen Holmes's claim. Religious anti-liberalisms draw on ancient and sophisticated theologies.

I cannot, of course, address all religious anti-liberalisms. I must focus. So I have chosen to concentrate on Catholic integralism. Integralism has intrinsic interest, but it also illuminates the strengths and weaknesses of religious anti-liberalisms as a class. What is integralism? Here is a gloss: Catholic integralists say that governments must secure the earthly and heavenly common good.[4] God authorizes two powers to do so, they assert. The state governs in matters temporal, and the church in matters spiritual. Since the church has a nobler purpose than the state (salvation), it may authorize and direct the state to support it with certain policies, such as enforcing church law. At times, the church may need assistance to advance its objectives.

This book has two goals: to assess religious anti-liberalisms in general and to assess integralism in particular. I argue at two levels: I build a case against integralism, and then I raise problems for religious anti-liberalisms as such. In the process, I compare integralism with its cousins in Sunni Islam and Chinese Confucianism. The book culminates in an *anti-liberalism framework,* a set of arguments that allow liberal and nonliberal readers to assess anti-liberal doctrines. The framework should help my liberal and nonliberal readers communicate.

A consequence of my focus is that I say almost nothing about liberalism, even though anti-liberals focus on criticizing it. Anti-liberals seldom defend their ideal since doing so raises awkward questions and requires shocking answers. But I want to know what they think and why they think it. So, in this book, *I will not defend liberalism at all,* save by criticizing its opponents. For all I say here, liberalism could be mistaken. None of my arguments presupposes liberal commitments. I have written in defense of institutional liberalism before,[5] but here I want to place religious anti-liberalisms under the microscope.

To My Three Audiences

Three groups have expressed interest in my project. The first group, liberals, might anticipate a horror story. After all, I claim that anti-liberal views are defensible and on the rise. Please don't read the text this way. I write to make religious anti-liberalisms more comprehensible.

---

[3] Holmes 1993, p. 3.

[4] Defenses include Waldstein (2016a), Pink (2018a), and Crean and Fimister (2020). For overviews of the position, see Schwartzman and Wilson (2019) and Brungardt (2020).

[5] Vallier 2019; Vallier 2020.

Today some people call themselves "postliberals" because they reject liberal values, though most accept liberal institutions such as constitutional democracy. Some postliberals cast about for an alternative, finding none.[6] They're searching for other options and doubt people with confident answers. They are not yet enemies of liberal order. They're merely on the fence.

Postliberals will find herein an assessment of radical religious alternatives to liberalism. I write to help postliberals assess these alternatives. But I also hope to dissuade them from opposing liberal institutions. Religious anti-liberals, again, face profound intellectual difficulties. If my arguments succeed, postliberals may conclude that liberalism is worth another look—or a first look.

Finally, I write to religious anti-liberals themselves. As noted, these groups often support an extensive state that adopts one of the great religions and shapes people to fit within that faith. Anti-liberals seek to alter or abolish liberal orders, and they oppose all liberal political and ethical theories. They are wrong to do so.

Since I focus on integralism, some readers may wonder whether this book is for them. I insist that it is. By examining integralism, readers can understand religious anti-liberalisms, so I encourage liberals and postliberals to stick around. You won't regret it. Integralism generates all manner of puzzles—philosophical, theological, political, economic, and legal. You will enjoy trying to solve them. I don't know anyone who finds the view boring once they understand it.

And while integralism is the least influential of the three theologies I examine, a new integralist movement is growing in the United States, and its unusual proponents have gained remarkable notoriety. Some of you are here because you want to read about them. I won't disappoint you in that either: I tell their story in Chapter 1.

Structure

After introducing the integralists and integralism in Chapter 1, I offer two arguments on their behalf. First, I review integralism's respectable historical lineage. I develop this *history argument* in Chapter 2. My second argument on integralism's behalf contrasts integralism with the new natural law theory, its closest philosophical and political competitor.[7] Natural law theorists believe

---

[6] Postliberals are diverse. They include followers of Leo Strauss, Protestant postliberals such as Stanley Hauerwas, Anglo-Catholics such as John Milbank, Eastern Orthodox writers such as Rod Dreher, and political scientist Adrian Pabst (see Pabst 2021).

[7] New natural law theorists include Germain Grisez, John Finnis, Joseph Boyle, and Robert P. George.

that governments should promote natural goods such as health and education but not spiritual goods such as salvation. The integralist disagrees: governments should treat these goods more symmetrically. Integralists have a point, which I develop into the *symmetry argument* in Chapter 3.

I then critique integralism, beginning with the main plan for reaching integralism—integration from within. I show that integration from within requires the violation of Catholic moral teaching. I also claim that integralism serves as a poor guide for social reform because it leads strategists in the wrong direction. This *transition argument* occupies Chapter 4. It addresses the most obvious objection to integralism—its manifest infeasibility.

Most readers will reject integralism if it cannot guide social change. But others want an ideal that inspires them, however impractical it proves to be. We may figure out how to reach integralism one day (this argument goes), so we must prepare. To address these integralists, I analyze integralism as a pure ideal.

Integralists say their ideal is a stable regime: a just and moral peace. But this is not so. Integralists justify their ideal by arguing that the fall injures our minds. Owing to sin, we cannot always distinguish right from wrong. Sinners will descend into profound moral disagreements—Babel born again. So I argue that integralism predicts disagreement, and future conflicts, that undo integralist order. The result? Integralist regimes will become repressive or decay into milder establishmentarian regimes. I defend this *stability argument* in Chapter 5.

Many will share the moral intuition that integralism is unjust since it allows governments to restrict religious liberty. The truth is more complex. Integralists have two inconsistent commitments concerning religious freedom: they oppose forced baptism, but they permit the state to punish Christians who dissent from dogma and leave the church. I claim that if justice requires the liberty to enter the church, it demands the liberty to exit. Chapter 6 develops this *justice argument*.

Chapter 7 assesses Confucian and Islamic anti-liberalisms. We can also ask questions about transition, stability, and justice within their theologies. I focus first on the Confucian constitutionalism of Chinese political theorist Jiang Qing and then turn to the Islamic Democratic ideal of the Tunisian politician Rached Ghannouchi. We will see striking similarities between these doctrines and note their related strengths and weaknesses. I argue that instability plagues Jiang's Confucian constitutionalism, whereas Ghannouchi's Islamic Democracy contains conflicting norms of justice.

A Framework for Discussion

An intellectual framework for engaging religious anti-liberals will come into view by the end of this book. We can use the framework to ask five questions of a particular religious anti-liberalism: Does the religious tradition support its adherents' politics? Which spiritual goods should the state promote, and why? How can any society transition into an anti-liberal regime—and at what cost? And can such a society be stable even if we reach it? Finally, can these governments establish justice, even on their own terms?

The purpose of the framework is to see whether liberals and their increasingly radical critics can have a conversation. Many on both sides are skeptical, some to an extreme. But I am optimistic. If liberals stop dismissing illiberal ideals, we might persuade our critics to help us uphold liberal institutions. The case for liberal institutions is sound, but we must make that case to diverse points of view, including nonliberal ones.

But first it's time to introduce integralism and, of course, the integralists.

1

Catholic Integralism and the Integralists

Pink's Quest

"My soul for *De legibus!*" I yelled from my Tucson office. It was 2007 and I was in graduate school, studying philosophy at the University of Arizona, and desperate to solve a problem: How should Christians think about the relationship between the good life and obligation? I thought that the philosopher and Counter-Reformation theologian Francisco Suárez had the answer, but there was no adequate translation of his work on the matter at that time.

That's why I had been delighted to learn about a new translation of Suárez's work. The book would include most of Suárez's famous treatise on law, *De legibus*. But there were delays. In my youthful impatience, I wanted the translator, British philosopher Thomas Pink, to hurry up.[1]

Little did I know that translating *De legibus* was not Pink's only project. He was on a spiritual quest to bring renewal to the Roman Catholic Church.

Surveying the empty husk of Western European Catholicism, Pink wondered what had gone wrong. What had happened to the Church? As a philosopher and historian, Pink had an idea. The Church had forgotten who she was, and she must be *reminded*. If she could remember, she might be reborn.

What sacred truth required recovery, according to Pink? That the Church is a *political order*: the Church creates law and administers grace to secure the salvation of the whole human race. Earthly polities aim to secure the earthly common good, but the heavenly polity is nobler. It saves souls.

The Church's salvific mission, then, is both spiritual and political at once. At minimum, the Church had long demanded independence from earthly

---

[1] Suárez 2015 is the magisterial, eleven-hundred-page final product.

All the Kingdoms of the World. Kevin Vallier, Oxford University Press. © Oxford University Press 2023.
DOI: 10.1093/oso/9780197611371.003.0002

government in matters of religion. Only God's representatives—the pope and his bishops—may govern the Church.

The Church, you see, had come to see itself as a voluntary organization, a sort of club. It recognized its goals as noble but did not consider itself sovereign over all other institutions. Pink found this odd. Christ is the King of the whole world, after all. As the nobler institution, the Church even has some authority over earthly governments to protect Christians from spiritual harm.

But Pink faced an obstacle. The Church had not only forgotten its history as a polity; it had set that self-understanding aside. In 1965, the Second Vatican Council had adopted and promulgated a declaration on religious freedom known as *Dignitatis humanae* (*DH*). This document discarded the Church's self-understanding as a polity and embraced a degree of religious liberty that endangered the Church's mission. If everyone has complete religious freedom, the Church cannot properly discipline and govern its flock.

Some Catholics had recognized this danger and gone into schism. They insisted that Vatican II had erroneously propagated *DH*. For Pink, division would not do. His goal became establishing *continuity* between historic and contemporary Church teaching; to his mind, the Church cannot set aside her identity as a heavenly polity. Her identity comes from God.

And so Pink developed a new interpretation of *DH* and began to spread it worldwide. Others often accompanied him in this endeavor, but Pink, more than anyone, saw resolving the tension as his mission.

Pink's work did not fall on deaf ears. He conducted two high-profile debates: first a written discussion with Catholic philosopher John Finnis and then a debate with Catholic theologian Martin Rhonheimer in person and in print. The new interpretation of *DH* was on the map.

Pink's passion comes with a love of philosophical inquiry and a richly British sense of humor. He appreciates the oddity of what happened next. Pink gave a lecture in Trumau, Austria, in 2012 that had massive ramifications.[2] A young priest, Father Edmund Waldstein, was in the audience, and he would turn Pink's torch into a bonfire.

Father Waldstein's Dream

Father Waldstein is the son of two Catholic theologians—a born-and-bred son of the Church. After spending most of his youth in the United States and

---

[2] Alan Fimister, one of the other leading integralist thinkers, organized the conference. Other integralists were in attendance, such as Fr. Thomas Crean. In some respects, integralism first revived in Europe.

attending Thomas Aquinas College in California, he had decided to become a Cistercian monk. Waldstein moved to a monastery in Austria to take up an intense series of religious duties.

Unlike his parents, Waldstein had political interests and felt that Catholics must oppose American liberalism. Indeed, even in college, Waldstein had begun formulating a critique of "Whig Thomism"—his term for American Catholic conservatism. His political interests continued to flourish even within the cloistered walls of the Heiligenkreuz monastery. But as a Cistercian and life-long Catholic, Waldstein had internalized a desire to obey the Church in all she commands. He knew the traditional teaching of the Church and opposed liberalism on that basis. But he had not quite figured out how to reject all liberal commitments. Among other things, *Dignitatis humanae* stood in his way.

As Waldstein listened to Pink, he became firmly convinced that *DH* has a nonliberal reading. If Pink was right, Waldstein could embrace anti-liberal Catholicism fully *and obediently*. *DH* no longer stood in the way of a principled and pious anti-liberalism. And so Waldstein and his friends got to work. Waldstein had joined Facebook in 2013 and began networking with like-minded Catholics across the world. He and others felt that Catholic traditionalists took an overly oppositional stance toward church leadership. The traditionalist attitude was counterproductive, they felt—even impious. The new Catholic illiberals would be something more, something nobler.

The new illiberal Catholics created a Facebook group, which in time moved to a private, live Slack chat. During this period the integralists planned and launched *The Josias* blog. The plan was striking. Blog entries were not simply chronological, but thematic. In time, the organizers thought, a manual of integralist thought would emerge from the posts. As of 2022, they have published two volumes of blog posts.

The blog developed a fan base and the ongoing Slack conversation gradually drew in some of these new fans, as well as figures from Twitter. Different participants in the Slack conversation developed diverse goals. Some wanted a more political approach to integralism—they wanted to make it happen. Others were content to think through what their faith required of them politically but not take immediate action. Through it all, Father Waldstein remained the gentle, pious, and passionate soul tying everyone and everything together.

Trump: A Time for Choosing

Waldstein succeeded—for a time, anyway. Each year, new and influential personalities entered the Slack conversation, and one man, political theorist Gladden Pappin, marshaled those inclined to make integralism politically relevant. I interviewed many people for this book. Almost all agreed that Pappin was critical in ensuring that the politically ambitious integralists won out. He began to manifest serious organizational talent, which he devoted to the cause. He also made the young community more unstable. In 2016, it shattered.

Many of the young integralists were quite left-wing economically, defending democratic socialism and Bernie Sanders's candidacy for the US presidency. They found Donald Trump repulsive—everything a Catholic should oppose.

Other integralists saw things differently. Trump had the world-historical power to displace the liberal consensus. If he commanded the American state, he could energize a new illiberal movement. Indeed, some lauded Trump as a new Constantine prepared to remake a pagan empire into a Christian one. The Trumpist integralists converted a group of friends into a radical political faction dedicated to turning the US government into a Catholic state.

Trump represented, for so many of us, a time for choosing, a turning point that set us all against one another. He empowered many strange groups, the integralists foremost among them.

The left-wing integralists, now a minority faction, became despondent: in their eyes, a once noble project now served dark ends. One told me that the Trumpist integralists are on a "demonic" path.

I cannot say what the Prince of Darkness is up to, but I can say that the integralists found a home within the intellectual stew created in 2016. They would even try to hijack the New Right. This process would amplify when a certain Harvard law professor entered the Slack conversation, though his initial role was passive. His time had not yet come.

Meanwhile, the European integralists watched with mixed feelings. The revival of integralism was exciting, but integralism mixed with American right-wing populism posed real risks. Still, few spoke out, preferring to focus on intellectual work. I started following the integralist movement in 2017. I found it amusing, creative, innocuous, and fascinating—I am no disinterested observer!—but I never expected it to grow.

Then 2018 gave integralists a right-wing stage—*and they used it*. In that year, Catholic intellectual history and American conservative history collided in the pages of *First Things*.

First Controversies: Mortara and French

First Things is the leading periodical for Christian intellectuals on the American Right. It has been for decades. From its founding until quite recently, however, the magazine usually defended Catholic fusionism ("Whig Thomism"). Its writers have used natural law theory to justify markets and limited government.

The founder of *First Things*, Richard John Neuhaus (1936–2009), defended the position, having come to it slowly. He found allies in Michael Novak (1933–2017) and George Weigel (1951–). But when leadership changed to R. R. Reno, the magazine's approach to liberal order shifted as well.

In February 2018, *First Things* published Father Romanus Cessario's book review of Edgardo Mortara's letters.[3] Edgardo, the son of Jewish parents, was born in the Papal States in the late nineteenth century, during the pontificate of Pius IX.[4] His Catholic caretaker baptized him as an infant when she feared he was on the brink of death. The law of the Papal States guaranteed a Catholic education to every Catholic. Upon learning of Edgardo's baptism, Pius IX thought that Edgardo's parents would raise him Jewish, which would break the law and deprive Edgardo of a Catholic education. So Pius IX removed Edgardo from his family.

The Mortaras vigorously and thoughtfully criticized Pius IX's actions, and Europe heard them. Pius IX had created an international uproar. But he held firm, raising Edgardo as his own child. Pius IX provoked those who disagreed with him, parading the boy in front of foreign diplomats who opposed his actions. Here is historian Eamon Duffy's recounting:

> Despite the serious misgivings of many Catholics, including the pope's own Secretary of State, the appeals of the family, of the Roman Jews, the intervention of the Emperor of Austria and Napoleon III of France, and the protests of the anti-clerical press, Pio Nono [Pius IX] resolutely rejected all pleas. . . . The pope's French protectors were so acutely embarrassed by the whole affair that the French ambassador seriously discussed with [Italian prime minister] Cavour the possibility of kidnapping Mortara and returning him to his parents.[5]

Despite this, Edgardo Mortara became a priest, and he died grateful, as his letters indicate.[6]

In his book, Cessario defended Pius IX, creating a conflict among *First Things'* readership. A few defended the kidnapping. If Pius IX had allowed the Mortaras to raise their son, they argued, then he would not have become a priest. Pius IX helped secure Mortara's salvation. Everyone else cited the manifest evil of

---

[3] Cessario 2018.

[4] Tapie (2018) provides a theologically informed review of the case and offers Thomists an opportunity to avoid defending Pius IX. If only integralists would take it!

[5] Duffy 2014, pp. 289–90.

[6] Duffy 2014, p. 290. For the memoir, see Messori (2017). For a compelling case that the memoir was fraudulently altered, see Kertzer (2018).

removing a child from his parents. The promise of salvation cannot legitimize breaking up a family.[7]

Another controversy also sprang from *First Things'* pages around the same time. In 2019, a young Iranian-American Catholic, Sohrab Ahmari, published "Against David French–ism," which attacked the political principles of the American conservative David French. Ahmari's piece exposed the new fault lines on the political Right. It inspired dozens of conservative think pieces.[8]

Some followed French in defending "right-liberalism." Conservatives should seek political success within the guardrails of liberal democracy, they argued, and they should pursue a peaceful resolution of the culture war. Ahmari found this naive: the "woke" left will not rest until the church ceases to exist, he contended. Religious conservatives have been fools for playing by liberal rules. The Right must fight fire with fire.

The controversy led to an in-person debate between French and Ahmari.[9] French, a trained lawyer, had argued before the Supreme Court. He prepared. Ahmari, in contrast, did not recognize the intellectual threat posed by his rival. He floundered. In doing so, he wounded his cause. The New Right would require more intellectual rigor to justify its existence.

Nonetheless, Ahmari made a critical argument consonant with integralist thought: societies should orient themselves around the authentic human good, even if others disagree. The position sounds intuitive. If Catholicism is true, why not make all institutions Catholic?

French defended liberal order as compatible with Christianity and argued that Ahmari exaggerated threats from the Left. But Ahmari was young—and in possession of a certain spirited charisma. His fight had only just begun. To this day, he claims that the spread of events like Drag Queen Story Hour vindicates him. He will undoubtedly lead future fights. Even his friends described him in the *New York Times* as someone who prefers to respond to conflict with a "Molotov cocktail."[10]

Around the time of this controversy, Ahmari appeared comfortable with integralism. However, he has said little on its behalf since then, and the term "integralism" does not appear in his latest book, *The Unbroken Thread*.[11] But he remains, after Adrian Vermeule, the most famous person associated with the

---

[7] I review the controversy in Vallier (2021b).

[8] My favorite balanced response is Anderson and George's (2019).

[9] "Cultural Conservatives: Two Visions Responding to the Post-Liberal Left" (event by the Institute for Human Ecology, Catholic University of America, September 5, 2019), YouTube video, 1:29:20, https://www.youtube.com/watch?v=fAG28K0nGAU.

[10] Schuessler 2022.

[11] Ahmari 2021.

view. Of course, without Adrian Vermeule, you and I would not be having this conversation. You may never have heard of integralism, and I may have seen only a flash in the pan.

The Rise of Adrian Vermeule

One of the most shocking features of the young integralist movement is that it converted one of the world's leading scholars of administrative law, Harvard law professor Adrian Vermeule. Vermeule converted to Catholicism around 2016 and quickly adopted integralism. He joined the integralist Slack conversation and would sometimes use Twitter to develop thoughts discussed in private. With time, he found a powerful digital voice.

By all accounts mild-mannered in person, Vermeule's social media presence nonetheless combines a rapier wit with a national reputation for blocking people by the thousands. Vermeule fused his intelligence, cleverness, and high social status into a fierce digital personality and became de facto leader of the new movement. Strikingly, Vermeule has little to say about integralism as an ideal. He has instead focused on transition theory—how we arrive at integralism— helping integralists develop a serious theory of the state and a theory of *state capture*.

Vermeule's rise came on the heels of another major intellectual event on the American Right: the publication in 2018 of political theorist Patrick Deneen's *Why Liberalism Failed*. Deneen provides an anti-liberal conservative critique of liberal ideals. According to Deneen, liberalism failed because it succeeded. Its perverse aim of constant liberation demoralizes and atomizes the populace. These aims manifest in left-liberal cultural crusades and right-liberal free-market crusades. Left- and right-liberalism enrich elites that cannot see their hegemony.

Deneen's conservatism prevented him from embracing integralism. Yet he strengthened the movement. His critique of liberalism proved influential, yes, but he also indirectly helped Vermeule solidify his status as leader of the integralist movement. For Vermeule would position integralism as *the* Christian alternative to liberalism. In his review of Deneen's book, Vermeule rejects localist answers to liberalism. Christians should indeed build strong religious communities to resist liberal elites.[12] To protect these communities, though, Catholics must dominate political life. They must take over the state and destroy liberalism from the top down, not so much with coercion but with other forms of persuasion and soft power.

---

[12] Vermeule 2018b.

Vermeule means business. Catholics must find "a strategic position from which to *sear the liberal faith with hot irons*, to defeat and capture the hearts and minds of liberal agents, to take over the institutions of the old order that liberalism has itself prepared and to turn them to the promotion of human dignity and the common good."[13] Vermeule's strategy, "integration from within," had been born. Integralists now distinguish themselves from all other postliberals, for they defend a radical ideal and have a plan to reach it.

These controversies have not earned integralism a good reputation, but they have put the view on the map. Vermeule seized an opportunity for ideological entrepreneurship. In large part owing to his efforts, the movement includes thousands of young, passionate Catholic anti-liberals. His movement remains small, but many know Vermeule and his views. Integralism has become a topic of intellectual conversation. The discussion has grown so intense that Oxford University Press sought someone to write about it. One day the invitation came to me.

In the meantime, Vermeule has ingeniously achieved three goals. The first: selling a synthesis of integralism and twentieth-century German legal theorist Carl Schmitt's critique of liberalism. Vermeule's movement has a unique spirit—deeply, self-consciously illiberal. Integralists often share Schmitt's view that politics is war and relish political combat.[14] Indeed, in their love for the fight, many integralists despise their fellow conservatives more than they despise the "woke Left." Yet integralism and Schmitt have no philosophical connection. One can accept integralism and reject Schmitt's views, and vice versa.

The second goal Vermeule achieved was to distinguish the integralist community from other Catholic traditionalists. Unlike other traditionalists, Vermeule expresses no strong preference for the Latin Mass over the *Novus Ordo*. Traditionalists criticize Pope Francis. Vermeule dissociates from integralists he finds overly critical.[15] This has been another ingenious move. Vermeule knows that the popes often mistrusted earlier integralist movements. Pius XI condemned Action Française in 1926.[16] By defending Francis, Vermeule ensures the viability of his movement. Yet integralists could condemn Pope Francis without contradicting their doctrine in the slightest.

---

[13] Vermeule 2018b, p. 2, emphasis added.

[14] Holmes 1993, pp. 39–41.

[15] In some respects, Vermeule's movement behaves like new ultramontanism. Ultramontanists defend enormous papal power. Some insist on the pope's impeccability (the absence of sin). For a discussion of the ultramontanist movement, see Duffy (2014, pp. 305–18).

[16] For discussion, see Hittinger (2007a, p. 17). Hittinger points out that the condemnation brought the great French Catholic political thinker and philosopher Jacques Maritain "out of his slumbers" on political matters.

The third goal Vermeule achieved was to connect integralism and American legal philosophy. While Vermeule is one of the world's premier scholars of the administrative state, he also works on judicial interpretation.[17] American conservatives think judges should read the Constitution according to its framers' intent or the text's plain meaning. Vermeule defends a non-originalist, non-textualist approach that directs judges to interpret the Constitution according to the common good.[18]

"Common good constitutionalism" will create a judiciary more open to religious establishment. Integralism fits tidily within common good constitutionalism because it offers an ancient, sophisticated conception of the common good. Vermeule's judicial philosophy may become a suitable vehicle for American integralism, but first he must displace the right-wing consensus.[19]

Catholics have enormous intellectual influence among right-wing elites: if integralists can convert them, they can rule. With one US Supreme Court justice, they can change constitutional law. Justices have spectacular power. Two-thirds of them are already Roman Catholics.

In my view, Vermeule is building a new anti-liberal elite designed to steer the New Right. By running a movement, the new elite can assail liberal order. This emphasis has become quite clear in Vermeule's new alliance with Deneen. Vermeule and his allies have transformed the integralist movement. Its fate now depends on the success of Vermeule's political plans, his team's ability to forge enduring political alliances, and the team's reputation on social media.

Integralism began as a movement for spiritual renewal, but today it labors under the yoke of a digital clique in search of political power. Pink, the movement's founder, surveyed the decimated Western European Church and devoted himself to reviving it. Vermeule, the movement's leader, observes the decay of American culture and fights to redirect that culture. The contrast is stark. Pink wants the church to *remember*; Vermeule wants the church to *rule*.

Here things stand in 2023. Despite setbacks in the 2022 midterm elections, the integralists soldier on by offering many on the New Right hope that they can defeat the Left—not just now, but forever. Their goal is *victory*, not compromise. Perhaps a new Catholic Christendom can arise from the ashes of doomed American liberalism.

[17] Breyer et al. 2017.

[18] Vermeule 2022a.

[19] I wrote this paragraph before the ruling in *Dobbs v. Jackson Women's Health Organization*, which handed the conservative legal movement the greatest victory of its entire existence, diminishing interest in and motivation for Vermeule's alternative.

Fissures

But fissures within the integralist movement have begun to manifest themselves. Many integralists have reservations about Vermeule's "big government"
integralism; these include Catholic historian Andrew Willard Jones. Jones
argues that integralism is a kind of post-sovereignty theory. Or perhaps it is a
pre-sovereignty theory. The integralist wants, in some sense, to do away with
the state in favor of a feudal order. Father Thomas Crean and theologian Alan
Fimister have their own integralism-based suspicions of the modern state.

Vermeule, Pappin, and others have decided that integralism requires
legitimizing illiberal states, which famously involves normalizing Hungarian
prime minister Viktor Orbán on the American Right. But Vermeule expresses
occasional enthusiasm for the Chinese government as well. Pappin, Ahmari, and
Deneen described China as a "civilizational equal" in the *New York Times*. Most
integralists know that China is a genocidal, anti-Catholic state, and they recoil
from the association between integralism and the Chinese Communist Party.

Today the integralist movement is led by a tight-knit group focused on political strategy. This group includes Vermeule, Pappin, Chad Pecknold, Pat Smith,
and now Deneen. Then there is a much looser confederation without political
ambition but rather interested in integralism as an ideal. This group includes
Pink, Crean, Fimister, Waldstein, and others.

I also already noted the ex-integralists, mainly from the Left. I keep their
names out of these pages, but they include foundational figures in the movement. While they defend aspects of integralism, they see the movement as ir-
redeemable. They think Vermeule, Pappin, and others have made the project so
toxic that they want nothing to do with it.

Theorists and Strategists

I have now introduced two integralist camps: theorists and strategists.[20] Theorists
defend the ideal while strategists pursue it. I will engage the strategists, because
part of assessing integralism is assessing integralists' political plans. However,
we will gain more insight by addressing the theorists. So this book engages the
theorists more than the strategists. The reason is that the strategists strive for the
ideal. If the ideal is defective, they should pursue other projects. Addressing the
ideal, then, addresses all integralists at once.

---

[20] Strategists include Vermeule, Sohrab Ahmari, Gladden Pappin, Chad Pecknold, and others.
The ideal theorists include Pink, Edmund Waldstein, Thomas Crean, and Alan Fimister.

While the integralist revival contains a dozen or so main characters, I will focus on two. I engage Pink as the chief theorist.[21] I shall address Vermeule as the chief strategist.[22]

Two Catholic intellectuals, however, play no role in this book. Patrick Deneen and Sohrab Ahmari are associated with integralism, but they say little about the view. Deneen shares integralists' disdain for liberalism, a disdain that he defends in his book *Why Liberalism Failed*,[23] but he has called integralists "crazy."[24] I suspect his conservatism rejects all radical ideals, integralism included. Deneen's work lies outside my book's scope.[25]

Ahmari seems to affirm integralism, but he says nothing about it.[26] And he has claimed that he does not want to make the United States into a Catholic country, which is not what you would expect to hear from an American integralist.[27] So I do not know how he would answer the questions I raise.

Vermeule and Pink have made profound intellectual contributions in other fields. Vermeule is one of the great scholars of American administrative law, and Pink is one of England's most accomplished philosophical historians. Here they receive sustained attention as the two leading lights of the integralist community. Later chapters highlight their differences. I now turn to explain integralist doctrine and the arguments made on its behalf.

The Integralist Narrative

Integralism, in my experience, appeals to two kinds of inclination. One is philosophical and theological, especially within the tradition of thought initiated by Thomas Aquinas. However, the most energetic integralists seldom draw out the political implications of some form of Thomism. In my experience, they are on an *adventure*. As Stephen Holmes notes, "nonmarxist antiliberals have a burning sense of *mission*."[28] These integralists see themselves as engaged in a cosmic, spiritual struggle. They view integralism as a narrative of salvation history, which explains integralism's appeal beyond certain Catholic philosophical circles.

---

[21] See Pink 2012b, 2013a, 2017, 2018a, 2020.
[22] See Vermeule 2017a, 2017c, 2018b, 2018d.
[23] Deneen 2018.
[24] "Closing Colloquy: Higher Powers Catholicism and the American Project" (Center for Ethics and Culture Fall Conference, "Higher Powers," November 9, 2018), YouTube video, 1:20:11, https://youtu.be/SVpiKpm6hDA.
[25] Indeed, Deneen could accept every one of my criticisms of integralism.
[26] The word "integralism" does not appear in Ahmari (2021).
[27] See Zerofsky (2021) quoting Ahmari: "I don't want to turn this into a Catholic country."
[28] Holmes 1993, p. 7, emphasis added.

I will for this reason provide the more active narrative of salvation history, and I will then explain integralist thought as philosophical theology. The next part of the chapter unfurls integralism as a kind of mythos; the rest conveys integralism as an abstract tradition of thought.

I start by speaking in what I take to be the integralist's voice, not my own.

The Church

In the beginning, God created the heavens and the earth (Gen. 1:1), including humankind, who fell from grace through sin (Rom. 5:12). We reject God. We refuse to unite with him. The consequence? We are subject not only to death (Rom. 5:12), but also to the devil (1 John 3:8)—the leader of the fallen angels and the governor of hell. The billions who have walked the earth, and (perhaps) the trillions to come, face the second death (Rev. 20:14).

Yet God did not abandon us (John 3:16).

He created a stiff-necked people (Exod. 32:9), the ancient Israelites, as his own. For two thousand years, he made them profoundly aware of their failings (Eccles. 7:20; Rom. 3:23), preparing them to receive and recognize Jesus Christ, the Word (John 1:1), the second person of the Trinity, conceived by the Holy Spirit and born of the Virgin Mary (Matt. 1:18–25). Jesus is the Messiah sent to forgive people of their sins (1 John 2:2) and lead them to eternal life (John 3:16).

The afterlife was not central to the Israelite faith, nor was conflict with the fallen angels. Jesus changed this. He expanded our understanding of heaven, hell, and spiritual warfare. Humanity is a battlefield; our fight is to love God with all our heart, mind, and soul, and to love our neighbor as ourselves (Matt. 22:35–40; Mark 12:28–31; Luke 10:25–28). We must imitate Jesus Christ (Eph. 5:1) in cooperation with God's promise of grace to all who believe (Titus 2:11).

Central to our story is the bride of Christ: the church he founded (Matt. 16:18). The earthly church is his army—the church militant—directed to spread the kingdom of God to all the earth (Matt. 28:16–20). Jesus gave the church the authority to teach (John 21:17), to forgive or to withhold the forgiveness of sins (John 20:23), and to dispense the means of grace (Matt. 16:17–20; John 21:15–17). He promised to guide the church until the end of the age (Matt. 28:20), ensuring that the gates of hell will never prevail against it (Matt. 16:18).

God structured the church hierarchically to keep it in fighting form. He appointed Peter as the first pope (Matt. 16:18), the general of the church, to govern in union with the other apostles and their successors (Acts 15). Jesus created the ruling body of the Catholic Church—the pope and the college of bishops. He ordained this hierarchy in the Gospels. It never changes. Time has only enriched and expanded it.[29]

All the Kingdoms of the World and Their Splendor

In the Gospel of Matthew (4:1–11), the Holy Spirit leads Jesus into the wilderness to be tempted by the devil. After Jesus has fasted for forty days, Satan tempts him three times. Recall the final temptation: "The devil took him to a very high mountain and showed him all the kingdoms of the world and their splendor; and he said to him, 'All these I will give you, if you will fall down and worship me.'"

The demons do not ignore human institutions.[30] They attempt to govern. And at times they rule. Ungraced polities, like their subjects, will sin, age, and die.

To establish the kingdom of God, the church must contest demonic rule and seek the spiritual governance of the entire world.[31] God instituted earthly political power for the good order of the human race, to punish evil and reward good (Rom. 13:1–4). But these mere human powers are too vulnerable to a relentless demonic assault. The church cannot abandon earthly rulers to stand alone against the darkness.

Governments, like their citizens, can be infused with grace—that is, divine favor. When the temporal order submits to the church in matters spiritual, grace flows through its veins—its law—teaching us right from wrong, leading us to repent of our sins, and sharing the sacraments that heal our hearts: baptism, confession, and the Eucharist chief among them. The church saves the polity from demonic rule.

The Ideological Enemies of the Church

The church has faced many enemies in its two millennia—the great heretics, Islam, persecution, and schism—but a new calamity befell the church in the sixteenth century: the Protestant Reformation.

---

[29] An overwhelming majority of Catholic theologians, officials, and apologists argue that Jesus's giving of the keys of the Church to Peter (Matt. 16:19) establishes the papacy as a divinely ordained position.

[30] Waldstein (2018): "Every part of the world has to be converted and exorcised in other to liberate it from demonic power. That includes political institutions." Pink (2018c) argues that this is magisterial teaching at the Council of Florence that "the unconverted world remains under the dominion of the devil." Crean and Fimister (2020, p. 263) say that "since the devil is the *prince of this world*, it follows that even were it not necessary for the temporal power to be subjected to Christ in virtue of His universal kingship . . . it should be done from simple prudence, as protection from a powerful and malevolent foe who would use every means to damn human souls" (emphasis original).

[31] Vermeule 2018b.

The Catholic Church is a spiritual military. The pope leads the church's spiritual soldiers by directing councils, cardinals, bishops, priests, and the laity. Each group has a unique authority and mission, but the final governing authority lies with the papal throne, as demonstrated by Scripture, tradition, and reason.

Unlike earlier heretical movements, the Protestant Reformers proposed a doctrine as pernicious as it was absurd—the priesthood of the believer.[32] Protestants interpret this passage as allowing individuals to determine for themselves what to believe by studying Scripture. In so doing, Protestants abolish the leader of the spiritual military, forcing each soldier to decide when and where to engage the enemy. By themselves, these soldiers cannot prevail.

Catholic theologians recognized from the beginning that this doctrine would destroy the working order of the church.[33] Protestants predictably collapsed into infighting and endless schism. Meanwhile, dark secular ideologies poured forth from the new cracks in Christendom.

The most virulent of these is socialism. The socialist seeks to transform the individual into a truly social being—one free from sin, hierarchy, and domination, who will join with others to create a new economic system organized cooperatively and planned scientifically. Socialist movements sought to liberate people from organized religion, Catholicism above all. Some socialists were friendly to Christianity, some even contributed to the common good, but these were always a minority. The socialist movements that came to power persecuted the church with unheard-of ferocity.

Socialism, however, has two weaknesses. Its unworkability is manifest and its opposition to the church unmistakable. This goes for Marxist socialism most of all. As soon as socialism reared its head, its days were numbered. It flourished for a few decades, killed millions, and died.

The elder child of the Reformation still lives, however, more patient and strategic than its little brother. Today it governs much of the world. It has even infiltrated the church. Its name is *liberalism*—the most successful enemy of the church in its history.

Liberalism takes the priesthood of the believer to its logical extreme. It asks each of us to make up our own minds about what matters most. Integralists seethe in response to Justice Kennedy's famous words in *Planned Parenthood v. Casey*: "At the heart of liberty is the right to define one's own concept of

[32] Protestants draw on verses such as 1 Pet. 2:9 ("But you are a chosen race, a royal priesthood, a holy nation, God's own people") and Rev. 5:10 ("you have made them to be a kingdom and priests serving our God"). For an early statement, see Luther ([1520] 2016).

[33] Bossuet (2018) develops an extended argument to this effect. I'm grateful to Edmund Waldstein for the reference.

existence, of meaning, of the universe, and of the mystery of human life."[34] People must reject the liberal claim that each person is a separate, free, and equal individual, born under the authority of no one, left to form political order with others by way of a social contract.[35]

As John Locke wrote in the *Second Treatise*, the natural state of humanity is one of "perfect freedom to order their actions, and dispose of their possessions, and persons as they think fit within the bounds of the law of Nature, without asking leave, or depending upon the will of any other man. A State also of Equality, wherein all the Power and Jurisdiction is reciprocal, no one having more than another."[36] The contract recognizes individuals' right to live their own lives in their own way. As John Stuart Mill (though not a social contract theorist) proclaimed in *On Liberty*, "The only freedom which deserves the name, is that of pursuing our own good in our own way, so long as we do not attempt to deprive others of theirs, or impede their efforts to obtain it. Each is the proper guardian of his own health, whether bodily, or mental or spiritual."[37]

Among liberalism's other doctrines: Liberals reject the fall of man, proposing that persons are originally and naturally good and rational, as Jean-Jacques Rousseau postulated in his *Discourse on the Origin and the Foundations of Inequality*.[38] Liberals march tirelessly into a glorious future of rational social progress, insisting on ever more egalitarian and "free" social forms, discarding the masses as unscientific and backward, marking them forever with social stigma.[39]

Liberalism ingeniously masks its own violence and sectarianism. That is its superpower. It stands above our conflicts, proposing procedures that can fairly resolve social disputes. Liberals dare to judge disputes between the church and its enemies, claiming impartiality even there. The liberal alone can serve as grand arbiter. The liberal alone is neutral.[40]

---

[34] 505 U.S. 833, 851 (1992), available at https://www.law.cornell.edu/supct/html/91-744. ZO.html.

[35] This is an unfair gloss on John Locke's doctrine in the *Second Treatise* (see Locke [1690] 1988). Locke's considered view is far richer and subtler. See Simmons (1994) for a stunning contrast with the brief presentation of Locke in Deneen (2018).

[36] Locke (1690) 1988, p. 269. That "within the bounds of the law of nature" bit should give anti-liberals pause.

[37] Mill 1978, p. 12.

[38] Rousseau 2018, pp. 115–93. For an exploration of liberalism's theology as Pelagian, see Nelson (2019). There is controversy over whether Rousseau was a liberal; I will not address that here.

[39] Vermeule 2017d.

[40] For a review of conceptions of neutrality in various figures, see Gaus (2009). Interestingly, integralists have been criticizing liberal neutrality for a while, even among American Catholics: "The state cannot avoid taking an attitude toward religion" (Ryan and Millar 1930, p. 30).

These are lies. The liberal is not peaceful. The liberal is not neutral. The liberal drags pious Christians out of their own story, as in a poorly acted movie, forcing them to compare the truths of Christianity with the myths of others. The liberal distances us from our values—from God—weakening our resolve and increasing our doubts.

The pious Catholic who seeks to govern pursues the divine mission of the church. We cannot delay in our quest to sanctify the governments of the world by bringing them into the kingdom of God. Christian soldiers must expose the pretensions of liberalism, refuse to distance ourselves from the faith, and wage spiritual warfare, both in our persons and in our polity.

Rejecting liberalism is sweet. The illiberal Christian can have honest debates about who has the right vision of the common good, about how to organize a Christian society. Such Christians no longer have to prattle on about how they have one "reasonable" view among others. They are free to take their own perspective and to draw everything and everyone into the kingdom (Matt. 28:16–20), just as the Lord directed.

The integralist promise: shed liberalism and pursue your values without apology.

The Allure of Integralism

Returning to my own voice, I hope you can see integralism's *narrative* allure. Liberalism, I admit, requires that people adopt restraints on their behavior that are, well, no fun. Liberals *do* demand that people take the perspective of others into account as they decide how to conduct their political lives. Liberals *do* say that we should refuse to coercively pursue our values when sincere and informed people contest them.[41] Liberals *do* insist on impartiality between different points of view. *Liberalism is burdensome.* The temptation to shed those burdens can be irresistible.

Integralists also draw energy from the seeming hypocrisy of left-liberal elites. The integralists tell us that the liberal elite demands the church's unconditional surrender. Liberals do not want to govern with those who think differently. They want to *rule.*[42] "Cancel culture" demonstrates the insatiable liberal desire for power and domination, among many other things. Conservatives often point out that left-wing elites don't practice what they preach. Vermeule has a famous retort: "It's not hypocrisy, it's hierarchy." Liberal elites are our betters; they play

---

[41] At least nonperfectionist liberalisms say this. Perfectionist liberalisms embrace this condition for religious disagreements, but not for most moral disputes. See Raz (1986) and Wall (1998) for discussion.

[42] Vermeule 2018b.

by a different set of rules. Get used to it. Vermeule and others claim that liberals will never rest until they dominate all social institutions. Christians must stop them by replacing them.[43]

The integralists have given a voice to young Christians, many of whom have grown up alienated from their institutions. These young people, often on the political Right, are not traditional small-government conservatives. They are not especially enamored of the Constitution, and they do not care about reading it according to original public meaning. They are not proud defenders of the market economy but demand a new American political order, one devoted to the spiritual care of the populace. They are not conservatives at all. We can better describe them as *counterrevolutionaries*.[44] Their first goal is to reverse the social revolutions led by Western elites, even with means that most everyone else rejects.

Integralists have also gained a hearing because American civilization seems on the decline. It is a cliché but true: we live in a polarized age. We trust each other less and hate each other more. Our values seem under attack, support for democracy erodes, economic progress has stalled for many but expanded for others. In rural parts of the country, most indicators of social progress have reversed.[45]

While these trends have created great hostility to liberal order, integralism offers the alienated something positive: an ultimate goal, a vision, a dream. This is why integralism is the premier radicalism on the New Right. For many young people, integralism has supplanted free-market libertarianism. The goal is no longer individual freedom, but a radical spiritual overhaul of the country, until liberals find themselves an irrelevant minority. Indeed, the most prominent integralists now style themselves postliberals. They have seen through the lies of liberal order and forge something new.[46]

The Elements of Integralism

Integralism departs radically from modern political thought.[47] Moderns begin political theory from reassuringly sanitized and austere principles of freedom and equality.[48] But one cannot understand integralism apart from revelation and the theory of the church.

[43] Deneen 2020.
[44] De Maistre 1995, pp. 77–105.
[45] Carney 2020.
[46] This rebranding is unfortunate. Most postliberals oppose integralism.
[47] Pink 2020.
[48] Gaus, Courtland, and Schmidtz 2018.

Integralists nonetheless boil their doctrine down to philosophical fundamentals—and so will I. Let's begin with what makes integralists Catholic and end with what makes them unique. Here I continue speaking in my own voice and not on behalf of Catholic integralists.

Catholic Social Teaching

God is not merely perfectly good; God is goodness itself.[49] As Jesus said, "No one is good but God alone" (Mark 10:18). Anything good partakes or "participates" in the divine nature (see 2 Pet. 1:4).[50] All human choices—even bad ones—aim at some good.[51] My choices have an ultimate goal: my flourishing, which the ancient Greeks called *eudaimonia*. Plato and Aristotle agreed with Jesus that God is the good. Eudaimonia consists in contemplating him.[52]

Plato and Aristotle thought God self-absorbed: since God is so great, he thinks only of himself. Jesus revealed that our relationship with God is not so one-sided. Eudaimonia consists in an intimate union with God, a union of love and mutual indwelling.[53]

God unites with us through generating his law and enabling us to follow it. But Christian tradition conceives of God's law differently than we normally do. When we use the term "law," we generally mean one of two things: human laws, which tell us how we *should* act, or laws of physics, which tell us how we *do* act. But not so long ago, people spoke of "law" in both senses at once: natural laws describe both *how* we choose and how we *ought* to choose.[54] How could this be? After all, we can disobey a rule we should follow, but not one we must follow.

The idea of a law that is both natural and breakable may strike you as odd. But the idea made perfect sense to many for more than two thousand years. Creatures with free will—and only such creatures—can act against their natures. Not for long, though: the consequences are too severe. How many fingers do we have? Ten. But not every human has ten fingers. I could cut one of mine off. But that violates my nature, and I will suffer for it. I would be making a mistake. It is natural for us to have ten fingers, so we should not cut them off.

---

[49] Stump and Kretzmann (1991) explain the sense in which God is goodness. Yet they distinguish this from God being the form of the good.

[50] Russell 2004, p. 77.

[51] This claim stretches back to the ancient Greeks. See Aristotle (2000, 1094a1–2).

[52] For an excellent new translation of Aristotle's theology and doctrine of God, see Aristotle (2021).

[53] Stump 2018, p. 118.

[54] Murphy 2011.

Today, many conservative intellectuals love to play detective. They seek the criminal who stole natural law from our collective consciousness. Some blame George Edward Moore;[55] others blame David Hume[56] or Martin Luther.[57] William of Ockham, a Franciscan friar from fourteenth-century England, endures the most abuse.[58]

I don't know what happened. But what you need to know is that the Christian idea of law tells us both what we do and what we ought to do.

Eternal law is the highest; it directs all creatures to seek good and avoid evil. God creates and promulgates the eternal law by being goodness. God then creates beings that can choose the good, and the eternal law applies to them.[59] The eternal law does not depend on divine commands; rather, it is the immediate logical consequence of God's existence.

The natural law is the eternal law applied to material creatures with a free and rational will: human beings. It directs us to choose what we have good reasons to choose. God makes natural law by forming human nature; our nature determines what is good and bad for us. Good choices fit our natures; bad choices distort them.

Natural law directs us to pursue goods that help us flourish as humans. These include bodily goods, such as health; relationships, such as friendship; and virtues, such as courage.[60] A good human life secures these natural goods. Reasoned reflection reveals the natural law to us: we can identify certain general rules that, when followed, secure natural goods. These rules usually have exceptions, but some do not. The natural law prohibits unnatural and wicked acts. We must not misuse the body or kill the innocent.[61]

---

[55] Moore 2004. The standard interpretation of the "naturalistic fallacy" claims that normative statements cannot derive from nonnormative ones. If we are more careful, the fallacy involves defining the "quality" of good by other qualities (see Moore 2004, p. 9). I thank David Gordon for discussing this point.

[56] Hume thought it impossible to derive moral claims from descriptive ones (Hume 1978, p. 469).

[57] For a more accurate discussion of Luther's nominalism, see Stern (2020, sec. 3).

[58] The standard story is that Ockham paved the road to modernity by denying the existence of universals. This denial undermines the idea of human nature, a nature that explains our objective good and our final end. Denying human nature undermines the notion of natural law in turn. For a richer and more accurate discussion of Ockham's nominalism, see Spade and Panaccio (2019, sec. 4.2). And for a masterwork undoing many misunderstandings, see Marilyn McCord Adams (1989) on Ockham. For the most famous attempt to blame modernity on nominalism, see Weaver (2013).

[59] I work from Mark Murphy's summation of Aquinas's doctrine of natural law from here forward. Murphy (2011, sec. 1) contains all the relevant citations. See also Finnis (1998).

[60] These basic goods continue to feature in modern natural law theory (see Murphy 2001; Finnis 2011).

[61] Finnis (1991) discusses the natural basis for absolute moral prohibitions.

God did not intend for humans to be alone: we are a hypersocial species. Humans form and flourish only in groups: first families and then tribes and villages. We even create cities, states, and empires. Natural law establishes what is good and bad for members of these groups. But it also determines the good for each group as a whole—the *common good*.[62] The common good accrues to the group and its members, but it is not diminished thereby.[63] An effective criminal justice system is good for the community and for its members. We profit from it together without loss.

Humans act from our reason, yet we disagree about what is best. We need an authority to harmonize our choices and orient them toward the common good. We also fall: we willfully break the natural law. We deserve punishment. For these reasons, God institutes governments for human communities (Rom. 13:1–4). And governments create positive law—law as we commonly use the term. Governments have authority when they resolve ambiguities in the natural law and when they help us follow it.[64] The positive law thereby advances the common good of the community. When the positive law completes the natural law, we must obey it.

Contemporary Catholic social thought stresses the importance of the common good.[65] But it contains moral principles, chief among them the dignity of the person as made in God's image.[66] As free, equal, and rational creatures, we partake in the divine nature by being what we are. Our God-likeness makes us inviolate; we owe one another respect and honor akin to that which we owe to God.

Our individual dignity also limits legitimate positive law, and laws that violate dignity aren't laws at all. Any legitimate government must advance the common good and respect human dignity.

The common good and human dignity ground human rights.[67] To have a right is to say that the right-holder is entitled to a certain good.[68] A right to dignified work means that government must supply everyone with a decent job. The Catholic Church embraces many such rights. These include the right to

---

[62] For a classic discussion of conceptions of the common good, see Murphy (2005).

[63] Murphy calls this the "distinctive good" conception of the common good.

[64] Finnis 2011, pp. 231–53.

[65] Catholic Church 1997, pp. 464–66.

[66] Catholic Church 1997, pp. 424.

[67] Hittinger 2008. A minor branch of integralism departs from Vermeule by preferring local communities over the state (see Jones 2020). This strand is consonant with the micro-integralist society I noted above.

[68] Hohfeld 1919.

healthcare, the right to vote, and freedom of religion.[69] Catholic social thought claims that governments exist to protect universal human rights. The church has not set natural law aside, though. When we talk about human rights, we thereby talk about natural law.[70]

The doctrines I have thus far discussed are those a person can determine through ordinary reasoning. The following doctrines require divine revelation; no one can infer them without divine guidance.

Again, we have a fallen nature: we are inclined toward sin. But, through Jesus Christ and his church, God heals our fallen nature. This regenerative process begins with our baptism. Through baptism, God gives us a great gift. We gain better access to our natural flourishing and become aware of our ultimate, supernatural end: eternal loving union with God. To offer this gift to all, God grants his church the authority to make law for His children—canon law.[71] The church uses canon law to articulate dogma and advance its mission. Canon law assigns rights and responsibilities to the church's members.

God authorizes governments to protect the temporal common good. But God has authorized the church to protect the spiritual common good. The spiritual common good consists of a corporate union with God. By joining the church, we become part of Christ's bride in an eternal marriage (John 3:29). This good is common because it accrues to the church and its members and *amplifies* thereby. God fashions us into his dwelling place by healing our sin and sanctifying our souls. And the more, the merrier.

The church insists that governments protect its right to pursue its mission, including preaching the gospel everywhere on earth. It also claims rights over its members, such as the right to discipline them for sin. Punishments range from minor penances to excommunication.[72] But the twenty-first-century church does not call on states to add civil penalties to its spiritual ones.

The church preaches free faith. Natural law prohibits forced baptism and precludes baptizing a child against the parents' will.[73] States may not prod people into any religious activity, even to save souls. The church affirms a universal right of religious freedom. No earthly government has the authority to coerce for religious purposes. While the church directs governments to follow natural law, it tolerates religious error among the unbaptized.

---

[69] Catholic Church 1997, pp. 444–69. Many Catholic classical liberals stress that the right to these goods is the right to receive them through private charitable organizations, such as the Catholic Church.

[70] Finnis 2011, pp. 198–200. For a helpful discussion of how personal dignity and the common good interface, see Mary Keys's (2008) work on Aquinas the common good.

[71] See canon law section below for much more explanation.

[72] See Catholic Church 1997, p. 368.

[73] For discussion of the relevant canons, see Tapie (2018).

Thomas Aquinas provides the foundations for these central claims, starting from his theory of the natural and eternal law.[74] But Aquinas draws on both Aristotle and Saint Augustine. One of Aquinas's aims was to combine their insights into a single system. Aristotle provides theories of human nature and virtue[75] while Augustine contributes his synthesis of Neoplatonism and Christianity[76] and his views on sin and grace.[77] These ideas may have inspired Aquinas as much as Aristotle did.[78]

Nearly all integralists are Thomists, so they too draw on Aristotle and Augustine. However, their influence passes through the work of later Scholastics. Here, as we will see, Francisco Suárez and Robert Bellarmine loom large.[79]

I mention these interpretative details only to set them aside. Here I have space only to identify the elements of integralism, not to trace their lineages. Fortunately, others tell the historical story better than I could.

Religious Freedom Disputed

Today church leaders believe that religious freedom extends to every human being. They base this right on human dignity and our duty to pursue the truth about God. The church defends this comprehensive right of religious freedom in *Dignitatis humanae*.[80] The standard reading of *DH* claims to revive the early church teaching about free faith, implying that the medieval church often forgot to protect this ancient liberty.[81]

Integralists claim that the standard interpretation of *DH* contradicts earlier church teaching. They point to encyclicals of Pope Pius IX (especially *Quanta cura* and its appendix, *The Syllabus of Errors*) and Pope Leo XIII (especially

---

[74] Aquinas 1920, I–II, q. 93 and q. 94.

[75] Perhaps most famously, *The Nicomachean Ethics* (Aristotle 2000, 1097b22–1098a20) contains Aristotle's famous *ergon* or function argument about the content of human nature and the conditions for human flourishing. Though describing Aristotle as a natural law theorist is controversial, pointing out that this argument shaped natural law theory is not controversial at all.

[76] See Augustine's *Confessions* (2009, 7.13), where Augustine describes the influence the "books of the Platonists" had on him. The "Platonists" included, among other figures, Plotinus, whose views on the immateriality of God and the superiority of the unchangeable derive from Plato (see Plato 1997, *Timaeus* 28d). A full list of influences is provided in Tornau (2019, sec. 4).

[77] For how his doctrine of sin changed his ethical theory, see Augustine (1998, 19.4). For one interpretation of Augustine's moral theory developed, see Wolterstorff (2012, pp. 180–206). Paul is Augustine's greater influence. Augustine's mature view of grace can be found in *Ad Simplicianum* 1.2.

[78] For an extended discussion of Augustinian themes in Aquinas, see Dauphinais et al. 2007.

[79] Key texts I explore below are Francisco Suárez ([1612] 2015) and Bellarmine (2012, 2016).

[80] Paul VI 1965a.

[81] Rhonheimer (2014) outlines the case for the standard reading.

Immortale Dei), as well as to a canon from the Council of Trent (defined in 1562).[82]

Theologians see an *apparent* tension between Leo's teaching and Vatican II's. Most resolve the tension in a *DH*-first direction. They follow the lead of John Courtney Murray, Jacques Maritain, and Saint John Paul II.[83] They argued that Leo XIII's integralism permits recognizing universal religious freedom. Leo XIII defended integralism only to resist sectarian, anti-Catholic liberalism. But Catholics may reject his particular institutional judgments.

Integralists resolve the tension in a Leo-first direction. They interpret *DH* so that integralism remains the political ideal.[84] A tiny minority of theologians and high-ranking church officials take this approach.[85]

Some fifteen years ago, Pink began developing a Leo-first resolution of the tension.[86] *DH* recognizes a right of religious freedom only against secular governments. *DH* calls them *human* powers. Our dignity prohibits states from abridging religious freedom. Given its spiritual foundation, the right to religious liberty transcends all human authority, and every human power must respect it. But the church is *divine* power. *DH* never denies that the church has authority over its subjects. It may excommunicate heretics, for instance. *DH* does not address church authority. And so it also does not address whether the church can license the state to punish its members. While the church no longer calls on states to advance its mission, it could reverse course.

Pink's reinterpretation made the integralist movement possible. If Pink is correct, Catholics can adopt integralism and remain in good standing with the church, and Catholics disillusioned with liberalism can embrace an anti-liberal ideal.

Pink's interpretation permeates the integralist movement, and so in this book I assume he is correct.[87] If Pink is incorrect, either integralism conflicts with

---

[82] I discuss these teachings in more detail in Chapter 2.

[83] Murray 1993, pp. 199–219; Maritain 2012, chap. 6. Saint John Paul II gave many speeches on this matter. For one of the most famous statements, see John Paul II (1995).

[84] Pink 2017.

[85] For discussion on this point, see Lefebvre (1994). Archbishop Lefebvre famously rejected *DH* as heretical, stressing that the council that promulgated it was pastoral, not ecumenical. The new Catholic integralists distinguish themselves from Lefebvre and his followers in the Society of Saint Pius X (SSPX), which he founded. Integralists see themselves as combining traditional Catholicism with pious obedience to the Church as she is and see SSPX as engaged in schismatic or near-schismatic behavior. The Catholic University of America maintains an archive documenting the history of SSPX.

[86] Pink appears to have presented his view first in public draft in 2008, eventually published as Pink 2012b.

[87] Waldstein (2014) declares for Pink, as do Crean and Fimister (2020, p. 108n14).

authoritative church teaching or *DH* is not definitive. Either way, integralists must take issue with their church, and they hope to avoid doing so.

For Pink, the church must not tell the state to restrict the liberty of the unbaptized. Jews and Muslims, for instance, have rights of religious freedom against all governments, including integralist ones. Historical integralist regimes repressed religious minorities, but integralists agree that such repression was unjust. The church can, however, call on the state to punish all baptized persons. Note that non-Catholics, such as Orthodox and Protestant Christians, often have valid baptisms. The population of the baptized is far larger than the population of Catholics.

While the state should protect the religious liberty of the unbaptized, it should also protect the baptized from spiritual harm.[88] These duties can compete: the unbaptized could use their religious liberty to degrade Christian spirituality. So far, integralists have articulated no principle that resolves this conflict. But the proper resolution is of the first importance. Suppose the state prioritizes prohibiting spiritual harm. It might suppress the religious rights of non-Catholics. Yet if it prioritizes the unbaptized, it could endanger the souls of the faithful. The state also allows religious diversity, placing integralism close to liberalism. Integralists can embrace a repressive regime or a lax regime.[89]

Goodness, Authority, and the Ideal

Eternal law, natural law, and positive law—sacred and secular—draw everyone into God's embrace. According to the integralists, integralist societies alone harmonize this holy legal quartet. But how shall we define integralism?

Contemporary integralists seldom tell us what integralism is a theory *of*. It might be a theory of the political good—what is good for the human community. It might be a theory of authority—when the state and the church have the right to rule. It might be a theory of the ideal regime—what kind of government a society should optimally have. Integralism is, in fact, a theory of all these things, but we must define each of its parts. And before we do that, we must revive its theoretical contrast from modern political theory.

---

[88] This is a clear implication of Pink's interpretation of *DH*.

[89] I call these two regime types *thick* and *thin* integralism (Vallier 2021a). Thick integralism errs in the direction of protecting the church; thin integralism errs in the direction of protecting the unbaptized.

Two Polities

Modern political philosophers see their subject as focused on the theory of the state. According to modern political thought, society has only one final political authority: secular (i.e., non-ecclesiastical) government. But integralism is a *two-polity* political theory. According to integralists, society has two supreme political authorities: the church and the state. The church is an ecclesiastical polity, a political community like other political communities. The church is no mere voluntary association within a social order, but a political society with direct divine authority over its members. Indeed, the great historical integralists insist that the church is a *perfect society.*[90] It has all the power and rights it needs to secure universal salvation.

For centuries in Latin Christendom, two-polity political theory was dominant. And this form of inquiry continued down through Thomas Hobbes and John Locke. They are pivotal historical figures because they helped create *one-polity* political theory. Both argued that society properly has one ultimate authority: the state.[91] For Hobbes, the sovereign is the head of both church and state.[92] For Locke, the church is merely a voluntary association and has no central role in governance.[93]

Integralists reject one-polity political theorizing. It treats the church as equal to any other social organization. Since the church is the only perfect society, it is the center of social life, or should be. And so they hark back to the two-polity political theorizing of centuries past.

Political Values

Integralists contend that state action must advance the natural common good. The state has the right and the duty to promote the natural good of the individual and community. The church has the complementary right and responsibility to promote their supernatural good. Finally, the church will sometimes need help achieving its mission. If so, integralists contend, the church may direct the state to assist it. It must enact policy and impose civil penalties. Integralism's moral standard is the whole common good: natural and supernatural, temporal and eternal, earthly and heavenly. A society that ignores the spiritual is inferior to one that supports it: "The spiritual and eternal interests of men are surely

---

[90] Bellarmine 2012, pp. 269–77. Leo XIII 2014, p. 112. Most nonintegralist Catholics also consider the Catholic Church a perfect society.

[91] Or, more aptly, the people have one ultimate representative: the state.

[92] See Hobbes 1994, books III and IV.

[93] This is a theme of *A Letter Concerning Toleration* (Locke 2009).

more important than their material and temporal interests; therefore, the society which deals with and promotes the former is more exalted than the society
which cares for the latter."[94]

Political Authority

The integralist theory of authority is arguably a theory of the right to rule. In general, if A has the right to rule B:

- A is morally permitted to coerce B to follow A's directives;
- B has a moral duty to follow A's directives; and
- A may create new directives, creating new moral duties for B.

In one-polity political theory, A is the state and B its citizens. But in integralist
theory, matters are more complex. Both church and state have the right to rule
in their own domains. The church's subjects are the baptized, whereas the state's
subjects are ordinary citizens. Any baptized person is under the authority of both
the church and the state. But integralism also postulates a right-to-rule relation
between church and state. The church may deputize the state to help advance its
mission. In that case, A is the church and B is the state. So, in an integralist society, there are *three* rights to rule. The church has the right to rule the baptized,
the state has the right to govern its citizens, and the church has the right to direct
the state in a confined range of cases.

These three rights to rule originate in divine sovereignty. Only God has the
ultimate or original right to rule. By assumption, everyone is under God's authority. So God can give his authority over humans to social organizations. For
integralism, God authorizes church and state, and the church may extend its
God-given authority to the state.

Political Ideal

For the integralist, any good society contains the church and the state. The state
can be democratic or monarchical—in short, God can authorize a king directly
or authorize the people to choose a constitution and rulers[95]—but church

---

[94] Ryan and Millar 1930, p. 39.

[95] Direct and indirect authorization of the secular polity have had their day in the Church. See
Ryan and Millar (1930, p. 26–7): "Ruling authority, divinely sanctioned, comes into existence as a
necessary consequence of the nature and end of human beings." Indeed, they claim that Suárez held
the following view: "the natural law directly received from Almighty God by the people, and thence
entrusted to the rulers of the State by constitutional consent." See Ryan and Millar (1930, p. 79). For
similar passages in Suárez, see Suárez [1612] 2015, p. 105; see also pp. 419–20, 432–33, 438–39,

structure is fixed. Whatever form the state takes, an integralist regime is one where the state submits to the church. Without submission, the government is not integralist. Such submission also implies a certain degree of integration between church and state; their constitutions, laws, and procedures aim at a certain harmony. Society is thus dually governed: it has a governing *dyarchy*.

The ideal integralist government is a *successful dyarchy*. Church and state effectively advance their aspects of the common good. When they join forces, they tend to achieve their shared goals.

Two moral imperatives apply to us all: we must advance the common good and obey divine commands. If the common good and divine commands require integralism, we should establish it. Or, rather, we should establish it when we can, while observing the constraints of natural law.

Definitions

We can now define three related integralist theses about the political good, political authority, and the political ideal:

1. The *complete political good*: Political order must advance the whole common good, temporal and spiritual.
2. *Compound political authority*: God authorizes and commands (which I will combine under the term "directs") church and state to each advance their part of the common good. God also grants the church the authority to direct the state to assist it in fulfilling its mission.
3. The *political ideal*: The best regime includes the partial subordination of the state to the church, which together form a dyarchy that successfully promotes the whole common good.[96]

Ideal Background Conditions

Assessing integralism requires specifying the social conditions under which integralism is morally appropriate. Historical integralists defended integralism for overwhelmingly Catholic societies with rich Catholic cultures. But is

---

441–43, 446, 449—that is, III.1.3, 2.4, 3.6, 4.1, 4.5, 4.8. For a review of Suárez's contractarianism, see Campos (2019).

[96] Pink has argued that integralism is also a theory of how states function; it is a theory of what states do and how they tend to flourish, stabilize, and decay. I focus on integralism as a normative theory in this chapter, but I address what Pink has to say about integralism as a theory of state function in Chapter 5.

integralism an ideal for other kinds of communities? Integralism's great Catholic critics, such as John Courtney Murray, have used this ambiguity to argue that integralism is, at best, an ideal for particular societies.[97]

Murray reasoned as follows. We cannot classify a community as Catholic if we know only that most people endorse Catholicism.[98] Other dimensions of evaluation matter, especially quality of faith.[99] Integralism cannot apply to a society composed of nominal Catholics. Integralist coercion might create an apostasy cascade—Catholics abandoning the church en masse because others have already defected from the faith.

Murray inferred that Catholics must give up integralist ideal theory.[100] He was wrong. Integralists can add a quality measure to the ideal by defining the ideal society as containing mostly observant Catholics. In a society that pious, we ought to establish the integralist ideal.

The integralist ideal is inappropriate when most members of society are unbaptized. There is a theological reason for this. Catholic theology supposes that everyone has a supernatural purpose: union with God. Some Catholics believe we have this purpose by nature. Yet, without God's aid, we neither know this purpose nor have the supernatural virtue to pursue it. If a community contains only unbaptized persons, they cannot see their supernatural purpose. Even a perfectly rational agent cannot infer the truths of revelation without God's help, though such a person can infer God's existence.

Unbaptized people cannot see integralism as rational from their own perspective, so they will see little moral reason to obey an integralist regime. Integralist order stabilizes owing to its observant Catholic citizens, since grace regenerates their reason. Catholics stabilize the regime when they act as natural law directs. Going forward, then, we can see that integralism is an ideal for all human beings, but one that should not be established in a non-Catholic society. A Catholic monarch in a rich institutional union with the church should not rule a society of Confucians. Society must become Catholic first.

---

[97] Murray 1993, p. 112.

[98] Even as traditionalist and integralist a theorist as Archbishop Marcel Lefebvre (1994, p. 93) argues that popes "condemned the separation of Church and State only in so far as it is a doctrine and in its application to the nations that have a *Catholic majority*." Pink, while no Lefebvrite, agrees on this point: Thomas Pink, "Reconciling Integralism, the Magisterium, and the Modern World," interview by Charlie Camosy, *The Pillar*, September 2, 2022, https://www.pillarcatholic.com/reconciling-integralism-the-magisterium-and-the-modern-world/.

[99] Murray 1993, p. 99.

[100] "It is time now to drop the categories of thesis and hypothesis completely out of the Catholic vocabulary" (Murray 1993, p. 214).

Catholic Integralism Defined

I can now provide a formal definition of integralism, one that combines its distinctive theses about the political good, political authority, and the political ideal. In this definition I offer a formal description of the set of integralist regimes. I combine key integralist theses into one schema that allows for variation across five variables (G, C, S, P, E). Box 1.1 lists the three principles of Catholic integralism.[101] I will use this formal characterization throughout the book.

The first two principles should be clear. We must expound on the third principle. The simple claim is that the church can direct the state to install policies and punishments to advance the ends *of the church,* within some limits. The church has, at best, *indirect* authority over the state.

Hence principle 3's historical name: the *indirect power.* I take the title from Cardinal Bellarmine's theory of the *potestas indirecta.*[102] Bellarmine provides the most famous defense of the indirect power, posed as a middle way between defenders of the direct power and those who reject even the indirect power.

Direct authority implies that the church can direct state activity in general, but the church has never defended a claim to the direct power, which some call *hierocracy.* Some popes have thought they had direct power. Innocent III (in office 1198–1216) illustrates. Historian Francis Oakley reads Pope Boniface VIII

Box 1.1 **Catholic Integralism Defined**

1. *Natural authority*: God directs the state to advance the natural common good, G, of a community, C.
2. *Supernatural authority*: God directs the church to advance the supernatural common good, S, of all baptized persons in C.
3. *Indirect supernatural sovereignty*: to advance S and only for this reason, the church may mandate state policies, P, backed by civil penalties, E, that advance S directly (i.e., not merely by advancing G) without excessively undermining G or S in some other respect.

---

[101] I'm grateful to many people for helping me refine the definition, including Will Combs, James Dominic Rooney, Xavier Menard, Zac Gochenour, Christopher Fleming, Bryan Cross, Tyler McNabb, and Tim Pawl.

[102] Bellarmine 2016, book 5, chap. 6.

similarly.[103] But the church has never dogmatized their claim and may well have dogmatized its denial.[104] Recent church teaching has confined the church's temporal authority to addressing spiritual affairs.

As Jacques Maritain puts it, the indirect power is a right to intervene in temporal affairs. Power over temporal affairs covers only moral and spiritual interests.[105] My definition above defines the indirect power as concerned with supernatural "interests."

Before I continue, I should set aside the most well-known definition of integralism. A popular blog post uses three sentences to define integralism:

> Catholic Integralism is a tradition of thought that, rejecting the liberal separation of politics from concern with the end of human life, holds that political rule must order man to his final goal. Since, however, man has both a temporal and an eternal end, integralism holds that there are two powers that rule him: a temporal power and a spiritual power. And since man's temporal end is subordinated to his eternal end, the temporal power must be subordinated to the spiritual power.[106]

As the preceding discussion demonstrates, this definition misleads. Catholic teaching, in general, rejects separating politics from the end of human life: political rule must respect the natural law, and natural law directs us to our final goal.[107] Catholic political theologians agree that we have both temporal and eternal ends and that God authorizes two powers—church and state—to promote their respective common goods. Catholics agree that the supernatural good is higher than the natural good. They also agree that spiritual power surpasses temporal power.

Integralism is unique because it interprets superiority as *rule*—legal and political superiority.[108] Superiority entails that the church may direct states to enforce canon law via civil law (more on this later). They may then prosecute canonical crimes, such as simony and heresy. The church is the "soul" that animates the "body" of the state: the church initiates, and the state responds.[109] But one

---

[103] Oakley 2012, p. 191–2. Maritain, by contrast, denies that Boniface VIII was a hierocrat, arguing that hierocracy was an innovation of some thirteenth- and fourteenth-century theologians (Maritain 2020, p. iv).

[104] Oakley 2012, p. 182.

[105] Maritain 2020, p. vii.

[106] Waldstein 2016b.

[107] Maritain 2012, pp. 147–87. Murray affirms these principles in many essays (Murray 1993, pp. 97–100).

[108] "For Leo XIII, authority is rule," whereas for Vatican II, "authority is service" (Murray 1993, p. 221).

[109] Leo XIII 1885, p. 114.

can interpret superiority more broadly to mean having "a higher place in the scale of values, a higher dignity," avoiding any "connotation of domination and hegemony."[110]

The blog post definition also runs together several matters which must be kept separate. A good definition should distinguish between values, authority, regimes, and ideals.

The Diversity of Integralist Regimes

My broad definition of integralism conveys the vast range of possible integralist regimes. For instance, I allow the common good to vary significantly in form and content. Integralists might adopt John Finnis's definition of the common good, according to which the common good does not surpass the good of persons in the community.[111] Others say the common good surpasses the good of each person.[112] The church defines some of the content of natural and supernatural common goods, but church doctrine can accommodate some variation in accounts of the common good.[113]

The integralist ideal specifies no societal scale. The ideal might be a federation of nations, a position Vermeule adopts.[114] Or one could set a low population ceiling, no more than ten thousand persons. The range of policies and punishments also lies open. Integralists could favor a narrow set of policies and light penalties for violations. Banning bad books might not figure into the integralist policy toolkit.

The subordination relation is also indeterminate in several respects. Do duties of submission occur naturally or arise by agreement? We do not know. Perhaps the state comes under church authority whenever exercising such power becomes feasible: the state is under church authority as soon as the right preconditions occur. Alternatively, the church and state may need to establish submission through a treaty.

This question seldom arose for the great historical integralists. During the time period I shall call High Integralism, European rulers were baptized. Further, their kingdoms were their private domains—much like their possessions. Feudal submission to the church is not mysterious. If King John submits to the church, he also submits his possessions. But modern societies operate differently because they distinguish sharply between offices and officeholders: the United States is

---

[110] Maritain 2012, p. 153.
[111] Finnis 2011, pp. 154–56.
[112] Murphy 2005.
[113] Catholic Church 1997, part 3, chap. 1, art. 2; chap. 2, art. 2.
[114] Vermeule 2019c.

not the personal fief of President Biden. I am thus unsure how state submission would awaken in a modern democratic state.

Another ambiguity: the state can support the church in many ways. State support goes beyond coercive force. The Christian state made "its jurisdiction available, for religious ends."[115] The authoritative powers of the state involve many tools, such as the provision of information and moral leadership.

Penultimately, and critically, integralism is compatible with a democratic state. Nothing in the natural authority condition precludes it. Some integralists think monarchy the best form of government, but not on integralist grounds. Indeed, one can see the case for constitutional democracy arise as early as the sixteenth century, when some Thomists developed a "translation theory" of authority according to which God vests political authority in the body politic, who then vest it in a constitutional order.[116] And once Pope Pius XI died in 1938, "the translation theory had triumphed within most of the schools and eddies of neo-Thomism."[117]

Finally, the integralist ideal leaves open the percentage of observant Catholics in their ideal social order.[118] The ideal might only need 51 percent—or maybe it needs 95 percent. The percentage matters. It bears on how to establish integralism and whether integralist regimes can stabilize. I address these matters in Chapters 4 and 5, respectively.

Envisioning Integralism: Law and Policy

Integralist regimes can vary greatly. That is one reason why we struggle to imagine them. Another source of confusion is that some features common to integralist regimes are unfamiliar to most readers. In my view, we can best envision an integralist regime if we understand its special use of canon law. Integralist orders put canon law at the center of social life. Canon law can even affect public policy, since the church may help shape legislation—say, legislation regarding education and mass communications. So, to imagine an integralist regime, let's explore the complex idea of canon law. I will build up to integralist public policy.

[115] Pink 2021.
[116] Hittinger 2007a, p. 19. For Bellarmine's proof text, see *De laicis* III.6.
[117] Hittinger 2007a, p. 19.
[118] Catholic citizens recognize that most others are Catholics. They agree on their underlying unity as a church.

Definition of Canon Law

Integralists claim that the church may authorize the state to help enforce church law, also known as canon law. In one sense, everyone wants the state to enforce some of the church's laws: consider marriage contracts or property titles. Modern states may enforce the church's own internal rules when these rules become relevant to civil legal disputes. Integralists distinguish themselves by the subset of canon law they want the state to enforce. Integralists hold that governments may punish perpetrators who violate canon laws that orient the faithful to salvation. Canon law, for instance, prohibits heresy, which can destroy charity (love of God) in the soul. Heresy invites damnation. Accordingly, integralists want the state to punish heresy with civil penalties if church penalties prove ineffective.

To be more precise, integralists want the state to use its own civil law to support the enforcement of canon law or at least to avoid undermining canon law. Most directly, the state could make it a civil crime to violate canon law (by, for instance, prohibiting heresy). The state should not enforce canon law directly. Such an act would constitute arrogation, because the state would usurp church authority. In the integralist ideal, the state shapes its civil law to support canon law and the purpose of canon law. The goal: make canon law more effective. The integralist envisions two interwoven bodies of law—civil law and canon law.

To understand integralism, then, we must understand canon law. I am no canon lawyer, so my summary must stay at the surface level. But it should prove adequate to understand and evaluate integralism.

So what is canon law? Definitions abound. Here is a classic statement from Italian jurist and legal scholar Vittorio Del Giudice. According to Del Giudice, canon law is "the set of juridical norms, laid down or adopted by the competent organs of the Catholic Church according to which the church itself is organized and operates and by which the activity of the faithful is governed, in relation to the purposes proper to the church."[119] Let's understand *juridical norms* as legal norms. They are binding rules that a legal system issues to achieve its aims. Along the same lines, canon laws help the church accomplish its purpose—the corporate salvation of the whole human race. These norms govern all the faithful and only the faithful, here understood as the baptized. And they necessarily order us to our supernatural end: eternal union with God.[120]

The body of secular law orders us only to our natural end: that is, it helps us flourish in an earthly sense. But canon laws serve the church's nobler purpose.[121]

---

[119] Errázuriz Mackenna 2009, p. 33; Giudice 1970.

[120] Errázuriz Mackenna 2009, p. 143. See also Corecco 1992, p. 137.

[121] Errázuriz Mackenna 2009, p. 212. Canon law also serves more mundane, temporal purposes, such as enforcing certain contracts between church members. But the church's earthly goals are necessarily ordered toward spiritual goals. The church has spiritual ends by nature, and its temporal ends

Canon law is the highest law governing the human person and the ultimate source of social order. Integralists would restore canon law's exalted status.

I have turned to integralist philosophy of law—what integralists think the law is.[122] Integralists have recently put much thought into the nature of law, and not only because they are led by a law professor. Integralists think that Catholics must recover a "natural law" theory of law, according to which positive law exists only when it orients social life toward the true human good. One cannot identify law with social facts—the laws on the books. Some immoral and unjust practices resemble law, but they are not law, because they conflict with divine and natural law. Thus, what positive law *is* corresponds to what morality *requires*. At minimum, law may never contradict true morality.

Canon law is the same, according to this view: you cannot grasp what counts as canon law by reading the *Code of Canon Law* alone. The code can be mistaken. Any part of it is mistaken if it frustrates the church's aims.

Instead, what counts as canon law depends on justice and the common good. Integralists often speak of *ius*. This Latin term can refer to legislation or to a "moral faculty of requiring something [right]."[123] *Ius* incorporates into one complex term a considerable part of integralist doctrine: namely, that what law is depends partly on what morality requires. This concept provides the background for Augustine's famous but oft-misunderstood dictum that an unjust law is no law at all.[124]

Thus, the aim of canonical legal institutions is not merely to enact legal norms but to evaluate practiced norms on the basis of a broader legal order of divine origin.[125] According to canonist Carlos José Errázuriz Mackenna, canon law addresses "what is just in the church." The moral and theological foundations of canon law must be plain. A positivist approach to law will not do.

Canonical Legal Authorities

The church not only has law, it *makes* law. But who makes church law besides God? Initially, church councils were central sources of canons, which took the form of conciliar legislation.[126] Bishops would gather, deliberate, and collectively

---

are intermediate ends toward those spiritual ends. States, by contrast, have only worldly ends by nature. They can also have spiritual ends, but only via integration with the church. I thank a friend for discussing this point with me.

[122] For a review of the different philosophies of canon law, see Errázuriz Mackenna 2009. Errázuriz Mackenna defends a rich natural law approach congenial to integralism.

[123] Aquinas 1920, II–II, q. 57.

[124] Augustine 1993, bk. 1, ch. 5.

[125] Errázuriz Mackenna 2009, p. 99.

[126] Rennie 2018, p. 21.

issue canon law.[127] Subsequently, canon law acquired many functions and became the possession of the entire clerical class.[128]

Beginning in the eleventh century, popes expanded their legal, judicial, and administrative powers, such as by designating other church officials to serve as legates.[129] Popes also enlarged the ecclesiastical court system.[130] In time, the church and its jurists began collecting canon law in detailed sourcebooks, starting with Gratian's decretals (the *Decretum*) in the twelfth century and its promulgation in the thirteenth. Scholasticism then gave canon law even more precision.[131] Once collected and promulgated, canon law became a vital public good and shared resource: priests, monks, bishops, and others could use it for specific purposes.[132] The consequence was that canon law governed social life. Medieval canon law in particular "had as much influence on the daily life of Europeans as secular law has on life in the modern world."[133]

During the same period, the church expanded its use of a legal document known as the papal decretal. A papal decretal is a letter that rules on some matter of canon law. Decretals could make or interpret canon law. They could also rule on disputed questions and assign punishments to violators.

The centralization of papal power gave decretals enormous influence.[134] Indeed, in the Middle Ages, the pope took "a central role in law-making and law-giving." The pope became the "chief author of the canons."[135] By the twelfth century, papal decretals had reached the same level of authority as conciliar canons.[136]

Integralists think that governments should reinforce some conciliar legislation and papal decretals. They affirm the church's supreme legal authority, and they would make such authority palpable for entire societies.

Sources and Types of Canon Law

Canon law has two sources: God and the church. In other words, canon law involves the action of God and the action of human persons. Canon law includes

---

[127] Humfress 2022, p. 26.

[128] Rennie 2018, p. 18.

[129] Popes claimed many of these expanded powers before the Middle Ages, but institutional developments in the Middle Ages made these powers much more effective.

[130] Winroth and Wei 2022, p. 3.

[131] Winroth and Wei 2022, p. 4.

[132] Austin 2022, p. 46.

[133] Winroth and Wei 2022, p. 1.

[134] Rennie 2018, p. 26.

[135] Rennie 2018, p. 26.

[136] Rennie 2018, p. 27.

the natural law. But it also includes divine positive law, since God can make further law at will. God also created the church to publicize and enforce that law on its members. Whereas divine law remains general, the church makes law by applying divine law to concrete contexts—the church makes law, then, by *determination.*

Consider marital law. If God has instituted marriage—and God had the power to not do so—then canon law includes the law of marriage. Similarly, canon law includes specifications of marriage law. Suppose the church allows only Catholics over the age of eighteen to marry. Here, canon law specifies God's will for marriage. If the church decrees that eighteen-year-olds may marry but not seventeen-year-olds, it *determines* marital law.[137]

Remember: integralism recognizes the church as a polity. Indeed, it claims that the church is the noblest polity. So the church must have law and legislative authority (the capacity to make or unmake law). But the source of canon law is God. God issues the natural law through his reason and divine positive law through his will. Canon law recognizes, promulgates, and specifies divine law, natural and positive.

And so the church recognizes four types of canon law for its members. These include the natural law, divine positive law, and church determinations of both.[138] But all four varieties orient the baptized toward salvation and communion with God.

Some laws serve multiple roles. For instance, Christian natural lawyers treat the Ten Commandments as natural laws. But God also enacted them by divine will, and he orders humans to observe them, so the Ten Commandments are also divine positive law.

Canon Law That Integralists Would Enforce: Heresy and Apostasy as Illustrations

Integralists, almost alone among Catholics, want states to enforce specific canon laws (via civil law). But which canon laws? Let's answer this question by considering the criminalization of heresy and apostasy. The 1983 *Code of Canon Law* defines *heresy* as follows: "the obstinate denial or obstinate doubt after the reception of baptism of some truth which is to be believed by divine and Catholic faith." It defines *apostasy* as "the total rejection of Christianity by a baptized person who, having at one time professed the Christian faith, publicly rejects

---

[137] Note that the natural law state also operates by determination. Here church and state run parallel.

[138] Errázuriz Mackenna 2009, pp. 258–59.

it."[139] A heretic rejects one or more Christian doctrines but remains loyal to Jesus Christ. An apostate abandons Jesus completely.

Laws concerning heresy and apostasy illuminate integralism because neither is a natural crime.[140] That is, according to Catholic teaching, one cannot detect the wrongness of heresy or apostasy by natural reason alone, because natural reason cannot verify the Christian faith. So integralists want the state to help enforce canon laws beyond the natural law: this is the commitment that separates them from almost all other figures in Catholic political thought.

Now, some ecclesiastical crimes are also natural crimes. Most medieval authorities considered heresy threatening to the spiritual *and* secular order, so they held that the state could punish heretics on natural grounds.[141]

Enforcement and Punishment

Canon law can also set policy in an integralist order—for instance, by dictating the curriculum for religious instruction. More on this below. But to understand integralism, we must explore how integralists would enforce canon law. Integralists are not champing at the bit to use state coercion for spiritual ends.

Like secular law, canon law assigns rights to those accused of an ecclesiastical crime, including the right to a fair trial. Also—and this is important—the accused have the right to a canonical trial. The church conducts trials with its own courts. Beyond that, the church has the right of refusal to try canonical criminals. For the integralist, the modern state would serve as backup, for the church is nobler. Sometimes the church would instruct the state where the state lacks the competence to determine violations.

If the church finds Reba guilty of a canonical crime, it will punish her. Church punishments are spiritual and therapeutic.[142] For instance, the court may assign Reba certain penances. By accepting her punishment, Reba will do her part to

---

[139] Code of Canon Law 1983, canon 751.

[140] Another crime that requires state support is schism. Schism occurs when a member or group of the faithful creates division within the church. Integralists would have states help prevent or end a schismatic act. A fourth crime—one with some real complexities—is blasphemy. Some blasphemies are natural crimes, since reason alone can determine that God exists. Or so Catholics believe. But other blasphemies, such as blaspheming the Trinity, are spiritual crimes. We know the Trinity only by revelation.

[141] Müller 2022b, p. 329 outlines how states could punish heretics. Other work indicates that heresy was the worst of canonical crimes. That was why heretics sometimes received "extraordinary" prosecution. Sometimes prosecutors could use torture to secure confessions. For a detailed discussion of the legal rights of heretics, see Fudge (2013). For further discussion of medieval criminal law, see Kéry (2022).

[142] Punishments also have an educative function. The church teaches the faithful by enforcing divine law, natural and positive. The baptized learn about moral and spiritual reality.

repair her relationship with God. The church thus punishes with an eye to the salvation of souls. However, if penances do not deter Reba from future crimes, the church may excommunicate her to protect the faithful from the spiritual damage Reba could cause. Still, excommunication comes with the hope that Reba will repent and reform.

Now suppose that excommunication fails. In that case, especially if the canonical criminal threatens public order, the church may direct the state to impose civil penalties. Or, rather, it will direct the state to do so where the civil law allows.[143]

This order of juridical procedure fits integralist theory. The church has the nobler purpose, so it has the first right to enforce its law. Also, the church can protect the faithful from the state. If the church finds Reba guilty and she reforms, the state lacks the authority to punish her. If the church finds no grounds to convict Reba of a canonical crime, the state certainly lacks punitive authority. The church calls on its "secular arm" chiefly when the canonical justice system fails to deter a convicted criminal.

In the late medieval period, penalties came in five varieties. Two affected all church members: excommunication and interdict.[144] Excommunication deprives a baptized person of the sacraments, centrally the Eucharist, and may also impose exile or other forced separation from other Christians. Interdict suspends the spiritual benefits of the church, such as participation in most sacraments, but it does not sever one's relationship with the church. The person under interdict does not lose all the rights and privileges of church membership.[145]

Either punishment may apply to large groups. Popes once placed entire cities under interdict and excommunicated whole nations.

From Law to Policy

The church may use its law to enact policies and instruct the state to enforce them, both directly through state activity (coercive or noncoercive) and indirectly by punishing violations (which, in many cases, follow the directives of an ecclesiastical court). But now let's turn to the types of distinctively integralist public policies that integralist regimes will make.

---

[143] Fr. John Kimes notes that civil and canon law have interacted in a variety of ways. The relationship between them has varied even within Catholic confessional states. The relationship I describe prevailed in the late Middle Ages. With time, strong kings reshaped that relationship, but we can focus on the late medieval arrangement because it best exemplifies integralist ideas.

[144] Müller 2022b, p. 339. The other three—suspension, deposition, and degradation—apply only to ordained clerics.

[145] Clarke 2022, p. 550.

Education

Integralist states control education. Baptized children have a right to Catholic education, even against their parents' will.[146] The government may direct schools to teach Catholicism to baptized students and may prohibit baptized children from attending non-Catholic schools. (It could close even home schools.) Education might extend into adulthood through mandatory religious practice. The dyarchy may force the baptized to attend Mass to expose people to the gospel and teach them the liturgy.

Communication

Integralist states must protect the baptized from temptation, which could require controlling mass communications.[147] Integralist states will ban or restrict heretical ideas. Given citizens' costless communication via the internet, integralist states will have to spend significant resources to surveil the populace. They might adopt a policy like China's Great Firewall.

Containment

Integralist states must thwart social movements that violate church teaching, including heretical movements among the baptized, such as Protestantism.

Deposition

Monarchs posed grave threats to historical integralist regimes. In response, the church deposed heretical monarchs and monarchs who tolerated heresy.[148] Sometimes this policy worked; other times not so much. Twenty-first-century integralists must contend with democratic officials. The church has no procedure for deposing them and has never attempted it.

Since democratic states foster pluralism and cycle through leaders, integralist democracies cannot stabilize.[149] Indeed, the possibility of an integralist democracy raises a host of odd questions. President Biden is Catholic. Can Pope Francis depose him for supporting abortion rights? Integralists can avoid these

---

[146] Recall the Mortara incident.

[147] I assume that the church would create a new, digital *Index librorum prohibitorum*.

[148] See canon 3 of the Fourth Council of the Lateran, discussed in Chapter 2. I leave open whether deposition may occur without a constitutional pact allowing it.

[149] One could have a regime with competing integralist parties: the administration would remain integralist yet cycle through leaders. But that supposes a degree of consensus unlikely to occur even in the Catholic ideal (see Chapter 4). I thank David Gordon for discussing this point.

problems by opposing democracy, as they sometimes do. But other regimes invite other problems.

Integralist states may tolerate sin and heresy, but only if suppression will do more harm than good. Again, practically speaking, integralist governments may resemble liberal ones. Indeed, some integralist regimes may be more tolerant than some liberal regimes.[150]

Why Integralism? The Quick Case

The quick case for integralism is the case for its three central principles (see box 1.1). The natural and supernatural authority conditions suffuse Catholic social thought, so I do not need to defend them here. So the case for integralism is the case for the indirect supernatural sovereignty condition. I will review four intuitive reasons to adopt it.[151] I expand upon these arguments in the following five chapters.

Integralists defend the indirect supernatural sovereignty condition on at least four grounds. The first defense draws on dogma and tradition. The church practiced integralism for centuries, or at least it attempted to do so. And it has supported integralism for centuries longer than it has embraced liberal institutions. Great theologians and popes defended integralism, such as (some contend) Saint Thomas Aquinas.[152] Great integralists have included theologians such as Francisco Suárez and Cardinal Bellarmine. More importantly, the list contains many popes, especially those of the late nineteenth and early twentieth centuries: Pius IX, Leo XIII, and Pius X. I explore this point in Chapter 2.

Twentieth-century Catholics often proposed liberal work-arounds to address the historical dominance of integralism. Some of these are insightful; I will address them in Chapter 4.[153]

---

[150] An integralist regime could adopt liberal constraints for its own reasons. For instance, the regime might recognize that the church is currently unable to conduct ecclesiastical trials effectively, and so the regime might observe liberal religious freedom norms. In that case, liberalism and integralism might overlap—a problem for my definition. I have two replies. First, I am defining integralism as an ideal, so I think I am free to assume that the integralism-in-liberal-clothing option applies integralism to unfavorable circumstances. Second, the integralist regime would act for very different reasons than the liberal regime, so it could be distinguished on that basis as well. I thank Christopher Eberle for discussing this.

[151] For a related approach to defining and defending integralism, as well as an original argument for the permissibility of religious coercion, see McNabb 2022, pp. 33–42.

[152] Despite Finnis (1998, pp. 228–31), Aquinas's *De regno* (2014, pp. 89–103) places him in the vicinity of integralism. Also see McCormick 2022.

[153] Murray is the most innovative. See the essays in Murray 1993.

The second defense of indirect supernatural sovereignty is the social kingship of Christ.[154] Christ's reign is not limited to individuals, families, civil society, and the church. It extends to every human institution, including political ones. Indeed, as two Catholic authors put it, "To deny these propositions is to maintain the illogical position that man owes God religious worship under only one aspect of his life, in only one department of his life."[155]

Since Christ rules through the church, the church must govern states, at least insofar as their activities bear on its mission. Nonintegralist Catholics will respond that human dignity prohibits religious coercion of the baptized. I explore different aspects of this reply in Chapters 2, 3, and 6.

The third defense relies on the Catholic distinction between nature and grace. Sin corrupts nature; grace—God's unmerited aid—heals it.[156] Grace also reveals a more excellent end: eternal loving union with God. Without grace, we fall victim to sin and never grasp our higher purpose. The same is true of the state. Sin corrupts the state, and grace heals it. Grace also reveals that the state has a nobler end: to help the church prepare its subjects for heaven. Without grace, the state will fall victim to sin. It will never grasp its higher purpose. And it will rule through fear and oppression.

The fourth defense also draws on the nature-grace distinction. Integralists argue that we can grasp the natural law only in a state of grace. Otherwise, our knowledge of the natural law degrades. But by receiving the sacraments, God infuses grace into the soul and thereby clarifies our moral vision.[157] Pious Catholics can distinguish right from wrong and choose moral actions. If the state assists the church, it helps its subjects to follow the natural law. A just and moral peace abounds.

The third and fourth defenses of indirect supernatural sovereignty imply that integralist regimes alone can be well ordered. I assess this claim at length in Chapter 5.

Transition

The most common objection to integralism is that it is a hopelessly utopian ideal and we have no way to transition to it. Integralists are sensitive to this worry, and Vermeule has developed a transition theory to help answer this concern.

---

[154] Crean and Fimister 2020, pp. 104–5; Lefebvre 1994, p. 89.

[155] Ryan and Millar 1930, p. 29.

[156] For Pink, the nature-grace distinction is critical to the case for integralism. He emphasizes the view as taught by, among others, Francisco Suárez. For Pink's lengthiest essay drawing out these themes, see Pink (2018c).

[157] Pink 2018b, 2020.

A complete integralist political theory applies Catholic principles to imperfect circumstances. Nonideal theory specifies how to transition to the ideal. In
Catholic terms, integralism distinguishes between *thesis* and *hypothesis*. The
thesis is the political ideal; the hypothesis (literally "below-thesis") applies political principles to imperfect circumstances.[158] Integralists also have a transition
theory. It explores how to move from an American hypothesis to a Catholic
thesis.

Some integralists adopt Carl Schmitt's critiques of the liberal state and follow
Vermeule in applying these critiques to American political life. They tend to favor
powerful rather than limited governments along the same lines as Schmitt, and
some even repudiate their limited-government forebears. Therefore, their transition theory stresses capturing and using a large and powerful state. This strategy
also requires convincing the Catholic Church to revive support for integralism
and to persuade the state to submit to the church.

The government does not submit to the pope and his bishops alone, but to
the entire spiritual administrative state, including councils, committees, and
courts. Vermeule would integrate the church bureaucracy with a modern anti-
liberal administrative state (here analogies with the Chinese government are not
uncommon). A modern dyarchy must synchronize the law of the state and the
church: two gigantic institutions, one global in scope.[159]

As noted earlier, Vermeule calls his transition strategy "integration from
within." Integralists should assume office and prepare for and even hasten
liberalism's collapse. When liberalism falls (*when*, not *if*), the state will become an ideological wasteland. Integralists can inhabit the carcass of the liberal
state, which they can then reanimate to advance the complete common good.
Vermeule and others have an almost apocalyptic vision.

Integralists have reason to agree with Vermeule. Small states may struggle to
reach integralist goals. Modern societies are large, diverse, educated, and individualistic; small governments cannot reshape them into pious and obedient
subjects.[160]

But do not lose sight of the fact that Vermeule's strategy requires capturing
the state, *ahead of creating* and *in order to create* a Catholic society.[161] He allows
Catholics to impose integralism on a non-Catholic population, which is inappropriate, as I argue in Chapter 4.

But suppose I'm wrong, and morality permits integralists to capture the
state. If so, integralists cannot fear acquiring political power. Catholics shrink

---

[158] Bévenot 1954. I discuss this distinction at length in Chapter 4.

[159] Vermeule 2019c.

[160] Strong governments can't either, as I argue in Chapter 4.

[161] I thank Xavier Menard and Micah Schwartzman for a discussion on this point.

from it, but their competitors do not, integralists claim. Muslim regimes seldom flinch from promoting Islam, and Chinese leaders do not hesitate to exercise incredible power. Progressive egalitarians use their "spiritual" powers to govern American culture, such as the academy and the entertainment industry, and they rule without shame. All three groups rejoice in sovereignty—Catholics should too.[162] Vermeule's popular writing focuses on encouraging Catholics to take this positive posture toward power.

A Model Integralist Regime

Like adherents of other movements, integralists disagree. But, unlike members of other movements, they seldom highlight those disagreements. They disagree about Vatican II, the Latin Mass, President Trump, and Pope Francis, but it is often hard to tell.

Integralists disagree about three more factors, and these matter for our purposes. First, many integralists like reactionary thinkers, such as Joseph de Maistre and Schmitt, but not all do. Second, some integralists prefer Catholic authoritarian regimes to liberal democratic ones, but others do not. Third, some integralists embrace the medieval state, whereas others prefer a modern one.[163]

Since Vermeule is the chief strategist of the integralist movement, in this book I address his stances on these matters. Vermeule is one of the world's leading Schmittian legal theorists. He is perhaps the leading Schmittian on the American Right.[164] His writing implies that Catholic authoritarian regimes are superior to liberal democratic ones.[165] He hopes to transform large, liberal states into integralist polities.

But the bulk of this book criticizes the ideal and sets transition theory aside. I also argue that integralism is not quite anti-liberal if it remains local. Right-liberalism is historically friendly to federalism and could allow local integralist regimes to exist combined with the freedom of exit. So I will assess the case for extensive integralist regimes.

I also will critique the ideal assuming a culture filled with observant Catholics, say north of 80 percent. It is easier to refute the ideal if it contains only a small Catholic majority, since the populace may engender great religious conflict. Let's not take the easy way out.

---

[162] For an expression of this sentiment, see Calleja (2020). The title? "Dare to Command!"
[163] For classic texts, see de Maistre (1995) and Schmitt (2007).
[164] Vermeule "demystifies" Schmittian concepts in Posner and Vermeule (2017).
[165] Vermeule 2018b. But see discussion in Chapter 3.

I also presume that integralist regimes enforce their laws with modest punishments, only scaling up when necessary. We should not assume that integralist states use gruesome punishments. Nor should we assume that integralists are eager to use excessive penalties. Let's avoid lurid hypotheticals.

In other words, I address the core subset of integralist regimes: I don't focus on peripheral cases, such as a global federation or a micro-polity, nor on regimes that are perfectly or barely Catholic, nor on regimes that are lax or severe in their punishments. And so I do not assess the case for every possible integralist regime—only for the core cases. Indeed, I would be happy for integralists to adopt localist restraints. I argue that they should in the epilogue.

2

History

I have two interwoven aims in this chapter. I review the history of integralist thought and politics: integralism's life, death, and resurrection. I also relay the first argument for integralism: authoritative figures, church documents, and institutional practice support it. The history argument is cumulative—no historical datum proves it, but a full picture of the evidence strengthens the integralist's case. I am not a Catholic (though I am as sympathetic as Eastern Orthodoxy allows), but in my view, the data favor integralism over its chief competitor.

Integralism's chief competitor follows the mainstream reading of *Dignitatis humanae*. According to article 1 of *DH*, the state must recognize religious truth and the truth of Catholicism in particular.[1] But religious coercion of the baptized violates their dignity, church authorization notwithstanding. The church directs and advises the state to observe the natural law—that is its chief political role.[2]

One can formulate the history argument in comparative terms: Catholic teaching and history favor integralism over the "soft establishmentarianism" of the Catholic mainstream.

The history argument has two strands: history and teaching. Historically, the church operated as a coercive authority in political matters for centuries. Catholicism rests partly on church tradition, so if a practice forms part of the tradition, Catholics have some reason to deem it appropriate. As for teaching, several authoritative church documents accord with integralism. These teachings are highlighted throughout this chapter as they become relevant to the discussion (see Boxes 2.1–2.9).

I'll walk through a series of events, beginning in Late Antiquity and proceeding through the Middle Ages and the modern period down to the nineteenth

---

[1] Paul VI 1965a, art. 1.

[2] Interestingly, this is how Ryan and Millar (1930, p. 44) characterize the three main theories of the role of the Catholic Church in civil affairs: "The Church has direct power over States; her power in this field is only indirect; her power is merely directive and of counsel."

All the Kingdoms of the World. Kevin Vallier, Oxford University Press. © Oxford University Press 2023.
DOI: 10.1093/oso/9780197611371.003.0003

century. I'll then proceed more carefully through twentieth- and twenty-first-century developments. You must understand the remarkable process by which the church embraced institutional liberalism while it rejected social liberalism. I focus most on the Second Vatican Council's teaching on religious liberty and how Thomas Pink revived integralism with his new interpretation of *DH*. The trials and tribulations of American conservatism, especially the formation of the current New Right, also aided integralism's rise. These events set the stage for the neo-integralist revival.

The Roman Empire and the Early Middle Ages

The integralist story begins with Constantine's conversion to Christianity and his decision to legalize Christianity in the Roman Empire. The empire circumscribed the Mediterranean, with bishoprics spread from the coasts outward. Some bishops had great authority. The central four were the patriarchs of Rome, Antioch, Jerusalem, and Alexandria. After founding Constantinople, Constantine created his own archbishopric, thus creating a five-patriarch group that many call the *pentarchy*.[3] The pope of Rome was lead bishop.[4] I will not address the pope's ancient authority,[5] but Constantine called the Council of Nicaea in 325, and at Nicaea the bishops ruled as a college.[6] Six other councils, also called by Byzantine emperors (and one empress), promulgated Christianity's central Trinitarian and Christological doctrines.[7]

Conflicts erupted about the respective powers of bishop and emperor. Constantine and his successors often gave the church latitude in matters of dogma.[8] The church embraced its authority. Many advocated a governing dyarchy: emperors govern ordinary life; councils and bishops govern spiritual life.[9]

I cannot, of course, present early church-state arrangements as though both parties possessed clearly defined roles and sought mutual cooperation. One reason is that the Christian episcopacy challenged the Roman Empire in a novel manner. Bishops could defy the emperor on the basis of their status and office,

---

[3] The degree of their primacy, the doctrine of their primacy, and the character of their primacy have varied with time (see Schatz 1996, esp. pp. 17–38).

[4] The patriarch of Alexandria also has the title of *pope*.

[5] Obviously, this is a long-disputed issue between Protestants, Catholics, and Orthodox.

[6] To remain fair to Catholics, one might add that the pope rules the college of bishops. Communion with the pope specifies college membership.

[7] Davis (1990) reviews the history of the first seven ecumenical councils.

[8] Constantine did interfere in the Arian controversy, one of many examples of imperial interference (Davis 1990, pp. 56–69).

[9] Again, Catholics will stress that the pope is the head of the other patriarchates.

Box 2.1 **Pope Gelasius I on the Two Powers**

There are two, august Emperor, by which this world is chiefly ruled, namely, the sacred authority [*auctoritas sacrata*] of the priests and the royal power [*regalis potestas*]. Of these, that of the priests is weightier, since they have to render an account for even the kings of men in the divine judgment. You are also aware, most clement son, that while you are permitted honorably to rule over human kind, yet in divine matters you bend your neck devotedly to the bishops and await from them the means of your salvation. In the reception and proper disposition of the heavenly sacraments you recognize that you should be subordinate rather than superior to the religious order, and that in these things you depend on their judgment rather than wish to bend them to your will. If the ministers of religion, recognizing the supremacy granted you from heaven in matters affecting the public order, obey your laws, lest otherwise they might obstruct the course of secular affairs by irrelevant considerations, with what readiness should you not yield them obedience to whom is assigned the dispensing of the sacred mysteries of religion?

Source: Gelasius I, "Famuli vestrae pietatis," in *Epistolae Romanorum pontificum*, vol. 1, edited by Andrew Thiel (Braunsberg, East Prussia: Eduard Peter, 1868).

---

they had the right to a trial by their peers, and no one could legally torture or execute them. The ultimate punishments to which bishops were subject included deposition and exile. In one early clash, Athanasius of Alexandria (ca. 296–373) and Emperor Constantius II (317–361) fought over the orthodoxy of Arianism. This illustrates how disputes about the authority of priest and emperor (or king) created great disputes from at least the fourth century onward. It continues to create them today.

Constantine ruled a united Roman Empire, but the Latin Western half collapsed in the fifth century and fell outside imperial control. State capacity—the power to perform critical social functions—crumpled. In response, the church expanded to provide public services. Clergy often occupied imperial offices: *dioceses* were first Roman designations; only later did they become ecclesiastical ones. But ecclesiastical governance differed between East and West. The West had a super-patriarch—the pope; within the pope's domain the church had more power and prestige than any king.

During this period, Pope Gelasius I (in office 492–496) sent a letter to the Byzantine emperor Anastasius (quoted in Box 2.1). In this letter, he claims that God ordained a dyarchy between the Christian priesthood and the imperial throne.[10] Gelasius does not use the papal title. He merely casts the priesthood as higher than the monarchy. In his letter, we read little about the two parties' relative powers[11]—much remains ambiguous, which again provoked conflict. The chief novelty was the letter's approach to monarchy: as Oakley puts it, the letter denies the emperor "any sacerdotal status."[12]

Gelasius indeed wanted a dualism of powers, but we do not know whether he sought more authority than that.[13] His more immediate successors seldom made such claims, and the East usually ignored them. Whatever the case may be, no one should import papal claims from the thirteenth century into this fifth-century document.[14]

The papacy would gradually centralize the appointment of bishops, wresting control from corrupt local political officials.[15] Catholics theorized that the pope was the chief priest over all others. They would eventually argue, against Greek authorities, that popes must ratify the decisions of councils or else the decisions are invalid. These include decisions of the universal or "ecumenical" councils of bishops.[16] In the Latin West, then, the "dyarchy" became the joint rule of pope and crown.[17]

Sacred Kingship

Until the eleventh century, the dominant political theology was *sacred kingship*.[18] Monarchy arises by divine ordinance and performs religious functions. The king might represent a deity, descend from a deity, or even *be* a deity. In most cultures and faiths, no independent ecclesiastical authorities existed, and so no institution other than kingship would claim divine authorship. In some ways, kings' claim of divine authorship conflicts with Christianity's Jewish inheritance. Ancient Israel famously desacralized kingship.[19] One need only read 1

[10] Gelasius I 1868. Ullmann (1981) claims that Gelasius universally placed royal authority under spiritual authority. I gather that this is a minority position.

[11] Oakley 2010, pp. 100–10.

[12] Oakley 2012, p. 69.

[13] Oakley 2010, p. 100.

[14] Oakley 2010, p. 205.

[15] Duffy 2014, pp. 155–56; Schatz 1996, pp. 97–99.

[16] Davis (1990) discusses the concept and practice of ecumenical councils at length.

[17] Schatz 1996, pp. 79–94; Duffy 2014, pp. 110–50.

[18] Oakley (2010, pp. 143–76) records the international ideal of sacred kingship, which Christianity threatened but then partially readopted in the early and High Middle Ages.

[19] Oakley (2010, pp. 41–55) reviews how the ancient Israelites desacralized the monarchy.

Samuel 8 to see this. God tells the Prophet Samuel that the monarchy will prove more curse than gift.

Christians also have a Roman inheritance, and sacred kingship lay at the heart of imperial authority. The Roman emperors called themselves "supreme pontiff" (*pontifex maximus*) long before popes did.[20] The office held enormous religious importance.[21] Postimperial Christianity struggled to reconcile these divergent and conflicting influences.[22]

Constantine inherited the Roman legacy, but his conversion would create social upheaval complicating the nature of his office. Christian emperors convened councils and supervised their proceedings. Constantine famously said of himself, "I am a bishop for those outside the Church."[23] (*Bishop* simply means *overseer*.) The early Christian historian Eusebius "portrays Constantine as a quasi-priestly figure, 'like a universal bishop appointed by God.'"[24] Emperor Justinian held a similarly high view of his office. He wrote on theology and pressured Pope Vigilius to accept the decrees of the Fifth Ecumenical Council (AD 553). Many kings called themselves "vicars of Christ," a claim we hear only from popes nowadays.[25]

We must recognize, of course, that the popes had long claimed more than a "primacy of honor" among other bishops. They saw themselves as the successors of Peter, chief of the apostles. They would eventually claim jurisdiction over other bishops. However, as Francis Oakley notes, for centuries "the gap . . . between theoretical aspiration and practical reality remained immense." Roman emperors long held the "stronger claim to be the functioning supreme leaders of the Christian world, even in spiritual matters."[26] Leo the Great (in office 440–461), one of the first popes to offer a strong statement of papal primacy, still ascribed "a priestly character to the emperor."[27] And Emperor Leo III told Pope Gregory II (726), "I am emperor and priest."[28] Emperors appointed and deposed patriarchs, changed the boundaries of dioceses, legislated on ecclesiastical matters, and convened and validated general councils.[29]

---

[20] The pope's Twitter handle is @pontifex.
[21] Oakley 2010, p. 35.
[22] Oakley 2010, p. 39.
[23] Oakley 2010, p. 99.
[24] Oakley 2010, p. 92.
[25] Oakley 2010, p. 76. Michael Hollerich informs me that Innocent III is usually given credit for the titular upgrade from *vicarius Petri* (vicar of Peter) to *vicarius Christi* (vicar of Christ).
[26] Oakley 2010, p. 72.
[27] Oakley 2010, p. 99.
[28] Oakley 2010, p. 102.
[29] Oakley 2010, p. 103.

Let's now recall Justinian's reconquest of much of the old Western Roman Empire. Oakley notes that, as a consequence, "from 556 on into the eighth century the legal form of papal election was itself determined by imperial decree."[30] Even more remarkably, the emperor stationed a Byzantine official, called an exarch,[31] in Ravenna, who supervised papal elections. Indeed, an elected candidate could receive consecration only with imperial confirmation.[32]

Charlemagne's Crown

Carolingian and Ottonian kingship resembled Constantine's sacred-kingship model. I will now slow down and focus on the tale of Charlemagne's coronation. Some may see the fact that Pope Leo III crowned Charlemagne as evidence that popes could make and unmake kings. But the real story shows how the doctrine of sacred kingship blazed through the ninth century.

Charlemagne (747–814) played a pivotal role in the prehistory of integralism. He aimed to build a new Christian Roman Empire, and his legendary status owes much to his success. Charlemagne gradually accumulated territory and influence. He rose from a paltry king of the Franks (768) to king of the Lombards (774). Charlemagne then ascended to emperor of the Carolingian Empire (800). Finally, Pope Leo III crowned him emperor of the Romans (800), a title he held until his death.

Our story concerns Charlemagne's final coronation. Popes spent centuries fighting kings for political and spiritual supremacy. An enduring controversy concerned who could bestow the title of Roman emperor (*imperator romanus*). The Eastern Roman (Byzantine) Empire flourished during the early and High Middle Ages, so the Byzantine emperor held the title. But in the late eighth century, Byzantine regent-empress Irene took power in Constantinople and ruled until her young son Constantine IV came of age. In response, Charlemagne seized the title of Roman emperor. The Frankish court thought "the Eastern imperial throne, constantly allied to heresy . . . was currently vacant."[33] The convenient implication was that Christendom had no protector and required a new one.

A central event in Charlemagne's reign was his coronation in Rome on Christmas Day, AD 800. Frankish historian Einhard's *Life of Charlemagne* falsely

---

[30] Oakley 2010, p. 215.

[31] In the Orthodox Church, an exarch is a bishop lower in rank than a patriarch but with a jurisdiction wider than that of the metropolitan of a diocese.

[32] Oakley 2010, p. 215.

[33] Duffy 2014, p. 95.

reported that Pope Leo III surprised Charlemagne with the crown. In fact, the coronation served the ambitions of both men.

Charlemagne's Gain

The coronation expressed Charlemagne's confidence that he was the caretaker of many peoples. His responsibilities extended beyond the Franks. Charlemagne was an emperor, and not merely a king. His adviser Alcuin thus called him *Imperator Augustus Romanum Gubernans Imperium* (august emperor governing the Roman Empire). Charlemagne was the rector of the whole Christian people. And indeed, Alcuin would describe Charlemagne as a new David—both priest and king.[34]

Many people thought Charlemagne possessed considerable ecclesiastical power. He had already called and presided over the Council of Frankfurt (AD 794), which, while not ecumenical, had doctrinal business. It rejected the promulgation of doctrine at the Council of Second Nicaea in 787.[35]

Nicaea II had condemned iconoclasm (the destruction of icons used for religious worship). Frankfurt rejected Nicaea II as heretical. Many Frankish leaders believed that the veneration of icons was tantamount to idolatry. Charlemagne listened to their testimony and issued his own decree. Charlemagne functioned as emperor. Six years later, the coronation in Rome ratified a title he already held.

Of course, it was not irrelevant that Irene, a woman, ruled in Constantinople. She also broke convention by refusing to remarry after the death of her husband, Emperor Leo IV. These factors buttressed the Western charge that the imperial throne was vacant. Pope Leo III was happy to transfer the title. He was so eager that he even did Charlemagne homage (*proskynesis*), lying prostrate before him.

Leo's Share

Leo III also benefited from Charlemagne's coronation. The coronation renewed the papacy's relationship of copaternity (godfatherhood) with the crown. Pope Stephen II had accepted the title from Frankish king Pippin (Charlemagne's father) in 754. Leo III thought that the coronation restored his copaternity. But in 813, Charlemagne signaled that he rejected Leo's claim by himself crowning his son, Louis the Pious.[36]

---

[34] Herrin 2021, p. 435; Oakley 2010, p. 161–2.

[35] Nicaea II did claim to be ecumenical. The Roman Catholic and Orthodox Churches recognize it as such today.

[36] This is reported in Einhard's life of Charlemagne (see Einhard and Notker the Stammerer 1969; Duffy 2014, p. 96).

By that time, forgers in Rome had created a document called the Donation of Constantine. It recorded that Pope Silvester had cured Constantine of leprosy by baptizing him. In return, Constantine had given the pope his diadem. This act implied that the pope could bestow the crown on someone else. The crown conferred authority to control "the regions of the West." The pope had significant political power. The forged Donation sustained the momentum of papal claims to temporal authority.

The Crowning of Charlemagne and Dyarchic Rule

The tale of Charlemagne's crown reflects the character of other flash points in integralist history. The coronation shepherded the development of dyarchic rule. But it sanctioned sacred kingship, not integralism. Kings acted as priests, and popes often legitimized such actions.

Charlemagne thought himself tasked with "leading his subjects to their eternal salvation." He did not see papal coronation "as in any way constitutive," even if popes thought otherwise.[37] The claim that papal coronation could create emperors would not solidify among European elites until the late ninth century.

By the tenth century, many thought papal coronations authoritative.[38] Some popes declared that they alone could award the title of *imperator romanus*. Conflicts arose when future Holy Roman emperors rejected papal claims. (In these cases, they denied that popes could bestow the title of *imperator Romanorum*, the title of Holy Roman Emperor.) The Holy Roman emperors insisted that the title passes through the monarchy, but popes countered that they were necessary intermediaries. These papal claims did buttress the evolution of the dyarchy.

Integralism developed from Gelasian themes, but one can take Gelasian themes in other directions. Theologians have often assigned monarchs greater ecclesiastical authority than integralism allows. Anglo-Norman Anonymous authored several influential treatises on political authority (ca. 1100). He defends royal power as superior to the power of the church.[39] This author argues that Old Testament kings foreshadowed Christ and that Christian kings imitate Christ. Bishops and priests are subordinate to the "royal Christus." What's more, popes lack jurisdiction over other bishops.[40]

---

[37] Oakley 2010, p. 179.
[38] Oakley 2010, p. 166.
[39] Oakley 2010, pp. 165–76.
[40] Oakley 2010, p. 175.

Kings and their apologists insisted on monarchical ecclesiastical authority. Indeed, they did so almost continuously from the birth of integralism until its death. Gallican Catholics defended royal supremacy for centuries.

The great modern nation-states often ignored the temporal demands of the pope. They did so not *merely* because they could. These new nation-states inherited centuries-old teaching that monarchs had great ecclesiastical authority. The doctrine of sacred kingship remained dominant in the Christian East, and some Orthodox Christians adopt it even today.

High Integralism

Sacred kingship survived the Middle Ages. We can see this in the horror early modern people had for regicide. But popes killed the idea, if slowly. The death throes began with the claim that popes can depose kings. This doctrine probably originated in the eleventh century. One finds it in the *Dictatus papae*, a series of twenty-seven statements on papal authority.[41] Pope Gregory VII (in office 1073–1085) entered it into his register in 1075. But how did popes triumph?

In the ninth and tenth centuries, papal authority deteriorated. Weak popes allowed corruption to flourish. But in the eleventh century, Gregory VII changed everything. Following the East-West schism, Gregory had free rein over much of Europe's legal order. He consolidated and streamlined canon law in Western Europe. Some historians, such as Harold Berman, argue that Gregory created a new kind of legal order, which birthed a distinctive Western civilization.[42]

Gregory insisted that the church has absolute liberty in ecclesiastical matters. At the time, kings often interfered with the appointment of bishops and even tried to name popes.[43] Gregory's attempt to end this practice secured his place in history as a towering contender in the Investiture Contest.[44]

The other contender was Holy Roman Emperor Henry IV (1050–1106). Henry insisted on appointing his bishops, but Gregory countered that only the pope had such authority. Henry withdrew his support from Gregory in response. A colossal struggle began. Henry IV increasingly refused to submit to Pope Gregory's demands. His opposition reached its zenith in January 1076

---

[41] Duffy 2014, pp. 121–22.

[42] Berman 1983, pp. 49–51. Contra Berman, historians now see the creation of this legal order as mostly a product of a mass clerical movement rather than the imposition of law from the pope. Gregory simply lacked access to state-like mechanisms to enact and enforce his will, but Gregory did help to lead a legal revolution even if he was not its principal cause. See Müeller 2022a, p. 91.

[43] At times, Catholic monarchs could veto candidates for pope before the cardinals began to vote.

[44] Tellenbach (1991, pp. 89–125) provides a classic recounting of the main events.

at a gathering of German and Italian bishops in Worms. Henry had them de-clare independence from the pope and demand that Gregory resign. The pope responded immediately. He deposed and excommunicated Henry and Henry's allied bishops, hobbling Henry politically.

Henry famously attempted to reconcile with Gregory. In 1077 at Canossa, he approached Gregory as a poor sinner who sought papal absolution. This dra-matic act solved nothing. Two years later, Gregory excommunicated and deposed Henry again. In time, Gregory banned all kings from investing ecclesiastics with any sacred authority. Henry now faced opposition from both German princes and allies of the pope; civil war followed. The conflict saw the election of an anti-king, Rudolf of Rheinfelden; meanwhile, Henry dared to appoint Antipope Clement III. Henry's forces then drove Gregory from Rome, and Gregory died in exile in Salerno.

Despite Gregory's seeming defeat, his prohibition on lay investiture of bishops held. He would forever transform church-state relations in Latin Christendom. Popes gained control over ecclesiastical appointments even though bishops still swore allegiance to their monarchs. The arrangement elevated the papacy's honor and prestige. The power balance between popes and kings increasingly favored the papacy. This development begins the crescendo of the dyarchy's influence—what I call High Integralism.[45]

Dyarchic rule expanded throughout the next two centuries. It arguably peaked under Pope Innocent III (in office 1198–1216) and began a long and ultimately permanent decline during the reign of Pope Boniface VIII (in office 1294–1303). This was a revolutionary period, which, as Oakley puts it,

> marked the birth pangs of something new in the history of humankind: a society in which what we now call the state was gradually stripped of its age-old religious aura and in which its overriding claims on the loyalties of men were balanced and curtailed by those advanced persistently by a rival authority.[46]

Did the papacy create the secular state? I take no position, save to prod readers to reflect.

Integralism's fortunes rose, partly owing to King Louis IX of France (reigned 1226–1270), later canonized as Saint Louis, a man renowned for his wisdom and holiness.[47] He had a close relationship with Pope Clement IV (in office

---

[45] Duffy 2014, pp. 138–50.

[46] Oakley 2012, p. 40.

[47] Jones (2017) provides an extensive account of Saint Louis IX's reign and holiness, though at times perhaps hagiographically.

Box 2.2 The Fourth Council of the Lateran on Deposing Kings

Secular authorities, whatever office they may hold, shall be admonished and induced and if necessary compelled by ecclesiastical censure, that as they wish to be esteemed and numbered among the faithful, so for the defense of the faith they ought publicly to take an oath that they will strive in good faith and to the best of their ability to exterminate in the territories subject to their jurisdiction all heretics pointed out by the Church; so that whenever anyone shall have assumed authority, whether spiritual or temporal, let him be bound to confirm this decree by oath. But if a temporal ruler, after having been requested and admonished by the Church, should neglect to cleanse his territory of this heretical foulness, let him be excommunicated by the metropolitan and the other bishops of the province. If he refuses to make satisfaction within a year, let the matter be made known to the supreme pontiff, that he may declare the ruler's vassals absolved from their allegiance and may offer the territory to be ruled by lay Catholics, who on the extermination of the heretics may possess it without hindrance and preserve it in the purity of faith; the right, however, of the chief ruler is to be respected as long as he offers no obstacle in this matter and permits freedom of action.

Source: From canon 3, Canons of the Fourth Lateran Council, 1215, available at https://sourcebooks.fordham.edu/basis/lateran4.asp.

1265–1268), who had once been one of his advisers. The French dyarchy drew strength from remarkable cultural achievements. Under its umbrella Saint Thomas Aquinas created his grand system of thought, and the Fourth Council of the Lateran (1215), the great medieval council, defined the doctrine of the Eucharist.[48]

A now-obscure canon from Lateran IV bears on our story. Canon 3 (quoted in Box 2.2) was not always so obscure: Francisco Suárez (1548–1617) and Cardinal Robert Bellarmine (1542–1621) cite it to defend integralism.[49] Thomas Hobbes (1588–1679) assailed it.[50] Canon 3 codifies when a pope may dethrone a

---

[48] Duffy 2014, pp. 138–50.

[49] Suárez (1612) 2015, pp. 786–7, 794; Bellarmine 2012, pp. 146–7, 161, 241. Neither passage refers to the canon by number, but it is clearly the canon under discussion. See also Pink 2015a, p. xv for discussion of Suarez's endorsement of the indirect power.

[50] Hobbes 1994, p. 392.

king.[51] If the king becomes a heretic or tolerates heretics, the pope may excommunicate him; if the king does not relent, the pope may release the king's nobles from their vows of obedience. The king could lose his crown—or his head.

Christians have forgotten Lateran IV, but we must remember it.[52] While canon 3 seems not to define doctrine, integralists need something like it to stabilize integralist regimes.[53] As we will see, since secular leaders can go rogue, the pope must have the power to remove them.

Back to our story. Over the course of the High Middle Ages, Islamic conquest devastated most of Mediterranean Christianity. Greek Christendom contracted. Latin Christendom contended with Islam in Spain, but Christendom appeared on the rise by the turn of the thirteenth century. The fourteenth century reversed course. The papacy moved to Avignon, laying the foundation for a ruinous church conflict. For when a pope returned to Rome, the church suddenly found that it had two popes.

Here is what happened, in brief. Pope Boniface VIII and King Philip IV (1268–1314) of France were not fast friends, unlike Clement IV and Saint Louis. Early in his reign, Philip stripped the French clergy of legal authority and taxed them. Boniface saw this as an affront and forbade it in a papal bull, *Clericis laicos*, in 1296.[54] Philip decided that Boniface had overstepped. The king thought that he alone had power over temporal law. He retaliated: the French crown would no longer fund the papacy. Defiant, Boniface responded in 1301 that "God has set popes over kings and kingdoms."[55] Philip didn't care. He proceeded to confiscate church wealth to fight the English.

Boniface dug in. In 1302, he brought down the hammer. He issued *Unam sanctam* to undermine Philip, but it booms across the ages with a firm declaration: "It is absolutely necessary for salvation that every human creature be in submission to the Roman Pontiff."[56]

---

[51] It draws on the *Dictatus papae*, a series of twenty-seven statements of papal authority. Gregory VII adopted it in 1075. From what I can tell, there is no precedent for Gregory's claim, but by Lateran IV, Gregory himself was precedent.

[52] Canons of the Fourth Lateran Council, 1215, available at https://sourcebooks.fordham.edu/basis/lateran4.asp. Canon 68 claims that Jews and Muslims must wear different clothes from Christians, to avoid confusion, supposedly. Saint Louis enforced this canon (see Jones 2017, p. 96). He also followed directives to burn all available copies of the Talmud. He filled more than twenty wagons "with the manuscripts, containing more than twenty thousand copies in all, and publicly put them to the torch in the Place de Greve" (Kertzer 2001, p. 139).

[53] Pink (2021) indicates that these canons were binding following their ratification. But he does not say whether canon 3 is still in effect today. Crean and Fimister (2020, pp. 234n55, 241) point out that the power was "upheld by ecumenical councils," which also implies that they believe it still holds.

[54] Boniface VIII 1296; Duffy 2014, pp. 159–63.

[55] Boniface VIII (1301) 1921.

[56] Boniface VIII 1302.

Philip didn't budge. So, in 1303, Boniface effectively, if unofficially, excommunicated Philip. Boniface first excommunicated anyone (including Philip) who prevented clergy from visiting the Holy See. He then declared that no Frenchman could name people to certain offices. Boniface hoped to deprive Philip of the sacraments. Surely *that* would work.

Philip sent an army to Rome to capture Boniface, and the invaders almost killed the pope. Boniface VIII died from a fever a month later. In 1305, Philip pushed the papal conclave to elect Clement V as pope. It was Clement who moved the papacy to Avignon. For sixty-seven years, seven popes resided there—the papal bureaucracy moved nearby.[57]

But in 1376, Pope Gregory XI left Avignon for Rome. He died in 1378, leaving behind a rocky relationship with his successor, Urban VI. The papal schism began when French cardinals tried to rescind their election of Urban VI in 1378, withdrew from Rome, and elected a new pope, a Frenchman, who took the title Clement VII. The French cardinals then opted to return to Avignon. The cardinals who stayed in Rome, supplemented by Urban VI's new cardinals, elected Boniface IX after Urban died in 1388.[58] Hence two papal lines coexisted. And, indeed, two popes ruled until 1417.

Three popes reigned simultaneously before the schism ended: Gregory XII at Rome, Benedict XIII at Avignon, and John XXIII at Pisa. The Council of Pisa had met in 1409 to choose a new pope. It had deposed both currently reigning popes and elected John XXIII. But Gregory and Benedict had ignored the council. Five years later, the Council of Constance (1414–1418) finally ended the schism: Gregory XII resigned and the council deposed the other popes, then elected Pope Martin V.[59]

I cover this conflict, and the Investiture Contest, for two reasons. First, integralism's rise makes sense in light of these events. Christianity's second millennium began with a papal revolution, the end result of which provided popes with the political authority integralists claim for them. The second reason I cover these events is to illustrate dyarchic instability: pope and crown routinely disputed their relative authority. Integralists celebrate the thirteenth century (as well as Saint Louis), but the long fourteenth century weakens their case for the stability of union between the two powers. When they praise Saint Louis IX, remember Philip IV.

I now turn to examine the Council of Constance in more detail, in part to explore its adoption of conciliarism. According to conciliarism, bishops acting as a college have divine authority over the pope.[60] Popes must obey them in matters

---

[57] Oakley 2003, p. 27; Duffy 2014, pp. 163–64.
[58] Today Catholics call these bishops "antipopes."
[59] Oakley (2003, pp. 20–59) provides an authoritative overview of the controversy.
[60] Oakley 2003. See also Schatz 1996, pp. 100–13.

Box 2.3 **The Council of Constance on the Superiority of Councils**

Legitimately assembled in the Holy Spirit, constituting a general council and representing the Catholic Church militant, [a council] has power immediately from Christ; and everyone of whatever state or dignity, even papal, is bound to obey it in those matters which pertain to the faith, the eradication of the said [papal] schism, and the general reform of the said church of God in head and members.

Source: "Council of Constance 1414–18," available at https://www.papalencyclicals.net/councils/ecum16.htm.

---

of faith. Since the council deposed and appointed popes, its position appeared to be reasonable.

Conciliarism poses another intellectual and historical challenge to the dyarchy. Exhibit A: *Haec sancta synodus* (1415), quoted in Box 2.3. Though this document was promulgated at Constance, Catholics nonetheless regard it as invalid. The papacy never accepted it, after all. Yet, partly on the basis of this document, conciliarists denied that councils required papal approval. They held firm through the First Vatican Council (1868–1870).[61] Until then (and to a lesser degree afterward), Catholic theologians still disagreed about the authority of popes. If we introduce conciliar authority into our discussion, the alternatives to integralism expand. One can object to integralism on conciliarist grounds. We can also see that, while integralists prevailed, they always faced dissent.

History remembers Constance for yet another reason. It conducted the heresy trial of Jan Hus, a Bohemian priest. Hus defended the public promulgation of John Wycliffe's proto-Protestant doctrines, though without adopting them. Following Hus's trial, the council branded Hus a "contumacious heretic."[62] It then turned him over to Holy Roman Emperor Sigismund (1433–1437) for punishment—by incineration. Christian rulers seldom burned heretics in the first millennium. The practice had begun in the West in the eleventh century and had become common within the Catholic Church in the thirteenth century. By the fourteenth century, the burning of heretics had become unremarkable.

Unfortunately for the council, the incineration of Hus proved remarkable indeed. Hus's deviations from church teaching were mild, so many observers saw his punishment as severe and unjust. Hus's Bohemian supporters revolted

---

[61] Schatz 1996, pp. 155–65; Oakley 2003, pp. 207–16.

[62] Fudge (2013, pp. 50–52, 140–43, 221–23, 314–20) provides an extensive discussion of the charge of contumacy.

Box 2.4 **The Council of Trent on Baptism**

If anyone says that when they grow up, those baptized as little children should be asked whether they wish to affirm what their godparents promised in their name when they were baptized; and that, when they reply that they have no such wish, they should be left to their own decision and not, in the meantime, be coerced by any penalty into the Christian life, except that they be barred from the reception of the eucharist and the other sacraments, until they have a change of heart: let him be anathema.

_____

Source: Canon 14 of the Council of Trent.

---

in response to his execution. They protested with such ferocity that future popes called four crusades to put down uprisings. The Hussite rebellions also laid the groundwork for the Reformation. The decision to punish a single heretic created massive political instability. It commenced the destruction of (purportedly) integralist regimes.

The Counter-Reformation and the French Revolution

The Catholic Church recognized early on that the Reformation required a theological response.[63] The Reformers influenced millions, and they had powerful royal support. The church answered with the Council of Trent, the most significant council since Lateran IV. Trent had seismic effects on dogma and liturgy. It reinvigorated defenders of the faith. It also anathematized Protestant doctrines, further contributing to inter-Christian conflict.

Twenty-first-century integralism owes much to a Tridentine canon as obscure as Lateran IV's canon 3. Erasmus of Rotterdam (1466–1536) had suggested that authorities ask young Catholics whether they affirmed their baptismal vows. If they did not, he said, states should not punish them for ecclesiastical crimes.[64] Trent condemned Erasmus's teaching (as quoted in Box 2.4). In doing so, it

---

[63] Duffy 2014, pp. 208–29.

[64] Erasmus 2008, p. 20; Pink 2019. Erasmus does not mention the state expressly, nor does the Trent canon, but—given the legal practice of the day—I think it fair to assume that it refers to the secular authority. The state was engaged in such activities, and so parties to the dispute arguably thought the permissibility of such governmental activities was at stake in the debate.

appears to affirm a key integralist plank—baptism subjects one to civil censure for violating canon law.

In this canon the church legitimizes integralist coercion—or seems to. States could penalize people for violating their baptismal obligations. This includes people baptized as infants. Catholics dispute the interpretation of this canon, as illustrated by an interpretative debate between Thomas Pink and John Finnis.[65] Trent establishes, at most, that integralist coercion is morally permissible, which falls short of vindicating integralism as a political *ideal*. Other sources must sync with Trent to justify integralism as the best regime. We will encounter such sources in the following pages.

Trent launched the movement known as the Counter-Reformation, which fought to recover Catholic losses from Protestantism. Catholics succeeded at times, but contests with Protestants proved disastrous overall. The Counter-Reformation ended with the Peace of Westphalia in 1648, following the ruinous Thirty Years' War (1618–1648).

Meanwhile, Catholics still disagreed about the relative authority of pope and crown. Some defended *hierocracy*—arguing, with Boniface VIII, that the church has extensive temporal power.[66] Others, especially French Catholics, thought monarchs could appoint bishops. Many describe this view as Gallicanism.

Integralism influenced the seventeenth century, but it came under severe strain. Another flashpoint occurred during the Venetian Interdict (1606–1607). Venice started prosecuting clergy for certain crimes, but the church objected, as it had three hundred years earlier. The church had sole authority to try clergy, the church maintained. The Venetians defended their jurisdiction as a matter of practical necessity—to maintain a unitary order. But apologists for the papal side made integralist arguments: given the nobler end of the spiritual power, only the church had jurisdiction over the clergy. As Bishop of Molfetta, Giovanni Antonio Bovio, argued at the time:

> Who does not see clearly, therefore, that just as man is subject to God and the body to the soul, and just as this life is ordained as the way to the heavenly fatherland and these earthly things as a stairway to celestial, so politics is subject and subordinate to religion, and the prince and temporal government to the head of religion and of the church?[67]

By this time, even an Italian city-state could resist papal power. At one point, it even appeared that the Venetians could count on the support of the French

---

[65] Pink 2013b, 2019; Finnis 2013. Crean and Fimister (2020, p. 233) appear to agree with Pink.

[66] Boniface VIII and Innocent III seemed to be hierocrats (see Duffy 2014, pp. 138–60).

[67] Quoted in Bouwsma 1990, p. 102.

king Henry IV, the ruler of a deeply Catholic nation. Gallicans and Venetians agreed that the monarch's divine right to rule includes jurisdiction over clerical crimes.

Cardinal Bellarmine defended integralism as a compromise position in response to such conflicts. He found historical middle ground between hierocracy and Gallicanism.[68] Integralists alone properly delineated the original authority of both the temporal and spiritual power. While Bellarmine's teachings irritated some, including Pope Sixtus V, Bellarmine died in good standing with the church.[69] Indeed, his position became orthodoxy. The church canonized him in 1930 and made him a Doctor of the Church in 1931.

Francisco Suárez was Counter-Reformation integralism's most extraordinary mind, owing to his rich theory of political life.[70] He wrote an extensive critique of King James I of England (who reigned 1603–1625). Starting in 1606, James made English Catholics swear allegiance to him over the pope. He defended his position thoughtfully. Partly in response, Suárez developed what remains the greatest defense of integralism.[71]

The Oath of Allegiance debate initiated further debates, some of which remain of great consequence for us today. Half of Hobbes's *Leviathan* (1651) concerns political theology. The only figure he addresses at length and by name is Bellarmine. Hobbes had seen Bellarmine at a Mass in Rome in 1614, and the cardinal apparently made quite an impression.[72] Hobbes thought Bellarmine provided the chief intellectual alternative to his theory of sovereignty. Temporal sovereigns could resolve disputed interpretations of natural law, but Hobbes admitted that spiritual rulers could too—so long, of course, as pope and crown did not divide power. That would court disaster.

John Locke (1632–1704) also contended with integralism, though specifically the Anglican integralism of Jonas Proast (1640–1710).[73] Jean-Jacques Rousseau (1712–1778) resisted Swiss and French integralism and excluded

---

[68] Bellarmine 2012, pp. 253–58, 270, 296–97, 304. Maritain (2020, p. iv) argues that Bellarmine expressed "the traditional doctrine of the Papacy."

[69] Maritain 2020, p. x; Pink 2015a, p. xiv.

[70] Pink 2015a, p. xv. Much of the defense can be found in *A Defence of the Catholic and Apostolic Faith*, book 3: "Concerning the Supremacy and Power of the Pope over Temporal Kings." See chaps. 5 and 23 in Suárez ([1612] 2015).

[71] See Suárez 2015, pp. 803–28 (book 6: "Concerning the Oath of Allegiance Exacted by the King of England").

[72] Martinich 1999, pp. 34–35. At that time, Bellarmine was seventy-one, and Hobbes was twenty-six.

[73] Locke 2009 (expressly in the *Second Letter*, pp. 67–107).

integralists (and many other Catholics) from the social contract.[74] Rousseau justifies his view in part with a plausible argument against integralism: "This dual power has given rise to a perpetual jurisdictional conflict that has made all good polity impossible in Christian states, and no one has ever been able to know whether it is the priest or the master whom one is obliged to obey."[75]

Opposition to integralism helped create the liberal tradition. Liberals celebrate religious toleration and oppose the coercive establishment of religion. For early liberals, integralism was the enemy. It disparages tolerance and demands the coercive establishment of Catholicism. Liberalism and Christianity might harmonize, but liberalism and integralism cannot.[76]

After Westphalia, the great European nation-states had enough power to ignore the church. Yet popes remained influential in Catholic regions. These included France, Italy, and much of the Holy Roman Empire, which was ruled by the Habsburg royal family, an old ally of the pope.[77]

I must note the illiberalism of early modern political thought. Protestant regimes—then called confessional states—ruled where Catholic regimes did not. Europe had several Calvinist and Lutheran states. England was Anglican. Europe grew religiously plural throughout the seventeenth and eighteenth centuries. Locally, though, intolerance prevailed.[78] The first liberals were thus a lonely bunch. They fought valiantly for toleration. Nonetheless, they opposed Catholicism as much as Protestants did. Later Enlightenment liberals supported freedom of religion in some respects, but many embraced targeted intolerance—especially French Revolutionary liberals.[79]

Horror at the French Revolution created two strands of conservative thought: the anglophone conservative tradition of Edmund Burke (1729–1797) and the European conservative tradition of Joseph de Maistre (1753–1821).[80] The Burkean strand has dominated the Anglosphere ever since. But some integralists prefer continental conservatism. They see modern-day liberalism as a natural extension of French Revolutionary liberalism.

[74] Rousseau wrote in *The Social Contract*, "Whoever dares to say *no Salvation outside the Church*, has to be driven out of the State; unless the State is the Church and the Prince the Pontiff. Such a dogma is good only in a Theocratic Government, in any other it is pernicious" (2018, p. 155).

[75] Rousseau 2018, p. 148. I thank Matthew Young for reminding me of this passage.

[76] They are not incompatible if integralism is small—more on this in the Epilogue.

[77] Rady 2017, chap. 4. The Habsburgs grew liberal until their dethronement after World War I. Nonetheless, integralists celebrate them as rulers of a multiethnic Catholic empire. They even have a soft spot for living Habsburgs.

[78] Johnson and Koyama 2019, pp. 9–12.

[79] Johnson and Koyama 2019, pp. 245–48.

[80] Their great works on the topic were Burke (2003) and de Maistre (1994).

Box 2.5 **Pope Boniface VIII on the Temporal Power of the Pope**

That spiritual power surpasses in dignity and in nobility any temporal power whatever, as spiritual things surpass the temporal. This we see very clearly also by the payment, benediction, and consecration of the tithes, by the acceptance of power itself and by the government even of things. For with truth as our witness, it belongs to spiritual power to establish the terrestrial power and to pass judgment if it has not been good.

Source: Boniface VIII, *Unam sanctam*, November 18, 1302, available at New Advent, http://www.newadvent.org/library/docs_bo08us.htm.

Some support the same remedies that Maistre favored, such as monarchy and a Catholic confessional state.[81] Integralists think traditional American conservatives cannot resist the revolutionary Left. They say that traditional conservatives instead ratify leftist impieties, within a decade or a generation at most.[82] (I will say more on integralism's role in twenty-first-century conservatism below.)

The Revolution helped create other European states. State capacity expanded everywhere. The new Italian state would eventually consume the pope's political domain—the Papal States. Indeed, Italy backed the popes into a corner more than once.

The Nineteenth-Century Popes

Many popes have defended the dyarchy. Leo the Great (in office 440–461) said popes rule the church, but honored the emperor's temporal authority.[83] Saint Gregory the Great (in office 590–604) argued that the spiritual power must inform the temporal power: "The earthly kingdom [must] be a service which subordinates itself to the heavenly kingdom."[84] Pope Innocent III (in office 1198–1216) called the church the "sun" and the state the "moon" that reflects the church's glory. The heavens had a major body to "dominate the day and a minor one to dominate the night," and so did society.[85] Boniface VIII

---

[81] On the hopes for restoring the monarchy, see de Maistre (1995, pp. 77–85, also p. 89).
[82] For one recent example, see Roach (2021).
[83] Leo I 2015.
[84] Gregory I 2012, p. 173.
[85] Innocent III 1954.

Box 2.6 **Pope Pius IX on Temporal and Spiritual Power**

The faith teaches us and human reason demonstrates that a double order
of things exists, and that we must therefore distinguish between the two
earthly powers, the one of natural origin which provides for secular affairs and the tranquility of human society, the other of supernatural origin,
which presides over the City of God, that is to say the Church of Christ,
which has been divinely instituted for the sake of souls and of eternal salvation. . . . The duties of this twofold power are most wisely ordered in such a
way that to God is given what is God's (Matt. 22:21), and because of God
to Caesar what is Caesar's, who is great because he is smaller than heaven.

Source: Pius IX, *Quanta cura: Condemning Current Errors*, 1864, available at Papal
Encyclicals Online, https://www.papalencyclicals.net/pius09/p9quanta.htm.

---

wrote about the temporal power of the pope in *Unam sanctam* (1302), quoted
in Box 2.5.[86]

These popes had greater power than their nineteenth-century successors.
European nation-states undermined the nineteenth-century papacy's political influence and rejected the pope's authority over many matters once considered within
his jurisdiction. The nineteenth-century popes never gave in. Popes Pius IX (in office 1846–1878) and Leo XIII (in office 1878–1903) rearticulated integralism as a
universal political ideal. They repudiated liberalism.

Pius IX's *Quanta cura* (1864), with its appendix, *The Syllabus of Errors*,
condemns liberal ideas (see Box 2.6).[87] Pius insists that the church has authority
in temporal affairs. Catholicism must become the sole state religion of every nation and exclude "all other forms of worship." The best societies reject complete
religious freedom, he asserts; they should adopt integralism (though he does

---

[86] In one way, this is not integralist teaching; it appears to be hierocratic, as noted earlier.

[87] Nonintegralists read Pius IX as condemning secular continental liberalism, especially French
liberalism. In response, integralists point to Joy (n.d.). But see Joy (2017, pp. 125–28), which reviews
deep theological disagreement about the *ex cathedra* status of *The Syllabus of Errors*, given that it
includes propositions drawn from a range of other documents. Joy (n.d.) admits that this complicates
his argument. The *Syllabus* may have been more a reminder than a decree. In *Man and the State*,
Maritain suggests that the *Syllabus* was such a narrow condemnation (see Maritain 2012, p. 159n13).
Other figures, such as Hittinger, seem to think that its nondogmatic status is obvious. Hittinger
(2007a, p. 9) called Pius IX's decision to issue the decree "rather impulsive" and driven by political
frustration.

Box 2.7 **Pope Leo XIII on Temporal and Spiritual Power**

The Almighty, therefore, has given the charge of the human race to two powers, the ecclesiastical and the civil, the one being set over divine, and the other over human, things. Each in its kind is supreme, each has fixed limits within which it is contained, limits which are defined by the nature and special object of the province of each. . . . There must, accordingly, exist between the two powers a certain orderly connection, which may be compared to the union of the soul and body in man.

Source: Leo XIII, *Immortale Dei: Encyclical of Pope Leo XIII on the Christian Constitution of States*, November 1, 1885, available at the Holy See website, http://www.vatican.va/content/leo-xiii/en/encyclicals/documents/hf_l-xiii_enc_01111885_immortale-dei.html.

---

not use that name). Pius conducted the First Vatican Council. Under his direction, the council proclaimed papal infallibility and ecclesiastical supremacy over every Christian bishop.[88] Pius told the world that the church was who it claimed to be: the one true faith.

Leo XIII added his great intellectual authority to Pius IX's intransigence, and Leonine integralism prevailed within the church.[89] The encyclical *Immortale Dei* contains the passage quoted in Box 2.7. The soul-body union analogy is critical to Leo XIII's argument. And it more than suggests that the pope believed in the indirect power, at least as *thesis*. Jacques Maritain claims that Leo XIII never endorsed the indirect power openly. But he thinks this passage comes close. Further, Leo XIII "said nothing which was not in perfect harmony with that doctrine."[90]

Leo XIII disagreed with reforms proposed by American Catholic authorities to support universal religious freedom. They claimed religious liberty explained the vitality of American Catholicism. The pope admitted that American Catholics used their liberty well, but *Longinqua* (1895) preserved the integralist ideal.[91] (continued in Box 2.8):

---

[88] This included even Eastern Orthodox bishops, who can confer valid sacraments (see First Vatican Council 1870).

[89] Leo XIII 1885, art. 13. Suárez influenced Leo XIII through his "post-1815 restoration Jesuit intellectual formation" (Pink 2021).

[90] Maritain 2020, p. iv.

[91] Leo XIII 1895, sec. 6.

Box 2.8 **Pope Leo XIII on the Deficiency of American Catholicism**

It would be very erroneous to draw the conclusion that in America is to be sought the type of the most desirable status of the Church, or that it would be universally lawful or expedient for State and Church to be, as in America, dissevered and divorced. . . . [The Church] would bring forth more abundant fruits if, in addition to liberty, she enjoyed the favor of the laws and the patronage of the public authority.

Source: Leo XIII, *Longinua: Encyclical of Pope Leo XIII on Catholicism in the United States,* January 6, 1895, available at the Holy see website, https://www.vatican.va/content/leo-xiii/en/encyclicals/documents/hf_l-xiii_enc_06011895_longinqua.html.

Owing to Leo, integralism remained influential into the twentieth century. Pius X (in office 1903–1914) embraced the view in condemning modernism in his 1907 encyclical *Pascendi Dominici gregis*.[92] The 1917 *Code of Canon Law* included Protestants among its subjects: they received valid baptisms. They were heavenly citizens.[93] The church could still direct states to punish Protestants for ecclesiastical crimes, at least in principle.

I think Leo XIII thought that integralism was no longer feasible, and his encouragement of French Catholics to engage the Third Republic, after Pius IX had forbidden them from doing so, was a concession to that reality. Leo XIII was a former Vatican secretary of state. He had a keen sense for diplomacy and surely understood that the days of his hero, Pope Innocent III, were long past.[94] However, *Immortale Dei* and *Longinqua* strongly suggest that, like Pius IX, Leo XIII affirmed integralism as *thesis*. The soul-body union he describes is the best earthly regime for the human person, even if we cannot reach it, and even if attempts to reach it would end in disaster. That, in my view, suffices to deem him an integralist.

From what I can tell, the Catholics who pushed hardest for religious freedom, like John Courtney Murray and Jacques Maritain, thought that integralism was their target.[95] And in Murray's many articles on Leo XIII, it seems that he

[92] Pius X 1907.

[93] For discussion of heavenly citizenship, see Pink (2012b).

[94] I find it striking that Leo XIII decided that he should be buried next to Innocent III in the Lateran, suggesting something more than mere admiration—perhaps agreement (Hittinger 2007b, p. 40).

[95] Maritain was abandoning *his own* embrace of integralism in *The Primacy of the Spiritual* (2020, pp. 6–36). Indeed, in that book, and as late as 1939, he claims that, while Leo XIII does not expressly reference the "indirect power," the balance of evidence favors Leo's embrace of the position (see pp. iii–iv).

thought that the reigning "Leonine" orthodoxy corresponds to integralism. The liberals knew what they were up against.[96]

Some scholars deny that Leo XIII was an integralist. They cite Catholic philosopher Russell Hittinger's claim that Leo XIII did not favor religious establishment. But for Hittinger, Leo XIII "certainly did not abjure a union of church and civil commonwealth." He cites the soul-body passage quoted in Box 2.7.[97] Hittinger's read does not draw the thesis-hypothesis distinction (as noted in Chapter 1), so his arguments show only that Leo XIII focused on protecting the church from modern states. The integralist can concede this and argue that Leo XIII worked within his hypothesis (non-ideal circumstances) but saw integralism as thesis (the political ideal).

This section contains central dogmatic data for integralism. While it falls short of proof, consider that integralism may fit these teachings better than it fits the Catholic mainstream.

The World Wars and Catholic Illiberalism

In the late nineteenth century, many Catholics thought that the church should articulate an economic philosophy that contrasts with liberalism, socialism, and feudalism. Leo XIII's masterwork, *Rerum Novarum* (1891), inaugurates this tradition. It grants much to several economic philosophies, though it repudiates socialism.[98] Most importantly, *Rerum Novarum* commenced papal reflection on a wide range of social issues. Papal encyclicals on such matters do not typically define dogma. They nonetheless drive church thought and activity.

Leo XIII also taught that Catholics were free to embrace monarchy or democracy.[99] With respect to democracy, then, Catholicism was officially institutionally neutral. Even in the 1930s, "Catholics were doctrinally indifferent to political form,"[100] a condition that continued until the beginning of World War II.[101]

The interwar period saw secular intellectuals lose faith in democracy, a process accelerated by the Great Depression. Liberalism declined, owing to constant criticism from democratic socialists, fascists, and communists. We cannot forget the many intellectuals who defended fascist doctrines and regimes, which included

[96] See Murray 1993, pp. 130–37, where the term "The First View" connotes an integralist-like position.

[97] Hittinger 2007b, pp. 62–63. I am grateful to Jennifer Frey for the reference.

[98] Leo XIII 2014, esp. pp. 211–15.

[99] See Pope Leo XIII 1892.

[100] Chappel 2018, p. 93.

[101] Chappel (2018, pp. 22–58) makes this point especially clear with respect to "paternal" Catholic modernism.

a huge number of European Catholics. Most rejected Nazism but supported the milder fascist regimes in Austria, France, Italy, Spain, and Portugal. The church opposed communism and sectarian liberalism, so Catholics often chose between supporting fascists and supporting social democrats. They sometimes chose fascists because fascists promised to defeat both communists and liberals.[102] The democratic inclination became dominant with time, but only after World War II.[103]

Meanwhile, Catholics created modern integralist parties. *The Syllabus of Errors* influenced the agenda of Partido Católico Nacional, a Spanish political party founded around 1890. (It was also called Partido Integrista Español.)[104] The term *integralism* arose among French Catholics who called themselves "integral Catholics." An Italian priest named Umberto Benigni founded a secret society in 1909 known as La Sapinière. This integralist organization lobbied Pius X for support.[105] The party of French author and politician Charles Maurras (1868–1952), Action Française, welcomed antidemocratic Catholics, including the young Maritain.[106] Portugal and Brazil had integralist movements too. During the First Portuguese Republic, Integralismo Lusitano rejected parliamentary democracy in favor of Catholic monarchy.[107]

We must understand how these parties arose. In nineteenth-century Europe, the fortunes of democracy matched the misfortunes of the church. Democratic power grew as Catholic power shrank. In response, Catholics often collaborated with antidemocratic leaders and supported authoritarian one-party rule in Italy, Germany, France, Austria, Portugal, and Spain. The most famous collaborators were Pope Pius XI (in office 1922–1939) and Benito Mussolini himself.

Mussolini wanted the church out of political life, so he offered Pius XI a deal. He would compensate Pius for the Italian seizure of the Papal States, confer sovereignty on the Vatican, and recognize Catholicism as Italy's official religion. Pius XI accepted, given his lack of enthusiasm for popular sovereignty. He hoped that public disillusionment with liberalism and with war would restore church prestige.

Pius XI won little from his deal with Il Duce. He had no moral authority when Mussolini dropped poison gas on Ethiopia, nor could he effectively resist Mussolini's anti-Semitic legislation in 1938. Pius XI came to regret his collaboration ("I am ashamed, not as pope, but as an Italian!"[108]). Pius XI's history is a cautionary tale for modern integralists.

---

[102] Chappel 2018.

[103] Chappel 2018, pp. 144–81.

[104] See van der Krogt 1992, pp. 123–35, esp. p. 125. See also Salvany 1993; Real Cuesta 1985; Schumacher 1962. For an overview, see Menard and Su (2022).

[105] Van der Krogt 1992, pp. 125–26.

[106] Rémond 2006.

[107] Ramos Ascensão 1943; Machado 1991.

[108] Kertzer 2015, p. 334.

Fascist and authoritarian (that is, both anti-liberal and antidemocratic) sympathies suffused many integralist movements. These included Action Française. In the 1930s, integralists supported Plínio Salgado's Brazilian Integralist Action and Engelbert Dollfuss's assumption of dictatorial power in Austria. Spain's Falangist movement had integralist sympathies, and it exercised great influence throughout the course of Francisco Franco's forty-year dictatorship. The American *Triumph* magazine, a periodical with integralist sympathies, supported Franco.[109]

Early-twentieth-century integralist movements have rich ties with anti-Semitism (though anti-Semitism was widespread at that time). Unlike many anti-Semites, Catholics did not derive their anti-Semitism from race theory; it arose primarily from long-standing Christian beliefs, particularly the belief in Jewish complicity in the crucifixion.[110] One can read about how popes confined Jews to ghettos in the Papal States for centuries,[111] including most of the nineteenth century.[112] According to Jewish historian David Kertzer, both Pius IX and Leo XIII "believed that the Jews' divinely ordained place was in the ghetto, and that healthy Christian society required protection from Jewish depredations."[113] I won't wade into the contentious issue of Catholic complicity in Nazism here.[114] That is not my topic, and I do not wish to tar integralists with unfair allegations.

I raise these issues because integralist movements did not adopt these views *wholly* by accident. In Chapters 4 and 5, you will see why integralists would overthrow or hollow out democracy and why they worry about large unbaptized communities, such as Jews. Indeed, Pope Gregory XVI (in office 1831–1846) justified many restrictions on Jews, including confinement to ghettos, "to guarantee Christian religion and morality." These prohibitions are "founded in the Sacred Canons" (which I mentioned above).[115] What's more, as historian John Connelly argues, Catholics alone may not have changed their beliefs. Indeed, Connelly notes that "from the 1840s until 1965, virtually every activist and thinker who worked for Catholic-Jewish reconciliation was not originally Catholic. Most were born Jewish. *Without converts the Catholic Church would not have found a new language to speak to the Jews after the Holocaust.*"[116]

---

[109] Patterson (2020) discusses the relationship between integralism and fascist movements in the twentieth century.

[110] Kertzer (2001, pp. 205–12) both discusses the theological aspects of anti-Semitism and challenges the distinction between religious and racial hatred of the Jews.

[111] Kertzer 2001, pp. 60–85.

[112] Although the Papal States ceased to exist on September 20, 1870, the Italian state did not abolish the ghettos until 1882.

[113] Kertzer 2001, p. 222.

[114] For a detailed and careful discussion, see Connelly (2012).

[115] As quoted in Connelly 2012, p. 82.

[116] Connelly 2012, p. 5, emphasis original.

Democracy and religious minorities stymie integralist politics. Integralists will face theoretical pressure to abolish democracy and mistreat religious minorities on the basis of commitments *internal* to integralism. Integralists need not support fascism, and they can fully oppose the persecution of Jews. Nonetheless, their desire for religious hegemony will tempt them. Catholic mistreatment of Jews ended *only* owing to the contributions of those who had once thought Judaism was true.

This is John Stuart Mill's revenge.[117] Learning the moral truth might require frequent engagement with "false" points of view. A political theology that places such laser-like focus on institutionalizing the moral and religious truth could easily miss this insight. Indeed, it *did* miss the moral truth, for centuries.

Toward Catholic Liberalism

In the early twentieth century, Catholicism looked politically flexible—and it was. Catholics supported many types of political regimes.[118] One intellectual noticed: German legal theorist Carl Schmitt (1888–1985) praised Catholicism for this flexibility.[119] Schmitt would later join the Nazi Party, and his membership ended only when the party ceased to exist. Schmitt was one of the twentieth century's leading anti-liberals. He supported Catholicism as liberalism's counterweight.

We cannot overstate Schmitt's influence in the interwar period. As German historian Heinrich Lutz lamented, Schmitt had a "fateful role as destroyer of the faith of young Catholics in the rule of law and in parliamentary democratic forms."[120] Schmitt attacked liberalism at every point.[121] He dismissed liberal confidence that market exchange and democratic deliberation produce good outcomes. He rejected the liberal doctrine of the rule of law. He defended "decisionism": the authority of law stems from its promulgation by the sovereign and not from the law's content.[122] Schmitt loved Joseph de Maistre and his "reduction of the state to the moment of the decision, to a pure decision not based

---

[117] Mill 1963, vol. 17, pp. 223–50.

[118] Again, see Chappel (2018).

[119] This was the major theme of Schmitt (1996).

[120] As quoted in Müller 2003, p. 73. With fortune, Schmittian intellectuals will not have the same effect on young Catholics today.

[121] For discussion, see Holmes (1993, chap. 2). For an excellent list of rejoinders to Schmitt, see Holmes (pp. 56–57).

[122] Holmes 1993, pp. 46–47. Holmes (pp. 37–60) provides what remains an excellent overview of Schmitt's anti-liberal commitments. See Müller (2003) for discussion of how Schmitt's objections to liberalism far postdate World War II.

on reason and discussion and not justifying itself, that is, to an absolute decision created out of nothingness."[123]

Schmitt cast all secular political philosophy as covert theology. Liberalism and socialism were secular religions. He thought all politics operates as conflict between friends and enemies. Liberalism falsely promises harmony between necessarily competing groups.

But, despite Schmitt's hopes, the church had lost its political power. Its influence must now come through reason and inspiration. This owes much to the church's transformation in the 1930s from "an *antimodern* institution into an *antitotalitarian* one."[124] Its embrace of liberal democratic institutions arose from its concern to avoid communist totalitarianism. The consequence was that the church began cooperating more with nations of different faiths and ideologies. Catholic intellectuals helped write the UN Universal Declaration of Human Rights (1948).[125]

The most important Catholic intellectuals who pushed for institutional liberalism were French philosopher Jacques Maritain (1882–1973) and American priest and theologian John Courtney Murray (1904–1967). They contended with Leo XIII's political thought and used Catholicism's role in the postwar order with the aim of moving the church toward liberal institutions. Owing to its international experience, the church embraced many universal individual and group rights, including the right to vote. Many Catholics hoped to convince the world that the church supports religious freedom. Catholic countries (though not the Vatican) signed the Universal Declaration of Human Rights. Murray hoped *Dignitatis humanae* would help non-Catholics trust Catholics as fellow citizens.[126]

Maritain's *The Primacy of the Spiritual* (1927) contrasts with his *Man and the State* (1951) on the church's public role in politics. Between the two books, Maritain shifted from integralism to institutional liberalism.[127] Indeed, following World War II, Maritain pushed for the Universal Declaration of Human Rights and may have affected the text.[128] According to Maritain's later thought, the Catholic Church should renounce all political rule. Integralism was once appropriate—but only for a "sacral" age, in contrast to our "secular" one.[129]

---

[123] Schmitt 2006, p. 66.

[124] Chappel 2018, p. 11, emphasis original.

[125] Sweet 2020, pp. 158–77.

[126] Murray 1993, p. 27.

[127] Maritain 2020, pp. 113–17, 123–39; 2012, pp. 147–87 (anyone who wishes to see a nonintegralist grapple with integralism should read every page of that chapter).

[128] Sweet 2020, pp. 158–77.

[129] Maritain 2012, pp. 157–62; Pink 2015b.

Maritain thought all humanity could grasp natural law. He saw different nations endorse human rights despite disagreeing on their justification.

In the secular age, the distinction between the body politic and the church is more stark, and indeed better reflects the gospel under conditions of religious pluralism. Religious divisions are unfortunate. But once we accept the semi-permanence of religious pluralism, we will see that, should integralism return, it will fuel "new despotisms and totalitarianisms."[130] Universal religious freedom allows for political freedom too.[131] And indeed, even the *supremacy* of the church is "more purely" applied when the church rules "by moral authority over consciences alone." The purest supremacy arrives when individuals "freely bear judgment, according to their own personal conscience, on every matter pertaining to the political common good."[132]

Murray also helped the church embrace religious freedom for pluralistic societies.[133] He published dozens of articles defending his position. American Catholic authorities first censored his work, but soon after they relented, his influence exploded. Like Maritain, Murray had many disciples.

Maritain and Murray argued that religious toleration fits Leonine principles. At the time, the church upheld integralism as the political ideal, as the thesis:[134] integralism is the thesis, toleration the hypothesis. Murray criticized the thesis-hypothesis distinction.[135] I focus on one of Murray's more ingenious arguments, because it bears on the rest of this book. Murray realized he could justify religious toleration without refuting integralism. Instead, he assailed the thesis-hypothesis distinction itself. We cannot speak of any transhistorical thesis, he argued; we can only identify hypotheses applicable to various times, cultures, and places. There is no such thing as Catholic ideal theory—integralism is as much a hypothesis as other arrangements.[136]

In Murray's hands, the thesis became a set of principles rather than a model of the ideal social world.[137] The immutable principles of the thesis mostly correspond to my definition of integralism. They include divine authorization of the temporal and spiritual powers. They stress the primacy of the spiritual, and they apply the ideal to Catholic societies. But they deny that spiritual primacy implies political sovereignty.

---

[130] Hittinger 2007a, p. 17.

[131] Maritain 2012, p. 108.

[132] Maritain 2012, p. 164.

[133] Murray 1993, pp. 42, 133.

[134] Bévenot 1954. I discuss the distinction between *thesis* and *hypothesis* in far more detail in Chapter 4. But see Maritain 2012, pp. 154–57.

[135] Murray 1993, p. 214.

[136] Levy 2016.

[137] Murray 1993, p. 112.

Vatican II and *Dignitatis humanae*

Church leaders accepted liberal democratic order. Today the Catholic Church embraces a range of human rights and supports democracy. But the right of religious freedom came to it late. The Second Vatican Council (1962–1965) composed and debated *Dignitatis humanae*, which, again, recognizes universal religious freedom.

Many council fathers sought to recover the ancient tradition of the church. The ancient teachings, in their view, opposed forced conversion. Yes, forced baptisms had occurred. But they had never received dogmatic sanction; indeed, the Fourth Council of Toledo (AD 633) had prohibited the practice. On the other hand, coercing the baptized also has an ancient lineage. The central authority on the matter? Saint Augustine (354–430). Augustine long supported suppressing heresy.[138] Still, his experience with ex-Donatists led him to an even more hard-line position—that religious coercion could change beliefs. Augustine favored such coercion, and used it.[139]

The Second Vatican Council fathers understood the church's complex relationship with religious coercion, but most regarded the anti-coercion strand as dominant. The church's role as a coercive authority—that is, the question of whether the church should use coercion *at all*—was so controversial that the council avoided addressing it head-on. The council may never have reached consensus.

The council fathers disagreed about the reasons that justify religious liberty. They redrafted *DH* many times. Once the council fathers settled on the final draft, however, they used *DH* to send the world a unified message (quoted in Box 2.9): human dignity forbids religious coercion. Pure and simple.

DH recognizes extensive religious liberties. Religious communities may "govern themselves according to their own norms."[140] They may establish their own educational institutions. The civil law may not interfere with how religious communities go about selecting, training, appointing, or transferring ministers, nor may it bar the construction of houses of worship. Religious groups may teach their faith in public through speech and print.[141] Parents have the right to live their own domestic religious life. They determine how they educate their children. Governments must not force children "to attend lessons . . . not in agreement with their [parents'] religious beliefs."[142]

---

[138] Bowlin 1997.
[139] Bowlin 1997.
[140] Paul VI 1965a, art. 4.
[141] Paul VI 1965a, art. 4.
[142] Paul VI 1965a, art. 5.

Box 2.9 **The Second Vatican Council on Religious Freedom**
in *Dignitatis humanae*

This Vatican Council declares that the human person has a right to religious freedom. This freedom means that all men are to be immune from coercion on the part of individuals or of social groups and of any human power, in such wise that no one is to be forced to act in a manner contrary to his own beliefs, whether privately or publicly, whether alone or in association with others, within due limits.

The council further declares that the right to religious freedom has its foundation in the very dignity of the human person as this dignity is known through the revealed word of God and by reason itself. This right of the human person to religious freedom is to be recognized in the constitutional law whereby society is governed and thus it is to become a civil right.

<hr>

Source: Paul VI, *Dignitatis humanae* (Vatican City: Libreria Editrice Vaticana, 1965), art. 2.

DH states that the common good requires equal treatment before the law. States may not treat anyone as inferior "for religious reasons," nor may they discriminate on the basis of religion.[143] Restrictions on religious freedom violate "the will of God and of the sacred rights of the person." States sin when they "destroy or repress religion."[144]

DH gives moral reasons in favor of these liberties. The right to religious freedom "has its foundation in the dignity of the person." The church also grounds religious freedom in divine revelation.[145] The argument is this: "Man's response to God in faith must be free." And so the state may not force conversion—"the act of faith is of its very nature a free act."[146] We cannot obey God unless we offer him the "free submission of the faith." In religious matters, "every manner of coercion on the part of men should be excluded,"[147] and "the person in society is to be kept free from all manner of coercion in matters religious."[148]

These claims sound universal. They sound even more universal when we note *DH*'s major premise: humans adopt religion only when we adopt it as true from

---

[143] Paul VI 1965a, art. 6.

[144] Paul VI 1965a, art. 6.

[145] Paul VI 1965a, art. 9. *DH* admits that it lacks a biblical basis for religious freedom. Yet it acknowledges no biblical obstacles to recognizing such liberty.

[146] Paul VI 1965a, art. 10.

[147] Paul VI 1965a, art. 10.

[148] Paul VI 1965a, art. 12.

our own perspective. True faith comes to us through our own point of view. God respects our freedom to reject him and places us "under no compulsion." Jesus did not compel submission.[149] Divine revelation—the very acts of Jesus Christ—demonstrate the injustice of religious coercion.

Many council fathers extended these arguments to the unbaptized and the baptized alike.[150] *DH* gives the impression that it does so. Apparently the church had left integralism behind forever.

Or had it? *DH* claims to contradict no previous church teaching, which surely includes Leonine doctrine. Murray, Maritain, and their followers spent decades resolving the tensions. *DH*'s defenders argue that teachings like *The Syllabus of Errors* did not express dogma.[151] (Incidentally, Cardinal Henry Newman also argued this.) Popes issued these teachings against sectarian European liberalism. Pius IX and Leo XIII did not dogmatize religious intolerance, the liberals claimed.

Some council fathers remained concerned about *DH*, and a handful even broke with the church over it (among other issues). The dominant schismatic group is the Society of Saint Pius X.[152] Still, integralism withered, and the church came to associate it with schismatics and hostility toward Vatican II. Pope Francis has called integralism a "plague."[153]

American Conservatism and the Rise of Right- and Left-Liberalisms

In this and the next two sections, I pause the cumulative case for integralism to unite the historical narrative of this chapter with the revival of integralism discussed in Chapter 1. To understand contemporary integralism, we turn to political developments in the United States. Integralism is also an outgrowth of developments within American conservative thought.

Before World War II, American liberalism shed its commitment to the free market.[154] The new liberalism combined liberal constitutionalism and

---

[149] Paul VI 1965a, art. 11.

[150] The two chief responses to Pink are Finnis (2013, pp. 566–77) and Rhonheimer (2014). Both share this intuition.

[151] Murray (1993) explores this strategy at length. Here Murray follows, of all people, Cardinal Henry Newman. See Newman 2015, p. 60.

[152] Vere 1999.

[153] Quoted in Catholic Sat (@CatholicSat), "At Audience with participants of a meeting promoted by the Institute for the Interreligious Dialogue of Argentina, Pope Francis says 'Integralism is a plague,'" Twitter, November 18, 2019, 6:21 a.m., http://twitter.com/catholicsat/status/1196 388035962834944.

[154] Witcover 2003.

democratic socialism. This hybrid—progressivism—created policy regimes
such as the New Deal, as well as the alliance that opposed it. The New Deal coalition excluded three groups:

- defenders of the free market (who called themselves "individualists");
- traditionalist religious believers (chiefly Catholic intellectuals);
- anti-communists.[155]

William F. Buckley (1925–2008) drew them into an alliance of convenience, as illustrated in his famous magazine, *National Review*.[156] These intellectuals interacted.
Some found common cause, while others denounced one another. A third group
synthesized an ideology. This view, often called *fusionism*, has served as the center
of intellectual gravity within American conservatism.[157] It orients conservative
intellectuals and politicians. They define themselves by whether they accept or reject it.

Fusionism has philosophical difficulties.[158] But this makeshift ideology enjoyed
political success after decades of struggle. From 1955 to 1976, the new "conservative" coalition lost many political battles, especially the 1964 presidential election.
Yet it created an army of young intellectuals and political organizers.[159] By 1980, we
can almost equate fusionism with American conservatism, so I will now use the
terms synonymously.

Conservatives sprang into action when American history gave them a chance.
The 1960s, 1970s, and 1980s witnessed the civil rights movement, second-wave
feminism, *Roe v. Wade*, massive increases in abortion and divorce rates, and
skyrocketing violent crime. Conservatives united voters concerned about these
changes; by the late 1970s, such voters included evangelical Christians. The coalition elected Ronald Reagan as president in 1980 and 1984.

Margaret Thatcher, British prime minister from 1979 to 1990, also embraced
fusionist ideals. She drove the United Kingdom toward the free market and
fought the Labour Party's robust administrative and welfare state. She joined
Reagan in opposing communism. With Saint John Paul II, they waged ideological

[155] Continetti (2022, pp. 32–91) reviews the formation of the coalition. George Nash (2022)
adds two further groups—neoconservatives and the Religious Right—but I see these groups as
joining the alliance later.

[156] Continetti 2022, pp. 99–130 (on Buckley), pp. 115–34 (on the founding of *National Review*).

[157] Even Warren G. Harding, Calvin Coolidge, and Herbert Hoover could fall under its banner,
despite the fact that most of the ideological welding occurred decades after they were in office (see
Continetti 2022, pp. 15–32).

[158] I think these difficulties can be resolved.

[159] Continetti 2022, pp. 170–71.

and spiritual warfare against the Soviet Union.[160] Coupled with a US military buildup, this campaign accelerated the Soviet Union's collapse. After 1991, much of the world moved toward markets. The United States became the world's global superpower and helped create a global economy. Anglophone conservatism triumphed, and Western Christianity was the wind at its back.

Meanwhile, some traditionalist Catholics chose integralist-adjacent ideals over fusionism. Brent Bozell Jr. (1926–1997) attempted to create an American integralist movement and founded *Triumph* magazine.[161] The magazine eventually failed, but Bozell's group then created and expanded Christendom College in Front Royal, Virginia. Integralism failed to capture hearts and minds.

The anglophone Left adapted to the new ideological environment by adopting many policy ideas from the Right. Bill Clinton (1946–) and Tony Blair (1953–) embraced markets. With conservatives, they opposed large fiscal deficits, excessive social welfare spending, and nationalized enterprises. They expanded free trade and supported international institutions that facilitated it.

For decades, liberalism formed the consensus of the world's most powerful nations. Conservatism functioned as market-leaning liberalism friendly to Christianity, while left-liberalism fought for social equality, welfare, sexual liberation, and privatizing religion. But both sides agreed that liberal democratic welfare-state capitalism was the best political and economic regime.

The Collapse of the Liberal Consensus

Historian Matthew Continetti argues that, over the last one hundred years, American conservatism has always contained many competing factions. But anti-communism had nonetheless united them.[162] Neoconservatives, religious conservatives, and libertarians agreed that communism was evil. The collapse of the Soviet Union put their disagreements on center stage in conservative politics. The movement began to attack itself—its factions grew further apart.

Then the twenty-first century wrecked their credibility, one by one. The Iraq War crushed the authority of the foreign policy hawks who had instigated it. These "neoconservatives" co-opted American military power to impose democracy on Muslim nations, but their war went worse than anyone had imagined.

The Great Recession challenged defenders of markets. Unlike during the Great Depression, elites did not shift to socialism. But the downturn knocked the wind out of the promarket elite; even the center-right wondered whether

---

[160] O'Sullivan (2008) tells the tale.
[161] Popowski 2011.
[162] Continetti 2022, pp. 69–85.

American economic policy had moved too far right. Rising economic inequality, together with a shrinking manufacturing base, reinforced these concerns. Opposition to markets grew.

The LGBT movement convinced American elites to oppose Christian sexual ethics. Evangelicals and Catholics who opposed same-sex marriage unintentionally convinced millions of people that Christians hated gays and lesbians. In 2013, the Supreme Court, staffed with Republican appointees, legalized same-sex marriage. Social conservatives had lost.

Indeed, social conservatives lost most battles in the culture war. They could not ban abortion despite staffing the judiciary with many conservative judges, at least not until the landmark 2022 decision in *Dobbs v. Jackson Women's Health Organization* reversed *Roe v. Wade* and *Planned Parenthood v. Casey*. Many Christian leaders discredited themselves through self-made scandals.

One must understand how greatly these losses affected conservative Catholic intellectuals. The mid-century Catholic liberals thought the constitutional liberal democracy would recognize the precepts of natural law. But natural law theory (purportedly) opposes abortion, while liberal democratic states legalized it. To Pope John Paul II, this was a betrayal. The liberal democratic state would not sanctify us and perfect our virtue, but it did promise "to protect fundamental human rights."[163]

Meanwhile, the center-left faced its own challenges. The Great Recession revived the fortunes of the economic Left, which drew the center-left away from markets and foreign policy interventionism. The Left foiled attempts to downsize the American welfare state and privatize Social Security. The cultural Left, in contrast, carried out a revolution. The academy shifted from economic socialism to a new and radical social egalitarianism—they focused more on race and gender than economic class. The new egalitarians rejected many liberal doctrines. They grew wary of free speech, robust religious freedom, and state neutrality. The critical legal studies movement pushed these ideas into popular culture,[164] including critical race theory[165] and other "critical" movements.

As the center-left aged, the academic and entertainment elites who replaced them leaned further to the left. Pretty soon, Democratic Party elders jumped on board, including Joseph Biden, who had been a senator or vice president for over forty years. In 2020, he tweeted, "Let's be clear: Transgender equality is the

[163] As quoted in Hittinger 2007a, p. 31.

[164] Alcoff 2021, sec. 1.1.

[165] Alcoff 2021, sec. 1.2.

civil rights issue of our time. There is no room for compromise when it comes to basic human rights."[166]

Consider the contrast with earlier liberals. The Left of the 1960s and 1970s fought for radical free speech, such as in the Berkeley free speech protests.[167] The American Civil Liberties Union had fought for the freedom of assembly of the Ku Klux Klan.[168] In 1993, the Democratic Party had supported religious exemptions for religious minorities from a range of laws and policies. It had collectively endorsed the Religious Freedom Restoration Act.[169]

Midway through the Obama administration, these commitments reversed. Speech codes spread across elite college campuses, universities grew concerned about conservative Christian student groups,[170] and the American Civil Liberties Union became a shadow of its former self.[171] Religious exemptions grew unpopular as orthodox Christians asked for them. Hostility toward exemptions arose in response to features of the Affordable Care Act (2010).[172] Left-wing illiberalism became orthodoxy in many elite social circles. Today this includes the corporate world. Elite Americans by 2023 have grown less liberal than they were even ten years ago. This illiberalism fuels political polarization.

In the mid-2010s, younger conservatives became increasingly aggravated by continuous political losses. They called their forebears soft and weak. They complained that the older generation, whom they dismissed as "right-liberals," wanted the Left's acceptance more than its defeat.[173] Right-liberals shared too many commitments with left-liberals. *Liberalism* became the problem.

Fusionism weakened. New anti-liberals began filling the ideological vacuum that opened on the Right. And in 2016, the political earth shook. The United Kingdom voted to leave the European Union and Donald Trump won the US presidency. A new right-wing populist movement converted many, especially right-leaning youth, and today has given rise to movement of "postliberals."[174]

---

[166] Joe Biden (@JoeBiden), Twitter, January 25, 2020, 1:20 p.m., https://twitter.com/joebiden/status/1221135646107955200.

[167] Cohen and Zelnik 2002.

[168] See *Brandenburg v. Ohio*, 395 U.S. 444 (1969).

[169] H.R. 1308, 103rd Congress (1993), available at https://www.congress.gov/bill/103rd-congress/house-bill/1308/text.

[170] See, e.g., *Christian Legal Society v. Martinez*, 561 U.S. 661 (2010).

[171] Michael Powell, "Once a Bastion of Free Speech, the A.C.L.U. Faces an Identity Crisis," *New York Times*, June 6, 2021. https://www.nytimes.com/2021/06/06/us/aclu-free-speech.html.

[172] See, e.g., *Obergefell v. Hodges*, 576 U.S. 644 (2015), which legalized same-sex marriage throughout the United States. Another controversy arose in *Little Sisters of the Poor v. Pennsylvania*, 140 S. Ct. 2367 (2020). This case concerned challenges to the Affordable Care Act's contraception mandate.

[173] Hale 2021.

[174] Continetti 2022, p. 379.

The New Right and the Rise of the New Catholic Integralism

Let's return to Catholic intellectual history. Recall that, after Vatican II, church leadership associated integralism with schismatic groups, hostility toward the council, and frankly, fascism. This position remains the overwhelming consensus. With the formation of the American conservative movement, however, Catholic intellectuals began to imbibe fusionism. They defend it in summer institutes, conferences, journal articles, and books. Their aim: harmonize American institutions with traditional Catholicism.

The older Catholic Right drew energy from many new Catholic converts. As anti-Catholic bigotry in the United States declined, the Catholic intellectual network grew. Catholic apologists evangelized traditional Protestants. These Protestants felt that their theologically liberal parishioners had betrayed the faith. Many "swam the Tiber" (that is, they converted).

Pope John Paul II's pontificate created intellectual gravity around conservative Catholicism. Despite grave challenges on the ground, Catholicism's intellectual domination continues to grow on the American Right. But elite Catholicism remains deeply liberal democratic. Given the elite Catholic consensus, where did integralism come from? As noted in Chapter 1, it began with British philosopher Thomas Pink's new interpretation of *Dignitatis humanae*.[175] But I have already told that story.

The Cumulative Historical Case for Integralism

Thus ends our history. We can now revisit the history argument. You may have met integralists who use historical proof texts to support their position, typically *Quanta cura* and *The Syllabus of Errors*. They can do better by making a cumulative argument, where one adds up data from history and dogma to vindicate integralism based on the balance of evidence. I think this argument should worry non-integralist Catholics. Integralism might fit the historical teaching and practice of the Catholic Church. Here's why: the balance of church teaching and practice may favor coercing the baptized. The standard reading of *Dignitatis humanae* provides strong counterevidence. However, Pink's read blunts *DH* as a source of evidence for the mainstream view. Only the other data

---

[175] Pink 2017. Besides Pink, John Finnis, and Martin Rhonheimer, many others have weighed in on the tension. For recent discussions, see Guminski and Harrison (2013), Guminski (2015), Lamont (2015), and Storck (2021).

can settle the disagreement, and those data favor integralism. Church practice and papal teachings in the medieval and early modern periods tilt against religious freedom for the baptized. Together they conflict with the standard reading of DH. Historically, the Catholic Church distinguished between the liberties of the baptized and the unbaptized.

I should note Martin Rhonheimer's response to Pink.[176] Rhonheimer argues that *DH* conflicts with earlier church teaching and practice, but he claims that the conflict poses no problem for the mainstream position. We need not read *DH* as continuous with Leonine integralism but may instead read them both with a "hermeneutic of reform." Here Rhonheimer draws on Pope Benedict XVI's hermeneutic for reading Vatican II documents.[177] According to this understanding, *DH reforms* teachings like Leonine integralism. Of course, if Leonine integralism were dogma, no one could reform it, but Rhonheimer denies that Leonine integralism has high dogmatic sanction. The church can contradict itself—just not at the dogmatic level.

I find debates about the dogmatic status of Catholic teachings bewildering.[178] Maybe one can reform *Immortale Dei*. I don't know. But I can see no way to water down the authority of the Trent canon XIV, not without opening the floodgate to theological liberalism. John Finnis has argued that Pink misreads the canon and that the church can reform the canon (if reform is necessary).[179] I cannot settle that debate here—it is too difficult. I leave the determination to you, but ask yourself the following question: If *DH* reforms the Trent canon, what preserves the dogmatic status of Trent's other canons?

---

[176] Rhonheimer 2011. Pink replies in Pink 2013a, and Rhonheimer responds in Rhonheimer 2014. For their lively in-person debate, see "Vatican II's Declaration on Religious Freedom: Revision, Reform, or Continuity?" ("For Freedom Set Free," Notre Dame Center for Ethics and Culture Fall Conference, November 24, 2015), YouTube video, 1:58:58, https://youtu.be/KvoTYBOTz1g.

[177] Benedict XVI 2005. For discussion, see Rhonheimer (2011).

[178] For a treatise on modern divisions, see Joy (2017). Some of the distinctions Catholics use today did not exist before the nineteenth century. At a minimum, they had no names. If Joy is correct, it is harder to know how popes and bishops understood the weight of their teachings. The distinction between the extraordinary and ordinary magisterium did not appear until 1863. Indeed, Joy (2017, p. 164) argues that the distinction is actually two distinctions: "This leads to what is perhaps the most important conclusion of the present study on the nature of the distinction between defined (extraordinary) and 'non-definitive' (ordinary) doctrines taught infallibly by the Church."
Joy proposes that theologians follow Vatican II and avoid using the terms. They should use "solemn judgment" and "definition" for an "extraordinary" judgment. The term "authentic magisterium" should replace the "ordinary magisterium" to name "non-definitive" teachings (Joy 2017, p. 165).
I place this information in a footnote because it detracts from the flow of the chapter. But distinctions between levels of dogma remained disputed even in the twenty-first century, which casts a fog over the fundamental question of the dogmatic status of integralist teachings.

[179] Finnis 2013, pp. 566–77; in response to Pink 2013b. For Pink's reply, see Pink 2019.

Integralists usually defend their position on dogmatic grounds alone. They also appeal to a smaller range of data than I have reviewed here. I hope I have strengthened their argument. It merits consideration.

Even so, the history argument is incomplete. It tells us that integralism fits Catholic teaching and history better than alternatives, but it doesn't explain the merits of integralist governance. Chapter 3 provides this explanation. Integralist states advance the whole human good—temporal and spiritual. Integralism alone treats goodness *symmetrically*.

Interlude: Augustine and the Coercion Argument

I have chosen not to examine the famous "coercion" argument against religious intolerance.[180] The familiar line runs as follows: Yes, if we could forcibly change the beliefs of others, such coercion might be justified. After all, coercion could produce beliefs that save souls! But coercing belief doesn't work because we humans lack any direct control over our own beliefs. Direct coercion of belief harms us without any benefit.

Integralists do not dispute this point; indeed, they oppose the direct coercion of belief, even for the baptized. But integralists have long supported indirect coercion of belief. Examples of indirect coercion include policy interventions that clear away temptations to false and heretical opinions. Many states (all states?) create environments conducive to some views over others, and some states deliberately control the flow of information for these purposes. Francisco Suárez argues that natural justice permits such indirect coercion of the baptized.

Assessing the efficacy of indirect coercion is fraught. While Suárez defended it, French philosopher Pierre Bayle wrote against it at length.[181] John Locke and Jonas Proast conducted a similar debate.[182] My takeaway is that indirect coercion of belief sometimes works and sometimes does not. But succeed it can. Conquest and propaganda often change the beliefs of a given population, sometimes radically. I see no way around that fact. So refuting indirect coercion of belief would be quite an undertaking. I henceforth focus on other criticisms.

---

[180] The locus classicus here is Locke (2009, p. 28): "pretense of saving their souls." But the argument has received much recent development. For one important such discussion, see Waldron (2010).

[181] Suárez (1612) 2015, p. 853; Bayle 2005, esp. pp. 541, 589 (in direct response to Suárez and Bellarmine). For a discussion of Suárez and Bellarmine's position, see Pink 2016.

[182] Locke 2009, pp. 3–46 contains Locke's first letter, whereas pp. 54–66 contain Proast's first response.

Readers may notice I say little about Saint Augustine in these pages. After much waffling, I decided that introducing his thought into the book would introduce the same multiple layers of complexity that one finds in his corpus. Fortunately, my arguments need not rely on his works. Were I to address the coercion argument, discussing Augustine would be indispensable. As I mentioned earlier in this chapter, Augustine was a longtime proponent of religious coercion, and he grew even friendlier with it over time.[183] He advocated forcing Donatists back to orthodox Catholicism. Grateful ex-Donatists helped convince him to take this position!

So I set Augustine aside, but not before I provoke the nonintegralist Christian. Augustine's views on religious coercion support the cumulative case for religious coercion, including coercion that the standard interpretation of *DH* rules out.

Whether Augustine provides support for integralism is another question. Given his pessimism about the feasibility of moral order, Augustine might help refute integralism. And yet Augustine powerfully argued that sin damages nature. He could help motivate the claim that the church must heal the damaging political effects of sin.[184]

---

[183] Bowlin (1997) remains the classic interpretation of Augustine's view on religious coercion.

[184] I discuss religious coercion briefly in Chapter 3.

3

Symmetry

The integralists have two powerful arguments in their arsenal. My brief history contains the first: popes, councils, and eminent theologians support integralist doctrine. Since few follow integralist interpretations of these authorities, integralists cannot rest their case. They need an argument for their position independent of these dogmatic disputes. I give them one in this chapter.

The *symmetry argument* defends integralism on the grounds that *integralism treats goodness symmetrically*. Modern Catholic natural law theory claims that the state should promote natural goods but not the supernatural goods of union with God; the theological virtues of faith, hope, and love; and the sacraments. Contemporary natural law theory treats natural and supernatural goods *asymmetrically*. The integralist offers a more coherent political theology.

If Thomas Pink reads *Dignitatis humanae* correctly, he has cleared away a sizable doctrinal obstacle to integralism.[1] I argue that integralists can mount a powerful philosophical argument against natural law perfectionism—the *symmetry argument*. Natural law perfectionists cannot justify their asymmetric treatment of goodness. Integralism, in contrast, treats the good symmetrically.[2]

We cannot dismiss the symmetry argument with the charge of infeasibility. We need only limit its scope: the argument shows that states should advance the supernatural good *when they can*. Integralism is not wholly utopian, either. Integralist regimes once existed, and so integralism may describe a feasible ideal.[3]

---

[1] Miller (2018) disputes Pink's interpretations of the relevant encyclicals.

[2] Strictly speaking, the inconsistency is *justificatory* rather than *logical*. A natural law perfectionist does not adopt strictly incoherent theses. Instead, the same considerations that *justify* promoting the natural good also *justify* promoting the supernatural good. I thank Peter de Marneffe for clarity on this point.

[3] Below I follow Catholic doctrine and distinguish between *thesis* and *hypothesis*. The thesis describes the Catholic political ideal, whereas hypothesis determines how we approximate the ideal in unfavorable conditions. For discussion, see Bévenot (1954).

All the Kingdoms of the World. Kevin Vallier, Oxford University Press. © Oxford University Press 2023.
DOI: 10.1093/oso/9780197611371.003.0004

I ignore liberal arguments against integralism, such as the claim that the state should not take sides on issues where people reasonably disagree.[4] Natural law perfectionists reject this constraint on state action.[5] I explore a disagreement among nonliberals.[6] And again, I also take Pink's interpretation of *DH* for granted; if Pink is wrong, integralists should return to hibernation.

Natural law perfectionism comes in different flavors. I address the most well-known and politically influential version: the "new" natural law theory of philosophers Germain Grisez, John Finnis, Robert P. George, and many others.[7] New natural law theorists cannot reject symmetric treatment of the good—or so I claim.[8]

I will now review the new natural law (NNL) theory, introduce the symmetry argument, and defend its central premise—the symmetry conditional. The chapter then assesses three replies: an objection from *authorization,* an objection from *religion,* and an objection from *prudence.* These replies fail. I conclude that the symmetry argument succeeds. The bold consequence? Catholic natural law theorists must take integralism seriously.

New Natural Law Theory

I characterize natural law theory first as an ethical theory, a theory that classifies actions as morally required, permitted, or prohibited. According to philosopher Mark Murphy, paradigmatic natural law theories hold the following:

(1) The natural law is given by God.
(2) It is naturally authoritative over all human beings.
(3) It is naturally knowable by all human beings.
(4) The good is prior to the right.
(5) Right action is action that responds non-defectively to the good.
(6) There are a variety of ways in which action can be defective with respect to the good.
(7) Some of these ways can be captured and formulated as general rules.[9]

---

[4] For a discussion of the class of such claims, see Vallier (2022).

[5] Or they hold that liberal restraint applies only to civility in public discourse. See George (1999, pp. 220–21).

[6] Nonliberals do not classify autonomy as a basic good.

[7] Grisez 1983; Finnis 2011; George 1995. I place "new" in quotation marks because these theorists think that their view is more consonant with Aquinas than were the natural law theorists who preceded them.

[8] Again, they cannot reject it on pain of a justificatory, not logical, inconsistency.

[9] Murphy 2019, sec. 1.4.

God issues the eternal law through the divine intellect—a law that becomes *natural* when applied to creation.[10] Natural law does not derive from the divine will, commands, or attitudes.[11]

Natural law specifies behavioral patterns and the conditions for creaturely flourishing. Humans alone have free and rational wills, so natural law also defines what we *ought* to do. Natural law describes our behavioral patterns, our flourishing, and how we *should* act. How does it do so? By specifying our final end—our ultimate purpose.[12] Our final end determines which acts, practices, and habits make our lives go better or worse.[13]

Not only do natural laws direct behavior, we can tell that they do so. Ordinary human reasoning reveals the natural law. We do not need divine revelation to grasp its requirements.[14]

Natural law theory places the good before the right—that is, it grounds right and wrong in facts about the good. Consequentialists agree, but the two views contrast in other respects. Consider three. First, consequentialism typically treats goodness agent-neutrally: a state of affairs can be good even if it is not good *for* any particular individual.[15] Natural law theory treats goodness as agent-relative: goodness is always goodness for a being or creature. Second, consequentialism claims that one can aggregate and then maximize goodness; hence the familiar slogan that the right thing to do is to maximize the good. NNL theory, in contrast, rejects the aggregation of natural "basic" goods. Aggregation is incoherent. And if we cannot aggregate goods, third, we cannot maximize them either. Consequentialism collapses.

Morally right actions respond appropriately to natural goods in one of two ways. Some goods merit production.[16] We respond appropriately to the good of health by healing the sick. Other goods deserve respect. We respond appropriately to the good of friendship by keeping our promises. Immoral actions—such as actions that weaken the sick or betray our friends—fail to respond appropriately to goods.

---

[10] Aquinas 1920, I–II, q. 93.

[11] Adams (1999) develops the most sophisticated contemporary divine command theory.

[12] Some NNL theorists may want to stress that the idea of natural law applies *only* to the structure of practical reasoning, and so to the free choices of rational beings. But I see no reason to deny that natural law has these other aspects.

[13] For Aquinas, our natural purpose is our *final cause*, and everything in nature has a final cause.

[14] For an exception, see the discussion below about grace and the knowledge of natural law.

[15] Though Douglas Portmore defends a version of consequentialism that appeals to agent-relative value (see Portmore 2011).

[16] Finnis 2011, pp. 118–25; Murphy 2011, sec. 2.4.

When we obey natural laws, we tend to acquire or enjoy natural goods. Not always, though; most natural laws have exceptions. That said, a few natural laws remain moral absolutes—ones we must never transgress.[17]

According to NNL theorists, humans live well when we enjoy certain *basic* human goods. Basic goods have their own worth; we should choose to promote or protect them for their own sake, and when we do so, our actions make sense. Knowledge is a basic good with its own worth. We can choose to promote or protect it for its own sake, and when we do, our actions make sense.[18] Cutting grass with scissors *lacks* its own worth, so we should *not* do it for its own sake; when we do, our actions make *no* sense.

Natural law theorists draw up different lists of basic goods. Grisez selects self-integration, practical reasonableness, authenticity, justice and friendship, religion, life and health, knowledge of truth, appreciation of beauty, and playful activities.[19] Finnis chooses life, knowledge, aesthetic appreciation, play, friendship, practical reasonableness, and religion.[20] Murphy picks life, knowledge, aesthetic experience, excellence in work and play, excellence in agency, inner peace, friendship and community, religion, and happiness.[21] Remember that all three lists identify "religion" as a basic good.[22] Religion helps assess the symmetry argument.

NNL theorists argue that the basic goods are incommensurable: no one can rationally rank aesthetic appreciation above the pursuit of knowledge.[23] Reason does not mandate that I become an artist rather than an academic.[24] We can represent choosing between incommensurables as choosing a basic good *for its own sake* without weighing it against other basic goods.[25] Incommensurability will resurface later in this chapter. It too helps us assess the symmetry argument.

NNL theorists apply natural law to politics. The state should help people pursue and enjoy the basic goods in a life of integral fulfillment. It should also establish the common good: the social condition where both individuals and

[17] On the foundations of moral absolutes within the new natural law theory, see Finnis (1991).

[18] I do nothing wrong in opting for a basic good for some further purpose.

[19] Grisez 1983, pp. 121–22.

[20] Finnis 2011, pp. 86–90. More recent lists include marriage as a basic good.

[21] Murphy 2001, p. 96.

[22] Here they follow Aquinas (1920, II–II, q. 81), although Thomists dispute whether Aquinas takes the NNL "basic goods" approach to natural law.

[23] Murphy 2001, pp. 182–98; Grisez 1978; Finnis 2011, p. 92. Formally, basic goods do not bear preference or indifference relations toward one another.

[24] Without incommensurability, new natural lawyers think their view collapses into egoism or utilitarianism.

[25] Murphy 2001, p. 193.

groups enjoy and pursue the basic goods.[26] The state may discourage choices that undermine basic goods.

Many people associate NNL theory with social conservatism. Understandably so. Finnis and George draw on NNL to defend conservative social policy. Examples include restrictions on same-sex marriage, euthanasia, and abortion.[27] Yet this association is not an intrinsic feature of NNL, so I set it aside for our purposes. Doing so clears the mind.

Classical Natural Law Theory: Excursus

Some call the new natural law theory "new" to contrast it with "classical" natural law theory.[28] Classical natural law theorists begin ethics with a theory of human nature, whereas NNL theorists begin ethics by asking what practical reason grasps as basic goods. Classical natural law theorists start ethics with metaphysics. NNL theorists begin ethics with principles of rational choice, which then classify our actions as reasonable or unreasonable.[29]

Classical and new natural law theorists can overdraw their differences. Murphy argues that their respective "metaphysical" and "practical" perspectives describe the same underlying moral reality.[30] I agree with Murphy.

Classical natural law theorists might fare better against the symmetry argument. What have I to say to them? The truth is, I am unsure. Here's why. Recall that classical natural law theory identifies moral truths via metaphysical ones.[31] We discern the metaphysical nature of persons and then delineate the resources, activities, and habits that actualize that nature. Ethical norms are rules that, when observed, realize human potential. But humans have a supernatural good too. The most important moral norms help humans reach their supernatural end. Such norms might justify a political order that facilitates such realizations—an integralist order, perhaps.

---

[26] Finnis 2011, p. 120. For a list with Finnis and Grisez on the same page, see Grisez, Boyle, and Finnis (1987).

[27] For a compilation of George's essays on the question, see George (1999). Critically, Gary Chartier—no conservative—embraces NNL (see Chartier 2014).

[28] Murphy calls this position "inclinationism" and contrasts it with the classical view: "derivationism" (Murphy 2001, pp. 6–45).

[29] Finnis 1998, pp. 91–92. For an excellent defense of classical natural law moral epistemology, see Jensen (2015, esp. pp. 44–60).

[30] Murphy 2001, pp. 40–45.

[31] For a somewhat recent defense of this "derivational" approach—to use Mark Murphy's (2001, pp. 6–13) term—see Lisska (1998).

Here we proceed from a metaphysical reality about persons to the duties of states. The NNL theorists can stress human interiority in realizing the good of religion, and they can draw on their account of first-person practical rationality. Classical natural law theory begins ethics from a third-person perspective. It thus lacks the resources to justify the asymmetric treatment of natural and supernatural goods.

This argument is too quick. Classical natural law distinguishes spheres of authority for different social groups, spheres that rest on the natures of these groups.[32] The family has its own nature. The state does too. Their natures ground limits on the powers of each. The church may have similar limitations; it may violate its nature by authorizing religious coercion.

Classical natural lawyers might argue that the church can authorize the state to use religious coercion. I will examine what I call the *authorization argument* later in this chapter. If the argument succeeds, then I think that classical natural law points toward integralism. But in Chapter 6, I will critique the authorization argument, thereby outlining how classical natural lawyers might resist integralism.

The Symmetry Argument

The symmetry argument draws on three types of supernatural goods. The first is union with God: our incorporation into Christ, where we enjoy sanctifying grace and receive the beatific vision. The second type of supernatural goods consists in the supernatural *virtues* of faith, hope, and love. These virtues empower us to unite with God: faith trusts God, hope relies on God's promises, and love desires and seeks union with God.[33] The sacraments form the third type. They relate us to God through material means, such as baptism, the Eucharist, and confession. A "supernatural good" indicates a good that falls into any of these types.

Supernatural goods are basic goods even though we do not grasp them through natural reason. Union with God has its own worth; we should pursue it for its own sake; and when we do so, our actions make sense. New natural law theorists may claim that we never choose supernatural goods for their own

[32] Crean and Fimister (2020, pp. 40–62) provide an excellent illustration of how classical natural law can establish the authority of different social spheres, even if they would reject a classical natural law argument that the church lacks indirect supernatural sovereignty.

[33] For Grisez on faith, see chap. 1, question A, in Grisez (1992, available at http://www.twotlj.org/G-2-1-A.html); for Grisez on hope, see chap. 2, question A, in Grisez (1992, available at http://www.twotlj.org/G-2-2-A.html); and for Grisez on love of God (charity), see chap. 3, question A, in Grisez (1992, available at http://www.twotlj.org/G-2-3-A.html). All involve union with divine persons.

sake.[34] Every choice of supernatural goods includes a natural good: that is, all supernatural goods *pair* with natural goods in the act of choice.[35] If this is correct, we never opt for supernatural goods alone.

Consider the good of *true* religion. According to the NNL theory, true religion is *two* goods: the natural good of religion and the supernatural good that comes from complete union with God. When we participate in Catholic religious life, we simultaneously choose natural religion and corporate union with God. For the NNL theorist, every choice of a supernatural good is like this. Supernatural goods come paired with natural goods in every case.

I can accept this point. Vindicating the symmetry argument only presumes the following: we can choose a supernatural good for its own sake even if we thereby also choose a natural good for its own sake. Choosing union with God, for instance, entails choosing religion. Our option for choice is to enjoy the natural-supernatural good pair, choosing both goods for their own sake.

The symmetry argument rests on the intuition that states must promote the whole good, natural and supernatural. It explains integralism's attraction: integralism treats goodness more symmetrically than the NNL theory does.[36] I formulate the symmetry argument as follows:

The Symmetry Argument
1. States should promote natural goods (natural law premise).
2. If states should promote natural goods, they should promote supernatural goods (symmetry conditional).
3. States should promote supernatural goods (proto-integralist conclusion).[37]

Integralists and NNL theorists agree that the state should promote natural goods, hence proposition 1. This *natural law premise* assumes that states "promote" natural goods by creating conditions where citizens can enjoy them.[38] I take the natural law premise for granted.

---

[34] God could bestow supernatural goods in response to our choices; our choice *occasions* a divine response. That means we can act so as to occasion a supernatural good, which is one way to choose a supernatural good.

[35] NNL theorists often describe choices as choices between *options to enjoy* goods. I prefer the less bulky locution of *choosing goods*. Here I treat these locutions as equivalent.

[36] Integralists do not treat the natural and supernatural goods *wholly* symmetrically. The church governs the distribution of supernatural goods, although these goods accrue chiefly to baptized persons.

[37] States could promote supernatural goods through a monarch (caesaropapism). But I take the integralism form for granted owing to its centrality in church tradition.

[38] "Promotion" does imply *maximization*; the state might not stand under any requirement to maximize the set of goods but rather to satisfice. Yet, either way, states have a powerful reason to prioritize infinite goods over finite goods.

I call proposition 2 the *symmetry conditional*. Here states enable the reception of supernatural goods, but not in the same way they promote natural goods. States cannot promote union with God *at all*. As Scripture teaches, God chooses us, not the other way around (John 15:16). God grants his church supreme authority over supernatural goods, which it must then extend to the state. The state's task? Help Christians choose to *remain in God's grace*.

The church-authorized state assists the church by devising coercive policies. It establishes Catholicism as the religion of state, and its schools instill the Catholic faith. Integralist states may also punish heresy and apostasy.

The symmetry conditional does not pit nature against grace. Grace only enhances nature. The state does not choose supernatural goods over natural goods. It sometimes chooses between a mere natural good and a *pair*—a natural good and a supernatural good together.

To illustrate formally, let N be a natural good unpaired with supernatural good S, and let N_S be a natural good paired with S. Suppose N is physical health and N_S is the good of religion paired with being in a state of grace. The state must now choose N or N_S and should consult all aspects of N_S in its decision. The state must not ignore that N_S pairs with a supernatural good. Again, if states should advance natural goods, they should also advance natural-supernatural pairs of goods.

To illustrate informally, recall Catholic teaching that most Protestant pastors (if not all) lack proper ordination. The disastrous consequence: they cannot confect a valid Eucharist and so cannot offer their parishioners the true body and blood of Jesus. Suppose that John is Methodist and receives the Lord's Supper during weekly services. He misses the true Eucharist. But John enjoys the natural good of religion by obeying Christ's command to remember him (Luke 22:19).[39] Five years later, John converts to Catholicism. Since Catholic priests can confect a valid Eucharist, he now receives the genuine body and blood of Jesus. John enjoys religion *and* the supernatural good of greater union with God.[40]

If the symmetry conditional holds, states must consider John's reasons to receive the Eucharist rather than the Methodist substitute. These reasons have great power: union with God is the greatest good of all. Yet the NNL theory orders the state to *ignore* these reasons. How odd. The integralist state honors these reasons by elevating religious truth over falsehood. Why? True religion is both a natural good and a tremendous supernatural good. The good of false religion pales in comparison. Catholicism, for instance, provides the true Eucharist.

---

[39] Obedience and remembrance may also be supernatural goods.

[40] I thank an anonymous referee for pushing me to clarify this point.

Buddhism does not. Practicing Buddhism is still a natural good, but it pales in comparison to practicing Catholicism.

The symmetry conditional seems true. If states should advance natural goods, they must keep citizens Catholic. Or, rather, they must create conditions where its baptized citizens can readily choose to remain in grace.

Proposition 3 is the *proto-integralist conclusion*. The symmetry argument cannot prove integralism: no one knows whether integralist regimes promote the supernatural good better than alternatives. If church and state integrate, increased church corruption could undermine the church's authority. Or Catholicism may flourish when it competes with other faiths.[41] Integralists must argue that their states best promote supernatural goods. Where do they even begin? No empirical work shows that "dyarchies"[42] best promote supernatural goods.[43] God distributes supernatural goods as he wishes and shrouds his gifts in mystery. Integralist arrangements crested in the thirteenth century, but historians doubt that thirteenth-century Western Europeans were especially pious.[44] For all we know, nonintegralist regimes advance the supernatural good more effectively.[45] And we know next to nothing.

Still, the proto-integralist conclusion helps the integralist shift the debate. We no longer ask *whether* states should promote supernatural goods but *how* they should do so. We know that states should promote supernatural goods *when they can*.

Reasons to Accept the Symmetry Conditional

From here forward, I will defend the symmetry conditional on four grounds. First, supernatural goods outweigh mere natural goods. Receiving the Eucharist trumps reading a novel, and eternal salvation trumps worldly fame. States have strong reasons to promote supernatural goods (which are always paired with a natural good).

Second, supernatural goods grant eternal life. In heaven, we can enjoy a wide range of natural goods forever.[46] We experience permanent aesthetic enjoyment

---

[41] Finke and Stark 2005.

[42] Here a dyarchy is a church-state union that governs a human community.

[43] Indeed, much work contradicts this claim (see Toft, Philpott, and Shah 2011).

[44] Johnson and Koyama 2019, p. 43.

[45] A supernaturalist politics could advance supernatural goods indirectly and noncoercively.

[46] At least, we can enjoy some natural goods. Grisez thinks we lose the natural good of intimacy with others who are in hell (see Grisez 2008, chap. 1, available at http://twotlj.org/OW-4-Ch1.pdf).

in God's presence. If that is true, states should support goods that help us enjoy natural goods without end.

Third, sin obscures our ability to identify natural basic goods. We miss what morality requires. Supernatural goods can heal our moral sight by bestowing God's grace upon us.[47] With grace, we can better pursue natural goods. We can *see* them. Surely, then, the state should secure the goods that enable us to identify natural goods.

Some Catholic teaching supports the third argument.[48] Consider Pope Pius IX: "Where religion has been removed from civil society, and the doctrine and authority of divine revelation repudiated, the genuine notion itself of justice and human right is darkened and lost."[49] And Pope Leo XIII: "When Jesus Christ is absent, human reason fails, being bereft of its chief protection and light, and the very end is lost sight of, for which, under God's providence, human society has been built up."[50] Francisco Suárez agrees:

> For grace also has an essence and a nature of its own, to which the infused light is connatural, and to which it is nonnatural not only to direct men towards righteous, good, and fitting behaviour in supernatural matters, but also to dispel darkness and errors relating to the purely natural law itself and to enjoin on that basis of a higher reason the observance of that same natural law.[51]

Grace helps us identify natural goods. With church authorization, then, states should organize society to enable the full saturation of grace in our institutions. If the state should help us enjoy natural goods, it should create an environment where we can more readily detect those goods. If the state wants to heal us, it should give us the cure. Pink adds that nonconfessional states have forgotten the natural law, as shown by their embrace of abortion, contraception, and euthanasia.[52] States that act from natural law alone lose grace and moral knowledge thereby.[53]

Finally, even if we grasp the natural law, we cannot follow it always, or even most of the time. Without sanctifying grace, "fallen men" cannot even keep the natural laws they recognize, but since grace restores virtuous motives, it

---

[47] Pink 2018a.

[48] Pink (2018a) covers a number of historical dogmatic sources of this claim.

[49] Pius IX 1864.

[50] Leo XIII 1900.

[51] Suárez ([1612] 2015), p. 46.

[52] Pink 2018a.

[53] Here society surely loses grace, but for the integralist, the political regime also loses it.

helps us achieve natural goods.[54] Grace creates virtues that aid moral choices. Put another way: if the state gives us medicine (grace) to cure a disease (sin), it should help us take this medicine. We cannot achieve natural ends unless the spiritual power teaches and sanctifies us.[55] The imparted supernatural goods help us *know* the moral law *and* follow it so that we can attain our natural ends.

We have excellent reasons to accept the symmetry conditional. I now examine three arguments against it: what I call the objections from *authorization*, *religion*, and *prudence*. For clarity, we can list objections to the symmetry conditional as follows:

1. The authorization objection
2. The religion objection
   a. The incommensurability reply to the religion objection
   b. The noncompetition reply to the religion objection
   c. The intending-harm-to-a-good reply to the religion objection
3. The prudence objection.

The Authorization Objection to the Symmetry Conditional

New natural law theorists may respond that states lack authority over supernatural goods. The state must establish only peace and justice.[56] Finnis reads Aquinas as claiming that the state should limit itself to pursuing peace—which is not a mere modus vivendi. Peace is rather "concord . . . and willing agreement between one person or group and another, but also harmony amongst each individual's own desires."[57] The law should "secure friendship between people,[58] and efforts to maintain peace by laying down precepts of justice."[59] Peace furnishes the benefits of social life and avoids contention. It does so even if it "falls short of the complete justice which true virtue requires of us."[60] Finnis accepts this position: the state lacks authority even over some natural goods, much less supernatural goods.

---

[54] Crean and Fimister 2020, p. 78.
[55] Crean and Fimister 2020, p. 18.
[56] Finnis 1998, pp. 219–33.
[57] Finnis 1998, p. 227.
[58] Aquinas 1920, II–II q. 99, art. 2c.
[59] Aquinas 2018, vol. 14, appendix p. 43.
[60] Finnis 1998, p. 228.

If the state lacks authority over supernatural goods, the symmetry conditional is false. The state cannot secure supernatural goods. It must not use religious coercion, even if coercion helps people keep the faith. Even if the state should promote natural goods, then, *it has no right* to promote supernatural goods.

The integralist agrees that states have no authority over supernatural goods *on their own*. The church has authority. Contra NNL, however, the church can expand state jurisdiction. The church could authorize the state to use civil penalties to support church law and policy.[61]

Objection: the church cannot expand state authority because it has no authority to coerce. It cannot give what it does not have. Note, though, that the church spiritually coerces its members all the time, excommunicating impenitent sinners to secure their repentance. Believers may *prefer* physical coercion. Civil punishment affects only this life; spiritual punishment could last forever. The church uses spiritual coercion. Perhaps it can authorize the state to use physical coercion.

Spiritual and physical coercion may differ *in kind*.[62] The authority to use spiritual punishments might not automatically extend to physical punishment. What then? The church may coerce physically owing to its status as a perfect society (*communitas perfecta*). According to Cardinal Bellarmine, "The [Church] ought to have every power necessary to attain its end. But the power of using and disposing in regard to temporal affairs is necessary to a spiritual end, otherwise wicked principles could foster heretics with impunity as well as overturn religion. Therefore, the [Church] has this power too."[63]

Leo XIII agrees:

> [The Church] is a society chartered as of right divine, perfect in its nature and in its title, to possess in itself and by itself, through the will and loving kindness of its Founder, all needful provision for its maintenance and action. And just as the end at which the Church aims is by far the noblest of ends, so is its authority the most exalted of all authority, nor

[61] One might wonder whether the church can take over state functions. Integralists claim that God authorizes the state to enforce the natural law. The church would usurp the state's divine authority by taking over state functions.

[62] Matthew Young helpfully suggests that even if believers experience spiritual penalties as more coercive, that does not imply that any authority may wield a lesser penalty simply because it has the authority to wield a greater penalty. Suppose, for instance, that Max's class paper deserves a failing grade. His teacher has authority to evaluate Max's paper and punish him with an F. Yet, given Max's desire for good grades, he would experience an F as a worse punishment than a literal slap on the wrist. The fact that Max's teacher can give him an F does not mean that the teacher can dole out the lesser punishment by slapping him on the wrist.

[63] Bellarmîne 2016, book 5, chap. 7, p. 308.

can it be looked upon as inferior to the civil power, or in any manner dependent upon it.[64]

Leo XIII teaches that the church holds every power needed to maintain itself and its mission. The church has authority to legislate on all matters concerning religion. Archbishop Marcel Lefebvre agrees. The church is a perfect society "supplied by its divine Founder with all the means to subsist by itself in a stable and independent fashion."[65] Thomas Crean and Alan Fimister also agree.[66]

But hold on. One could claim that the church can authorize the state only in matters that fall "within its competence."[67] If physical coercion helps advance its mission, the church may use it, but otherwise not. One could argue that physical coercion goes beyond the church's competence. Russell Hittinger argues that the Papal States were "comically incompetent" in their operations.[68] Integralists agree. Crean and Fimister argue that wielding "both swords" on behalf of a large public creates too many temptations to "avarice and pride."[69] For instance, they predict that simony would be more common if the church must wield the temporal sword.[70]

But even here, the church could have the power to authorize the state to act on its behalf because the church possesses a power it cannot competently wield. So the church could still extend its authority to a competent power—that is, the state.[71] If I am too weak to lift my couch, I can authorize a strong person to lift it. Similarly, if the church is too incompetent to wield the temporal sword, it can give the state the temporal sword on its behalf.

We have thus far assumed that the state can identify the true religion. Now let's question that assumption. If the state cannot identify true religion, it should not promote the supernatural good. It lacks the competence. A reply: The church

---

[64] Leo XIII 2014, p. 112.

[65] Lefebvre 1994, p. 85.

[66] Crean and Fimister 2020, pp. 16–22.

[67] Leo XIII 2014, p. 113.

[68] Hittinger 2007b, p. 40.

[69] Crean and Fimister 2020, p. 77.

[70] Crean and Fimister 2020, p. 77n23.

[71] This reply raises the question of whether the church could develop the competence to use physical coercion, which it presumably had in the Papal States. If the church could rule the Papal States, then can't the church rule in temporal affairs in general? Why would God then establish the state and place it over temporal matters if the church could govern everything? In short, why not make every state a Papal State?

knows the religious truth and can inform state officials. Officials can then respond accordingly.[72]

Let's grant that a state with Catholic leaders can trust church testimony. But what if a state is religiously diverse? If the state is led by Catholics, maybe Catholics can override objections from their subordinates.

Or not. State officials may affirm Catholicism as citizens. But they may remain unable to accept Catholicism in their office as state representatives. In medieval societies, monarchs often mixed private and public powers. The mix arose from institutional degradation. The Roman Empire had sharply distinguished between holding an office and owning property. In the medieval period, "the very notion of office . . . came to be assimilated to that of proprietary right"[73] as symbolized by the single word "dominium," which denoted "both proprietary right and governmental authority."[74] Thus, a king could submit his whole "dominium" to the church in the medieval period. Some did.[75]

In contrast, modern polities distinguish people from their offices. Many constitutions prohibit officials qua officials from accepting and acting on church testimony. Integralism is manifestly unconstitutional in the United States. The Roman Empire had separated "proprietary and governmental authority," as modern states often do. Integralism arose only when societies did not draw those distinctions.[76]

To institute integralism, state officials will have to consult their private convictions and support a concordat—a contract that codifies state obedience. If the constitution bars a concordat, officials can advocate constitutional change. This is quite the barrier. High-ranking officials must adopt integralism and advocate constitutional change through processes fixed by a nonintegralist constitution.

NNL theorists can offer three other authorization objections. They can appeal to the standard interpretation of *Dignitatis humanae*, which I have set aside, or they can argue that church authorization will permit the state to act *unjustly* or *incompetently*. Unfortunately, all three replies show that the authorization objection depends on successful prior objections. The first reply depends on the proper interpretation of *DH*. The second reply depends on what justice requires. And the third reply dissolves into the objection from prudence, which I address below.

---

[72] Citizens can receive this knowledge by faith, so state actors can too, even if states are not agents.

[73] Oakley 2010, p. 77.

[74] Coleman 1983, p. 212.

[75] One oft-cited example is King John's submission to Innocent III. This ended the papal interdict on England.

[76] Oakley 2012, pp. 200–201.

The Religion Objection to the
Symmetry Conditional

The chief objection to the symmetry conditional draws on the character of the natural good of religion. Here I outline this *religion objection*. The next three sections examine integralist responses to it (2a, 2b, and 2c in the outline above). Some readers may find these replies overly technical. You can skip them. But they engage the intricacies of NNL theorists in ways that strengthen the symmetry argument, so I include them. Here's the religion objection: In recruiting the state as its secular arm, the church may permit the state to threaten religion. If so, the church authorizes a violation of natural law, which is impossible.

We enjoy religion when we achieve "harmony with the more-than-human order, those aspects of the ways things are that transcend the world of human making, doing, and acting."[77] New natural law theorists argue that we can enjoy religion even if our faith rests on false beliefs. Any sincere pursuit of religious truth realizes this basic good.[78]

Finnis and George argue that states may promote religion only by ensuring that people may choose religion freely.[79] In *Making Men Moral*, George claims that religion "can indeed provide a reason for political action. It cannot, however, provide a reason for compelling or forbidding religious belief or practice."[80] If we do not freely choose religion, we do not enjoy it.[81] Since people can enjoy religion within different faith traditions, the state must not coercively favor one faith.[82] It should tolerate many religions, while encouraging religious reflection, faith, and practice.[83] Natural law forbids coercion that undermines the good of religion, which means that integralist coercion violates natural law.

Before I assess this argument, remember that the integralist state may religiously coerce only baptized citizens. Others have complete freedom of religion.[84]

Philosopher Terence Cuneo criticizes the religion objection. A person can choose a religion that undermines other goods, which could make the person's

---

[77] Murphy 2001, p. 131. Grisez, Finnis, and George define "another category of reflexible good" as "peace with God, or the gods, or some non theistic but more-than-human source of meaning and value." See Grisez, Finnis, and George 1987, p. 108.

[78] Or, instead, regardless of which of a wide range of reasonable religions people choose.

[79] Finnis 2006; George 1995, pp. 219–28.

[80] George 1995, p. 41.

[81] George 1995, p. 221.

[82] I set aside symbolic (noncoercive) establishment of religion, which NNL theorists can accept.

[83] George 1995, p. 224.

[84] Save for exercises of religion that violate natural law.

life worse on the whole.[85] Suppose Reba espouses a religion that discourages knowledge. Religious authorities fear that knowledge will lead Reba to leave the faith. Here Reba enjoys the basic good of religion, but she loses the basic good of knowledge. Forgoing knowledge could "defeat the goodness of ordering her religious life freely."[86] The government should ensure that Reba pursues religion effectively and should discourage bad religions with that goal in mind.[87]

Let's strengthen Cuneo's point. If Catholicism is true, humans can unite with God.[88] If Reba becomes a baptized Catholic, she enjoys that union;[89] if Reba becomes Buddhist, she does not.[90] Pious Buddhists cannot access grace through the sacraments. The church-authorized state should discourage Reba from Buddhism, if it can do so without creating a greater harm.[91] To generalize: the state should promote true religion even over *excellent* false religions.

The state can coerce belief only indirectly. It could bar baptized citizens from reading and sharing heretical literature. It could ban baptized children from madrassas. Integralist state policies remove temptations in order to help people remain in grace.[92] Policy changes people's beliefs indirectly.

At first glance, then, natural law does not bar integralist state action. The religion objection fails; the symmetry conditional holds.

The Incommensurability Reply to the Religion Objection

New natural law theorists say we cannot commensurate the natural basic goods, meaning that reason cannot establish that natural good *A* is superior to natural good *B*, or vice versa. Indeed, reason cannot even assign them equal value. This *incommensurability thesis*, mentioned above, even applies to choices "between

---

[85] "False religion" for our purposes will denote any religion or denomination other than Catholicism. Yet, for the Catholic, no religion need be wholly inaccurate.

[86] Cuneo 2005, p. 116. Cuneo denies that religion is a basic good. States may also fail to distinguish between defeated religious goods and better ones.

[87] If a religion undermines knowledge, the state might limit it. According to the NNL theory, the state has authority over natural basic goods. But if the faith requires reducing knowledge, limiting knowledge is to suppress it. NNL theorists want to avoid this.

[88] Hittinger 1988, p. 120.

[89] That is, she enjoys a free choice to become Catholic, and not under duress.

[90] At least, she does not enjoy it as obviously, and not to the same degree.

[91] My argument does not assume that religion is a merely instrumental good. To say enjoying good *A* helps one enjoy good *B* is not to say that *A* is instrumentally good alone. *A* and *B* might both be basic goods.

[92] I am grateful to an anonymous referee for this point.

instantiations of one and the same basic good."[93] Reason cannot commensurate natural good A_1 and natural good A_2. We cannot commensurate across different persons.[94] Reason cannot say that it is better for Reba to enjoy natural good A than for John to enjoy natural good B. Reason cannot say that B is worse or that the two options have equal value.

NNL theorists can argue that we cannot commensurate John's true religion with Reba's false one. The integralist state needs a rational basis for prioritizing spiritual over temporal goods, but incommensurability means no such basis exists. If that is the case, NNL theorists can use the incommensurability thesis to reject the symmetry conditional.

The integralist can reply that integralist states help lead people to true re-ligion. And this is for their own good. The state need not commensurate reli-gion across persons, only within a single life. Integralist policies could be Pareto improvements, moving each person toward a greater realization of religion.

Many supernatural goods have infinite weight. Take union with God: an enormous good that endures forever.[95] As Grisez claims, "Nothing is more im-portant for the Christian than to be in unity with the love of God which comes to us in our Lord Jesus."[96] We should place God *above* all else. Once we know that Catholicism involves union with God, we should choose it.

Here we can surely commensurate a finite good with an infinite good. Denying this strains credulity.[97] I understand claiming that reason cannot commensurate finite goods. Perhaps we encounter two goods and can neither choose one over the other nor regard them as indifferent. But a practically reasonable person must choose an infinite good over a finite one. I illustrate in the next section with the case of Jan.

George denies that the good of religion overrides other natural goods. We can modify his argument to ask whether true Catholic religion outweighs mere natural goods. Consider John, a humble Roman Catholic with a standard nine-to-five job.[98] Suppose John believes that religion trumps other basic goods and concludes that he must attend church rather than get to work on time. We must squeeze in church whenever possible. The priority of religion would "entail that he behaves immorally if he opts instead to spend his time before work reading

[93] Grisez, Boyle, and Finnis 1987, p. 110. One can commensurate between goods within the life of a single person.
[94] Though we can commensurate choices for a single individual.
[95] Here I suppose that we can choose union with God *once God offers it to us.*
[96] Grisez 1983, p. 156.
[97] NNL theorists often claim that free will requires incommensurability. We can freely choose only between goods that we cannot commensurate. I cannot address this argument here; it is too complex.
[98] "John" is the name I link to George's argument.

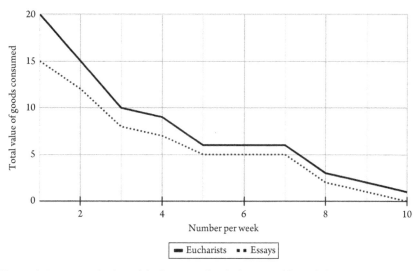

Figure 3.1. Marginal value of the basic goods of religion and knowledge.

the paper, or listening to some jazz recordings, or playing with his children." If religion has priority, he "must, if possible, act specifically for the sake of religion."[99] But John should not always pursue religion first. That would be unreasonable.

Yet we do not choose basic goods in classes but in marginal amounts. For example, we choose knowledge by units. We read one book and then another. The strength of our reasons to pursue a basic good diminishes at the margin. Each book has less value for us than the previous one.

True religion outweighs mere natural goods *at the same margin*. John should always choose the first Eucharist over reading an essay in *The Atlantic*. But he can forgo his seventh Eucharist.[100] John need only rank his first Eucharist over mere natural goods.[101]

Consider Figure 3.1, a map of John's choices in a single week. One of the curves represents the marginal value of receiving the Eucharist, whereas the other represents the marginal value of reading an essay in *The Atlantic*.[102] The first Eucharist has more value than the first *Atlantic* essay, which has more value than

[99] George 1988, p. 1427.

[100] He cannot value the eighth Eucharist since Catholics ordinarily should not receive the Eucharist more than once a day.

[101] Some basic natural goods are also instrumentally good. We may need them in order to enjoy supernatural goods.

[102] My utility analysis represents the logic of choice *as such*. I do not think basic goods have mere instrumental or subjective value. Neither do I suppose that the *objective* value of the Eucharist diminishes. Rather, additional units of objective good have diminishing returns *for us*. The curves represent the strength of our *objective reasons* for choosing basic goods.

the third Eucharist.[103] The summed value of Eucharists exceeds the summed value of essays. Yet one can still rationally choose to read an *Atlantic* essay rather than receive further Eucharists.[104]

If true religion trumps mere natural goods at the same margin, states should promote it. They should suppress dangerous heresies. If states protect religious freedom for the baptized, more Catholics may leave a state of grace.

The Noncompetition Reply to the Religion Objection

One can resist these trade-offs in another way: perhaps we never choose a natural good over a supernatural good. When we choose option *x* over option *y*, we opt for the natural good in *x* only absent from *y*. We act only for the sake of natural goods, and we make trade-offs only between them. The choice of a natural good over a supernatural good *never arises* for individuals *or their governments*.

Hence the *noncompetition thesis*. States cannot choose the supernatural good—*no one* can. The symmetry conditional presumes that the state can choose to promote supernatural goods. If the noncompetition thesis holds, that is impossible.

At times, Grisez seems to argue that we do not choose between natural and supernatural goods. Or, at least, God will never stick us with such a choice. In a commitment to Jesus, "there is no need to choose between human good and friendship with God."[105] Supernatural and natural goods do not compete with one another when we make practical choices. When we choose God, we choose the natural good of religion; we do not choose between divine goodness and religion.[106]

The symmetry conditional does not suppose that anyone chooses between natural and supernatural goods. States can advance true religion via natural religion. We have one reason to choose religion: it is a natural basic good. We have an additional reason to choose true religion: it comes paired with a supernatural

---

[103] I abstract from the fact that receiving the Eucharist once a week is a holy obligation.

[104] An anonymous referee protests against the claim that supernatural goods exhibit diminishing returns. I think we can at least say that the first Eucharist has more value than the second because the first Eucharist is one received under a holy obligation, and so one's reasons to receive the first Eucharist exceed in strength one's reasons to receive the second.

[105] Grisez 1983, p. 514. Grisez claims that we never choose union with God, not that we never choose the Eucharist.

[106] Grisez 1983, p. 588. Here we should read Grisez as referring to coming to faith, not to choosing to remain in grace.

good. We choose between acting on one reason and acting on two reasons, and the practically rational choice resolves in favor of the latter.

Grisez thinks we can keep supernatural goods once we have them. He claims that charity—loving God—is not something we do, but something God asks us to "*remain in*."[107] Russell Hittinger responds, "How one can remain in an attitude... without thereby choosing to act in such a way... is quite mysterious."[108] Remaining in an attitude *is* choosing between supernatural goodness and something else. I structured the symmetry conditional to accommodate this point. The state assists the church by helping people choose to remain in grace. Grisez allows that we can choose to remain in grace or to reject the supernatural good once we receive it.

Consider Jan, an aspiring twenty-first-century artist. God has given Jan a remarkable gift: she is a sculpting prodigy. Jan wants to attend the best art school in the world to develop her talent, but secular progressives run this school. They reject Catholic teaching on sex and gender. Jan grew up Roman Catholic and she affirms the teachings of the church. Her views may dim her bright future.

Jan must now choose between developing her talent to the fullest and openly affirming the teachings of her faith. Jan chooses her art career. She becomes Episcopalian, a denomination with progressive views on LGBT issues; through church involvement, she gradually changes her views on sex and gender.[109] From Jan's perspective, at least at first, she chooses artistic excellence over true religion. She leaves a state of grace for a natural good. Jan's choice is competitive.[110] She consciously chooses a mere natural good (excellence) over a superior pair of goods (religion and true religion).

Most Catholics can explain Jan's error: she wrongly discarded a supernatural good for a mere natural good. The supernatural good has greater weight, yet she threw it away.

NNL theorists cannot adopt this line of reasoning because of how they represent choices between goods. Grisez would represent Jan as choosing between excellence and religion. In so choosing, Jan intends harm to the good of religion: she acts immorally owing to her attitudes toward natural goods alone. Jan

---

[107] Grisez 1983, p. 588, emphasis added.

[108] Hittinger 1988, p. 137. I leave open whether Grisez claims that choosing to remain in grace is a choice. The point is that Hittinger thinks we have a choice about whether to remain in grace.

[109] Here Jan might deliberately change her mind, but more likely she engages in a host of actions that gradually change her convictions, such as openly criticizing Catholicism to her teachers, no longer attending Mass, etc. I thank an anonymous referee for pushing me to clarify this point.

[110] Though note that a choice between *A* and *B* can be competitive *even if A* and *B* are incommensurable. Even if *A* and *B* are incommensurable, one cannot enjoy them both simultaneously. *A* and *B* are still scarce alternatives.

means no harm to religion, though; she simply forgoes true religion for artistic excellence.

The NNL theory cannot explain Jan's error. We cannot aptly represent Jan as choosing between natural goods. She makes a competitive choice between a natural and a supernatural good by her own lights. Consider how Jan experiences her choice. Jan believes that God once revealed himself to her, creating a felt closeness with him. Then she pushes God away. Jan does not experience herself as rejecting a natural good; her faith suffuses her experience. If we explain her mistake as rejecting the natural good of religion, we have not explained her choice as she experienced it.

Turn from Jan to the state. Once the state learns that Catholicism is the true religion, it faces trade-offs. It must choose between building hospitals and establishing inquisitorial courts. In some cases, it chooses health. In others, it chooses the true religion. Like Jan, the state faces a choice between a natural good and a supernatural good. Integralist policy choice is competitive. If this is accurate, the noncompetition reply fails and the symmetry conditional remains unscathed.

The Intending-Harm-to-a-Good Reply to the Religion Objection

NNL theorists stress that one must never intend harm to a basic good.[111] We should not destroy a friendship to pursue knowledge, nor should we destroy our health to achieve athletic excellence. Integralist states, one might argue, require the authority to harm false religion among baptized citizens. States could force Protestants to attend Mass and could shutter Protestant churches. But those policies would intend harm to the good of (Protestant) religion, and intending such harm is always wrong.

The integralist state is not *trying* to harm false religion, though. The state simply advances the true faith. It punishes heresy to ward off religions with less value, much as the church already uses spiritual punishments for the same purpose. On analogy with the church, the state intends to preserve the true religion. It lacks an immoral intention.

Consider an analogy. The state must protect its citizens from harm. This duty permits using violence to deter enemy combatants, which harms the health of the enemy. The state does not thereby intend to harm the good of health. It preserves its citizens' health.

[111] Tollefsen 2008, pp. 8–13.

Integralists see church membership along the same lines. The church must protect its citizens from harm through reason, persuasion, and spiritual punishments. The church-authorized state adds civil penalties to the church's toolkit, and it no more intends harm to religion than it intends harm to the health of enemy combatants. The church intends no harm to religion when it uses spiritual punishments, nor need the state intend harm to religion by assisting the church.

The Prudence Objection to the Symmetry Conditional

The previous four sections form one argument. States must violate natural law to promote supernatural goods. Why? Because the state can undermine the good of religion. The integralist responds that states coerce only to help people remain in grace and so they must establish true religion over false religion. The church may expand the authority of the state beyond natural peace and justice.

The new natural lawyer can also offer pragmatic arguments against the symmetry conditional.[112] I have already argued that a Catholic state can overcome its ignorance by listening to the church. I now ask whether states can advance true religion once they recognize it.

Suppose states cannot reliably change beliefs through coercion. They may still protect Catholics from spiritual damage, say if they ban books advancing bad ideas.[113] Ongoing protection may then improve the lives of future generations. Philosopher Brian Barry elaborates the point by imagining persecutors who want to maximize adherents across time:

> Saving the souls of the present generation of adults is of trivial significance compared with what is at stake in saving the souls of their descendants. And here the historical record is extremely clear. Most of the contemporary adherents of Islam are the descendants of people who originally adopted it at the point of a sword, but the quality of their faith today is no less for that. The same goes for many Protestant and Catholic areas in Europe. The effectiveness of coercion in producing genuine belief over the course of a few generations is beyond question.[114]

---

[112] Cuneo 2005, p. 122.
[113] Waldron 1993, p. 109.
[114] Barry 1990, p. 5.

In other words, *conquer the infidel* and create sincere faith in the long run.[115] Then patiently expand the Catholic population. Society will come around.

Philosopher Christopher Wolfe defends religious liberty on natural law grounds by combining two arguments. He first argues on moral grounds against directly coercing belief, then he argues in favor of expanding religious liberties on pragmatic grounds. These arguments sum to a "principled prudential" case for religious freedom.[116] Suppose pragmatic concerns favor protecting religious liberties. Maybe religious freedom limits false piety because religious coercion pressures insincerity. Still, the state's incompetence is not a moral reason to respect religious freedom: pragmatic considerations tell us only that the prudent state respects religious freedom. Practical arguments cannot strengthen the truth of a moral principle.

Some may resist separating moral and prudential considerations. Yet recall once more that the integralists of old happily distinguished between principle and practice. They contrasted *thesis* and *hypothesis*.[117] Thesis describes the political ideal. Hypothesis then applies principles to less favorable conditions. Integralism is the political thesis. Wolfe's arguments target only *hypothesis*—unidealized, real-world conditions. And integralists accept his principled argument: they reject the direct coercion of belief.

Wolfe should advance his pragmatic objection against the *thesis*. Here's how. Historical integralist regimes had weak state capacity—states performed few functions and for a small populace. Even in these regimes, popes and kings fought like cats and dogs. For every friendship between pope and crown, European history contains a conflict. The legendary friendship of Saint Louis IX and Pope Clement IV[118] contrasts with the grand conflict between King Philip IV and Pope Boniface VIII.[119] These events occurred a mere thirty-five years apart. The latter conflict led to the Avignon papacy and, later, the papal schism.[120]

Medieval integralist orders proved unstable. The dyarchy invited conflicts between two powers with no superior to settle their disputes. Societies can stably divide political power.[121] But the integralist division of power produced instability as often as not.

[115] Of course, Catholics cannot kill off a generation of people. Here the point is more abstract: religious coercion can work to create the desired beliefs.

[116] Wolfe 2009, p. 246.

[117] Bévenot 1954. The Second Vatican Council set the distinction aside, but integralists must revive it.

[118] Jones (2017) reviews their relationship in detail.

[119] For an account of their contest, see Duffy (2014, pp. 164–75).

[120] Duffy 2014, pp. 166–75.

[121] Hobbes 1994, p. 392.

If economist Mark Koyama is correct, integralism appeared stable only when church capacity rivaled state capacity.[122] In the thirteenth century, the French state became more powerful. The pope now had reason to recruit the French state to advance his spiritual objectives. In exchange for favorable policy, he legitimized the monarchy. But by the fourteenth century, the French state had grown strong enough to ignore papal demands. It did so, and worse.

Modern state capacity *greatly* exceeds papal power. As I argue in Chapter 5, this power inequality will destabilize integralist arrangements. Integralism cannot *stick*. These problems arise even for large, complex social orders under favorable conditions. They may apply to an ideal integralist order. Critics could reject integralism *as thesis*. I will do this in Chapters 5 and 6.

The Symmetry Argument Vindicated

Recall the symmetry argument:

1. States should promote natural goods.
2. If states should promote natural goods, they should promote supernatural goods.
3. States should promote supernatural goods.

We see integralism's attraction: it treats goodness symmetrically. It seems obvious. The state should promote the whole good under the proper conditions. Three powerful objections fail: authorization, religion, and prudence. Prudential objections have a further implication: they revive the thesis-hypothesis distinction. The distinction comes with a high price: the price of retreating into a radical form of ideal theorizing.

For now, though, the integralist rides high: the proto-integralist conclusion should please integralists. They have a powerful argument against their chief philosophical and political competitor, one that does not rest on contentious dogmatic disputes. The symmetry argument moves the debate in the integralist's direction.

---

[122] Johnson and Koyama 2019.

Defense Complete

Integralists have two powerful arguments: history and symmetry. These arguments show why some adopt the position. And notice that the arguments strengthen one another. The symmetry argument justifies the state promotion of supernatural goods on philosophical grounds, but it specifies no regime type. The history argument specifies a regime type, but it does not justify the state promotion of supernatural goods on philosophical grounds. The arguments bolster each other. They clasp.

But the integralist must now face three powerful objections. First, we cannot reach integralism through moral means. Second, even if we could reach it, we cannot stabilize it. Third, even if we could stabilize it, integralism treats baptized dissenters unjustly. I offer three arguments against integralism: *transition, stability,* and *justice.* I will conclude that integralism is false. Those who want society to promote the supernatural good must look elsewhere.

4

Transition

Integralist strategists, who are primarily American, want to create a new integralist state. They would subvert liberal order and substitute their values in its place. They also believe liberalism is on the brink of collapse, but they are happy to help it along.[1] The strategists face a familiar challenge: integralism is unrealistic. We cannot transition to integralism from a liberal democratic order or the price would be too high, some say. The strategists roll their eyes. Who, after all, can predict history? (Leaving aside their prediction that liberalism will fall, of course.) Institutions change, sometimes quickly.

Here I allow that integralism is feasible. I offer a related but new objection: the only transition plan on offer requires grave sin. The strategists must violate the strictures of their faith to secure a political victory. Economist F. A. Hayek once said that "socialism can be put into practice only by methods which most socialists disapprove."[2] My argument parallels his. Integralism can be put into practice only by methods that most integralists disapprove.

I scrutinize the main transition plan for three reasons. First, no one so far has created a concrete list of the social and moral barriers that integralists face. A compelling list might worry the strategists. Second, offering a list will provide the strategists with an opportunity to tell us where they get off the boat. (I hope it will be at the beginning.) Third, the transition barriers pose such severe problems that integralists must retreat to near-utopian political theorizing: what philosophers call radical *ideal theory*. Integralism becomes a theory of the preeminent political regime *alone*. It cannot recommend concrete social reforms. Yet an ideal beckons; it should tell us how to reach itself. If the ideal cannot guide us, its attraction fades.

Conservative readers may want to stop after this chapter. Most conservatives reject extreme ideal theory.[3] They propose modest reforms based on humility

---

[1] Vermeule 2018b.

[2] Hayek 2007, p. 159.

[3] Tosi and Warmke 2022.

All the Kingdoms of the World. Kevin Vallier, Oxford University Press. © Oxford University Press 2023.
DOI: 10.1093/oso/9780197611371.003.0005

about social change. Radical ideals endanger our fragile social order.[4] Integralism radicalizes right-leaning youth, whereas this chapter encourages their reformist impulses.

I examine *integration from within*, Adrian Vermeule's strategy for state capture.[5] (Other methods, such as forming pious local religious communities, fit a pluralistic liberalism that stresses toleration and respect for diversity.)[6] My argument culminates in a calculation of the probability that integration from within succeeds. Table 4.1 identifies fifteen categories of transition problems. Together, they demonstrate the spectacular improbability that integralists can overcome these barriers. After I have discussed these transition problems in detail, you can review the table to make your own estimate (see Table 4.2, near the end of this chapter).

The following section describes the Catholic distinction between utopian and realistic political theory—the thesis-hypothesis distinction. I then discuss integration from within, its preconditions, and its three phases. It is a plan to reach an integralist thesis. I then catalog three types of transition challenge: leadership failures, internal resistance, and external opposition. These challenges plague five transition stages: party capture, state capture, state stabilization, church capture, and church-state integration. Since Vermeule's strategy will fail, integralists must retreat into utopianism.

At the end of this book, I will present an alternative to *integration from within*. I call it *integration writ small*. This plan recommends that integralists form charter cities. Citizenship in such a city would require that one submit to a dyarchic government, but everyone has a right to emigrate. Integration writ small constrains state power to protect local polities—no mean feat. Further, the strategy requires convincing the church to readopt and pursue integralism—even harder. But integration writ small is at least morally feasible, unlike integration from within.

Many right-liberals will welcome integration writ small. They have long favored federalism, and some support radical forms of decentralization. Micro-integralism fits into their political vision. I see this as an advantage for integration writ small. It avoids political antagonism. But many may resist calling such a regime integralist because it has a quasi-liberal super-structure and complete freedom of exit.

---

[4] Deneen 2018, p. 78.
[5] Vermeule 2018b.
[6] Levy 2015; Gaus 2021; Kukathas 2007.

Table 4.1 **Evaluating Which Transition Problems Apply to Each Transition Stage**

	State-Side			Church-Side	Unification	
	Stage 1: party capture	*Stage 2: state capture*	*Stage 3: state stabilization*	*Stage 4: church capture*	*Stage 5: settle timing, boundaries*	*All stages*
Type of transition problem						
Leadership failures						
Internal resistance						
External opposition						
Chance of success						

Transition Theory

As noted, integralists distinguish ideal from nonideal theory with the thesis-hypothesis distinction. French Jesuit Maurice Bévenot puts the distinction this way:

> The thesis . . . considers the rulers and the subjects "according to their intrinsic essence, and according to the order established for both by the Creator, in the double economy of nature and grace." Thesis is "the perfect, normal, ideal state," but it is not "sheerly utopian." It existed in the past.[7]

---

[7] Bévenot 1954, p. 443, quoting from an unsigned article in *La civiltà cattolica*, series 5, vol. 8 (October 2, 1863): 129–49. (Bévenot guesses that the author was C. M. Curci; presumably Bévenot also translated the quotations into English.) For other discussions, see Craycraft (1999, pp. 130–31), Maritain (2012, p. 154), Carmella (2007, p. 197), Lefebvre (1994, p. 99), Chappel (2018, pp. 146–47).

Thesis gives way to hypothesis in a society that operates under unfavorable circumstances. Hypothesis examines matters "as they become by the intrusion of accidental circumstances—which are often criminal and always regrettable—in certain countries and nations."[8] Thesis, by contrast, describes the best Catholic social world this side of the grave.

The thesis-hypothesis distinction has an interesting history. Félix-Antoine-Philibert Dupanloup (1802–1878), the bishop of Orléans, drew it for a reason. He hoped to soften the blow of Pius IX's anti-liberalism in *Quanta cura*.[9] He wrote that "if we do not succeed in checking this senseless Romanism, the Church will be outlawed in Europe for half a century."[10] If Pius IX condemned liberalism as thesis, Dupanloup argued, Catholic anti-liberalism has few practical implications. Many bishops were grateful for Dupanloup's work; indeed, Pius IX said he was grateful (though he apparently thought otherwise).[11]

This distinction, designed to save liberalism, later became an obstacle. Until the Second Vatican Council, many Catholic authorities believed that integralism was the Catholic ideal. Since it was an ideal, they believed that Catholics should fight for it. Non-Catholics knew this, and it led them to doubt Catholics' allegiance to democratic regimes.[12]

Several influential twentieth-century Catholic theologians assailed the distinction. Their goal? Relativize integralism to bygone social conditions by destroying the thesis.[13] At times, John Courtney Murray pursued this strategy. He argued that Catholics should endorse liberal order as a modern, pluralistic hypothesis.[14] He famously called the First Amendment to the US Constitution an "article of peace." It reduces conflict in a pluralistic society, even if the thesis regime would not exhibit much pluralism.[15]

Murray and Jacques Maritain had subtle plans: to alter the concept of the thesis enough to abolish it. They identify the Catholic thesis with a set of abstract principles that take no transhistorical institutional form, not with a set of institutions.[16] The thesis affirms the divine authorization of the natural and supernatural powers. It even affirms the superiority of spiritual power. But supremacy is spiritual. And spiritual supremacy does not entail political sovereignty.

---

[8] Bévenot 1954, p. 443.
[9] Pius IX 1864.
[10] Duffy 2014, p. 296.
[11] Duffy 2014, p. 296.
[12] Murray 1993, p. 17.
[13] Murray 1993, pp. 199–219; Maritain 2012, chap. 6.
[14] Murray 1993, pp. 199–219; Maritain 2012, chap. 6.
[15] Murray 2005, chap. 2.
[16] Murray 1993, pp. 132–33. Maritain 2012, chap. 6.

Different circumstances warrant their own specific hypotheses: some of these hypotheses embrace the political superiority of the spiritual power while others do not. All historical contexts are hypotheses, for all are imperfect. And since the thesis-hypothesis distinction is not dogma, the church could discard it for a *hypothesis-only* approach.[17] And so Murray announced, "It is time now to drop the categories of thesis and hypothesis entirely out of the Catholic vocabulary. The future systematization of Catholic doctrine on Church and state will not have the disjunctive structure characteristic of the once-received opinion. Its structure will be unitary."[18] Murray thought that Pope Pius XII (in office 1939– 1958) was pushing the church away from seeing itself as a polity.[19] Pius XII had recast the church's self-conception. Following *Mystici corporis Christi*, Catholics should view the church more as a mystical body than as a polity.[20] When church leadership set the thesis-hypothesis distinction aside, Murray's supporters claimed victory. At least in part.

Maritain's strategy was different. He argued that the thesis lacks a "univocal sense" because it always applies to concrete historical periods.[21] Applying the thesis to actual conditions requires violence. Such an imposition then betrays the immutable principles and puts "a ghost in their place."[22] Any application of principles is analogical. Indeed, "the more transcendent the principles are, the more analogical is the application."[23]

Hypothesis is also problematic because it assumes that historical periods have no underlying principles. And so Maritain deploys the distinction between the secular and sacral ages, each of which warrants a distinct hypothesis because the secular and sacral ages have different underlying rationalities. Maritain proposes a path between thesis and hypothesis. We need "concrete historical ideals" that tell us what to hope for in our age. These ideals are "neither absolute nor bound to an unrealizable past" but are realizable relative to a given time.[24]

If Maritain was a liberal, he was a curious one. He argued that one could ad- mire integralist regimes in the Middle Ages even if they are "a dead letter in our age."[25] Integralism was appropriate in the sacral age but not in the secular age of religious pluralism. Today, the "supreme, immutable principle of the superiority

[17] Murray 1993, p. 112.
[18] Murray 1993, p. 214.
[19] Murray 1993, p. 32.
[20] Pius XII 1943.
[21] Maritain 2012, p. 155.
[22] Maritain 2012, pp. 155.
[23] Maritain 2012, p. 156.
[24] Maritain 2012, p. 157.
[25] Maritain 2012, p. 63.

of the Kingdom of God over the earthly kingdoms can apply in other ways than in making the civil government the secular arm of the Church."[26] But Maritain was no moral relativist. Instead, those applying abstract ethical principles to different societies must acknowledge colossal differences between them—differences so large that we cannot speak of a clear thesis.

Integralists must reject Murray's and Maritain's arguments and embrace integralism as thesis. But if integralism resurrects as the thesis, Catholics should create an integralist regime. It is the *best* regime, after all! Vermeule has responded to the allure of the thesis by explaining how to reach it.[27]

Integralist strategists want a revolution. So I analyze attempts to transition from something like liberal democracy to integralism.[28] In a *liberal* regime, citizens have broad, equal liberties that discourage interference from others and from the government. Central liberal rights include the freedoms of speech and religion. In a *democratic* regime, citizens choose their leaders by majority vote, or something near enough. Leaders select laws and policies similarly. Central democratic rights include the right to vote and the right to run for office.

Let's pause to note a unique feature of the integralist transition strategy. Integralists affirm original sin: all fall short of moral perfection. Everyone acts immorally sometimes, including political leaders. Other political ideals, such as the socialist ideal, reject original sin: they attribute immoral behavior to bad institutions. But Catholics follow Jesus in stressing that what comes out of a man's mouth defiles him (Matt. 15:11). Even the Catholic thesis contains some bad behavior.

On Assessing Vermeule

I issue some notes of caution about analyzing Vermeule's strategy. First, I freely admit that his plan is not the only possible plan. Some may respond with the argument that integralist transition theory survives the demise of integration from within. Fair enough. But no integralist offers an alternative plan. Few challenge Vermeule on this point—or on any other. But, if integralists want to propose a better statist strategy, I am all ears.

---

[26] Maritain 2012, pp. 162.

[27] Here's a dissertation idea for an enterprising young integralist: write on how to revive the thesis-hypothesis distinction in light of the ideal-nonideal theory debates in political philosophy.

[28] Despite Viktor Orbán's declarations, Hungary still protects a broad range of liberties for individuals and small groups, even if in some respects it restricts individual rights.

Second, Vermeule has extensive background in the social sciences. I think he has identified common contours of any large-state transition strategy, such as capturing a political party. His plan coheres in some respects. By critiquing him, we can critique statist transition strategies in general.

Third, integration from within is ambiguous with respect to time frame. If Vermeule has one generation in mind, we will see that there are few prospects for success without considerable violence. The longer-term the strategy, the more likely success can come from the use of reason, persuasion, and soft power. But, as the timescale grows, uncertainty expands by orders of magnitude. If integration from within occurs over a century, then its prospects become even more radically uncertain. So moral considerations push us to lengthen Vermeule's time frame, whereas practical considerations press us to shorten it.

Finally, there is the matter of sources. Many readers will come to this book familiar with what we might call the *informal information* about integralist strategizing, such as social media or public talks. In my view, the informal information indicates that the strategists do not mind strongman tactics. However, I omit the informal information. First, much of the information is fleeting and I do not know how seriously it is meant. Second, I am not sure people should be held to their social media in a work such as this. I would not want that standard applied to me. For my purposes, then, what happens on social media stays on social media! My interpretation of Vermeule will focus on articles and posts that indicate long-term and stable conviction. Since Vermeule has strewn his short strategic works about the internet, I do engage in some reconstruction. But I tie my claims to the text.

Here is my hermeneutic. Vermeule's research before and after his conversion to Catholicism fit together. In everything, Vermeule seeks to *redeem public power*. Vermeule wants traditional conservatives to abandon their opposition to the administrative state because strong states can advance the common good. Here Vermeule would redeem public power *politically*.[29]

Vermeule now understands the redemption of public power *theologically*. Integralism will grace the state and grace its subjects by extension. The state can help citizens grasp and follow the natural law, promote the earthly common good, and even *help* them pursue the heavenly common good—corporate salvation in Christ. The administrative state serves as the church's deputy for the salvation of souls.

So while I may not synthesize Vermeule's work as he would, I have nonetheless assembled the pieces consistent with the theme of politico-theological

---

[29] For a review of Vermeule's common good-based defense of the administrative state, see Casey 2023.

redemption. Integration from within is a redemption story: Vermeule tells us how liberalism will die and how integralism can rise from the ashes.

The tale I tell flows from the text and these background assumptions.

Integration from Within

Vermeule does not outline his transition strategy in a single book or article. Yet we can detect a clear pattern from his many short articles and blog posts on the matter. Integration from within attempts state capture. The goal? Install integralists in powerful positions in a liberal nation-state. As liberalism falls, integralists seize the state and turn it toward religious objectives.

Vermeule's now-famous article "Integration from Within" criticizes Patrick Deneen's *Why Liberalism Failed* for excessive localism.[30] Vermeule believes that the liberal state will overrun these small communities. It will destroy their capacity to resist. Those who yearn for a Catholic civilization must capture a liberal state. As I noted in Chapter 1, for Vermeule, the proper antiliberal strategy requires finding "a strategic position from which to *sear the liberal faith with hot irons*, to defeat and capture the hearts and minds of liberal agents, to take over the institutions of the old order that liberalism has itself prepared and to turn them to the promotion of human dignity and the common good."[31]

To understand Vermeule's strategy, I review both how he understands liberalism and his prediction that liberalism will perish. I then divide his positive plan into three phases: *community building*, *state staffing*, and *state capture*:

1. *Community building* trains integralists for liberalism's demise.
2. *State staffing* places integralists in positions of power to capture the state.
3. Integralists take over, completing *state capture*.

Compared to historical integralists, Vermeule is an outlier. Few integralists address the scenario where the integralist state governs a non-Catholic society. The conflicts that created integralism took place within baptized populations. An integralist state cannot create peace or justice in a non-Catholic populace—only strife and revolt. Too many people will dissent. But, as we will see, Vermeule thinks that humans yearn for powerful rulers. The masses may follow elites into the Catholic Church.

---

[30] Vermeule 2018b; Deneen 2018.
[31] Vermeule 2018b, emphasis added.

The rest of this section answers the following four questions:

- What is liberalism?
- Why must liberalism fall?
- How should integralists prepare?
- How should integralists capture the postliberal state?

Vermeule contra Liberalism

Vermeule defines liberalism as a sociopolitical regime, a concrete political-theological order.[32] It is a force that exercises social and political power. Liberalism is also a theory, "a clan of doctrines, of which theological, political, and economic liberalism are the main branches. All these are descended more or less directly from the fateful thought that the autonomy of the individual, of the individual's reason and desires, is of paramount importance."[33] Liberalism does not ignore the human good. But it does seek to produce human goods indirectly through spontaneous order mechanisms—institutions that produce order without central direction. Examples include democratic deliberation, checks and balances, and the competitive market.

Liberalism is also a religion, indeed a "fighting, evangelistic faith."[34] Some call liberal elites decadent and lustful, but Vermeule deems them ascetic fanatics.[35] They will sacrifice to liberate humanity from traditional, religious constraints. Liberals cannot "liberate" nonliberals until they subdue them, so they promise universal peace and prosperity. Liberals distract nonliberals with a "universal deluge of economic-technical decadence."[36] They shower nonliberals with temptation.

Liberalism preaches the fundamental harmony of human interests. It seeks peace through a "balance of opposing forces," to use Carl Schmitt's phrase.[37] Here Schmitt refers to several familiar decision-making processes: "the rule of law, the free market, and the inevitable triumph of truth in open discussion."[38] Liberals claim that these procedures balance interests and depoliticize our

---

[32] Vermeule 2019a; Vermeule 2019b.

[33] Vermeule 2019b.

[34] Vermeule 2018b.

[35] Here Vermeule could find a kindred spirit in Archbishop Lefebvre, who cited one Father Roussel as saying that "the liberal is a fanatic of independence" (see Lefebvre 1994, p. 30).

[36] Vermeule 2017a.

[37] Schmitt 2008, p. 221.

[38] Holmes 1993, p. 46. Remember I am quoting Schmitt, and next footnote.

fiercest conflicts—an ingenious lie. For in critical moments, "decisions may have to be made before a rational consensus has had time to emerge."[39]

Liberal elites know at some level that they need the nonliberal population. Nonliberals produce society's social capital—its seed corn. Liberals then destructively feed on it. Liberalism also needs nonliberals as the ultimate Other—a permanent foe that liberals can repeatedly conquer. Liberals then celebrate their victories with secularized religious services that praise hard-won liberties.[40]

Liberals' need to rule explains liberalism's schizophrenic attitude toward democracy. If liberals want to terminate nonliberal power, they must sell liberalism to nonliberals. Liberals do this by casting nonliberal democratic victories as undemocratic.[41] That way, the nonliberal public never notices that it has the democratic power to overthrow liberalism.

Liberal elites are parasites, alien organisms that colonize and rule the nonliberal population. Liberals berate nonliberals whenever they resist a proposed liberation. They punish the noncompliant to ensure that they will have low social status. Liberals thereby ensure that nonliberals cannot rule.[42] But the nonliberal populace remains large and could overthrow liberal control. It requires domestication. So liberal regimes lie to nonliberals when they promise universal freedom, safety, and wealth.

Liberalism Is Doomed

For Vermeule, *liberalism is always hungry*. Hungry for liberation. Nonliberals find "no lasting peace" with liberals, who always push for new liberties:

> Yesterday the frontier was divorce, contraception, and abortion; then it became same-sex marriage; today it is transgenderism; tomorrow it may be polygamy, consensual adult incest, or who knows what. The uncertainty is itself the point. From the liberal standpoint, the essential thing is that the new issue provokes opposition from the forces of reaction, who may then be conquered in a public and dramatic fashion by the political mobilization of liberal forces.[43]

To me, the old frontiers were fighting monarchy, aristocracy, slavery, racism, and sexism. But Vermeule starts the time line later and projects a repulsive culmination.

[39] Holmes 1993, p. 46.
[40] Vermeule 2017d.
[41] Vermeule 2018c.
[42] Vermeule 2017d. This worsens as liberalism decays.
[43] Vermeule 2017c.

Liberalism's desperation leads to its demise: "The sheer plasticity and restless liberationism of the regime exceed the populace's appetite for freedom, and a kind of rebellion against the principles of the regime itself will occur."[44] Contemporary progressivism is liberalism's apotheosis and terminus: "As the liberal imperium ages and decays, its sectarians become ever more anxious about internal rebellion and external threats, and the persecution of non-liberals becomes more aggressive, systematic, and widespread."[45] Liberals become frantic.

Vermeule analogizes his view with Karl Marx's claims about capitalism: "Liberalism is inherently unstable and is structurally disposed to generate the very forces that destroy it."[46] Liberalism cannot liberate society forever. Further, the liberal false promise of peace and prosperity cannot survive. Liberal capitalism is so relentless and destructive that it threatens the legitimacy of liberal order. Capitalist life will become intolerable. The economic-technical state undermines itself because "it rests upon a defective psychology and anthropology." Nonliberals will "[crave] the return of 'strong gods'" and will summon these gods rather than wallowing in the liberal mud of toys and titillations.[47]

Another destabilizing force arises when liberals oversell spontaneous orders. Liberals say the best social processes emerge through human action, not human design.[48] Markets serve as paradigm cases. Vermeule responds to these claims with two arguments. First, we cannot verify the market's success; liberal economics obscures rather than clarifies the outcomes of the market process. Second, liberal order depletes social capital and so atomizes society.[49] The liberal state cannot provide the prosperity or the community it promises to nonliberals.[50]

Vermeule characterizes liberal elites much as Marx describes capitalist elites. For Marx, capitalist elites are always hungry. And, because of the tendency of the rate of profit to fall, the capitalist class becomes more desperate with time.[51] Capitalists make the proletariat so miserable that it overthrows them. Marxists also argue that capitalism and parliamentary democracy legitimize themselves with false promises. But elites lie to the working classes, not to nonliberals.

---

[44] Vermeule 2017a.

[45] Vermeule 2017c.

[46] Vermeule 2017c.

[47] Vermeule 2017a.

[48] Ferguson 1782, p. 205; Hayek 1945, p. 527.

[49] Vermeule 2019b.

[50] Vermeule 2019b. Most elites in most societies overpromise what they can accomplish. Also, it is not clear whether Vermeule thinks liberalism is a proper ideology. He offers no theory of ideology.

[51] Marx and Engels 2011, chap. 32.

When liberalism collapses, Vermeule argues, it does not take the state with it. The administrative state survives by necessity. The state becomes an ideological wasteland, open to capture. The halls of power empty, creating room for a new ruling class:

> But even within liberal-democratic political orders there are always institutional forms that long predate liberalism, that have no necessary connection of principle to liberalism, and that will certainly survive liberalism's eventual disappearance. One candidate for such an organizational form—and there are others as well—is bureaucracy, which has flourished in non-liberal regimes from Song China to Salazar's Portugal. . . . The ideal-type principles of hierarchy and unity of top-level command that animate bureaucracy, especially but not only military and security bureaucracies, are not obviously the sort of principles that threaten to inscribe liberalism within the hearts and minds of participants.[52]

When liberalism fails, massive bureaucracies open wide, and nonliberals can capture the levers of power.

More parallels with Marx emerge. Marx thought that capitalism would be replaced by a proletarian dictatorship that would transform society's means of production to serve its interests. For Vladimir Lenin, a vanguard must lead the proletariat, one that understands workers' interests.[53] For Vermeule, nonliberal, religious masses will capture the state. They will need leadership from anti-liberal intellectuals attuned to the common good.

My aim is not to assess Vermeule's critique of liberalism's social dynamics.[54] I will argue that integration from within cannot counter liberalism. The plan cannot respect ordinary morality.

Phase 1, Community Building: Vermeule's Ark

While liberalism must die, no one knows the day or the hour. So Catholic integralists must prepare now. To do so, they must create an enduring, cohesive, self-conscious microcosmic political society. The political organization trains Catholics to see through liberalism's lies. And it develops strategic plans.

---

[52] Vermeule 2018d.

[53] Lenin 2013.

[54] But here's what I think: Vermeule accurately describes a subset of the modern Left. That group, though, is not nearly powerful, coherent, and wily enough to overwhelm other social forces.

Vermeule describes the Catholic Church as a kind of ark. This Ark can survive liberalism's self-undermining dynamics. An ark is not a museum, which contains only dead or frozen things, nor is it a zoo, which traps living beings in a static space. An ark "houses living beings, who breed, reproduce, and change over time," and moves forward "with a discernible aim."[55] The vocation of the church "is to preserve the living tradition of the Verbum Dei [the Word of God] amidst the universal deluge of economic-technical decadence, and the eventual self-undermining of the [liberal] regime."[56]

When the liberal state collapses, the Ark can capture the remains of the state. Indeed, it may garner historically unprecedented power. To illustrate, Vermeule cites Schmitt's book *Roman Catholicism and Political Form*:

> Should economic thinking succeed in realizing its utopian goal and in bringing about an absolutely unpolitical condition of human society, the Church would remain the only agency of political thinking and political form. Then the Church would have a stupendous monopoly: its hierarchy would be nearer the political domination of the world than in the Middle Ages.[57]

Catholics spring from the Ark into the administrative state and the judiciary. Victory will not come quickly, but all faithful Catholics will soon pay the price for their faith. They may even experience "a kind of low-temperature martyrdom."[58] But fear not. The Ark will re-emerge one day. In the meanwhile, it incubates a new Catholic civilization.

Vermeule stresses how quickly circumstances change. "[o]ur political world is far more fluid, far more malleable and susceptible to shaping through intentional action, especially the action of committed political minorities, than the putative realists can conceive at any given time."[59] Given our chaotic political era, the denizens of the Ark must face uncomfortable facts about how the future might unfold.

Catholics must strip themselves of ideological and institutional attachments, be these attachments conservative, progressive, or libertarian. Catholics must push for a regime that protects and elevates the church. Liberals will grow more aggressive, which requires "hard counsel." Catholics must surrender all "political

---

[55] Vermeule 2017a.
[56] Vermeule 2017a.
[57] Schmitt 1996, pp. 7–8. Quoted in Vermeule 2017a, 2017b.
[58] Vermeule 2017c.
[59] Vermeule 2021.

and institutional loyalties, and . . . ideological commitments, that . . . potentially constrain or compete with the mission of the Church."[60] These loyalties hamper their ability to serve.[61] This would return Catholics to their politics one hundred years ago, when they were "doctrinally indifferent to political form."[62]

Note well: Vermeule ranks institutions by their friendliness to Catholicism. Other factors play a small role in ranking institutions—and in ranking leaders. Suppose that Catholics must choose between Generalissimo Francisco Franco's Spain and President Biden's liberal democracy. Given Vermeule's proffered evaluative standards, how could he avoid recommending Franco, who afforded Catholicism special political privileges for decades?

The *true* Ark is not yet the whole Catholic Church, as the church battles liberal threats from both without and within. The true Ark is part of the church—those who grasp the truth about liberalism. In my view, the integralist community forms the Ark's foundations. In the early 2010s, the movement consisted of a community of bloggers focused on reviving nonliberal aspects of Catholic social thought. Shortly after his conversion, Vermeule joined the conversation and began expanding the community of social media. He assumed de facto leadership. His efforts have paid off. Without his leadership, integralism may have gone nowhere.

Vermeule may not see integralists as the founding generation of a postliberal Ark, at least not under that description. But no one can deny that he has spent years engaged in ingenious digital organizing. He does not hide it. Nonetheless, you could miss his astonishing accomplishment: building on the work of others, he has created a new faction in American political life. The faction attempts to influence the American Catholic Church and the Republican Party. It is small. But Vermeule does not think his sect needs numbers to have influence. In a recent piece, Vermeule cites a revealing passage from Joseph de Maistre, who once said, "the people count for nothing in revolutions, or at most count only as a passive instrument. Four or five persons, perhaps, will give France a King."[63] This passage comes from chapter 9 of Maistre's *Considerations on France*. The chapter's title: "How Will the Counter-Revolution Happen If It Comes?" Vermeule is clear: a small, devoted cadre can instigate a Catholic-led American counterrevolution against liberalism.

Make no mistake: Vermeule means to install a ruler. Vermeule has recently argued that right-liberals miss an obvious point. He says that "if the right views do not control the state, the wrong ones will."[64] He agrees with J. F. Stephen,

---

[60] Vermeule 2017c.
[61] Vermeule 2017c.
[62] Chappel 2018, p. 93.
[63] De Maistre 1995, p. 77.
[64] Vermeule 2022a.

one of the great critics of liberalism: "I am right, and you are wrong, and your view shall give way to mine, quietly, gradually, and peaceably; but one of us two must rule and the other must obey, and I mean to rule."[65] We can capture the strategists' aims as a slogan: "I mean to rule." Why? Much is at stake: the whole common good. We have only two options: become rulers or become subjects. Collective self-rule, I'm afraid, is not on Vermeule's menu. Nor is it an option for his prominent followers.

Vermeule's faction helps young Catholics rediscover true Catholic political theology, which they treat as irreformably anti-liberal. They offer continuous commentary on American politics, create paywalled publications, and sell tickets to conferences for their supporters. They try to push society, and the GOP, to abandon liberalism. Vermeule et al. know that they must connect with the nonliberal populace they wish to lead—though their values differ from the values of those they would govern.

The faction—the Ark in utero—is an organized digital community. It has several distinguishing characteristics, which I noted in Chapter 2. First, Vermeule has distinguished it from Catholic traditionalists ("trads"). Traditionalists often take an oppositional stance toward liberal popes, especially Pope Francis. But Vermeule knows that popes can ruin political movements. As I mentioned in Chapter 1, in 1926 Pope Pius XI condemned Action Française, an integralist party in France.[66] For this reason, among others, Vermeule writes almost nothing about the Latin Mass. He avoids condemning the church hierarchy for any reason.

Vermeule's faction also crosses swords with traditionalists over the modern nation-state.[67] Trads often hope to return to medieval institutional structures. Vermeule resists these attitudes. As noted, Vermeule encourages Catholics to embrace and expand the modern state. Indeed, he dreams of building a "robust administrative state, of a sort that St. Louis IX could never have imagined."[68]

Vermeule does not blame the liberal state for promoting substantive moral values. Every state does that. No, the problem is that the liberal state has *bad* values. The integralist faction will give the state a proper purpose: pursuing the true common good.

Vermeule pushes the American right wing away from Burkean conservatism. He and others argue that conservatives have only preserved the liberal revolution. But liberal institutions were born in sin. Vermeule hopes the new

---

[65] Stephen 2018, p. 40.

[66] For discussion, see Maritain (2020).

[67] The chief scholarly example is Jones (2017). Vermeule (2018a) raises worries about Catholic trad nostalgia.

[68] Waldstein 2018, p. 2.

generation of conservatives draw more on Maistre and Schmitt. The New Right will not make peace with the Left; it will seek the Left's conquest and obliteration. The goal is not gradualism but counterrevolution. Vermeule has convinced thousands that these Schmittian and Maistrean objectives fit with the radically distinct philosophy of Thomas Aquinas.

We must understand the function of Vermeule's faction to assess integralist strategy. Here's what the faction must do next.

Phase 2, State Staffing: Vermeule's Colony

Those who yearn for a Catholic civilization must staff the liberal state. In Vermeule's view, the proper anti-liberal strategy requires defeating and capturing "the hearts and minds of liberal agents" and taking over "the institutions of the old order," turning them to integralist purposes.[69]

Marxist parties illustrate. They worked to hasten the demise of capitalism. They were certain of capitalism's doom, but they pushed for socialism anyway. Revolution will lead to social transformation, but activists can ease capitalism's death and socialism's birth. Integralists operate similarly. They work to hasten the demise of liberalism. They are certain of liberalism's doom, but they push for integralism anyway. Counterrevolution must do most of the work, but integralists can ease liberalism's death and integralism's birth. So the integralist faction is not a passive force.

The community must place its members in positions of power. Vermeule encourages integralists to take positions of influence in executive-type bureaucracies. These bureaucracies will survive liberalism's collapse. Vermeule downplays working through "parliamentary-democratic institutions," for which he displays no enthusiasm.[70]

Integralists cannot win by taking over the administrative state alone; they must also co-opt the federal judiciary. Vermeule has been subtler here. He never tells judges to make the law integralist. Yet judges should sometimes bend the law toward the true common good. And he argues, with all other integralists, that the common good has a spiritual component. He leaves it to the reader to connect the dots.

Vermeule's strategy for subverting the judiciary involves propagating a new judicial philosophy. As I have noted, he calls this doctrine "common good constitutionalism."[71] With progressives, Vermeule recommends interpreting the

---

[69] Vermeule 2018b.
[70] Vermeule 2018d.
[71] Vermeule 2020; Vermeule 2022a.

Constitution according to its (purported) underlying aims. Vermeule rejects originalism. Judges should not read the Constitution by identifying the text's original meaning alone. They must sometimes directly consult the common good. But Vermeule thinks that appeals to the common good vindicate certain right-wing policies (and some left-wing ones).

This chapter does not assess common good constitutionalism, but, if followed, the philosophy should conform law to the common good over time.[72] It can also bypass the democratic process. Judicial review can use the common good to justify reshaping the law.[73] Integralist order can grow from the rules and policies Vermeule's new jurists create.

Vermeule does not directly discuss the relationship between integralism and common good constitutionalism. However, his book on the topic is telling. Vermeule claims that the common good has a supernatural part. Indeed, our highest happiness is supernatural. Vermeule sets the issue aside, but not without tipping his hand: common good constitutionalism addresses only the "*secondary ends*" of the political community. How his doctrine applies to the *primary* ends of the community should be clear by now.[74]

This claim is significant. Imagine that you're a judge who agrees to "presumptive textualism,"[75] but in hard cases, you consult facts about the common good as you determine how to rule. Now imagine that you're also a Roman Catholic judge and believe that the highest good of the community is corporate salvation. When you consult the common good, why limit yourself to its secondary aspect? Why not also consult its primary part? In this case, Catholic theology will bear on your interpretative strategy.

How might this look? Vermeule does not say. Nonetheless, we can tease out some implications. In the United States, a *complete* common good constitutionalism should provide further motivation to clip the separationist implications of the establishment clause. The Catholic judge recognizes the great good of established religion. And so, in hard cases, this judge reads the establishment clause as allowing more, rather than less, establishment.

Vermeule could deny that judges should consult the supernatural common good. After all, integralism teaches that the state has no authority over the supernatural good. Only the church has divine sanction in such matters. So, even if a

---

[72] For a strong critique, see Pojanowski and Walsh 2022. For another excellent, and indeed powerful critique, see Mancini 2023.

[73] Mancini 2023 brings this point out well.

[74] Vermeule 2022a, p. 29, emphasis added. Vermeule also says that "canon law" is part of the classical legal tradition, which indicates that Vermeule sees canon law as part of advancing the spiritual common good. He mentions canon law on the first page of the book.

[75] Vermeule 2022a, pp. 8, 80, 84, 110.

judge—let's call her Judge Mary Bennett Coyne—grasps the supernatural good, she knows she has no authority over it.

This response is not fully persuasive. First, judges can respond to the super-natural common good through subtler legal maneuvers. Judge Coyne might think she should ease legal barriers to a Catholic establishment. She greases the wheels for church dominion. Second, Judge Coyne will have revelatory grounds for certain moral judgments. She might grow more opposed to the death penalty or to same-sex marriage.

The point here is simple: common good constitutionalism directs judges to consult the common good in hard cases. The common good includes the super-natural good. And so judges should consult the supernatural good in some hard cases. Even a cursory read of Vermeule's work makes the connection obvious. He reveals his political goals. One need only do the reading.

We can see how common good constitutionalism leads to integralism. Imagine that Vermeule trains a new legal Right. The next generation of integralist legal scholars co-opt the Federalist Society. Vermeule's jurists grad-ually alter the law while other integralists change the makeup of the GOP. Future judges insist that the common good is Catholic, thereby enabling an integralist takeover. The GOP remains a likely vehicle for integralist opera-tions via its judicial nominees.

Is Phase 2 Strictly Defensive?

Vermeule wants to protect the church from malignant states. His method: train strong Christian leaders who will take power and defend the church. When I have spoken with Vermeule's defenders, often young people, they characterize his strategy as concerned chiefly with *defense* rather than *offense*. I do not think Vermeule's theory of liberalism allows for any such distinction. Vermeule would not suppress liberalism with violence. Liberalism will destroy itself. But liberals and the liberal state can still do significant damage in the meanwhile. Further, once liberalism dies, it could revive.

As Vermeule so evocatively claims, we must "sear the liberal faith with hot irons."[76] It must not rise again. Only a strong state combined with a strong church can complete this urgent task. Vermeulean protectors must become conquerors. They must then rule with an iron rod. And so, however much Vermeule wants to avoid coercion, he is stuck with it. Integralists must exer-cise hard power.

---

[76] Vermeule 2018b.

Phase 3, State Capture: Vermeule's Victory

Suppose that Vermeule is correct: liberalism falls, and the state becomes an ideological wasteland. The church has incubated a powerful subcommunity that survives the liberal apocalypse, and it now releases its members, who co-opt the state.

How does this work? Vermeule bases his plan on Leo XIII's advice to French Catholics. Leo encouraged French Catholics to take part in French politics in order to improve the Third Republic. Leo XIII called this *ralliement*.[77] Vermeule says little about how hard integralists should fight for the ideal. I suspect that he thinks it won't matter much, since liberalism will destroy itself.[78] Integralists need only prepare to co-opt remaining state capacity, specifically executive-type bureaucracies.[79]

The nonintegralist population of any co-opted society, such as the United States, will remain large. What if they resist? Vermeule seems to think they will fall in line:

> Just authority in rulers can be exercised for the good of subjects, if necessary even against the subjects' own perceptions of what is best for them—perceptions that may change over time anyway, as the law teaches, habituates, and re-forms them. Subjects will come to *thank the ruler* whose legal strictures, possibly experienced at first as coercive, encourage subjects to form more authentic desires for the individual and common goods, better habits, and beliefs that better track and promote communal well-being.[80]

We will thank our rulers because they make us more virtuous. We yearn for a strong sovereign; we want not equality but hierarchy (we are "subjects" and not citizens, after all). And so we will obey a robust administrative state and learn to love its "ordered relation of temporal and spiritual power."[81] This new state deliberately pursues the whole human good. Political doors will one day open, but only if integralists begin preparation now.

I have questions. First, even if liberalism falls, liberals will still command some governmental wreckage. They will resist integralism with a zealous fervor. That is what we should expect—assuming Vermeule has captured the character of

---

[77] Leo XIII 1892. Leo XIII thought French Catholics should try to improve the Third Republic, not destroy it and replace it with integralism.

[78] Vermeule 2019b.

[79] Vermeule 2018d.

[80] Vermeule 2020, emphasis added.

[81] Waldstein 2018, p. 2.

the liberal mind. Remember: liberals have a "fighting, evangelistic faith," which drives "ascetic and highly motivated" activity.[82] Vermeule's analysis implies that liberals will violently resist integralist rule. They might start with behind-the-scenes assassination and espionage, support a military coup, or launch a civil war. Integralists will struggle to contain nonviolent unbaptized resisters.

Vermeule's forces must observe Catholic moral constraints. They cannot lie, harm the innocent, and so on. Vermeule must insist that his agents follow these ethical constraints. Consider a comparison he draws with Saint Paul:

> Despite his tactical acumen, Paul never lies or violates other moral norms. His identity claims, and the political and legal claims following from them, are all true or valid, and his flexibility is openly professed.
>
> The strategic Christian need only emphasize, truthfully, one or another of his multiple political loyalties and identities as relevant and helpful to the audience and the occasion.[83]

Integration agents never need to lie, nor sin otherwise, to maintain their position. Instead, they strategically emphasize their different political loyalties and identities. (Even though Vermeule asked them not to have any political loyalties and identities other than to the church.)

How can integralists peacefully resist the violent and enraged liberal remnant? We lack a "just integration" theory. (I have tried to work one out.) But whatever its principles, integralists must violate Catholic teaching to seize power. The simple reason is that they must overcome political factions that will use violence to defend themselves. The integralist party and the integralist state must respond with sufficient violence to succeed. But Catholic social teaching cannot legitimize the level of violence required.

Integration from within probably requires abolishing democracy. But Vermeule likely believes that democracy will either collapse or become a formality. All the same, integralists must one day win elections. And, owing to the competitive party system, sometimes the party will lose, even if integralists steer it. Liberal elites will sometimes regain power. With democratic majorities, liberals will expel integralists from power. They will know that integralists yearn for the glorious death of liberal democracy. The academy excludes conservatives from positions of influence; the liberal administrative state has far more power at its disposal.

---

[82] Vermeule 2018b.
[83] Vermeule 2017c.

If Vermeule is right, liberals will create a de facto inquisition. Integration agents will stand trial once unmasked. Liberals won't care that integralists share a country or a faith or use the same pronouns. They will demand that integralists reveal their plans, knowing that integralists are loyal to the Catholic Church alone. How can integralists keep their jobs? They must stop liberals with force; votes won't work.

Vermeule and his fellow strategists face a dilemma: they can sinfully succeed or they can fail. They can use tactics pioneered by fascists and communists, but they must use violence in ways that the Catholic Church rejects.[84] I am *not* saying that integralists relish violence, but I *am* saying that victory requires violence. Integralists have cast liberals as power addicts and fanatics. Their plan must treat liberals accordingly.

We can now ask whether integration from within has any prospects for success. Vermeule again emphasizes the fluidity of political constraints.[85] But I see no reason to believe that the fluidity of institutions works to his advantage. He has no story about why integralism must follow liberalism. Marx at least *argued* that capitalism would collapse into socialism, but Vermeule has not explored that dimension of his social theory.

We don't know which social conditions survive liberalism's collapse. The culture will probably remain inclined toward personal liberty and social equality. We can safely say that its institutions will exhibit great complexity and that communication costs will remain low. So we must assess Vermeule's plan as beginning from social conditions like ours. Vermeule may think that social conditions will prove hospitable to integralist takeover, but I see no such argument in his work.

Vermeule's model of liberal social dynamics is less compelling than Marx's model of capitalist ones. Marx had a deeply mistaken model to explain why capitalism must decline.[86] Vermeule has less. Marx had a story about the causal interaction between economic forces. Vermeule's theory appeals to a single, overwhelming social power. Marx developed a theory of ideology and explained how it interacts with economic forces. Vermeule ascribes great power to a "sociopolitical regime," a category I'm not sure picks out a social kind. Vermeule does not appeal to any familiar social kind, such as an ideology.

Perhaps Vermeule does not need a causal story before he creates a community. But we have little reason to think he can lead this community in the right direction. If liberalism collapses, integralists may not defeat competitor groups. So let's grant liberalism's demise. This is far from the claim that the Ark can succeed, because we don't know how a postliberal regime will look. The truth is,

---

[84] Piekalkiewicz and Penn 1995.
[85] Vermeule 2021.
[86] Marx and Engels 2011, chap. 32.

Vermeule's integralism has an apocalyptic dimension: spiritual forces ultimately foreordain liberalism's collapse.[87]

Background Conditions

As noted, we can begin our assessment of Vermeule's strategy with social conditions like our own. However, we have no idea how background conditions will change once liberalism dies. Let's now examine the background conditions for transitioning to integralism.

Integralists likely begin this transition from societies that have the following features:

- a liberal democratic constitution
- considerable pluralism
- moderate individualism
- high levels of education
- costless communication
- greatly differentiated institutions
- some institutions that are complex adaptive systems
- connections to a global church
- knowledge of the church's liberal period

I'll describe each feature in more detail.

A Liberal Democratic Constitution

The base society protects extensive individual and group liberties for everyone: freedom of speech, freedom of the press, freedom of religion, and the right to a fair trial. Everyone has the right to vote and run for office, elected officials choose legislation, and people vote for their leaders by majority rule. Social liberalism is in a state of decay, but the constitution remains in effect.

Considerable Pluralism

Society contains diverse value systems, religions, and political ideologies. It has many Jews, Muslims, Protestants, and atheists. Citizens disagree about sexual mores and economic ideologies.

---

[87] The strategy might be aptly described as Thomism-Leninism.

Moderate Individualism

Society is more individualistic than most historical civilizations. Despite the decline of social liberalism, many people still support rights to choose one's faith and moral values. Some disobey restrictions on their "deviant" moral behavior.

High Levels of Education

The base society has a high literacy rate. Most people have a college degree. Citizens of this society know far more than citizens of historic integralist regimes, and they process that extra information into new values and arguments.

Costless Communication

The base society communicates costlessly.

Greatly Differentiated Institutions

Medieval regimes had low state capacity. They had fewer functions and less power to perform them.[88] Today, states perform many tasks through diverse agencies; states exhibit high differentiation, as do extra-state legal and economic institutions. Large governmental and corporate bureaucracies have distinct and conflicting interests.

Some Institutions Are Complex Adaptive Systems

Differentiated institutions interact, which means that society resembles a complex adaptive system. Society is complex when it has the following characteristics:

- The system has a large number of constituent parts.
- There is feedback between the parts such that the behavior of one part affects the others.
- The parts are not homogeneous. The properties of the parts vary between the parts. (Or, at least, the parts display different behaviors in response to the same signal.)
- The behavior of agents can be seen as complying with rules. (Complex systems are rule-governed systems.)
- The interdependence of the parts is not so great that the system becomes chaotic.

---

[88] Johnson and Koyama 2019, chap. 1.

- The rules that govern the parts respond to how the parts behave. Specifically, the behavior of the parts shapes the rules that govern their behavior. There is system-level feedback.[89]

Experts face enormous challenges as they seek to predict the operations of complex adaptive systems. Indeed, they struggle to determine how *past* outcomes occurred.[90] Expert forecasters cannot predict changes in discrete social variables beyond five years—typically far less. Any integralist transition plan requires predicting system-level outcomes at each stage, but every stage will itself exhibit complexity, including the end state of integralism.

Connections to a Global Church

Society must coordinate activities with a billion-member global church, whereas medieval integralist regimes coordinated with a regional European church surrounded by enemies and competitors (Muslims, pagans, Arians, and Eastern Orthodox Christians). Catholicism has 5,600 bishops from nations and cultures worldwide, and none openly affirms integralism. No pope has embraced integralism since Pius X (in office 1903–1914). The vast majority of Catholic theologians and leaders follow *Dignitatis humanae*'s standard interpretation.

Knowledge of the Church's Liberal Period

Catholicism rests on tradition and understands itself as developing doctrine gradually.[91] Catholics emphasize continuities in church teaching and church structure, but today the church embraces most constitutional rights found in advanced democracies.[92] Integralists have decades of work ahead of them. By the time they win a regime, the church will have rejected integralism for a century. Perhaps Catholics will view this period as the church's great dark age. Other reasonable Catholics will wonder whether Christ's Church could be *so wrong* for *so long*. These Catholics may resist transitioning from liberal order and may push for liberalism once the church becomes nonliberal again, creating conflict.

---

[89] I thank Alex Motchoulski for this characterization of complexity. Also see Gaus 2021, pp. 118–28. For an excellent introduction to how complexity interfaces with the design of public policy, see Colander and Kupers (2014). Their idea of the "complexity frame" of policy making informs my remarks on complexity throughout this book.

[90] Colanders and Kupers 2014, pp. 252–55.

[91] Newman 1994.

[92] At least, it does if the catechism is any guide. See Catholic Church (1997), part 3, sec. 1, chap. 2, art. 3.

Soft Power

Vermeule's plan involves both hard and soft power. Hard power uses institutional coercion or economic incentives; soft power exerts social and cultural influence. Political scientist Joseph Nye explains that you have soft power when you can get others to do what you want apart from coercion or payment.[93] Here I prefer philosopher and behavioral scientist Cristina Bicchieri's social norms framework, which also models social control as soft power. We can understand soft power as the capacity to control on the basis of social sanctions, such as shaming and ostracism.

For Bicchieri, "trendsetters" exercise the greatest amount of soft power.[94] As high-status community members, they can change norms: they can impose new norms or flout old ones without negative social consequences. Integralists would deprive liberal trendsetters of soft power and create integralist trendsetters.

Soft power often matters much more than hard power. And political groups cannot easily wield hard power if soft power stands in the way. Those with soft power may direct members of their community to ignore some law or policy, and much evidence suggests that soft power will prevail.

The integralist argues that the influence of the progressive Left comes from its enormous soft power. In the United States, you won't suffer physical harm if you dissent from elite morality on issues of sex and gender. But you will face punishment from the progressive vanguard on social media. One might prefer a night in jail.

Integralists cannot capture hard power if the Left holds all soft power. They know this. Vermeule hopes that liberalism self-destructs and creates opportunities for cultural displacement. The goal, then, is to take soft power from liberals and wield it in favor of orthodox Catholicism. How would this go? Today one gets canceled for teaching that only two genders exist. In the Vermeulean era, one could get canceled for teaching that we are saved by faith alone.

Vermeule has not explained how integralists are to capture soft power. He says only that liberals will run out of steam. Liberals have competitors, though: powerful groups that Vermeule leaves unnamed. So, while liberalism may weaken, nonintegralist yet nonliberal groups might take over.

As noted above, Vermeule's analysis flounders because it focuses almost entirely on liberalism's internal dynamics and how they unfold. Opposing forces go undertheorized. I am attracted to political scientist Michael Freeden's approach

---

[93] Nye 2004.
[94] Bicchieri 2016.

to ideology.[95] For Freeden, ideologies are necessarily contested systems of ideals; one cannot describe liberalism without providing an account of opposing forces. So Vermeule's analysis often strikes me as nearly incoherent.

True, progressives have extraordinary influence in the arts, media, and higher education. But they have not always had this much control, and they do not stand unopposed in the culture. Yes, right now, many factors work in their favor. But, given the value of soft power, new groups will eventually fight for it.

Humans like to conform to shared norms, but—as I argue in the next chapter—conformity bias may not always create a single elite class. Most societies have competing elites with conflicting values. In some cases, trendsetters within those groups manufacture conflicts to claim power over one another.

Vermeule might offer a multiple force model by examining his current competitors. Let's focus on the New Right. This group includes the National Conservatives, led by Yoram Hazony, and more secular intellectuals affiliated with the Claremont Institute. Once we step outside the New Right, "fusionist" forces abound, such as the American Enterprise Institute. If the left-liberal vanguard collapses, fusionists could co-opt liberal power by positioning themselves as moderate alternatives to integralists.

So yes, integralists will use soft power to transition. But they need a better theory of how one captures it. The strategists do not have an effective strategy for capturing soft power. Indeed, they have a marked tendency to make political enemies. Where do they go from here?

Complexity Hypocrisy

Vermeule makes claims about system-level processes far beyond what anyone can know. Our American complex adaptive system disables system-level predictions. I critique Vermeule by predicting transition barriers, chiefly blowback mechanisms. But I'm in no better position to make predictions than Vermeule, right?

Although social scientists and expert teams can't predict system-level outcomes, they can trace short-term causal processes. These processes have unintended consequences, but one can foresee them as short-term phenomena. Knowing this, I do not predict system-level change. I stick to more modest, localized predictions, such as which groups will resist an integralist takeover. I thereby follow complexity theorists. Complexity theory suggests that no one

[95] Freeden 2003.

can foresee system-level changes but that one *can* predict short-term processes at the meso-level of social organization.

Further, complexity helps predict a kind of system-level outcome: *diverse niche construction.*[96] Complexity produces competing local hegemons. Hegemon multiplication occurs in much the same way as free ecologies produce ecological niches. The free development of plant life seldom leads to a uniform wheat field, free of all other fauna, but instead produces rich mixes of plants and animals. Complex systems tend toward local heterogeneity. This pattern troubles hegemonic strategies for social change, such as integration from within.

Transition Problems

Three types of transition problem can plague each transition phase: *leadership failures, internal resistance,* and *external opposition.* Leadership failures occur when party, state, or church leaders become corrupt or incompetent. Internal resistance occurs when actors resist integralism from within formal institutions, and external opposition when outside groups resist integralist governance. Each type of problem has subtypes.

1. Leadership failures
    a. Corruption
    b. Bad leaders
2. Internal resistance
    a. State dissensus
    b. Church dissensus
    c. Containing heretics
    d. Punishing heretics
    e. Military power
3. External opposition
    a. Democratic resistance
    b. Local resistance
    c. Educational resistance
    d. Banning/cancellation
    e. New diversity

---

[96] I thank Alex Schaefer helping me clarify my thinking on this point.

Leadership Failures

Leadership failures may take the form of corruption or bad leaders.

Corruption

Vermeule draws on public choice economics to critique liberal affinity for the market.[97] Public choice assumes motivational symmetry between market and government actors.[98] Both groups often act from self-interest and produce institutional failures—market failure or government failure. The transition to integralism must combat government failures, as predicted by Vermeule's own assumptions.

Sinful government actors will redirect funds to their private projects and enrich themselves by limiting market exchange (that is, by rent-seeking).[99] Such public choice problems plagued socialist bureaucracies, as bureaucrats gummed up the administrative works.[100] Anyone employed in higher education understands such behavior. And much worse occurs. Bribery can become a major problem, especially between citizens and law enforcement.[101]

Corruption interacts with social trust—our faith that strangers will follow established norms. Higher-trust countries have far less corruption.[102] When people trust each other more, they engage in less corrupt behavior; and when people behave more ethically, they can increase trust—positive reinforcement.

Liberal order creates trust between members of large, diverse societies.[103] Vermeule merely asserts that liberal institutions undermine social trust. In fact, our best evidence suggests that liberal regimes maintain social capital better than alternatives. We have good reason to think that an integralist authority would protect social capital poorly. Heavily Catholic societies have more corruption than historically Protestant nations, and not by accident.[104]

An integralist state resembles an "ideocracy," a regime structured around a monistic ideology. Such a society is led by ideologues, not a mere military junta.[105] Ideocracies include communist, fascist, and Islamic fundamentalist

---

[97] Vermeule 2019b; Mueller 2003.

[98] Buchanan 2003.

[99] Tullock 1993; Piekalkiewicz and Penn 1995.

[100] Boettke 1993, pp. 57–72.

[101] Tullock 2005.

[102] Bjørnskov 2011. See also Vallier 2020, chap. 2.

[103] Vallier 2020, 2019.

[104] Bjørnskov 2006.

[105] Piekalkiewicz and Penn 1995, pp. 25–27.

states. As an ideocracy, an integralist state may follow these regimes into widespread distrust and corruption.

States that pursue sectarian agendas sow distrust to gain power and reduce resistance. Integralists will unintentionally sow doubt between integralist officials and non-Catholics.[106] Non-Catholics will see their government as an alien hegemon and clandestinely ignore its directives. Catholic officials tasked with containing pluralism will mistrust dissenters.

We can easily envision lost trust. Consider distrust between American public health officials and the public over COVID-19 policy. Health authorities treated the people as untrustworthy: officials lied to the public but imposed draconian restrictions without cause and dragged their feet on new treatments. People distrusted public health officials: many people flouted basic guidelines and spread conspiracy theories. If COVID-19 sowed mutual distrust between ruler and ruled, integralism will, too; the disconnect between elite and mass opinion will produce mutual alienation.

Sectarian regimes that undermine social trust erode a precious social resource.[107] One such problem: low social trust invites more corruption, and so an integralist regime invites corruption from non-Catholics who reject its authority.

Unique forms of corruption arise at every transition stage. Some stages may even require corruption, since integralists might buy off semi-liberal officials or secure support from nonintegralist allies. During state stabilization, non-Catholic groups will have strong reasons to capture institutions. Integralists must discourage them from doing so.

Turn now to the church. Corruption already plagues Vatican finances. If integralists give the church more political power, they invite further deterioration. Corruption here poses great dangers. Heretical movements universally point to church corruption to justify their views and activities.

Corruption may crop up at the unification stage as popes and elected officials attempt to control each other. Contests for control suffused High Integralism, such as the many that arose from the creation of the Avignon papacy.

Bad Leaders

Another leadership failure involves incompetent or wicked officials in church or state. State officials may undermine political coalitions that keep their party in power. Integralists need allies with good political instincts, because they

---

[106] Murray 1993, p. 16.
[107] Vallier 2019, chap. 1.

cannot otherwise place their agents in key party and government positions. Incompetent or evil partners may make promises they know they cannot keep. Or they may betray the integralist faction in their coalition.

Bad church leadership poses a greater danger: one weak or corrupt pope can discredit any integralist attempt to take power. The church struggles to contain clerical sexual abuse. It may not regain political influence for decades, even centuries.

Politics affects how the church chooses its officials. If the church controls potent states, it will attract worse leaders.[108] The selection process will invite interference from other interested parties, as it routinely did in centuries past. Kings often had strong incentives to install servile popes, and at times they succeeded, as with Philip IV and the Avignon papacy (again an excellent illustration).

Internal Resistance

The second challenge involves quelling rebellion within the state and the church. Let's begin with the state.

State Dissensus

Plenty of groups will stop integralists from gaining power within a right-wing party, not to mention within the liberal democratic state. They cannot yet ban people from certain institutions. So suppose integralists capture a state. Modern states contain many entrenched factions, such as the American farm lobby and public-sector unions. Trump supporters said the "deep state" betrayed Trump's agenda during his presidency.

Internal groups will resist integralists owing to self-interest and ideology, so integralists must reduce the influence of these groups. Ideocratic regimes face such challenges from their inception. In response, they form elite military forces that share the regime's ideology. These ultra-loyal troops then subdue career military officials. (Hitler's SS springs to mind.) Historical ideocratic regimes have also created youth programs to increase loyalty to their leader. (Hitler Youth springs to mind.)

Even using these tactics, sects stabilize an ideocratic regime only with great difficulty. Political scientists Jaroslaw Piekalkiewicz and Alfred Wayne Penn claim the

---

[108] Here I expect the integralist to argue that empowering people ennobles them. It gives them a chance to act on their nobler impulses. I find no argument showing this. So I default to the assumption that, at the margin, power corrupts or selects for more corrupt leaders.

process takes ten to fifteen years.[109] The state must invest enormous resources to expel, subdue, or kill resisters. Worse, strategies that cleanse one bureaucracy may fail elsewhere. Modern state bureaucracies have various cultures and norms as well as diverse allies, such as weapons manufacturers.

Internal groups may violently resist integralist takeover. When integralists abolish democracy, intelligence agencies could become dangerous enough to assassinate integralist leaders or organize military coups. Many resistant officials might keep quiet rather than challenge integralist rule openly. Thus, if ideocratic leaders use too much fear, they will not know whom they can trust. The common consequence? Leadership purges, replete with execution, torture, and show trials.

A one-party state forgoes the great benefit of democracy: peaceful transitions of power. Integralist states must ensure that power transfers remain peaceful, yet even integralist elites may fight one another, as Catholic kings did.

And, to reiterate, Vermeule has publicly declaimed all such tactics. Indeed, even in "Integration from Within" he indicates hesitancy about coercion, though what he says is curious: "It would be wrong to conclude that integration from within is a matter of coercion, as opposed to persuasion and conversion, for the distinction is so fragile as to be nearly useless."[110] On the one hand, integration from within is not "a matter of coercion." But the distinction between coercion and noncoercion is "nearly useless"—which leaves one to wonder which tactics Vermeule has in mind.

Church Dissensus

If church history is any guide, the pope and the crown will dispute their relative authority. Consider some examples:

- Popes Boniface VIII and Innocent III claimed sweeping temporal power.[111]
- The papal schism led to conciliar supremacy at the Council of Constance.[112]
- Francisco Suárez and Cardinal Bellarmine tried to resist royal claims to ecclesiastical authority.[113]
- The First Vatican Council saw intense internal disagreement over papal infallibility: a third of bishops left the council rather than resist.[114]

---

[109] Piekalkiewicz and Penn 1995, p. 138.

[110] Vermeule 2018a.

[111] Duffy 2014, pp. 138–50.

[112] Oakley 2003, pp. 32–51.

[113] Suárez (1612) 2015, pp. 757–828; Bellarmine 2012, pp. 211–25. See also Pink's introduction to Suárez (Pink 2015a, pp. xiii–xviii, which is the introduction to Suárez [1612] 2015).

[114] They eventually relented. See Oakley (2003, pp. 207–16).

- Fears of excess centralism continued into the Second Vatican Council, such that Vatican II softened Vatican I's papal centralism.[115]

Today Catholics disagree on political matters as much as ever. They form voluminous competing factions that interact in surprising ways. Catholic integralism arose following a debate about the Catholic doctrine of religious liberty. Integralists have crossed swords with traditionalist Catholics who resisted Vatican II. They have fought other traditionalists by allying themselves with liberal Catholics who protect leading US Catholic officials from scandal.

Integralists must still contend with hostile Catholic factions even if they come to power. Some factions will resist integralist policies, such as deposing heretical prime ministers. If depositions fail, future popes will avoid them. These disagreements will occur in light of the church's liberal democratic century. Factions will oppose integralists by appealing to this tradition.

Containing Heretics

Integralist states invested considerable resources to suppress heresy. They sometimes used extreme violence.[116] Popes called crusades to quell heretical regions by directing kings to send in their troops. Popes placed under interdict cities that gave heretics sanctuary, prohibiting the entire city or nation from receiving the sacraments—including confession, which forgives mortal sin. Popes exercised political power by threatening pious Catholics with eternal damnation.[117]

New integralist states will identify heretics and discourage heresy with digital technology. Chinese-level tactics could prove effective. Even if people learn heretical ideas, the state might chill speech about them. It could punish the most dangerous heretics—make examples of them.

But it is hard to know what will happen. Jan Hus's execution provoked mass resistance. Martin Luther grew more opposed to the papacy when he learned what Hus taught.[118] Many feared that the church would treat Luther like Hus. In response, Frederick III, one of the electors of the Holy Roman Empire who shared Luther's ideas, shielded him from danger. Luther then built a mass

---

[115] Oakley 2003, pp. 250–63.

[116] The church formalized the death penalty for heresy in the late twelfth and early thirteenth centuries (Fudge 2013, pp. 112–13; Johnson and Koyama 2019, p. 44).

[117] This happened when Prague protected its favorite son, Jan Hus, from arrest, and it occurred again during the four Hussite rebellions (see Fudge 2013, pp. 293–95).

[118] Haberkern 2017.

movement that helped destroy most quasi-integralist regimes within two hundred years.

The integralist state could create martyrs who become national heroes. Czechs have celebrated Hus for six centuries. Saint John Paul II apologized for the burning of Hus, calling it "cruel."[119]

But assume heretics get what they "deserve." Today the state will struggle to identify and convict them. Heretics can still spread their messages and seek sanctuary in local houses of worship. Many will leave the country but pipe their views back in. Even when integralists catch them, new difficulties will arise.

Punishing Heretics

The Catholic Church has considerable canon law that governs heresy trials. Medieval heretics had few legal rights. They had no presumption of innocence, no right to defend themselves—not even a right to counsel.[120] The Council of Constance even revoked Hus's guarantee of safe passage. Incineration had become the standard punishment for heresy.

To convict a heretic, heresy trials first made two determinations.[121] They had to show that the defendant held heretical beliefs and that the defendant held to them with "contumacy"—that is, stubbornly and irrationally.[122]

Modern heresy trials may require severe punishments to stop heresy. Bellarmine was clear: you must kill heretics, or they can still spread their ideas.[123] The church could instead isolate heretics. But not before their followers distribute their work to the ends of the earth in seconds. Severe punishments may not discourage prominent dissidents, because they will martyr themselves. Hus faced death with great courage. He was not alone.

Military Power

During High Integralism, popes exercised military power to preserve political stability and religious uniformity. They allied themselves with monarchs for

---

[119] Quoted in John L. Allen Jr., "The German Shepherd Bids Farewell to a 'Wolf in Winter,'" *National Catholic Reporter*, September 25, 2009, https://www.ncronline.org/news/german-shepherd-bids-farewell-wolf-winter.

[120] His *salvus conductus*. Fudge 2013, pp. 182–86.

[121] Fudge 2013, p. 2.

[122] Fudge 2013, pp. 50–52.

[123] Bellarmine 2012, pp. 102–9.

their armies. Saint Louis IX and Pope Clement IV caught, interrogated, and executed (putative) Cathar priests.[124] Unless Catholic ecclesiastical authorities can
conduct military campaigns, heresy may erupt.

Unless the church regains military power, monarchs will ignore church
directives. Prime ministers more so. The church must build enough military
power to ensure that these political officials obey church directives. Spiritual
punishments often failed, even during High Integralism. Excommunication subdued monarchs in the past. Today the pope will need a few more troops than the
Swiss Guard to enforce his decrees.

The specter of the pope authorizing crusades anew will create global controversy. Many recall the Crusades with horror: Jews, Muslims, Protestants,
and Orthodox Christians. Church leadership must exercise its ancient military
power without triggering these associations. We must also consider the risk of
military conflict between states and a rearmed papacy.

Of course, in the past even these policies failed to contain heresy. Today an
integralist state will use mass surveillance and control its national internet. The
dyarchy could suppress dissent, but only at great cost.[125]

External Opposition

Integralist strategists must also subdue opposition force outside the state.

Democratic Resistance

Integralists must begin transition within a democracy. They must capture a party
by forming alliances with influential groups. American integralists aligned themselves with Donald Trump as critics of his critics. (Some have said they were
anti-anti-Trump.) They excoriated traditional conservatives and libertarians
within the GOP, which has earned them many enemies and brought them little
influence. Party leaders will keep integralists out of leadership, including leadership of the GOP in any form the GOP has taken. Any democratic society will

---

[124] Jones 2017, pp. 36–37. Johnson and Koyama (2019, pp. 61–63, 71–72) provide a contrasting
account of the Cathar persecution. They argue that we do not know how many people adopted
Catharism and that Louis's campaign may have aimed at subduing nobles in southern France rather
than Cathars.

[125] Here the natural objection is that progressives have already pulled this off, and thus so can
integralists. But, as I noted above, we do not know how soft power is captured from opposing groups.
The progressive coordination of opinion is mysterious. We do not yet know how it works because it
is not centrally coordinated.

consider integralism a threat, at least at first. Nonintegralists, including many Catholics, will fight integralist ascendency.

But let's keep imagining integralism. Suppose Vermeule convinces young right-leaning jurists to adopt his common good constitutionalism; even then, integralists have sent few people to the polls. If they cannot deliver votes, they will not matter in the GOP. And as they gather votes, they must contend with many competing political factions.

Small groups with unpopular beliefs struggle to take power, but they can wield significant influence.[126] Recall the neoconservatives who convinced George W. Bush to invade Iraq. They succeeded with small numbers. However, the neoconservatives built on existing military power and elite willingness to use it. Integralists must engage in decades of persuasion. Their public profile suggests that they have work to do.

We haven't talked about the Democrats yet. The Democratic Party lives in perpetual fear of theocracy, real or imagined. If integralists capture the GOP, Democrats will resist. (Remember Vermeule: liberals are fanatics.) They will peel people off integralist coalitions by focusing on those likely to suffer under an integralist regime, such as Jews and evangelicals.

Republicans may oppose integralists when they learn of integralist disdain for the Founders. Or when integralists propose reforming the First Amendment. Nonetheless, imagine that an integralist GOP wins many national elections. It will still lose elections to Democrats, who will resist the long transition toward an integralist regime. Frustrated, integralists must push for one-party rule and expel hostile factions from the GOP. (And they may *finally* destroy David French–ism, once and for all.)[127]

These events are not *unthinkable*. Communist and fascist parties pursued similar strategies, as have dictators the world over. But these "ideocratic" groups embraced a degree of violence that violates Catholic moral teaching on human rights. One-party rule reduces human rights protections vis-à-vis competitive party systems.[128] Catholic leadership agrees.[129] The integralist strategy assumes that the pope will ignore the destruction of democracy, support one-party rule, and dismiss anticipated human rights violations. Maritain joined Action Française only for the Vatican to denounce it soon thereafter. A pope could easily condemn a twenty-first-century integralist party.

---

[126] Doing so requires dominating cultural institutions, such as Hollywood and the academy.

[127] Ahmari 2019.

[128] Halperin, Siegle, and Weinstein 2010.

[129] Perreau-Saussine 2012.

Local Resistance

Now consider groups that resist integralism from outside the democratic process. Few of these will see reasons to obey integralist policies. Covert disobedience pervades authoritarian regimes. Indeed, disobedience is the lifeblood of civil society under authoritarian rule. An ideocratic government must crush these groups with propaganda, ideological education, and secret police. Here local niche construction synchronizes with economist Elinor Ostrom's important work on how local communities manage common-pool resources. People will find creative ways to govern themselves, even under the watchful eyes of authoritarian regimes.[130]

Let's envision which groups will resist most. Consider Jews, the LGBT community, and Black Protestants.

Jews know how they fared under the integralist regimes of old: poorly. Even as pious a ruler as Saint Louis IX persecuted Jews, burning all available copies of the Talmud.[131] Following the Fourth Lateran Council, he made Jews wear unique clothes to avoid confusing Christians. He even considered expelling Jews from France. Catholics debated baptizing Jewish children against their parents' wishes during that time.[132]

These practices continued for centuries. Pope Gregory XVI (in office 1831–1846) insisted on imposing the following restrictions on Jews: "Employing Christian servants or wetnurses, . . . owning real estate, . . . living—where there is a ghetto—outside of its walls mixed in and confused with Christians, are prohibitions founded in the sacred Canons. These, in order to guarantee Christian religion and morality, command the separation of Christians and Jews."[133] David Kertzer argues that Pius IX and Leo XIII thought that "the Jews' divinely ordained place was in the ghetto." Any healthy Christian society "required protection from Jewish depredations."[134]

When popes ruled, even in the nineteenth century, they made Jews second-class citizens—at best. Jews have every reason to oppose an integralist regime. Integralists must somehow assuage their worries.

---

[130] Ostrom 1990.

[131] Historians call this event the Disputation of Paris (1240). See Green (2013) and Kertzer (2001, p. 139).

[132] Tapie 2018.

[133] Quoted in Kertzer 2001, p. 82 and Paldiel 2006, p. 322. For a description of how Catholics viewed the claim that Jews required spiritual segregation, see Connelly (2012, p. 100).

[134] Kertzer 2001, p. 82.

Imagine them trying. Catholic integralism sprang into public view because some defended Pius IX's decision to remove Edgardo Mortara from his family.[135] When *First Things* published a defense of Pius IX, Jewish readers were outraged. Leading Jewish philosopher and conservative Yoram Hazony described the event as "sickening."[136] Jews *already* associate integralist strategists with oppression.

Remember: this chapter explores real-world transition theory. People don't always obey the teachings of their churches, and we should not assume that an integralist regime will treat Jews well—surely not enough to quell resistance. From a Jewish perspective, integralism was brought forth in iniquity and in sin did its defenders conceive it (Ps. 51:5).

Now consider the LGBT community. Catholicism teaches that same-sex attraction is "disordered" and that same-sex intercourse is a mortal sin.[137] Unless gays and lesbians repent of same-sex relations, they could suffer forever. Catholic leaders have often treated gays and lesbians badly. (I have not yet examined the abuse scandals, for which Catholic leaders took too long to claim responsibility.) From an integralist standpoint, the state must disperse LGBT communities to protect Christians from spiritual damage. The state should not physically harm LGBT persons, but it must prevent them from forming communities that tempt people to sin.[138] These acts will provoke resistance.

Finally, consider Black Protestants. Integralists claim that ecclesiastical law covers every baptized person, including Protestants. An integralist state might outlaw distinctive Protestant activities. Protestants could face heresy charges. So, according to integralism, Black Protestant churches have no right to exist. The state must decide whether to declare Black Protestant churches criminal organizations.

The Black Protestant church organized political resistance for centuries, and it remains one of the central institutions of the Black community. Integralists may tolerate Black Protestants for prudential reasons, and they may recognize the great moral value of resisting unjust oppression, but this will hardly reassure the Black church.

In the past, integralist states often mistreated religious minorities. They segregated some populations, often confining them to ghettos.[139] The integralist

---

[135] Cessario 2018. For discussion of the Mortara case, see Schwartzman and Wilson (2019) and Tapie (2018).

[136] Yoram Hazony (@yhazony), "In 1859 the Vatican kidnapped a Jewish child who was never returned to his parents. A crime that rocked the world then. Today @firstthingsmag publishes a defense of this sickening deed," Twitter, January 10, 2018, 7:25 a.m., https://twitter.com/yhazony/status/951067495213027328.

[137] Catholic Church 1997, p. 566.

[138] At least, the state will not harm them unless it catches them violating natural law.

[139] See Chapter 2; also Kertzer (2001).

state could suppress violence through strict segregation norms. But, as philosopher Elizabeth Anderson argues, integration failures come with a steep price. Even less-direct forms of segregation harm physical and psychological well-being.[140]

Integralists must protect the baptized from spiritual damage. As history suggests, they will feel pressure to segregate religiously diverse populations. Heathen and heretical communities may threaten the polity. But, insofar as the state must care for the common good, segregation must end.

Educational Resistance

To stabilize integralism, the church must instill dogma in baptized children.[141] Integralist states could ban many forms of Christian schooling, including Protestant schools and many home schools. The government may prohibit Jewish and Islamic schools from educating baptized children.[142] States must subjugate higher education. Universities will foster resistance, including rogue Catholic universities. (Integralists believe there are more than a few of those today.)

Banning/Cancellation

Again, integralists say that liberals are power addicts. But integration from within places pious integralists in a quasi-liberal state: a bit unsafe. Vermeule might convince some to staff the administrative state or the judiciary, and they might see this as missionary work or martyrdom. But if Vermeule understands the liberal mind, liberals will expel integralists—or fight them or force them to betray their conscience. Again, integralists don't get past step 1 of the state capture phase.

During state stabilization, remaining liberal elites will cancel integralists, just as some universities ban certain conservatives from college campuses. To garner political power, integralists must destroy liberal cultural dominance and be quick about it. Otherwise, liberal bans will hamper the transition to integralism.

The Catholic Church could cancel integralists, too, given that most Catholic theologians still associate integralism with schismatics and opponents of Vatican II. Moreover, as I've mentioned before, no Catholic bishop embraces integralism

---

[140] Anderson 2010, pp. 67–88.

[141] Crean and Fimister 2020, pp. 50–54.

[142] Pink's read of *DH* assigns unbaptized parents the right to use religious schools, as article 5 clarifies: "Parents, moreover, have the right to determine, in accordance with their own religious beliefs, the kind of religious education that their children are to receive" (Paul VI 1965a).

in public. Few accept Thomas Pink's interpretation of *Dignitatis humanae*, and most will view attempts to establish integralism as disloyal and disobedient. Integralists may not rise high in the church hierarchy.

New Diversity

Philosopher Gerald Gaus has argued that open societies exhibit autocatalytic diversity. Diverse perspectives tend to branch and we cannot predict their content ahead of time.[143] Donald Trump's political success came out of nowhere, Twitter was his megaphone, and the QAnon movement followed in his wake. Integralist social media illustrates unexpected diversity. Ten years ago, no one anticipated an integralist revival, and it would not exist but for social media.

Societies will develop other forms of diversity and new groups may devolve into fierce infighting. Consider the alarming clash between gender-critical and trans-inclusionary feminists.[144] Even ten years ago, feminists respectfully debated these matters, but social media has moralized the debate. Open societies generate new forms of diversity all the time—some good, some bad. This pattern will continue. Integralists must overcome diverse groups with new tactics.

I also expect innovations in baptism. Many will seek a new baptismal rite once the baptized become liable for heresy and apostasy. Non-Catholics may alter the rite enough to render their baptisms invalid in the eyes of the Catholic Church. Or they may pursue secret baptism. Or they may lie about their baptismal status.

Strategic Stages toward Integralism

I group the strategic stages required to reach integralism into three macro-stages: state-side, church-side, and unification. At a general level, integralists must capture and subdue a liberal or quasi-liberal democratic state, convince the church to reclaim military and political power, and then push the two entities to unify.[145]

Integralists must observe the laws of their societies. Integralists in ages past argued that infidel kings had authority over their subjects. Christian kings may invade heathen nations only to protect Christians.[146] Contemporary integralists might agree. They could cast liberal democracies as infidel regimes, ascribing

---

[143] Gaus 2021, pp. 109–17.

[144] For a review of the relevant positions and their history, see Bettcher (2014).

[145] Many integralists think that natural law requires a global state. See Vermeule (2019c), who claims that natural law requires world government.

[146] Suárez (1612) 2015, p. 800; de Vitoria 1991, pp. 84, 219.

them moral authority despite their moral failings. Integralists would then treat the US Constitution as legitimate. If I am correct, integration transition theory requires working within the Constitution. Integralists also have practical reasons to affirm the Constitution. If their willingness to break the law becomes public knowledge, integralists will become enemies of the state. The constitutional path is longer but safer.

If integralists follow this path, they must repeal the establishment clause or reinterpret it into irrelevance.[147] To do so, they must convince a massive majority to make this change. Otherwise the integralist must "hope" that liberal constitutions become partly or entirely moribund or that other social movements discredit liberalism. Integralists can then replace a dead liberal constitution with a living integralist one. This *might* happen. Democracies often adopt new constitutions, as do US states. Integralists could pursue constitutional reform. But if integralism requires waiting for Americans to adopt a new constitution, integralists will wait a long time.[148]

State-Side Stages

Integration from within contains three state-side stages.

Party Capture

Integration stage 1 entails capturing a political party. (I have already addressed the difficulties integralists will face in capturing the GOP.)

State Capture

I have discussed how integralists might capture a democratic coalition. Nonetheless, few political parties remain in power for long, and losing parties adjust to become more competitive. Integralists will lose many political battles before they win. Knowing this, they must create a one-party state, as other ideocratic groups have done. The executive can then limit the democratic process—at least, as long as integralists keep the executive on their side.

---

[147] Integralists might push to read the establishment clause as applying only to the federal government. Many mainstream conservatives would agree with them. Integralist Maryland, anyone?
Note also that integralists would have to limit First Amendment protections of speech, the press, and assembly.

[148] If they do not wait, and instead support a revolutionary government, they will almost certainly create conditions that they would consider outrageously oppressive. This is the way of the vast majority of political revolutions (Buchanan and Motchoulski 2022).

State Stabilization

Integralists next stabilize the new nation-state, which, again, could take more than a decade.[149] Here's how it goes. Fascist and communist states imprisoned and executed political enemies. They controlled media, spread propaganda, indoctrinated children, subdued the military, and expelled competing factions. Integralists must follow the path forged by other ideocrats.

Many groups will outlast state capture, including some of the unbaptized population. Integralists cannot eliminate them all. Suppose the percentage of gay, lesbian, and transgender persons remains around 7 percent. Few will baptize their children or seek baptism themselves. They will resist underground—or even rebel in the open. Others may join them.

The integralist state may preempt resistance through modern surveillance technology, such as drones and security systems (like China's Great Firewall). At this point I am unsure how to proceed. I don't know whether Catholic social thought permits mass surveillance. Even if mass surveillance proves permissible, though, states will pay a steep price to track citizens who threaten religious uniformity.

We must again distinguish between baptized and unbaptized subjects. Unbaptized subjects have a right to religious freedom, and I expect them to use it. But the integralist state can coerce the baptized. It must also build new educational, inquisitorial, and judicial institutions, and these institutions must discourage heresy and apostasy. In some respects, then, the church will contain far more heresy than it did in medieval Europe. Monitoring and punishment systems may prompt insincere piety, however. And fake piety is a grave sin. Integralists must not press nonintegralists to endanger their souls.

Again, Lateran IV claims that popes may depose heretical kings after a period of excommunication and a refusal to repent. Popes may also depose orthodox kings who tolerate heretics. But the church lacks the raw power to depose leaders of modern nation-states, especially democratic leaders. If the Vatican cannot depose rulers, states may allow heresy. Secular rulers will keep integralism at the starting line.

Church-Side Stages

Let's turn to church-side stages.

---

[149] Piekalkiewicz and Penn 1995, p. 138.

Persuasion Campaign

I have stressed that not one of 5,600 Catholic bishops embraces integralism in public. They may believe that *Dignitatis humanae* prohibits integralist arrangements on moral grounds. The bishops surely find integralism impractical and undesirable in other respects: opposition may approach 99 percent.

Right now, the group of well-known integralists is tiny. Few have any ecclesiastical authority. Integralists may expect that liberalism's malignancy will change the church's mind. The postliberal church might elect a pope prepared to build integralism, but we have little reason to humor this prediction.

The greatest barrier to integralism is converting the church. The persuasion campaign must occur under real-world conditions of sin and confusion. Leading integralists invest little time persuading the hierarchy. They spend hours a day on social media, create paywalled publications, and sell tickets to conferences they headline. Successful political movements lobby politicians and build alliances. Some leading integralists seem to prefer building a loyal fan base.

Leadership Changes

Once the persuasion campaign succeeds, the church must elect proper leaders. These leaders will have diverse priorities, especially since the church is a global organization. Cardinals must want integralism enough to select an integralist pope. The pope must then take the necessary steps to form an integralist order.[150]

I won't list all canon laws that the pope must change to create a new integralist regime. If we grant that they have been changed, barriers still abound. Since 1983, canon 11 has placed Protestants beyond ecclesiastical penalties.[151] Church officials cannot prosecute Protestants for canonical crimes despite their valid baptisms. The church must change this canon—but to do so, it must effectively declare all Protestants criminals.[152] The church will renew ferocious conflicts with Protestantism.

Acquisition of Political and Military Power

Even if the church endorsed integralist arrangements, it could not enforce them. Popes once governed polities and raised armies. Today, military power requires

---

[150] We could classify electing an integralist pope and changing policy as one event, which I will allow despite its implausibility.

[151] I am grateful to Tom Sundaram for helping me understand this point.

[152] The church might simply drop canon 11, allowing variation within integralist regimes. This *might* go down easier among Protestants. I am grateful to David Gordon for discussion about this.

more than assembling knights and trebuchets. Popes need support from states with modern weaponry or need to build weapons themselves (!).

Right now, bishops can't invest in arms companies. The current pope ferociously opposes the death penalty and has said that even just war theory legitimizes war too often.[153] Will future popes purchase tanks, missiles, jets, and submarines? Hire a cyber warfare division? Stockpile nuclear weapons? Will a future pope write an encyclical to the effect of "How I Learned to Stop Worrying and Love the Bomb"?

Modern states will stop the Vatican before it acquires modern weaponry. The power asymmetry is too vast. In the thirteenth century, integralism existed because of weak state capacity. States had enough power to affect social outcomes, but they had too little to forgo legitimation from religious authorities. As state capacity grew, secular leaders sold themselves on other grounds. They increasingly appealed to prosperity and popular consent. Why would any modern state place itself under the papacy's military authority? The Vatican must rely entirely on ideological influence.

Unification Stages

Nonetheless, suppose integralists capture church and state. Two more problems arise.

Timed Submission

No historical integralist regime arose from efforts to coordinate two enormous social groups. Small states came under papal influence through unique events. Today, a society can become integralist only with the submission of secular to spiritual power. This requires good timing. Each side must coordinate their activities in real time in order to integrate. Both the church and the secular world contain a massive array of competing sects, and either party might lose interest if the other drags its feet or falls into internal conflict.

[153] Joshua J. McElwee, "Catholic Activists Praise Pope's Move Away from Just War Theory," *National Catholic Reporter*, October 12, 2020, https://www.ncronline.org/news/justice/catholic-pacifists-praise-popes-move-away-just-war-theory.

Table 4.2 **Evaluating Which Transition Problems Apply to Each Transition Stage**

	State-Side			Church-Side	Unification	
	Stage 1: party capture	Stage 2: state capture	Stage 3: state stabilization	Stage 4: church capture	Stage 5: settle timing, boundaries	All stages
Type of transition problem						
Leadership failures						
Internal resistance						
External opposition						
Chance of success						

Boundary Problems

Even after submission, popes and kings must define their respective jurisdictions:[154] even old buddies Louis IX and Clement IV disputed their relative authority.[155] Thomas Hobbes famously thought that these boundary disputes cause political instability: neither side acknowledges a higher, third power to resolve their disputes.[156] And again, these conflicts plagued medieval regimes. As Jean-Jacques Rousseau reminds us, "This double power has given rise to a perpetual jurisdictional conflict that has made all good polity impossible in Christian states, and no one has ever been able to know whether it is the priest or the master whom one is obliged to obey."[157]

[154] And so we cannot compare the sovereignties of the pope and crown with those of different states. Each state has jurisdiction over a distinct group of subjects. Pope and crown, however, have jurisdiction over more or less the same citizens (Pink 2021).

[155] See "St. Louis IX," *Catholic Encyclopedia* (New Advent), accessed December 13, 2022, https://www.newadvent.org/cathen/09368a.htm. This article recounts conflicts between St. Louis IX and the papacy of his day, which includes the pontificate of Clement IV.

[156] Hobbes 1994, p. 392.

[157] Rousseau 2018, p. 148. I thank Matthew Young for reminding me of this passage.

The Probability of Reaching Integralism

We have three types of transition problem: leadership failures, internal resistance, and external opposition. Each problem could afflict any transition stage. I don't know which problems will arise; I can only help generate a rough probability judgment through educated guesses. I assume one can separate each stage into distinct causal substages, and likewise with each transition problem. We cannot be sure, though, so you must guess.

Table 4.2 lists problems in the first column and transition stages in the column heads. Consider the probability of success at each point. In the fifteen cells where transition problems and transition stages intersect, place an *x* where you think a transition problem afflicts a transition stage. (Yes, write in the book, if you like.) To keep matters simple, multiply the probabilities.[158] Remember: integralists must overcome these challenges while respecting natural law and the US Constitution (and state constitutions).

Make up your own mind. For my part, I cannot assign a probability of success greater than 1 percent for any transition stage, even if I ignore ordinary moral constraints. Keeping morality in mind, I cannot assign more than a 0.01 percent chance of success. (Party capture and state capture will violate Catholic moral teaching.) If these probabilities are accurate, the probability that a society like that of the United States becomes integralist is 1 in 1^{-24}. That is, it is infinitesimal. Play with the table to see if you get a different result.

If these probabilities seem too low, consider the following. Integralists must convert a national state and an international church, and then they must convince the former to submit to the latter. To succeed, Vermeule must solve three of the greatest coordination problems in the history of the human race.

Forced into Ideal Theory

Integralists have no idea how to overcome these transition barriers. They have said almost nothing about them. They merely argue that liberalism will fall, but this hardly diminishes transition problems.

Distrust their predictions! Political scientist Philip Tetlock has shown that experts can predict changes in discrete social variables. But the time horizons are short. Even elite prediction teams ("superforecasters") perform worse than

---

[158] Or use other formulae, and feel free to group some of these events together if you think they're not independent.

statistical models after a few years. *No one* can predict system-level outcomes in societies like the United States.[159]

Let's assume that integralists are expert predictors. (They're not.) The worst expert predictors are "hedgehogs." Hedgehogs apply one overarching theory to predict or explain certain events.[160] "Foxes," by contrast, draw on many models. They quickly revise their opinions when they receive new information. When Tetlock was developing his theory, he studied Sovietologists who tried to predict the future of the USSR.[161] Hedgehogs underperformed expectations.

Let's assume that the integralists have expertise in the relevant areas. (They don't.) They still operate like hedgehogs. Vermeule relies on the ideas of Carl Schmitt, as we have seen. Schmitt's thought changed over the course of his career, but Vermeule tends to rely on Schmitt's early thought.[162] The result: the hedgehog model of social change we explored above. Sadly, integralists are not foxy. They seldom update and revise their views in light of new information. Indeed, they shut out critics more than any political group I have ever encountered. Integralists have not organized themselves to generate effective predictions.

Suppose you read Vermeule's essays on liberalism. Now you ask whether liberalism will collapse. If Tetlock is correct, you may as well flip a coin to find an answer.

The integralist ideal does not illuminate a path to the best regime. No one knows how interacting social groups will respond to each transition stage. The ideal does not specify our proximity to it. I might know that the tallest mountain is Mount Everest, but if I have no idea how to reach it, this is not terribly useful information.

Allow me to introduce another challenge. Each transition stage can decrease the common good in the short run even if it paves the way to large future increases in the common good. Even if I know where Mount Everest is, I cannot determine the cost of finding it. Some paths may bring me to a small mountain nearby, whereas others will lead me into chasms I cannot escape. In the same way, even if I know that integralism is the best regime, I cannot determine the

---

[159] Tetlock and Gardner 2016, p. 17.

[160] Tetlock 2006, p. 76.

[161] Tetlock 2006, pp. xi–xvi.

[162] We have seen how often Vermeule appeals to Schmitt in his work. His affinity for Schmittian insights and models extends back before his integralist period (see Vermeule 2009; Posner and Vermeule 2011; Posner and Vermeule 2017). Vermeule appeals to multiple models of the social world in his legal writings—a degree of sophistication that evaporates in his work in political theology.

cost of reaching it. Some transition plans may promote the common good, but descending from those moral "peaks" could harm the common good. Other transition plans may lead to integralism but require grave harm to the common good in the process.

We can see that reaching *any* ideal in a complex order requires a fateful choice between local moral improvements and global improvements.[163] Reformers can sidestep these issues, but only if each transition increases a society's level of justice or goodness. We don't know how institutions operate in transition, so integralists may not face an inclining "landscape" of common goodness. Goodness may not increase per transition stage, so integration from within takes grave risks. By pursuing the moral best, integralists risk making society worse.

I do not know how Catholics should approach this challenge. Catholic moral teaching is stringent and so prohibits many efforts to transform society. Sensing these challenges, many Catholics adopt conservative attitudes toward social change. They invest their efforts into improving the common good in small ways. They have no ideal.[164] In any case, acts that decrease the common good risk grave sin.

The integralist ideal tempts integralists to damage nearby improvements in the common good. Integralists famously shower affection on Hungarian president Viktor Orbán. Has their support brought integralism closer to fruition because they have helped normalize Orbanist political tactics in the United States? Or have they created new lines of resistance to integralist ideas, given their association with authoritarian leaders? Who knows! (Not the strategists.)

Sometimes integralists provide policy insight. They suggest programs that could improve the common good, such as their proposals for supporting large families. But they can justify their best policy proposals without their ideal. They need only appeal to the common good. Worse, attempts to realize the ideal may draw energy away from their most reasonable proposals. Time is short, after all. Finally, Catholic dogma may forbid forgoing local improvements to reach larger ones.

The integralist ideal is more trouble than it is worth.

Theorizing about political ideals has value. Pursuing those ideals also has value, though this value depends on how we pursue them. Societies with competing ideals work better than ideocratic regimes. They also work better than societies where people have no great aspirations. I do not ask integralists to forgo their ideal. Instead I hope to convince readers to oppose Vermeule's state capture strategy, which is immoral and has no prospects for success. Vermeule's ideal has misled him. In this he follows the path of many utopians before him.

---

[163] Gaus 2016, p. 142. Gaus called this "The Choice."
[164] Here I take Russell Kirk to be representative (Kirk 1985).

Ideals can serve two other functions: they can rank nonideal regimes and identify defects in them. But even here integralists face challenges. First, Catholic social thought contains many moral principles, chiefly the common good, human dignity, solidarity, and subsidiarity, all of which determine how Catholics should rank social worlds, and all of which can conflict.[165] Second, integralists must grasp the character of complex social worlds well enough to rank them according to these four principles. Good luck with that.

Pink shows no sympathy for integration from within. He focuses on improving church teaching on religious liberty and explaining the moral decay of liberal regimes.[166] The challenge for Pink's analysis (as we will see in Chapter 5) is that many factors figure into social changes that integralists lament.[167] Artificial birth control may prove a far larger factor in changing behavior than any reduced presence of divine grace. We need more evidence to see whether religious decay alone leads to mass moral forgetting. And so it is unclear whether the integralist ideal can even perform the meager function Pink posits for it.

Integralism cannot guide reform, rank social worlds, or predict how regimes operate. What remains? The pure ideal—the Catholic thesis—a description of the best social world. Readers might put this book down now. Integralism is impractical. It tempts its proponents to support bad leaders and bad policies. Better to focus on other political proposals.

But others may find the ideal no worse for wear despite its impracticality.[168] And remember Chapter 3: we profit from asking whether the state should promote supernatural goods. Assessing the pure ideal may prove worthwhile. The question of the best human regime compels many of us, me included.

In the next chapter, I argue that the integralist ideal fails to meet its success conditions. An integralist order should create moral peace among its subjects, and social stability should arise from citizens' free decisions to follow the natural law. But the set of integralist social equilibriums is either relatively small or empty, which means that integralism will break down. If I am right, we should not aim at the ideal at all.

---

[165] Hittinger 2008.

[166] Pink 2018a.

[167] Pink 2020.

[168] Pink 2020. According to Pink, trouble reaching integralism bears not at all on its orthodoxy: Integralism rests on a metaphysics of the self that Catholics must affirm.

5

Stability

Catholic integralists characterize their view as a moral and legal *order*. States should order society toward the highest good. But society should also order *itself*, in that its main institutions must be stable. Integralist order corrects itself in response to challenges. The system must also reach an equilibrium based on its citizens' moral actions. Peace cannot rest on legal coercion alone. Integralism must have *moral stability* to count as a moral order.

This chapter asks whether integralist orders can maintain moral stability. I will focus on a large-scale social order that lasts at least two generations. If the order tends to gravitate toward equilibriums based on oppression and fear, an integralist regime is not a moral order. Similarly, it is not a moral order if it falls into disequilibrium.[1] In either case, integralism becomes a much less attractive ideal.

Integralist orders destabilize owing to factors that integralists themselves acknowledge and even emphasize. Integralists argue that sin corrupts our knowledge of the moral law. Only God's grace can heal our moral sight.[2] If church and state can limit sin and unbelief, they can help citizens grasp and obey the moral law. Citizens will then agree about what morality requires. The church-state union can then coordinate individuals to ensure that obeying the moral law serves the common good.

Integralists think moral disagreement is the normal tendency of *morally corrupted* human reason. That tendency persists in an integralist order, though the order can manage the fallout. Integralists also say that moral disagreement arises from *unguided* human reason. Even virtuous people will disagree about the moral law. They, too, need guidance. Free inquiry apart from church

---

[1] I offer an *infeasibility proof* for integralism.

[2] Pink 2018a. Integralists argue by way of natural law, but my argument only requires that individuals face objective ethical demands, whether those demands rest on natural laws or some other basis.

All the Kingdoms of the World. Kevin Vallier, Oxford University Press. © Oxford University Press 2023.
DOI: 10.1093/oso/9780197611371.003.0006

direction produces confusion, disagreement, and schism.[3] This second source of disagreement also persists in integralist order despite the regime's attempts to counteract it.

I call these tendencies toward disagreement *unnatural* and *natural* pluralism.[4] Sinful behavior produces unnatural pluralism; natural pluralism arises from causes that could confuse a saint. I will stress throughout this chapter that integralism *predicts* both forms of pluralism.

Integralism does not make angels govern humans, so officials will disagree too. Unnatural pluralism accompanies sin into power. Natural pluralism will also find shelter among political officials, leading to sincere controversy. Officials may support other relationships between church and state. Integralist leaders must also contain moral and political disagreement among citizens and among themselves.[5] None of this is easy.

Integralists hope to avoid suppressing pluralism with coercion. Order emerges from two chief factors: (1) individuals see and follow the moral law, and (2) they obey authorities. Punishment and coercion aid stability, but they are regrettable. Integralists will punish and coerce to halt destabilization, but only as a last resort.

Four forces determine moral stability. Grace and coercion preserve stability, while natural and unnatural pluralism corrode it. I claim that destabilizing forces outweigh stabilizing forces. Formally, the set of integralist social equilibriums is empty; informally, integralism will unravel.

In this chapter, I offer a simple model of integralist stability that, by and large, abstracts from many complexities. My model is a move in a discussion that does not yet exist: whether integralism is a moral order. My claim is that, based on a simple model of the ideal, integralism lacks moral stability. I call the case for this claim the *stability argument*.

We must begin with a simple model. After debate, inquirers can build a more complicated one. Integralists should respond by building a better model.

My critique unfolds as follows. I describe a well-ordered integralist society, its constitution, and its characteristic policies. I explain how grace and coercion create stability and how pluralism undermines it. I also develop a formal model to show how these forces create social equilibriums.

I then explain how pluralism creates more disagreement than grace can contain. Coercion cannot effectively supplement grace: moderate coercion is too

---

[3] Newman 1994, p. 181. Protestant sects are the "applications and results" of the principle of private judgment.

[4] I do not use the term "reasonable pluralism." I make no normative evaluation of the reasons why people come to disagree.

[5] They must also contain disagreement between citizens and officials—but I set this problem aside.

s67

weak, and intense coercion will produce a modus vivendi—an order based on a balance of power—or an equilibrium based on fear of punishment.

Integralists could adopt more generous modeling assumptions, and I outline the costs of doing so. I conclude that integralist regimes unravel of their own accord. They are not moral orders.

But first I owe a warning to nonphilosophical readers. This chapter centers my critiques. If the stability argument works, the other arguments do not matter. The transition argument won't matter: even if the strategists could construct an integralist order, it will collapse. The moral arguments won't matter much either: if integralist order is not an order, one can reject it apart from ethical considerations. Since this chapter is the book's heart, I offer the most rigorous argument. But I fear I may wear down the patience of nonphilosophical readers, so readers should feel free to skip the section that develops my formal model.

Theology and Economics: An Incongruous Method?

Many readers will experience this chapter as incongruous because its argument models the effects of sin and grace. While one might quantify sin as degree of moral infractions, *no one* quantifies grace but God, who distributes his favor gratuitously and mysteriously. But my model assesses only a claim *that integralists make* (or want to make).[6]

Remember a central rationale for integralism: mere natural-law states provide inadequate protection from sin. The church must exercise indirect sovereignty to infuse grace into politics. Otherwise, we should expect social decay. These claims amount to qualitative predictions, which my model only clarifies. We can sometimes test qualitative claims using quantitative analysis because the analysis identifies the parameters where the qualitative claims hold. If the range of parameters is relatively small, this casts doubt on the qualitative claim.

Yes, in the end, you can't model grace. But integralists make qualitative predictions about regime change, so they should not dismiss attempts to make those predictions precise.

Readers who balk at formal models in theology may also balk at my use of rational choice theory. I assume that people in my model of integralist order respond to incentives. One might object that rational choice theory assumes a false philosophical anthropology: few people act like *Homo economicus*.

[6] Pink 2018a; Waldstein 2016a.

My model makes no such assumption. First, I deny that rational choice theory carries any implications for the metaphysics of human nature; it has such implications only in conjunction with other claims.[7] Rational choice theory plus an impoverished value theory will imply a false anthropology. But since I allow for a rich, Catholic theory of value, my use of rational choice theory remains innocent.

Of course, I do argue that people respond to powerful incentives. Integralists assume as much. Why subject the baptized to civil punishments if those punishments don't change behavior? I claim that people will change their behavior to forestall eternal negative consequences for themselves and (some) others. I also assume that people will consider the price of resisting state coercion. They will sometimes disobey the state.

I conclude that my assumptions about human decision-making are innocent.

Success Conditions for the Argument

All regimes decay. So a successful stability argument must do more than prove integralism's instability. It must also show the following:

1. Integralism unravels where integralists say it holds firm.
2. Collapse occurs owing to the logic of the ideal regime itself. The model excludes external factors such as foreign conquest.
3. Destabilization must be prompt.

I will clarify conditions 1 and 2 at length below, but I can address condition 3 here. Integralists might accept slow decay and argue that integralism decays slower than competitor regimes. But if integralism decays quickly, that makes it far less attractive.

As I indicated in Chapter 2, history suggests a quick collapse. High Integralism was quite limited in time and space compared to other regimes, and it occurred in the brief period when church capacity matched state capacity. The balance did not last long, as the reign of Philip IV illustrates.

An integralist regime is one where the state submits to the church. Saint Louis IX was perhaps in submission to Clement IV, but it is hard to find any other monarchs who treated popes as their legitimate constitutional superiors. History does not record many kings who obeyed papal decrees in cases where integralism requires obedience. The set of regimes that *look* integralist seems small; the set of regimes that *were* integralist may be smaller still.

---

[7] Gaus and Thrasher 2021, chap. 2, esp. p. 50.

The Integralist Well-Ordered Society: Basic Elements

Integralists endorse an institutional dyarchy to advance supernatural goods. Popes and bishops reign in spiritual matters and have infallible teaching authority in matters of faith and morals.[8] They can also enact canon law. The church may then direct the state to enforce its law[9] and promulgate its teachings among the state's baptized citizens.[10] In predominantly Catholic societies, most citizens will fall under church jurisdiction. Church and state rule together—that's what it means to be a dyarchy. Pope Leo XIII described integralism as a "soul-body union" between church and state.[11]

Integralist regimes sometimes employed distinctive policies. They regulated communication about dangerous ideas and controlled religious minorities to protect Christians from spiritual harm.[12] From time to time, the integralist state failed to suppress heretical groups. Whole regions went rogue.[13] In response, popes launched crusades to conquer and convert these regions. Popes claimed the authority to depose heretical rulers. Even orthodox kings could lose their crowns if they refuse to suppress heresy.[14]

Integralist orders have constitutions. Constitutional rules determine how people choose political officials and how officials make policy. But integralist constitutions add *dyarchic* rules—rules that specify when the church may direct the state to help it advance spiritual goods.

Here I address integralism as an ideal for a large-scale society with more than a million members. If integralists confine their ideal to small societies, they might avoid my argument. Small societies preserve homogeneity and can better expel dissenters. Integralists have not yet specified the proper size of integralist orders, but they proceed as though integralism is ideal for any society. So will I.

An integralist regime is stable when order arises from free choices to follow the moral law.[15] Coercive punishments cannot produce moral order on their own. They can create only modi vivendi.[16] Integralist orders seek to restore

---

[8] Sullivan 2002, pp. 24–34.

[9] Again, via the state's civil law. See Chapter 1 on envisioning integralism section.

[10] Pink 2012b.

[11] Leo XIII 1885, p. 14; Pink 2017, p. 9.

[12] Suárez (1612) 2015, pp. 853, 863.

[13] For the Cathars, see Jones (2017, pp. 36–37). For the Hussites, see Fudge (2013, p. 41).

[14] Bellarmine 2012, pp. 211–25; canon 3 in Canons of the Fourth Lateran Council, 1215, available at https://sourcebooks.fordham.edu/basis/lateran4.asp.

[15] Pink 2018a.

[16] McCabe 2010.

moral knowledge and virtue lost because of sin, whereas a modus vivendi falls short of the integralist ideal. This is doubly true of a fear-based equilibrium.

John Finnis reads Aquinas as claiming that the purpose of the state is to establish peace.[17] Peace is "concord . . . and . . . agreement between one person or group and another." Peace even includes "harmony amongst each individual's own desires."[18] The law secures "friendship between people." Finnis argues that, for Aquinas, the state "maintain[s] peace by laying down precepts of justice."[19] Peace provides the benefits of social life and avoids the costs of contention.[20] Thomas Crean and Alan Fimister agree: integralism is a "just ordering" because it enables members of society to reach their extrinsic ends "by removing causes of quarrel between them and reasons for mental trouble within any one member."[21]

Pope Pius XI offers a more authoritative description of the perfect Catholic order.[22] If officials know they rule on God's behalf, they will promote the common good and respect human dignity. The result: "a stable peace and tranquility, for there will be no longer any cause of discontent." Citizens will obey their states if they believe that rulers act with Christ's authority. Pius continues:

> *Peace and harmony, too, will result*; for with the spread and the universal extent of the kingdom of Christ men will become more and more conscious of the link that binds them together, and *thus many conflicts will be either prevented* entirely or at least their bitterness will be diminished.[23]

Integralism's defenders claim that an integralist regime creates peace between church and state. Indeed, it harmonizes the general interest of citizens because church and state receive their due and distinctive authority.[24] They govern in their distinctive spheres.[25] An integralist regime thus advances society's complete common good—temporal and eternal.

---

[17] Finnis 1998, p. 227.

[18] Finnis 1998, p. 227.

[19] Aquinas 1920, I–II, q. 99, art. 2c.

[20] Finnis 1998, p. 228.

[21] Crean and Fimister 2020, p. 27.

[22] Though it is unclear whether Pius XI was an integralist, he still shares much with his predecessors.

[23] Pius XI 1925, emphases added.

[24] By "authority," I mean moral authority. Church and state have the right to exercise political authority, *auctoritas*. Scholars often contrast authority with *potestas*—namely, the capacity of states to exercise their power. The integralist state has both *auctoritas* and *potestas*.

[25] Pink 2021. Pink argues that Leo XIII defended integralism "to avoid conflict between sovereign authorities" and that dividing legislative competence was helpful in that regard. Also see Leo XIII 1885; Pink 2018a; Waldstein 2016a; Jones 2017.

The engine of integralist order is the free, moral action of its citizens. When the church is sovereign, it regenerates its citizens through God's grace, which helps people both see and follow the natural moral law. A dyarchy forms a peaceful order—a social equilibrium.[26] Integralist regimes create their own support rather than have it imposed from without.[27]

Moral citizens form the basis of moral stability. Moral citizens act for the sake of some good: their individual good and the common good. Their choices aim at their individual final end—their individual flourishing. Since humans flourish only in communities, their choices must also serve the common good.[28]

Moral citizens also believe that an integralist regime best promotes the good. They view the regime as legitimate and affirm its authority (*auctoritas*)—the right to rule. We could also call them *sincere integralists*. I presume that moral citizens dominate the integralist well-ordered society—at least at first. But the integralist ideal also contains citizens who oppose integralism. Non-Catholic citizens may recognize the regime's authority, but only if it advances the temporal common good. They might tolerate the regime's religious policies but oppose them nonetheless.

Historical integralist regimes restricted the religious liberties of unbaptized groups. Jews and Muslims were central targets.[29] Some states granted them rights against forced baptism for themselves and for their children. Other states did not concede even these rights.[30]

Recall that the Catholic Church today recognizes extensive religious liberties. As *Dignitatis humanae* teaches, humans have a universal right of religious freedom. Religious communities may "govern themselves according to their own norms."[31] They may establish educational institutions. The law may not interfere with selecting, training, appointing, or transferring ministers. *DH* permits the construction of houses of worship. Religious communities may teach their faith, whether in speech or in print.[32] Parents have the right to live their own domestic religious life. They decide how they educate their children. The government must not force children "to attend lessons" that contradict their parents' faith.[33] According to *DH*, the common good requires equal treatment

---

[26] Waldstein 2015, 2016a; Jones 2017. I will explore the character of this equilibrium below.

[27] Penal institutions supplement the forces maintaining stability.

[28] Waldstein 2015. For the baptized, their end and the common good are eternal beatitude.

[29] The regimes went as far as dictating the clothes that they wore. See canon 3 in Canons of the Fourth Lateran Council, 1215, https://sourcebooks.fordham.edu/basis/lateran4.asp.

[30] Tapie 2018.

[31] Paul VI 1965a, art. 4.

[32] Paul VI 1965a, art. 4.

[33] Paul VI 1965a, art. 5.

before the law and forbids religious discrimination. States may not treat anyone as inferior "for religious reasons."[34]

Integralist regimes protect the religious liberties of their unbaptized citizens. If they coerce the unbaptized, they order society, but poorly.

I should stress the Catholic teaching that governments may punish *anyone* who violates the natural moral law. Any rational person can grasp its objective moral requirements through the use of reason, so the state can hold them responsible for violations. In contrast, integralist states may punish only the baptized for violating canon law.[35] Baptism places Christians under canon law.

Some models of well-ordered societies assume that people follow state directives. Philosophers call this the *strict compliance* assumption.[36] Integralists reject strict compliance owing to the doctrine of original sin. Baptism frees people from the guilt of original sin, but it leaves behind concupiscence—a tendency to act on irrational passions and temptations.[37] Sinful persons will sometimes ignore institutional directives or fail to follow them in full. They need grace and correction. With grace, conferred by the sacraments, Catholics receive virtue and become moral citizens.

My model is nationalist. I analyze the stability of an integralist regime without considering international factors. I do this to keep the model simple. International factors greatly complicate matters. For example, integralist regimes have a relationship of subordination with the Vatican. This relationship has been volatile. In addition, the Catholic Church is a global organization with great cultural diversity. The church is fractious. If we model either factor, we cannot get a model off the ground.

I set aside migration policy for similar reasons. Integralists may object: their regime stabilizes if it draws Catholics in and forces others out. But if we allow migration, we cannot ignore other international factors. Isolating for global factors helps the integralist case, on balance.

A Model of Integralist Order

Assume that moral citizens and officials promote the complete common good. Yet sin pervades the integralist society. Citizens violate moral and canon law, though they sin less often than they would in nonintegralist communities.

---

[34] Paul VI 1965a, art. 6.
[35] Aquinas 2002; de Vitoria 1991.
[36] For recent discussion of the principle, see May (2021).
[37] Ott and Fastiggi 2018, pp. 108–12.

I limit the effects of sin on the church. Sin will not lead the church to teach in error on matters of faith and morals, nor will the church impose unjust canon law. I also assume that church officials avoid grave sin and crime. (To model an ideal, we must make unrealistic assumptions.) State officials submit to the church. They too avoid grave sin, apostasy, and heresy, though less often. They may disagree on other matters, such as whether to adopt policies that the pope recommends.

Ideal integralist orders contain seven groups. I have selected these groups because they existed in historical integralist regimes (save for group 5). I will not introduce atheists into this model because integralists argue that atheism is culpably irrational.[38]

1. *Non-Christian theists*: Jews and Muslims.
2. *Unbaptized Christians*: Any Christian not yet under the church's jurisdiction.[39]
3. *Baptized non-Catholics*: Orthodox and Protestant Christians.[40]
4. *Lax Catholics*: Catholics in grave sin or those who seldom receive the sacraments.
5. *Catholic liberals*: Catholics who affirm liberal democratic institutions. They appeal to the teachings and practice of the church in the twentieth and twenty-first centuries.
6. *Catholic nonintegralists*: Catholics who reject both liberal and integralist institutions.
7. *Catholic moral citizens*: Sincere integralist Catholics. Or Catholic citizens who otherwise affirm the regime as legitimate and just.[41]

Catholic moral citizens compose 80 percent of the well-ordered society; groups 1–6 compose 20 percent. The model allows minorities to become moral citizens, and vice versa. Catholic moral citizens, or their children, may join groups 1–6.[42] Citizens can cross groups.

I do integralists no favors if I assume that everyone is a moral citizen or sincere integralist. If moral stability requires unanimous agreement, the equilibrium is quite fragile.

---

[38] Tanner 1990, p. 810.

[39] Unbaptized Christians are those who affirm Christian doctrine but are not (yet) baptized.

[40] Protestants count as heretics, Orthodox as schismatics.

[41] Why not assume that group 7 adopts integralism? Because most who support regimes lack a political theology.

[42] I allow people to become moral citizens for diverse reasons.

Stabilizing Factors: Grace and Coercion

Understand grace as divine favor. Within Catholic theology, God can infuse grace into the soul. Grace helps us see the moral truth because sin can blind us to what morality requires.[43] Grace also heals the vices caused by original and personal sin. So grace makes moral citizens by helping people see *and obey* the moral law. Moral citizens then create moral stability.

The church communicates grace through reason, persuasion, and the sacraments. It imposes "spiritual" punishments on members that break its laws; these punishments range from minor penances to excommunication. Sometimes these punishments fail, so the church requests the state's help.

Integralists claim (or should claim) that grace produces social stability. Why? Suppose they denied it. The denial suggests one of two things. First, it may signal that the mere natural-law state can achieve moral stability. It needs no church-led infusion of grace. But stability rests on free compliance with grasped natural law. Sin damages this process, and we know that only grace can heal it. The integralist case against mainstream natural lawyers weakens if states stabilize without grace, since states can flourish without the papacy's indirect sovereignty.

Second, the denial may imply that, although the natural-law state decays, so does the integralist state. Grace is inadequate for its task. This claim sounds heretical because it denies that grace changes behavior. Integralists might retreat to the weaker claim that grace does not impact behavior in detectable ways, but then how could we tell that grace produces stability?

Coercion

Historically, states assisted the church through legal coercion and civil punishment. So, when spiritual penalties fail, the church directs the state to coerce on its behalf.[44] In ideal theory, assume that states coerce morally: they may punish anyone who violates natural law and penalize the baptized for breaking canon law.[45]

The integralist ideal assumes that states coerce effectively. States ensure external, public obedience. And they sometimes affect what people believe, given that the law operates as a teacher.[46] Effective states also avoid coercion that does not restore compliance.

---

[43] Pink (2018a) covers some historical dogmatic sources of this claim.
[44] Nozick (1969) provides an influential account of coercion.
[45] Insofar as the state crafts and enforces its civil law to criminalize canon law violations.
[46] Pink (2018b) develops Suárez's doctrine of how religious coercion can serve as a teacher.

Assume that, at first, a unified dyarchy coerces effectively. But allow coercion to become ineffective. For instance, the dyarchy may fall into infighting and impose immoral and imprudent controls. These conflicts can destabilize the dyarchy, even in ideal theory.

Fear and moral conviction do not always displace one another. Instead, I assume only that coercion degrades moral motivation as coercion becomes more pervasive and severe. This displacement may happen for any number of reasons. One is disproportionate punishment. People may want to stop heresy, but the threat of execution might seem, well, overkill. If citizens resent their regime as unjust, they may disobey it.

I should note here that coercion seldom involves the brute force of sending the police to one's home. Instead, I treat coercion as a parameter. The state can increase or decrease coercion in innumerable ways. I discuss some ways in which the state might use coercion below. To produce a manageable analysis, I must confine myself to a handful of methods. But states coerce in many ways. And, as Vermeule has noted, the baldest uses of force are, in some respects, a failure of the legal system, not a success.[47]

Destabilizing Factors: Natural and Unnatural Pluralism

If humans lack grace, we will exhibit two kinds of pluralism—unnatural and natural. Unnatural pluralism derives from sinful behavior, whereas natural pluralism derives from factors that could confuse a sinless person. God has not revealed the entire moral law to everyone; even virtuous people may adopt false moral beliefs.

Sin—the disposition or choice to violate moral requirements—causes disagreement. Reba, plagued by pride, may rely on her private judgment when she makes ethical decisions. Or she may harbor intemperance: she indulges all her basest passions. With time, Reba embraces her bad behavior. Sins then pass from her to others, who may then adopt her moral misperceptions.

We disagree owing to factors other than sin. First, the moral law contains ambiguities: it may not rank goods or help us secure them. Second, our limited rationality and ignorance may produce disagreement. Factors such as conflicting evidence, vague concepts, and distinct life experiences make disputes inevitable.[48]

---

[47] Vermeule 2022b.
[48] Vallier 2019.

Third, we must venture predictions about the consequences of our actions. But social outcomes flow from interdependent social choices.[49] We predict how others behave, and they do likewise for us. Our interactions can then produce surprising outcomes.

Fourth, like all of us, officials struggle to apply moral principles to their own lives. Applying these principles to order modern social institutions is much harder.[50] Modern societies exhibit complexity. Their parts feed back into one another. No one can predict the outcomes of these systems with any accuracy.[51] Since prediction is impossible, even people with shared values will disagree about which institutions best realize them. Public deliberation might help produce consensus, but deliberation can also exacerbate disagreement.[52]

The integralist can grant much of what I have said. Catholics have long condemned Protestantism on a straightforward ground: theological judgments without church guidance lead to pluralism. Again, unguided moral reasoning may lead people astray. The consequent pluralism may arise naturally (that is, without sin); even saints disagree.

When moral knowledge decays, disagreement expands. Humans do not collectively shift into several common moral errors. Those outside the church may agree with one another on some central ethical requirements, but they will diverge on others. And even when people share values, they will differ about their relative importance.[53] Overall, then, the sources of pluralism will produce divergent moral beliefs rather than a coordinated moral error.[54]

On the other hand, most people exhibit extreme conformity bias.[55] Humans conform to the group's beliefs; people will adopt beliefs merely because their group affirms them. But conformity bias is a double-edged sword for integralists.

---

[49] Bicchieri 2006, pp. 158–59.

[50] Even if individuals see natural law as a simple deontological rule, this will hold. Pluralism can arise from diverse rule applications alone.

[51] Gaus 2021, pp. 209–11.

[52] A fifth source of pluralism may be our social neurology. Humans tend to gravitate toward communities of about 50–150 members, and the vast majority of religious communities are this size across cultures and times. Robin Dunbar argues that wannabe religious leaders manufacture disagreements and conflicts and use these factors to justify creating new sects that they can lead unopposed (see Dunbar 2022, pp. 244–56). The result is a consistent centrifugal tendency within religious communities (and, I would add, ideological communities). We could call this factor natural or unnatural, depending on whether the leaders develop their new communities through moral violations. Dunbar's work is new—but if it receives validation, it might explain most religious pluralism.

[53] Gaus 2011, p. 180.

[54] One can maintain that reason vindicates certain goods as natural and intrinsic and still deny that the social exercise of reason is right reason.

[55] Gaus 2021, pp. 9–10.

If leaders flout the natural law, the masses may commit similar moral violations. Elite changes ignite population changes.[56] The same behavioral cascades can occur when elites disagree with one another. Conformity bias creates competing factions, not consensus.

Unfortunately for the integralist, pluralism will persist despite church guidance. Heresy will arise periodically. But the greater danger arises from disagreement about the powers of the pope. For centuries, many theologians thought that bishops' councils held supreme ecclesiastical authority, whereas others claimed that the pope was the greater power.[57] Other ecclesiastical doctrines persisted, such as the view that monarchs should play a central role in church governance.

Integralists might blame these disagreements on sin, but they arise from complex and subtle factors. Again, moral reasoning is complicated; even saints disagree. In the policy arena, popes may engage in imprudent political interventions, discrediting their authority.

Integralist Europe gave birth to proto-democratic thinkers such as Marsilius of Padua.[58] The Reformation arose from doctrinal disagreements that began around that time, owing in part to John Wycliffe. The early Reformers defended some doctrines that the church had yet to settle.[59]

Once we introduce mass communication, natural pluralism will expand. The printing press helped the Reformers convert thousands in short order, and as disagreements spread, many integralist regimes fell. During this time, most people faced severe illness and famine. They focused on day-to-day survival and local events, and in most cases, they had no idea what the church taught. Medieval peasants knew little of anything outside their villages.[60] The church coordinated the beliefs of a few hundred thousand elites, at most. And even these elites struggled to communicate.

The Reformation and liberalism might have exacerbated disagreement and dissension, but we cannot pin all the blame on them. Growing cities, rising literacy, and cheaper mass communication also created pluralism.

---

[56] For discussion, see Gaus 2021, p. 166.

[57] Burns and Izbicki 1997; Oakley 2003, esp. chap. 5.

[58] Marsilius 2005, p. 46–50.

[59] McGrath (2020) argues that the Protestant doctrine of justification was an innovation. However, it was not defined as heretical until the Council of Trent.

[60] Leijonhufvud (2007) describes villager social networks and connections in eleventh-century France.

The Formal Model: A Technical Discussion

I now introduce a model to identify social equilibriums, equilibriums that with-stand the behavioral currents of grace, coercion, and pluralism. The time horizon extends over several decades. The elements:

> y axis: potential thresholds of moral citizens (sincere integralists) required for moral stability; too few and the dyarchy loses moral stability, or stability simpliciter;
>
> x axis: morally and smartly applied coercion;
>
> p: the degree to which pluralism creates disagreement and deviant behavior;
>
> g: the degree to which grace contains disagreement and deviant behavior;
>
> y_1 = threshold of moral citizens required to keep the dyarchy morally stable;
>
> $y_2 = \sqrt{gx} - px^2$ (determines how coercion affects the percentage of moral citizens).

Here y_1 = 80 percent, which seems like a proper threshold for moral stability. A higher threshold implies that society stabilizes only with remarkable uni-formity, whereas a lower threshold allows too much dissent to count as an integralist ideal. I explore the rationale for the threshold further below.

Note also that I assume that 80 percent of actors are moral citizens. So the integralist well-ordered society meets the threshold. At first.

Curve y_2 outputs the proportion of moral citizens as a function of degrees of coercion. Coercion is the input, moral citizenry the output. Two factors shape the output curve: disagreement-generating pluralism (p) and agreement-generating grace (g).

In y_2, the *square root term* implies the following: states impose coercive policies with the highest returns first. Suppose they punish the most dangerous heretics. The returns to coercion fall as they punish more minor infractions. The *squared term* represents how coercion fails at higher levels and to an ever-greater extent (the quadratic term represents diminishing returns after some ideal level of coercion). Together, the two terms represent my claims (1) that moderate coercion produces too little stability to overcome pluralism, and (2) that high coercion undermines moral motivation, which worsens the effects of coercion. Consider Figure 5.1.

At .2 units of appropriate coercion, moral citizens stabilize the regime.[61] The regime reaches *moral equilibrium*. Stability originates chiefly from moral

---

[61] I chose .2 solely for purposes of illustration.

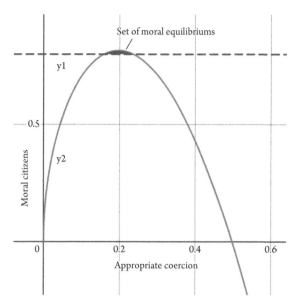

Figure 5.1. Moral equilibriums when pluralism is greater than grace.

motivation and then from social and legal punishment, such that no Catholic moral citizen has an incentive to deviate from obedience to the dyarchy's rules. But in Figure 5.1, the dyarchy cannot reach moral stability with more or less coercion. With too little force, grace cannot contain pluralism. With too much coercion, fear displaces moral motivation. Society misses moral equilibrium.

What happens when a society falls below the threshold? Three outcomes can occur (and they can mix). The first outcome is that society settles into a modus vivendi equilibrium. Stability originates from force and acquiescence, and the hoped-for level of moral motivation is not present.

The second outcome is worse—a fear-based equilibrium. Social stability rests entirely on fear of punishment, which greatly harms human flourishing. Philosopher Martha Nussbaum has recently argued that the harms of fear are not limited to its intrinsic undesirability; fear also corrupts and distorts other emotions, such as anger. Anger creates division, hatred, and recriminations.[62] The state might quash revolts, yes, but placing society in a state of enduring fear erodes cooperation. If the fear equilibrium is challenged, an entire regime can collapse overnight.

The third outcome is disequilibrium. Society degrades into increasing pluralism, confusion, and sin, and the number of sincere integralists falls. Baptisms

---

[62] Nussbaum 2018.

and consequent church citizenship contract.[63] If nonintegralists sense weakness in the regime, they may move to overthrow it.

The three outcomes mix when some disobey while others conform from fear and acquiescence.

Modus vivendi regimes destabilize more readily than regimes based on moral motives. Fear-based equilibriums crumble even faster. Once a small group dissents without punishment, the regime is doomed. Eastern European communism illustrates.

Political economists have long understood this: fear was never enough for enduring political stability. As David Hume said:

> No man would have any reason to fear the fury of a tyrant, if he had no authority over any but from fear; since, as a single man, his bodily force can reach but a small way, and all the farther power he possesses must be founded either on our own opinion, or on the presumed opinion of others.[64]

Conformity bias can produce stability if it secures widespread moral agreement. Tyrants can create moral consensus by suppressing open dissent, which prods conformity bias into supporting them. But the forces of pluralism are strong. In a complex adaptive system, local elites will rebel in order to lead their own splinter groups. New pockets of *conformists* will resist elites. As noted earlier, conformity bias can generate conflict as often as control.

Complex social systems resemble ecosystems. When left to themselves, they produce ever more refined and varied local niches. When we forget to mow the lawn, our problem isn't just tall grass: new weeds and new insect colonies bloom. Complex systems order themselves *fractally*.

Social media is a complex social system that exhibits the same patterns: social media integralism is a diverse niche construct par excellence. Catholic social media produces ever more diverse niches within itself, led by dissenting elites, as integralism demonstrates. In general, conformity bias produces elites jockeying for domination. No sect long prevails.

Moral stability requires recourse to moral motivation. Morality can overcome the less stable motivation of fear and provide further reason to follow the law. Punishment also becomes more effective: people will experience guilt and shame when they are sanctioned for public immorality.

---

[63] One could represent societal collapse with a Schelling S-curve model (Schelling 2006, pp. 102–10).

[64] Hume 1777, p. 34.

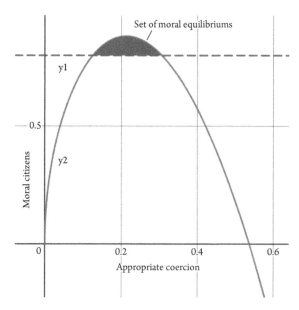

Figure 5.2. Moral equilibriums when grace is greater than pluralism.

In Figure 5.1, the set of moral equilibriums is small (the set of points where $y_2 > y_1$). The pluralism rate slightly exceeds the grace rate. If grace falls, no moral equilibriums exist; if pluralism rises, no moral equilibriums exist. The integralist hopes to maximize equilibrium points. Thus the integralist must defend a high g and a lower or equal p. Grace must overpower pluralism.

When grace exceeds pluralism, the set grows larger—see Figure 5.2. An integralist order can approach 100 percent moral compliance with only some (.25 units) of coercion. It can handle a bit more coercion and remain stable—or a bit less. The dyarchy has more room to maneuver.

A large set of moral equilibriums indicates that the integralist order is flexible. Once disrupted, the regime need only return to some moral equilibrium, not to the original one. The system can sacrifice stability—sticking to one moral equilibrium—and gain robustness—returning to some moral equilibrium after the disruption.[65] More moral equilibriums strengthen the ideal.

To show instability, I defend a high threshold, a high p, and a low g. I also argue that legal coercion cannot contain pluralism. Figure 5.3 (later in this chapter) displays the null set result.

We can establish the threshold as follows. In debates before *DH*, theologians disagreed about how to characterize the ideal Catholic society. They agreed

---

[65] Thrasher and Vallier (2018) define stability in an open society as having two components: constitutional rules have stability, whereas local legal rules have robustness.

that an ideal Catholic society is majority Catholic, but commitment *level* was disputed.[66] If a society is not Catholic—say, because it is less than 50 percent Catholic—the integralist model will not work. So the threshold must exceed .5.

Given the theological consensus, we should set the threshold higher, at some supermajority level. But not too high. As the threshold rises, the set of moral equilibriums shrinks. At the limit, one must say that integralist regimes stabilize only through unanimous agreement—not a plus.

I set the threshold at 80 percent to meet both desiderata.

High Unbaptized Pluralism

Consider again the seven groups that compose an ideal integralist order. Natural and unnatural pluralism deprive groups 1–4 of moral knowledge. Citizens disagree about morality and religion. Some favor regime change.

Dignitatis humanae grants groups 1 and 2 complete immunity from religious coercion. No one may baptize them (or their children) against their will.[67] Beyond this, the unbaptized have freedom of worship and can communicate with others about their faith. *DH* arguably forbids states from imposing economic disadvantages on the unbaptized.[68] But states must protect established Catholicism.

Group 3 presents an unappreciated problem. Imagine that you are a parent in an integralist regime. If you baptize your children, they incur severe criminal liabilities; if they preach heresy, they could go to prison—or worse. Faithful Catholics may still baptize their children. Members of groups 1–4 will hesitate. Non-Christian theists will grow even less interested in baptizing their children. The same goes for unbaptized Christians. Baptized Protestants may decide not to baptize their children at all. Lax Catholics may not baptize their children either; they may fear temporal punishment more than the risk of eternal punishment.

Many in these groups will practice secret baptisms. Citizens will often deceive authorities about their baptismal status. A mother might baptize her child in secret, doing her duty to God. Then she need only fail to report the baptism to state authorities, which she will regard as a small price to pay to protect her child.

---

[66] Murray 1993, p. 65.

[67] The Mortara case is a rare exception.

[68] Paul VI 1965a, art. 4. Vitoria argued that such taxes would constitute unjust coercion into the faith (de Vitoria 1991).

The regime's second generation will differ from the first. It will contain either fewer baptized citizens or more citizens baptized in secret. If the state figures out how to detect secret baptisms, many will forgo baptism in response. The result? The state won't know who falls under church jurisdiction.

If the church pressures citizens to be baptized publicly, it risks encouraging insincere conversion and insincere reception of other sacraments.[69] Christians sin gravely if they receive the Eucharist insincerely. If the church pressures parents to baptize their children, it creates similar risks.[70] The church must not incentivize sin.

Even widespread fear of punishment may produce insincere conversions. But if the regime weakens punishments, it invites more pluralism. In response, the church might mandate Mass attendance. But it cannot force sincere reception of the sacraments. Confession, for instance, can succeed only if it is sincere. The integralist state might affect its citizens' religious beliefs if it controls their exposure to information. But information control falls far short of integralist goals.

To avoid these problems, an integralist state might turn to positive incentives instead of negative ones. The integralist order could craft noncoercive policies that encourage baptism. These *baptism-benefit* policies must surmount powerful disincentives created by new civil punishments. But a thin line separates positive incentives from coercion. One must not, for instance, make healthcare services dependent on baptism, because such a policy pits one's health against membership in one's religious community.[71]

The church must not use financial incentives to encourage baptism. Such incentives invite insincere piety and appear to be simony under canon law.[72] They also convert one's relationship with the church into a fiduciary relationship, which undermines its spiritual significance. Nor may the church authorize the state to institute such incentives: it may not authorize the state to sin any more than it may choose to sin.

I doubt that any workable state policies meet these conditions. The state might strengthen Catholic public services vis-à-vis alternatives and people may seek baptism to access those services. With time to reflect, they may remain in the church for the right reasons. Or they may leave.

---

[69] For discussion, see Suárez ([1612] 2015, p. 861) on the Fourth Council of Toledo. Also see de Vitoria (1991, p. 229): "Freedom of choice … has always [been] given to potential converts."

[70] According to canon law, all baptized children have a right to Catholic education. Catholic schools can contradict heretical or lax parents. Of course, disrupting the family is a serious matter.

[71] Many people will remain uncommitted members of these communities. Some will have no affiliation. The results of the competition are hard to project.

[72] Canon 1380 of the 1983 *Code of Canon Law*.

These policies present a dilemma. If the quality of Catholic *essential* services drawfs non-Catholic services, people will feel inappropriate pressure. If the state makes Catholic hospitals superior to non-Catholic ones, people may get baptized to get in with the right surgeon. But high-quality *nonessential* services will provide poor incentives. No good parents will make their children liable to criminal prosecution in order to visit museums.

My takeaway: few baptism-benefit policies appear appropriate.

Readers might worry at this point that my instability predictions have grown too specific. But remember that, for Catholics, baptism has eternal consequences. The analysis involves infinite costs and benefits. One need only assume that citizens in their choices respond appropriately to these massive incentives. If they're even a tiny bit sensitive to such costs, they must focus on the circumstances of baptism. And so they will respond in one of three ways: by avoiding, altering, or anonymizing baptism. We cannot know which strategies they will pick. But we can assume they will choose at least one of these strategies.

High Catholic Pluralism

Groups 5 and 6 (Catholic liberals and nonintegralists) pose new difficulties, especially if they serve as state and church officials.[73] Disputes about integralism could split the dyarchy. Integralists might insist that influential officials adopt integralism. Yet the church has not defined integralism *de fide* (dogma deemed essential to the faith).[74] Indeed, most Catholic theologians think the church authoritatively rejects integralism. I grant that officials in a well-ordered society accept all *de fide* dogma. But they may disagree on many nondogmatic matters.

Some officials will reject integralism, arguing that states should protect the (nonliberal) good but refrain from integralist coercion. Virtuous Catholics debated integralism throughout the High and late Middle Ages. Nearby groups such as Eastern Orthodox Christians never accepted it. Influential officials might also prefer liberal democratic institutions to integralist arrangements. Officials may reject liberalism as an ethos but nonetheless think that human dignity grounds free speech and voting rights. To prove their orthodoxy, these officials may also point to the church's liberal period. Currently, the church embraces liberal institutions.

Pope Pius X (in office 1903–1914) was probably the last integralist pope. As I noted in Chapter 4, none of the Catholic Church's 5,600 bishops openly endorses integralism. Could the church err *that* much for *that* long?

---

[73] Since we focus on high officials, assume that they are familiar with integralist doctrine and either accept or reject it, contrasting with the public who will have simpler political beliefs.

[74] Some church declarations might make sense only if integralism is true.

Catholic liberals and Catholic nonintegralists will frequently oppose integralist policies. Expect them to disapprove of coercively containing pluralism. Owing to natural pluralism, they may acknowledge widespread reasonable disagreement on political questions. Respecting non-Catholic perspectives, they may expand the voting franchise.

The state could demand that Catholic officials support the regime's constitution. But that will go only so far. Officials disobey constitutions and use legal theory to justify it. With time, nonintegralists will find ways of bending constitutional rules to achieve preferred outcomes.

Monarchy

Thus far, I have assumed that an integralist society has a Catholic king. But monarchy creates problems. For a start, Catholic pluralism will arise even in the king's court. If many elites reject integralism, kings may feel free to oppose papal directives, breaking the dyarchy. In response, the church may ally with a royal family, as exemplified by the church's long alliance with the Habsburgs. Monarchs could limit the influence of nonintegralist and liberal officials.

But playing with kings is playing with fire. We see this in pivotal historical conflicts such as the Investiture Contest, the creation of the Avignon papacy, and the English Reformation. Perhaps integralist ideal theory would have helped society avoid these conflicts. But remember that the integralist ideal contains sin, and so we cannot assume that monarchs always behave. Even noble kings will chafe under their restrictions, and some may go rogue. And if you lose the king, you lose everything.

Consider three more problems. First, political scientists like democracy for good reasons. Democracies enjoy nonviolent transitions of power between competing elites and protect human rights better than alternative regimes do.[75] Second, effective public policy requires public trust. But data suggest that people trust governments more when they can influence them.[76] Monarchy severs that link.[77] Third, monarchs have a strong personal reason to interfere with papal elections. Philip IV illustrates. He helped elect Clement V, who then moved the papacy to Avignon. The Avignon papacy inaugurated a century of declining papal power, a decline that would eventually lead to three simultaneous popes.

---

[75] Achen and Bartels 2016, pp. 316–19.

[76] Vallier 2020, pp. 211–16. Also see Grimes 2017.

[77] Toothless monarchies may increase social trust (Vallier 2020, p. 64).

Problems with Democracy

If nonintegralists can vote and run for office, integralist democracies will destabilize. Voters may oppose integralist arrangements on many grounds. They will
push their leaders to shed integralist constraints, even constitutional limitations.
Anticipating democratic machinations, some integralists recommend restricting
voting rights to Catholics.[78]

Even if non-Catholics cannot vote, the integralist state must limit intra-
Catholic pluralism. Catholic liberals will extend the franchise to non-Catholics.
Integralists could disenfranchise Catholic liberals too, but then the state must
disenfranchise conservatives who would enfranchise the liberals.[79] The voting
public shrinks.

Yet I granted that Catholic moral citizens compose 80 percent of the populace. They could form an enormous majority to control nonintegralists. But
would they? Catholic moral citizens may have reasons to favor other parties.

Mixed Regimes

Integralists might combine a Catholic monarchy with a parliament. The king
could have the power to overrule legislation that conflicts with church teaching.
But mixed regimes invite boundary disputes. Parliament will have a strong interest in determining the faith of the monarch. English history is illuminating
here. Recall the great interest the nobility took in the king or queen's religious
affiliation, an interest that persisted for centuries.

Three current social conditions persist under integralism: (1) high levels of
education, (2) cheap communication, and (3) considerable urbanization.

Education

In historic integralist regimes, neither the church nor the state tried to educate
the entire populace. Peasants lived and died unaware of any political contests
between pope and crown, so the church could ignore popular opinion. Today
the church must convince millions of educated people to support integralism.
College-educated persons can grow attached to polarized and erroneous views,
given their augmented ability to defend any belief they hold. Integralist regimes
must propagandize the populace to suppress dissent. And propaganda often fails.

---

[78] Crean and Fimister 2020, p. 173.

[79] They need not do this if the liberal faction is not influential. Analogously, a liberal regime might
tolerate a nonthreatening communist bloc. The integralist must explain why liberals lack influence,
though.

Communication

Global communication will remain costless, so the integralist state must build a surveillance apparatus to track and control communication—easier said than done.

Urbanization

Today, most people live in cities with zones where heretics and dissenters can hide. Unbaptized groups may even give heretics and dissidents sanctuary. The regime must use violence in populated areas to stop dissenters, yet church teaching may prohibit the necessary force. Close, frequent urban interactions will spread heresy and dissent.

Boundary Disputes

The historical record is clear. Kings and popes routinely disputed their relative ecclesiastical authority, and thus the extent of their competing powers.[80] Popes tried to depose kings over such matters.[81] Consider once more the Investiture Contest and the Avignon papacy, as well as Henry VIII of England. Power politics created severe, long-standing conflicts.

If integralism returns, the church must contend with prime ministers, having never tried to depose a democratically elected leader. And for good reason. The people choose their prime ministers, so by deposing one the church must overrule a decision made by the public. A second problem is that democracies have more leadership turnover than monarchies. Even if one prime minister adopts integralism, the next prime minister may reject it. Third, parliaments tend to choose prime ministers. Parliaments are large and raucous, and their members are no saints. A parliament's obedience will not come cheap. To guarantee obedient integralist prime ministers, the church must exercise enormous political influence.

The integralist must grapple with two facts: the historical instability of medieval regimes and the challenges posed by democratic leaders. We should expect boundary disputes, especially between pope and prime minister.

---

[80] Pace Pink (2021), we cannot analogize a dyarchy to the sovereignties of different states. Under integralism, pope and crown have jurisdiction over the same subjects.

[81] Popes excommunicated kings, as Innocent XI did to King Louis XIV of France. Pope Innocent III put Norway under interdict for three years (1198–1202) in response to the actions of King Sverre.

State Capacity

The rise of state capacity in Western Europe explains the decline of integralist regimes.[82] Medieval kings could not project power far beyond their seats. Indeed, they had so little power that they sought legitimation from the church, which they received in exchange for pursuing church objectives.[83] Yet as nation-states grew, kings raised larger armies and legitimized themselves on new bases. They appealed to divine right, prosperity, and popular consent. They no longer needed church legitimation. Papal power declined.

Today states have far more power than the Vatican. Large states can and will ignore the church from time to time, which can break the dyarchy. No dyarchy can long survive dramatic power inequalities.

If church officials capture the state, they can police its subjects and encourage religious uniformity. But consider two problems. First, large states legitimize themselves on the basis of democratic propaganda. The public obeys the state because the public believes that the people authorize the state's activities. As the church restricts democracy, the state may lose its democratic legitimacy and people may ignore the integralist state's religious directives.

The integralist might respond that nondemocratic states will seek religious legitimation. But if the Vatican has a weak military, states may appeal to another source of legitimacy—or to numerous other sources, such as economic prosperity and military might. These societies may also pay the high price that comes with abandoning democracy, such as the loss of peaceful transitions of power.

Modern state capacity creates severe problems: large states will ignore the church. This worry applies to integralist states. The temptations of power can overwhelm the moral motives of top officials, and that is enough to endanger the dyarchy.[84]

Grace Does Not Contain Pluralism

Grace must contain pluralism to stabilize regimes. Even as grace abounds, we should doubt that it limits pluralism. Consider a few challenges.

---

[82] Johnson and Koyama (2019) explain how state capacity impacts religious persecution.

[83] The church arguably intervened because it had more state capacity. It had, after all, co-opted the administrative apparatus of the Roman Empire.

[84] Integralists might support vast reductions in state capacity. But this would come with many costs. The state might not be able to keep the peace or reduce poverty.

Pious Heretics

Heresy first arises from highly observant Christians who receive God's grace.[85] Martin Luther was intensely pious. He developed Protestant ideas because he found living out medieval Catholic theology impossible. God could not want him to live in fear. Luther's predecessor, Jan Hus, was also pious, singing hymns as he burned to death.

Heresy may originate from those in a state of grace. But if heretics resist correction, they must think that they're wiser than the church. Such radical pride is damnable, no? But notice that these originally pious Christians became heretics anyway. Grace failed to contain pluralism.

Pluralism in Catholic Christendom

Does grace best contain pluralism in integralist regimes? Perhaps not. Catholic societies often have huge internal disagreements. If anything, Catholicism seems to engender more internal disputes than other faiths. Compare Eastern Orthodoxy, which had no Reformation, and note the considerable theological consensus among Sunni Muslims. The integralists' social media content provides evidence for my claim. Catholic social media is notorious for broad-spectrum disagreement and a certain viciousness. An integralist society might not become one big happy family.

Catholic teaching is more centralized than that of any other faith. Yet Catholics continually manufacture disagreements. And they insist that these disputes require urgent resolution. Highly Catholic societies seem destined to collapse into pluralism. Some groups, such as modern progressives, can coordinate political control despite internal disagreements. But Catholics have forgotten how to rule.

Estimating Grace

Catholic doctrine teaches that non-Catholics receive grace.[86] The Orthodox have valid sacraments, and Protestants have valid baptisms. God also bestows grace on non-Christians. If grace is pervasive, non-Catholic pluralism thrives despite widespread grace.

---

[85] I assume that the heretics in question challenge defined dogma. Even many church fathers, such as Origen, defended beliefs later declared heretical.

[86] Paul VI 1964, art. 16.

Grace and Social Morality

Grace helps people apply the moral law to their personal behavior, as well as the behavior of their families and local communities. But, as Thomas Hobbes argued, we cannot solve our central coordination problems simply by agreeing on moral principles. Indeed, agreement may create those problems in the first place.[87] We dispute the proper interpretation of a moral law that we all recognize; we need a judge to help resolve our disputes. This point holds apart from Hobbes's metaphysics.[88]

Hobbes thought that Catholics could defend the church as the voice of public reason.[89] The church can create binding interpretations of the moral law. But having distinct sovereigns—popes and kings—is a recipe for civil war.

Assume that Hobbes is wrong and dyarchies can remain stable in the long run. Even so, dyarchic regimes cannot solve social conflicts with simple legal changes. First, legal solutions to social problems often fail because they violate local social norms.[90] Social norms invoke the fear of social sanction. We follow norms to avoid disapproval and punishment from other community members. If the law prods us to violate a social norm, community members may disobey it to avoid social sanction. Suppose an interpretation of the moral law becomes a social norm. Laws may fail to alter behavior.[91]

Second, the dyarchy fallibly interprets the moral law, which will sometimes yield flawed policies.[92] God commands us to obey the law (Rom. 13:1–2). Yet we must disobey the law if it requires us to sin (Acts 5:29). Dyarchies cannot dispel private judgment. Citizens must still use private judgment to decide whether to obey the law in cases where it seems to require sin.

Third, dyarchies may punish people by mistake. Popes excommunicated and then deposed kings, but depositions are not infallible. After a deposition, subjects face a dilemma: they can obey the church, which declares its deposition valid, or they can obey the king, who says the deposition is invalid. Whom should citizens believe? They disobey a divine authority no matter what. Subjects may make divergent choices and cause civil strife or civil war.[93]

---

[87] Hobbes 1994, chap. 5, ¶ 3, p. 23: "But no one man's reason, nor the reason of any one number of men, makes the certainty." Diverse interpretations of the natural law lead to the state of war.

[88] Here I follow the model of the state of nature as presented in Sharon Lloyd's work (2009).

[89] Hobbes 1994, chap. 42. Hobbes was engaging arguments in Bellarmine (2012, pp. 121–406), "On the Temporal Power of the Pope."

[90] Barrett and Gaus 2020.

[91] Bicchieri (2016) discusses several such cases.

[92] Early on I assumed that the church does not make grossly immoral policy, but that does not preclude all problematic policies.

[93] David Gordon wonders whether the integralist can argue that, if God wants an integralist regime, the grace rate will be higher under integralism than under alternative arrangements, all else being equal. Unfortunately, God does not appear to add grace in proportion to the scenarios

The Limits of Coercion

Integralist orders will face considerable pluralism. The state must coerce, but coercion has limits. Excess punishment will create a modus vivendi or a social order based on fear. Citizens will often act on motives other than moral conviction.[94] Remember that the unbaptized have substantial religious freedoms. Integralist regimes must not interfere with religious minorities, even to pursue central objectives. Under these conditions, boundary disputes and excess state capacity doom the integralist ideal. As the church advocates more coercion, it risks more significant harm, and in such cases, states may dispute church authority. States with that much capacity will ignore the church.

But let's assume away boundary and state capacity challenges and imagine that the integralist regime strays from equilibrium. It coerces to course-correct. Will coercion work? That's doubtful. Catholic education will face more resistance from citizens less committed to the regime. Parents may contradict the state's curriculum, and they may go to prison before sending their children to school. Worse, people might refuse baptism.

The result would be a larger dissenting population. Communication controls would become easier to circumvent, which would encourage dissent and sanctuary for dissenters. An extensive surveillance state might contain these problems. It would need enormous power, though, which would again risk creating fear and insincere piety.

The integralist state must preserve agreement and obedience among the baptized. It must punish apostasy and heresy, say by calling crusades or deposing rulers.

Punishing Apostasy

Some religious regimes make apostasy a capital crime. They buttress social norms that motivate families to shun their apostate members. States could adopt similar political priorities to maintain themselves.[95] But theocracies often create consensus when they place economic burdens on religious minorities. The Catholic Church prohibits these policies. They resemble simony. Such burdens

---

he prefers, given our tendency to resist grace. It is not clear, then, that grace will contain pluralism enough to create the right kind of stability.

[94] For concerns about fear-based motives, see Waldstein (2014, 2016a). I should stress here that liberalism may be as coercive as integralism. Liberalism may decay just as integralism does. My argument is that integralism is not a moral equilibrium. That suffices to refute integralism.

[95] Muslim spiritual policy is often enforced in a decentralized fashion. Sultans had only temporal authority.

can also create insincere piety and stoke nonintegralist opposition to integralist policies.

Punishing Heresy

A formal heretic embraces a heresy despite church correction.[96] The church often forbade heretics from preaching and burned their writings.[97] Today heretics can spread their errors through modern communication technology. Punishment can energize this process.

Natural law and canon law both imply that heretics have the standard legal rights of defendants. These include the right to counsel and a reasonable presumption of innocence.[98] Prosecutors must overcome significant obstacles.[99] Convictions require proving that a heretic holds heretical beliefs "contumaciously": that the heretic sticks to these beliefs owing to irrationality and pride.[100] Heretics may remain silent to avoid self-incrimination. In that case, courts must convict on the basis of prior behavior. Proving contumacy is tough: courts must determine whether heretics object both rationally and conscientiously. Defense attorneys will easily sow doubt. They need only show the court that their clients' beliefs are reasonable.

Here's a prior problem. Baptized people, especially heretics on trial, will cast doubt on the validity of their own baptisms. Consider Protestant baptisms that use defective liturgical elements or *one wrong word*. Catholic theology would not recognize the baptisms as valid. If the state must determine whether to punish a Protestant under canon law, it would face a new burden. It must decide, with solid evidence, that the Protestant's baptism was valid. Enforcing these canon law violations becomes harder.

Courts will declare most accused heretics not guilty if the state brings them to trial at all. Heretics will resume spreading heresy, emboldened by absolution.

---

[96] "Heresy," *Catholic Encyclopedia* (New Advent), accessed December 13, 2022, https://www.newadvent.org/cathen/07256b.htm.

[97] Fudge 2013, pp. 136–38.

[98] On due process in Catholic canon law, see Kenneth Pennington, "Due Process, Community, and the Prince in the Evolution of the *Ordo iudiciarius*," accessed December 13, 2022, http://legalhistorysources.com/Law508/procedure.htm. On the use of witnesses, see Hendrickson (n.d.).

[99] Successful convictions in ecclesiastical courts are difficult. Ecclesiastical courts have a high standard of evidence: "moral certainty." John Paul II, "Address of John Paul II to the Tribunal of the Roman Rota," Holy See website, February 4, 1980, https://www.vatican.va/content/john-paul-ii/en/speeches/1980/february/documents/hf_jp-ii_spe_19800204_sacra-rota.html. Also see "Moral Certainty," Legal Information Institute, accessed December 13, 2022, https://www.law.cornell.edu/wex/moral_certainty.

[100] Fudge 2013, pp. 50–52.

Other citizens will learn that heresy convictions are rare and will preach heresy themselves. Heretical ideas will spread. Heretics who are found guilty may become martyrs, creating civil unrest, as in Hus's case.

Calling Crusades

Medieval heretics spawned powerful movements. Examples include the Cathars in France and the Hussites in Bohemia.[101] These groups led popes to call crusades.[102] Following Hus's incineration, popes called four separate crusades to subjugate Bohemia and authorized similar military interventions to fight the Reformation. These campaigns often failed, and even when they succeeded, the church paid the price of enormous bloodshed. It squandered lives and resources.[103]

Even if the pope calls new crusades—an absurdity—Catholic military operations face many barriers. Heretics can flee to nations where the state cannot intervene.

Deposing Rulers

Suppose states ignore the church. Following Lateran IV, the church could claim conciliar authority to depose heretical rulers.[104] Francisco Suárez defended this right. Sometimes the church can suppress heresy only if monarchs assist it.[105] If a king succumbs to heresy or even tolerates heresy, he could damn his people.

Deposition runs grave risks. The pope might provoke a war or invite states to invade nations whose monarchs he has deposed. The public might defend its elected leaders. Influential nonintegralist officials may resist a deposition. Their objections may weaken the resolve required to restore an integralist moral equilibrium. Deposition is difficult. It requires considerable follow-through, which the church may lack.

If we reintroduce boundary disputes and state capacity, the dyarchy is doomed. Coercion cannot contain pluralism. No moral equilibriums exist.

---

[101] Jones 2017, pp. 36–37. However, see Johnson and Koyama (2019, pp. 61–63, 71–72). For a discussion of crusades against Hussite heretics, see Fudge (2013, pp. 293–95).

[102] A *crusade* is a military operation with expressly religiously objectives, not merely a military operation to recover the Holy Land.

[103] Johnson and Koyama (2019, pp. 153–66) discuss the price Spain paid for suppressing the Reformation.

[104] As canon 3 illustrates. Also note that Lateran IV even grants special spiritual merits to those who repress heresy.

[105] Suárez (1612) 2015, pp. 757–828; Pink 2015a, xv; Bellarmine 2012.

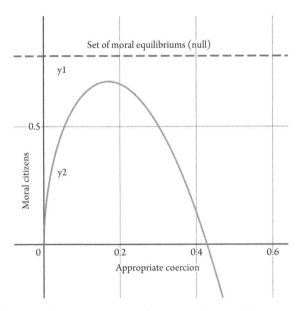

Figure 5.3. Moral equilibriums when pluralism is much greater than grace.

See Figure 5.3: pluralism is robust, and grace cannot contain it. Society settles into a modus vivendi, an equilibrium, of fear or decay.

Dropping Motive Transparency

I have thus far granted the integralist a powerful assumption: motive transparency. I have assumed that we can discern when and whether others act from a firm grasp of the natural law: Officials and citizens can tell whether anyone else acts for moral reasons. Lawmakers can then adjust policy to cultivate the right motivations. But, of course, this is an unrealistic assumption. The human capacity to mask our motives is one of our great talents as a species, and indeed, we are so good at it that we routinely fool ourselves. If integralist stability depends on motive transparency, that is terrible news for integralism.

So suppose we drop motive transparency. What happens to the model? We can no longer infer motive from conformity. Rulers can ensure that people follow the natural law to some extent, but they cannot determine why people follow it. Integralist stability depends on cultivating proper motives, so discerning motivation matters.

One advantage of the integralist theory is its account of our spiritual psychology. People seek eternal beatitude under some conditions, and their concern to avoid divine punishment and curry divine favor may keep them in line. A dyarchy could strengthen moral motives with proper education, especially for youth. It could instill obedience, inducing guilt and shame if people break the law of church or state. But even in this case, church and state officials may fail to produce moral motives and may even undermine them. Citizens can disagree about what church and state command. Pluralism will arise when the pope and, say, the crown issue conflicting directives. (For instance, the church deposes a king, and the king refuses to vacate his office. This happened many times.)

Disagreement can also result when people adopt a rapidly expanding heresy. Remember that the Arian heresy was influential and widespread. Whole nations were Arian Christians. The church strove for centuries to stamp out Arian belief. In subsequent integralist regimes, squelching heresy was an ordinary affair of the state, partly out of fear that a heresy could grow as widespread as Arianism.

Even during High Integralism, determining what people believed was tricky. And so, without motive transparency, rulers might produce a modus vivendi or a fear-based equilibrium. They cannot be sure that their policies have succeeded.

During High Integralism, these problems were less pressing. Most people obeyed the dyarchy unawares because it was not a part of their daily lives. The populace consisted almost entirely of villagers who kept to their locales. Few had the education or incentive to understand how their society operated. But the stability argument targets a complex, educated, and communicative order. The opportunity for fear-based motives is substantial.

Integralists pride themselves on their ability to see liberalism's dark heart. They equate liberalism with progressive cultural hegemony. They then suggest that integralists can capture progressive soft power for Catholic ends. But the character of left-wing power will not provide the motives integralists want. According to integralists (and many others), progressives wield outsized power through fear. Millions feign support for the newest progressive social trend or linguistic practice. And no one knows how many people agree with progressive elites. I doubt that corporate executives running anti-racism trainings entirely agree with these policies.

If integralists have the correct analysis, progressives are happy with conformity. They do not seek motive homogeneity. Indeed, they may want some people to act from fear. The possibility of fear could justify endless new rounds of progressive re-education. Progressives get to perpetuate their ideology and collect a permanent university paycheck. But the integralist ideal depends on people acting from a firm grasp of the true good. Progressive soft power will only give integralists the capacity to rule by fear, and we have little reason to think that soft power will transform fear into moral conviction.

A famous formal model helps deepen the problem. Václav Havel wrote on the character of "post-totalitarian" regimes.[106] Havel argued that Eastern European dictatorships were, as economic Kaushik Basu puts it, "dictatorships with no dictators."[107] Everyone complied with authoritarian social norms to avoid punishment. Basu has developed Havel's work into a formal model of *diffuse dictatorship*. If Basu is correct, the dyarchy could create perfect conformity with natural law, and yet no one acts from moral conviction—not even the king or the pope.

Motive opacity and fear of sanction can sustain mass conformity in some cases. And so, once we accept motive opacity, the possibility of diffuse dictatorship arises. Integralists cannot dismiss this possibility as unrealistic, for they, in effect, argue that diffuse dictatorship is an American reality. Worse, motive opacity will become common knowledge. Citizens will know that officials face difficulties learning citizens' motives, officials will understand that citizens know that officials have trouble, and so forth. Everyone will grasp the possibility of widespread deception. In such cases, diffuse integralist dictatorship is always on the horizon.

I do not want to overstate my case. Motive opacity does not mean that officials and citizens can never discern motives. But the opportunity for confusion and error is serious. Ideocracies were unstable because officials knew that people obeyed only because of threats. Indeed, *officials* often obeyed only because of threats. Eastern European tyrannies survived for a mere fifty years despite massive propaganda campaigns.

In our model, modest motive opacity implies routine policy error. Officials will often use too much or too little coercion to keep society in line, assuming that officials are themselves sincere integralists.

Modify the Model?

Integralists will respond by altering the model. They may lower the threshold of moral citizens or raise the initial proportion of moral citizens.

A first reply lowers the threshold of moral citizens to 70 percent. A regime counts as morally stable if 70+ percent of citizens are moral citizens. A lower threshold is easier to meet. But the ideal now allows more dissent and resistance. The now-larger minority requires more coercion, which will prove both less effective and harder to justify.

[106] Havel 2015.
[107] As quoted in Basu 2000, p. 145.

The second reply is to begin the model with a more homogeneous population. Integralist order could start with 95 percent moral citizens. Two problems arise. First, integralism can stabilize only with overwhelming agreement, making the ideal less appealing. Second, if pluralism is natural to humans, integralism may contradict human nature.[108] In this case, integralists lose the argument on their own terms.

Moral Decay

Integralist orders contain the seeds of their own destruction. Many citizens will lose moral knowledge, which will lead to honest disagreement. Integralist societies cannot manage pluralism enough to reach moral stability, owing to Catholic teaching itself.

Integralist orders will decay into *modi vivendi* or worse. To the extent that integralist regimes have existed, they could have easily become nonmoral equilibriums. Alternatively, in disequilibrium, society could shift to another regime type. History suggests the most likely outcome: by the twentieth century, most Catholic societies had become moderate establishmentarian regimes.

My argument grants the integralist a lot. I omit pluralism in the college of bishops and set aside the unpredictable results of papal elections. The college of cardinals might elect an integralist pope, but future popes may disagree. I set aside international sources of instability. A pope with political power may provoke negative responses from nonintegralist regimes. Consider how China would approach an integralist pope: Chinese Catholics may come under even greater suspicion.

Integralists will dismiss one or more of my modeling assumptions as inaccurate or crude. But all models simplify reality. Integralists should respond with a model of their own.

As noted above, integralists might admit that their order will decay but show that the decay rate is slow enough that we should still pursue the ideal. If an integralist order can last for a century, that's pretty good. Further, if other regimes decay, but more slowly, integralism may have enough value to justify establishing it anyway. An integralist century beats a liberal millennium. Integralism: a nonideal ideal.

I offer two replies. First, integralists will need to, at minimum, sketch how long their ideal will last compared to similar regimes. They could contrast integralism

---

[108] Gaus (2003) claims that radical pluralism has converted liberalism into a post-Enlightenment project.

with soft-establishmentarian states, which establish Catholicism as the religion of state but do not exact civil punishments for violations of canon law (beyond mundane cases). The faster integralism decays vis-à-vis these regimes, the less attractive it becomes. And, under a short duration, we cannot accurately describe the ideal as a moral peace. A decadal regime is not the integralist goal.

Second, if integralist regimes decay, societies must pay cyclical transition costs to restore them. Integralism must have enough value to justify its constant restoration.

These costs can compound. Suppose they require sacrificing some economic growth. A nonintegralist state will grow far wealthier than the integralist order within a century. The nonintegralist order can better fight poverty and guarantee healthcare. The stabilization costs to integralism include the opportunity costs of the regime's other priorities. Nonintegralists may resist paying repeated stabilization costs.

I conclude that integralism is not a moral order.

Instability is a problem for integralism, apart from a comparison with liberal orders. In this chapter, I explored whether the integralist ideal is attractive. If integralism is not a moral order, it is less attractive in itself. Transition concerns strengthen its unattractiveness. If we cannot stabilize an integralist society, that is an excellent reason not to push for it.

Integralists cannot rest their case by vindicating integralism over liberalism. Societies have taken many other forms. Integralism, to be ideal, must be superior to many different regimes. In my view, integralism is false if it is less stable than a milder confessional state. Many fathers of the Second Vatican Council preferred this gentler form of establishment. They expected less social strife and violence. They might have been right.

But no critique of integralism would be complete without assessing the morality and justice of an ideal integralist regime. So I turn to that assessment now.

6

Justice

One common argument against integralism is that it permits injustice. Integralism violates the human right of religious freedom, at least for the baptized. And integralists allow particular injustices. These include the Mortara kidnapping, the burning of heretics, and fascist dictators.

In my view, these claims will not persuade integralists. They have a well-developed doctrine of religious freedom. And, in my opinion, they can avoid the parade of horribles if they want.

But they cannot escape another kind of justice argument. If we zero in on integralism's political theology of baptism, the integralist adopts two norms of justice that seem to conflict. First, Catholic dogma states that no one may force anyone else into the faith. Yet second, and with the medieval church, the integralist allows religious coercion of the baptized: Christian states may press people to remain in the faith by punishing heretics and apostates. But if religious coercion is wrong at the start of the Christian life, why is it permitted after that? The integralist appeals to *baptism*. Baptism serves as a *moral transformer*: it transforms religious coercion from unjust to just.

My thesis is that baptism cannot serve as a moral transformer. If I am right, then two norms of integralist justice conflict. The norms do not strictly contradict one another. Indeed, integralists can resolve strict contradictions, but only if they postulate ad hoc harmonizing propositions.

To examine whether baptism is a moral transformer, I will first address the resolution proposed by Aquinas. Aquinas argued that baptism transforms the morality of religious coercion because baptism involves a vow to God to obey the church. People generally think it is wrong to force someone to make a vow, but they generally agree that one may enforce the vow thereafter.[1] If baptism involves a vow, then that solves the baptism dilemma.

---

[1] The state may sometimes compel vows, such as in criminal punishments. But Aquinas focuses on cases where such coercion is forbidden, which he thinks includes baptismal vows.

All the Kingdoms of the World. Kevin Vallier, Oxford University Press. © Oxford University Press 2023.
DOI: 10.1093/oso/9780197611371.003.0007

Aquinas reconciled the tension by examining the character of baptism. He argued that heresy and apostasy violate the baptized person's vow to obey the church. The church may direct the state to help it punish vow-breakers. Aquinas also argued that the state must protect people from spiritual harm, so we should punish baptismal oath-breakers for this reason too.

Aquinas thought enforcement could be severe. Heretics merit stern spiritual penalties, such as excommunication. He taught that the church may punish heretics after attempts to correct them fail.[2] If the baptized person does not relent, heresy deserves strict physical penalties, such as execution.[3] When setting a sentence, the state must also consider community salvation, which further justifies harsh punishment.

I argue that Aquinas's resolution fails, as infant baptism illustrates. Catholicism teaches that baptism changes the will, but not as the integralist requires—because infants make no promises at their baptism. Indeed, they make no promises at all.

Stopping spiritual harm cannot by itself justify religious coercion. The unbaptized can create spiritual damage, but that fact does not justify force; here Aquinas is clear: no person may baptize another against the second person's will.

After arguing that Aquinas's solution fails, I adapt contemporary theories of political obligation to explain enforceable religious duties. I focus on consent, gratitude, associative obligations, and natural duties of religion. But none of these theories works.

Some Catholic thinkers defended the religious coercion of the baptized for practical reasons. They wanted to keep society stable. At that time, Western elites agreed that a religiously plural society must destabilize, yet they recognized that forcing new people into the church did not work. So they devised a more modestly coercive solution: if the church-authorized state penalizes those *tempted* to apostasy, they could preserve agreement within homogeneous societies. The power to coerce the baptized became important during the Counter-Reformation for this reason. From a Catholic perspective, growing Protestant populations threatened endless civil wars. If the church did not coerce the baptized, Christendom would collapse.

Religious coercion of the baptized may have seemed reasonable when people believed it was essential for social order. But this policy solution to a practical problem generates a conflict at the level of moral principle. Catholic leaders could solve the problem of *stability* (discussed in the last chapter), but only if they create a problem of *justice* (analyzed here).

---

[2] Aquinas 1920, II–II, q. 10, art. 8.
[3] Aquinas 1920, II–II, q. 11, art. 3.

Religious Liberty Review

As we know, according to Thomas Pink's interpretation, *Dignitatis humanae* recognizes a universal right of religious freedom. No state may coerce people into the faith. But *DH* does not address the rights of the church over the baptized. *DH* permits the church to direct Christian states to punish some canonical crimes. (If you have recently read Chapters 1 and 2, you may skip the remainder of this section; it is review.)

Let's recall just how many religious liberties *DH* protects. Religious communities may "govern themselves according to their own norms." They may create their own educational institutions. The law may not interfere with selecting, training, appointing, or transferring religious ministers. It may not restrict the construction of houses of worship. Religious communities may teach their faith in public. They may do so through speech or in print.[4] Parents have the right to live their own domestic religious life. They may determine how they educate their children. The government may not force them into alien education systems.[5]

DH states that the common good requires equal treatment before the law, so the state may not treat someone as an inferior "for religious reasons."[6] *DH* prohibits religious discrimination. Restricting religious freedom violates God's will and the rights of the person. No one may use force to "destroy or repress religion" among humans within a country or in a "definite community."[7]

DH gives moral reasons, not prudential reasons, in favor of these liberties. The right to religious freedom "has its foundation in the dignity of the person." The church grounds religious freedom in divine revelation that affirms human dignity.[8] *DH* argues that our response to God in faith must be free. And so no one may force another "to embrace the Christian faith against his own will." The act of faith by nature is a "free act."[9] Individuals cannot affirm revelation unless they offer God "reasonable and free submission." For this reason, in religious matters, "every manner of coercion on the part of men should be excluded."[10] And again: "The person in society is to be kept free from all manner of coercion in matters religious."[11]

---

[4] Paul VI 1965a, art. 4.

[5] Paul VI 1965a, art. 5.

[6] Paul VI 1965a, art. 6.

[7] Paul VI 1965a, art. 6.

[8] Paul VI 1965a, art. 9. *DH* admits that it lacks a biblical basis for religious freedom. But it acknowledges no biblical obstacles to recognizing such a right.

[9] Paul VI 1965a, art. 10.

[10] Paul VI 1965a, art. 10.

[11] Paul VI 1965a, art. 12.

God respects our freedom to reject him. He places us "under no compulsion." Jesus did not use force or coercion to bring people to the Father.[12] Here we have a moral argument from revelation and not mere natural law. Natural morality and divine revelation show the injustice of religious coercion.

These claims sound universal. The claims sound even more universal when we note *DH*'s major premise. We adopt religion only when we adopt it as true from our own perspective, and we cannot come to the one true faith save from our own perspective.

The Second Vatican Council seemingly applied these arguments to the unbaptized—at least *DH* gives that impression at first glance.[13] So, if Pink is correct,[14] *DH* can seem misleading. I expect that Pink's interpretation will become more prevalent in time, but I also believe it will remain the minority position. The reason is that *DH* cites moral reasons for religious liberty, and these reasons apply to the baptized.

The Continuity Objection to the Standard Reading

Pink argues that the standard reading of *DH* contradicts earlier church teaching because *DH*'s first article claims that *DH* contradicts no earlier church teaching. In response to the standard reading, Pink argues that we should read *DH* as continuous with these earlier teachings. Pink's case for continuity relies on his reading of Leo XIII and the Council of Trent. The standard reading of *DH* contradicts Leo XIII and Trent, as we have seen in other chapters.

Pink focuses on Leo XIII's teaching in *Immortale Dei* and the earlier decree of the Council of Trent (session 7, canon 14).[15] Leo XIII explains:

> The Almighty, therefore, has given the charge of the human race to two powers, the ecclesiastical and the civil, the one being set over divine, and the other over human, things. Each in its kind is supreme, each has fixed limits within which it is contained, limits which are defined by the nature and special object of the province of each. . . . There must, accordingly, exist between the two powers a certain orderly connection, which may be compared to the union of the soul and body in man.[16]

---

[12] Paul VI 1965a, art. 11.

[13] The two chief responses to Pink are Finnis (2013, pp. 566–77) and Rhonheimer (2014). Both share this intuition.

[14] See Nutt and De Salvo (2021) for a recent defense of Pink.

[15] Pink 2017.

[16] Leo XIII 2014, p. 114. Suárez had a significant influence on Leo XIII. Leo grew up as part of the "post-1815 restoration Jesuit intellectual formation" (see Pink 2021).

Leo XIII teaches that God has established two polities (*potestas*). These are the spiritual and temporal powers. God has authorized the leaders of each government to advance their part of the common good. The state protects the earthly common good, and the church protects the spiritual common good. But the church has higher, eternal aims. And so, as the integralist reads Leo XIII, the church may tell states to advance its objectives, much as the soul directs the body. Leo XIII thought that the church might direct the state to discipline baptized Christians. The baptized have become citizens of the church, after all; and, like citizens of the state, they must obey the law of their polity. In this case, their polity is the church.

Owing to Leo XIII's authority, integralism remained influential into the twentieth century. Pope Pius X (in office 1903–1914) held to it.[17] The 1917 *Code of Canon Law* listed baptized Protestants as subject to ecclesiastical laws.[18] For Pink, this means that the church could, if it decided, direct Christian states to punish Protestants for canonical crimes.[19]

The Council of Trent appears to endorse integralist coercion. As I noted in Chapter 2, Erasmus of Rotterdam (1466–1536) had offered a brief policy recommendation in his commentary on the Gospel of Matthew. He thought authorities should ask young Catholics whether they affirm their baptismal vows. If they do not, only the church may punish them for ecclesiastical crimes, through denial of the sacraments.[20] Trent condemned Erasmus's teaching. By doing so, it appears to affirm a key integralist plank: baptism subjects one to civil censure for violating canon law.

> If anyone says that, when they grow up, those baptized as little children should be asked whether they wish to affirm what their godparents promised in their name when they were baptized; and that, when they reply that they have no such wish, they should be left to their own decision and not, in the meantime, coerced by any penalty into the Christian way of life, except that they be barred from the reception of the eucharist and the other sacraments, until they have a change of heart: let him be anathema.[21]

---

[17] Pius X (1907) also condemns modernism in a way consonant with integralism.

[18] See Pink 2012a.

[19] Though this practice had become quite rare. Interestingly, Ryan and Millar (1930, p. 35) think that baptized persons "born into a non-Catholic sect" should never be "coerced into the Catholic Church," as it would be "fundamentally irrational, for belief depends upon the will and the will is not subject to physical compulsion."

[20] Erasmus 2008, pp. 20–21.

[21] *Council of Trent*, Session 7, Decree on baptism, canon 14, 3 March 1547, in Tanner 1990, vol. 2, p. 686.

For Pink, Trent claims that baptism obligates everyone "to keep the faith as adults."[22] If they culpably refuse to keep the faith, that licenses temporal punishment, including—Pink argues—punishment by the state.[23] The church may go further than "denial of the sacraments" by deputizing the state to aid in the punishment. At least that is how the council fathers at Trent understood the canon.[24] Infant baptisms, Pink claims, were no exception.

Pink's reading arose from his attempts to square these teachings with *DH*. He argues that the Leonine and Tridentine doctrines apply to the church-authorized state, whereas *DH* applies to the state acting solely in its capacity as guardian of natural law.

Pink's Reinterpretation (Again)

In response to the threat of discontinuity, Pink provides a narrower read of *DH*. According to Pink, the declaration recognizes a universal right of religious freedom against states but not against the church: the state lacks the authority to use religious coercion, but the church does not.[25] Indeed, *DH allows* that the church may restrict the religious liberties of its members by calling on Christian states to assist it, even if that is no longer church policy.

If Pink is correct, the church can deputize the state to enforce canon law via civil law. But canon law covers only the baptized, not the unbaptized. So I assume that freedoms mentioned in *DH* apply to the unbaptized who live in integralist states.

Does the Church Have the Power to Coerce?

Suppose baptism renders baptismal coercion permissible. This entails that the church may authorize the state to use physical coercion. Here is a typical response: The church has no authority to use physical coercion and consequently cannot allow the state to use it. The church cannot grant a power that it does not have.

Integralists can argue that the church has the authority to use spiritual coercion and thus may extend that authority to physical coercion. Here is the integralist's argument formalized[26]:

[22] Pink 2019, p. 2.
[23] For counterargument, see Finnis (2013, pp. 570–72).
[24] Pink 2019, p. 2. Pink defends his interpretation of Trent at great length.
[25] Pink 2017. Also see Crean and Fimister 2020, pp. 107-8n14.
[26] I am grateful to Josh Cohen and Sarah Genob for discussion on this point.

1. The church has divine authorization to use spiritual coercion.
2. If the church has divine authorization to use spiritual coercion, it has divine authorization to use coercion that resembles spiritual coercion.
3. Physical coercion resembles spiritual coercion.
4. Therefore, the church has divine authorization to use physical coercion.[27] (from 1, 2, 3).

In other words, since physical coercion resembles spiritual coercion, the church may use physical coercion.

What should we make of this argument? Most Catholics affirm proposition 1, and proposition 4 follows from 1–3. So let's consider propositions 2 and 3. I have trouble assessing 3 because I don't know how to evaluate the claim that spiritual and physical coercion resemble one another. Obviously physical coercion resembles spiritual coercion because both are coercive. But does that observation suffice to show that physical coercion is permitted?

Further, church tradition has long distinguished between spiritual and physical coercion. Spiritual coercion is central to church functioning. Physical coercion is not. Similarly, priests may use spiritual coercion but not physical coercion.

Here's a case for proposition 3. To evaluate the similarity of physical and spiritual coercion, we could appeal to what justifies spiritual coercion. The justification is that spiritual coercion helps preserve the salvation of the church's members—and physical coercion might help with this. If so, physical and spiritual coercion can both discipline the errant.

What about proposition 2? Spiritual coercion keeps people upright, and so does physical coercion.[28]

We can expand on this point: the church may use physical coercion owing to its status as a perfect society (*communitas perfecta*). Leo XIII taught that the church holds every power needed to pursue its mission.[29] It may legislate on matters "within its competence."[30] If physical coercion helps advance its mission, the church has the authority to exercise it. Physical coercion may lie outside the church's competence. The church may still extend its authority to a competent power (i.e., the state).[31]

But consider the following. The church could learn to use coercion well. It ruled the Papal States for centuries. If so, the church could rule in temporal

---

[27] I thank an anonymous referee for this point.

[28] Of course, many argue that physical coercion is ineffective in matters of faith. Here I grant that it can work sometimes. If physical coercion always or usually fails, integralism is already false.

[29] Leo XIII 2014, p. 112.

[30] Leo XIII 2014, p. 113.

[31] I thank an anonymous referee for this point.

affairs if it chooses. But then we lose our grasp on why God would assign the state temporal authority if the church can rule well. Why not make every state a papal state? Why not hierocracy?

I would respond in this way: Today the church lacks the competence for modern governance. Further, it may have lacked competence even when it governed the Papal States. Temporal authority saddled the papacy with earthly temptations. So it may have governed well in temporal affairs, but earthly rule compromised its rule in spiritual matters. Any integralist can think the Papal States were a bad idea.

Let's summarize. If baptism is a moral transformer, integralism might be true. As a perfect society, the church may use physical coercion, though using coercion is unwise because the church lacks competence to use physical coercion well. The church may thus authorize the state to use physical coercion on the baptized.[32] We can see, then, why the church could have the power to use physical coercion against the baptized.

If baptism is not a moral transformer, *then* we face the baptism dilemma below. Integralists make two claims: religious coercion of the unbaptized is unjust, but religious coercion of the baptized is just. These two claims are not contradictory if baptism is a moral transformer. If not, however, integralists have a fateful choice: allow religious coercion of the unbaptized or prohibit religious coercion of the baptized. They can do neither. Integralism thus depends upon the claim that baptism is a moral transformer. And this claim is implausible.

The Baptism Dilemma

The baptism dilemma arises from integralists embracing two teachings that seem to conflict. The Catholic Church teaches that forced baptism is wrong.[33] People have a fundamental right to religious freedom because the choice of faith must be free. Yet, if integralists are correct, church-authorized states may prohibit the baptized from rejecting the Catholic faith, or at least from doing so in public.[34] But if faith must be free at the beginning, why not after that?

---

[32] I reject this "authorization" argument below.

[33] Even the arch-traditionalist Archbishop Lefebvre (1994, p. 242) claims that "the civil authority is not permitted in any way to compel consciences to accept the Faith revealed by God. Indeed, the Faith is essentially free and cannot be the object of any constraint." He also cites the *Code of Canon Law* of 1917 and points out that the Church can tolerate Jews but not heretics because "the Jews never accepted the Christian faith, while the heretics did" (p. 111). Heretics are "outside of the Church, but with the duty and obligation of remaining inside, and therefore they can be forced to come back as we force sheep when they leave the flock" (p. 118).

[34] *DH* allows forbidding religious freedom that threatens public peace and public morality. Paul VI 1965a, art. 7.

Again, baptism makes the difference: integralists say that it functions as a moral transformer, some state of affairs or act that "transforms an unjust situation into a just one."[35] Baptism changes a person's liberties. Before baptism, a person is free to accept or reject the faith, but not afterward.[36] If the state forces a person into religion, it acts unjustly, but it acts justly if it forces the person to remain in the faith.

But what is baptism? How does it work? To most, baptism is mere water and words. For certain Protestants, baptism signals a commitment to the faith. Or it signals the dedication of one's parents.

For Roman Catholics, matters are more radical: "Through baptism, we are freed from sin and reborn as sons of God; we become members of Christ, are incorporated into the Church, and made sharers in her mission."[37] Baptism is necessary for salvation, as commanded by Christ (John 3:5).[38] Baptism has two main effects: "purification from sins and new birth in the Holy Spirit."[39] God forgives all sins through baptism, including original sin. God also remits punishment for sin. Nothing stands in the way of salvation. Yet temporal consequences of sin remain. People still suffer, get sick, and die. And they keep an inclination to sin that theologians call "concupiscence."[40]

Baptized Christians now receive the grace of justification. We can believe in God, hope in God, and love God through the supernatural virtues of faith, hope, and love. We can live and act through the prompting of the Holy Spirit and experience the Spirit's gifts. Baptism makes us part of the church, the body of Christ. The baptized no longer belong to themselves but to "him who died and rose for us."[41] Baptism assigns new responsibilities in the church and the right to receive its gifts.

Baptism is an eternal seal, a spiritual mark, and no sin can erase it.[42] Further, people cannot undo their baptism. Expatriation from the church is impossible, in contrast to expatriation from the state. Following one's baptism, one has membership in the church at every point in space-time. A billion years in the future, a billion light-years away—it does not matter. This point matters greatly for my

---

[35] Chambers 2008, p. 21.

[36] Suárez thought that religious coercion could benefit the will. Yet these reasons do not apply to the act of faith itself (see Pink 2018a).

[37] Catholic Church 1997, p. 312.

[38] At least the desire for baptism is necessary, if baptism is unavailable.

[39] Catholic Church 1997, p. 321.

[40] Catholic Church 1997, p. 322.

[41] Catholic Church 1997, p. 323.

[42] Catholic Church 1997, p. 324.

purposes. The impossibility of exit means that baptized people cannot shed their enforceable obligations, even if they expatriate from the state.[43]

Another critical point: baptism gives the will new powers. Again, we can now cooperate and unite with God. But, while baptism gives infants new inclinations or capacities, it does not give them new acts. A promise is, by necessity, an action and not an ability.[44]

One cannot retreat to the claim that only adult baptism generates enforceable obligations. That position runs too close to Erasmus's. And, again, the integralist believes that the church permanently condemned Erasmus's view. Pink seems to say this.[45] Baptism suffices to make one liable for heresy and apostasy in an integralist state.[46]

The Tridentine teaching strikes many as unjust. But note that it legitimizes punishment only in some cases and does not license punishing the inculpable. Suppose that baptized Reba was raised outside the church. She grows up and preaches heresy. Here Reba's actions lack culpability, and so natural law forbids punishing her. She has "invincible ignorance"—nonculpable intellectual errors.[47]

This maneuver may help integralists avoid grim punishments, but it does not save them. Here I ask whether baptism creates legal liabilities, not when violations of canon law are culpable. Whether baptism creates legal liabilities has great importance, and one wants to know how it works. It seems strange that states cannot force people into the faith but can make them remain in it, and odder still to think that baptism makes the difference.

I can state the baptism dilemma more clearly. The reasons that ground a right of religious freedom apply to the baptized, so baptism must provide overriding reasons for religious coercion. These overriding reasons cannot license coercing the unbaptized. Baptism needs an element necessary and sufficient to assign legal liabilities, but no such element exists.

A Thomistic Resolution: Baptismal Vows

Contemporary integralists do not face the baptism dilemma alone. Aquinas also grapples with it. I engage Aquinas to illustrate the power of the baptism

---

[43] The integralist might maintain that one can shed one's *enforceable* obligations by expatriating from the state, but then all those subject to severe integralist coercion would emigrate.

[44] An infant has new powers of the will as part of the soul, even if the infant's body cannot exercise those powers.

[45] Pink 2019, p. 26.

[46] From here, I presume that baptized citizens have these liabilities.

[47] Jone (1946, p. 7) calls ignorance vincible when one can dispel it through appropriate "moral diligence."

dilemma: the most famous Catholic theologian took the problem seriously. (I follow philosopher Gregory Reichberg's interpretation of Aquinas on these matters. His read helps me formulate the problem, even if I would like to differ with him in some details.[48])

Aquinas addresses religious freedom in the *Summa Theologica*.[49] The church fathers and councils prohibit coercion into the faith.[50] Aquinas concludes that, as Reichberg puts it, "deliberate action to impede [religious] freedom" is unjust:[51] "These [unbelievers] are by no means to be compelled to the faith." The act of believing "depends on the will."[52] The context refers to a person who considers whether to embrace the faith for the first time.

Aquinas elaborates in his commentary on the Gospel of John.[53] No one believes "unless he wills to do so." Drawing near the Father "cannot result from violence." So one cannot use brute force or "the conditional violence of coercion" that comes from threats of harm. People must have freedom of choice to act on their budding desire for God.

According to Reichberg, for Aquinas, "Theological faith requires voluntariness in the strong sense of the term."[54] When I choose to believe in God, "my heart must be directed to the reason motivating faith—divine truth as source of my beatitude—*for its own sake*."[55] In this view, "Coercion is antithetical to the very nature of faith."[56] Aquinas claims that no one comes to the faith "by violence." He approvingly cites the Fourth Council of Toledo, which taught that "it is only willingly, not despite ourselves, that we are saved."[57] In so backing this canon, Reichberg argues that Aquinas strongly supports religious freedom.[58]

The first half of the baptism dilemma comes into focus: no one may force an unbaptized person into the faith. Now for the second half, as Aquinas justifies punishing heretics and apostates:[59] "Now it is not within the competency of the

---

[48] See Finnis (1998, 2013) for an alternative, integralism-incompatible reading. I should also note Jean Porter's (2016) important work regarding Aquinas on justice, where justice is understood as chiefly a virtue, only giving rise to principles of justice by extension. For an earlier helpful discussion of Aquinas on the virtue of justice, see Stump (2005, pp. 309–38).

[49] Aquinas 1920, II–II, q. 10, art. 8.

[50] Reichberg 2020, p. 10.

[51] Reichberg 2020, p. 11.

[52] Aquinas 1920, II–II, q. 10, art. 8.

[53] Aquinas 1951, p. 176 (no. 935).

[54] Reichberg 2020, p. 16.

[55] Reichberg 2020, p. 16. Emphasis in original.

[56] Reichberg 2020, p. 17.

[57] Fourth Council of Toledo (633). See Aquinas 1920, III, q. 68, art. 10.

[58] Reichberg 2020, p. 17.

[59] Aquinas 1920, II–II, q. 10, art. 8. I'm citing a specific part of the question, because the question as a whole addresses non-believers, not heretics and apostates specifically.

church to punish unbelief in those who have never received the faith . . . . She can, however, pass sentence of punishment on the unbelief of those who have received the faith."[60] Aquinas thinks some political authority (perhaps the church-authorized state) can force people to return to the church and that it can prohibit them from leaving.

Many Catholics think this practice has a basis in medieval canon law. The Fourth Council of Toledo prohibited forced baptisms but allowed the state to force baptized Jews to remain in the faith. Here's why:

> Those who have already been forced to convert to Christianity, . . . since they have accepted the divine sacraments, received the grace of baptism, the anointed [sic] with holy oil, and taken the body of the Lord, they must remain in the faith that they received whether by force or by necessity so that the name of the Lord and the faith they hold not be considered vile and contemptible.[61]

Leaving the faith after receiving it is akin to blasphemy, which states may prohibit. But Aquinas does not endorse this rationale, perhaps for the following excellent reason: the state should not force people to remain in the faith merely because their defections subject God to bad press.

The Thomistic baptism dilemma is plain: we cannot compel unbelievers to the faith, but in some cases baptized believers can be compelled to the faith.[62]

On this interpretation of Aquinas, how does he resolve the tension? His solution concerns the nature of vows: "Just as taking a vow is a matter of will, and keeping a vow, a matter of obligation," where "a matter of obligation" entails an obligation to keep the vow.[63] Vowing must be free, but keeping it need not be.[64] Aquinas explains, "[T]here are unbelievers who at some time have accepted the faith, and professed it, such as heretics and apostates: such should be submitted even to bodily compulsion, that they fulfil what they have promised, and hold what they, at one time, received."[65] Conversion to Christianity implies an unchangeable commitment to remain a Christian. The state cannot induce faith

---

[60] Aquinas 1920, II–II, q. 12, art. 2.

[61] Pennington 2014, p. 117. Some statements about baptized Jews omit the grounds for coercion (see p. 121).

[62] I take no stand on whether Aquinas in fact endorses integralist religious coercion.

[63] Aquinas (1920, II–II, q. 10, art. 8, ad. 3) compares baptism to vowing (again, not identifying the two).

[64] Aquinas does not *identify* baptism with a vow but *analogizes* baptism to a vow in the *responsum ad 3*. I am grateful to Finnis for this point.

[65] Aquinas 1920, II–II, q. 10, art. 8.

through coercion, but it can sustain faith: those who join the faith promise to stick with it.

Aquinas says little more about the promise-baptism analogy. We must stray beyond his text for a full exploration of his solution.[66]

Reichberg tries to resolve the tension as follows. He distinguishes between accepting the faith and professing it. Acceptance involves an incoercible act of the will. Professing faith consists in communicating one's beliefs and promises through outward signs. New Christians (or their parents or godparents) renounce the devil and consent to the faith in the baptismal rite. The state punishes people for violating this public vow. It punishes an external act alone, so the church-authorized state restricts apostasy and heresy in their public expression.[67]

If Reichberg's understanding is correct, the church may punish the unbelief of those who have received the faith. Even those baptized as children can merit punishment.[68]

I suspect that fear drove Aquinas's reasoning; we will see below that fear probably drove the reasoning of Trent's council fathers as well. They worried that authorities who allow heresy will thereby endanger civic peace and unity.[69] If authorities allow apostasy, they will effectively give competitor groups fresh recruits. Aquinas still tries to justify punishment on grounds other than good consequences—the state cannot punish John simply because he endangers civic unity. John might do so by accident. Punishment implies guilt, and innocent unbaptized people can unintentionally threaten civic unity. One must not punish the inculpable, consequences aside.

Pink does not attempt to resolve the baptism dilemma, but—as the leading living integralist—he needs a rationale. He mentions punishments such as removal from office. Yet he downplays capital punishment, exile, and restrictions on public worship.[70] Pink needs to provide a further justification for drawing the dividing line as he has.

A final point concerns the relationship between a vow and baptism. *Someone* makes a vow at one's baptism. But the act of baptism is distinct from the act of vowing. Christians can perform both acts separately. I can validly baptize a baby without an express vow as long as I baptize the baby in the name of the Father, the Son, and the Holy Spirit. Again, baptism is necessary and sufficient for legal

[66] Reichberg 2020, p. 19.

[67] Reichberg 2020, p. 20.

[68] Suárez appears to follow Aquinas. See Reichberg (2020, pp. 38–9) and Suárez ([1612] 2015, pp. 333–40/685–702).

[69] Reichberg 2020, p. 47. Johnson and Koyama (2019) claim that many religions believe that civic unity requires shared faith (see de Vitoria 1991, p. 343–4). Suárez ([1612] 2015, p. 479/763) defends religious uniformity to preserve peace and natural justice.

[70] Pink 2013a, pp. 94, 104.

liability in an integralist regime. Vows can resolve the baptism dilemma only if baptism is necessary and sufficient for a vow to take place. What a strange claim! Vows involve actions, but baptism only bestows habits, powers, and dispositions.

Godparental Vowing

Trent drew the canon on baptism from a censure of Erasmus issued by the Parisian Faculty of Theology. The censure is informative. The Parisian theologians write:

> [Erasmus's] advice, in so far as it urges us to seek out those baptized as infants when they are grown up and to ask them whether they assent to *what their godparents promised in their names at baptism*, and, if they do not approve, finds it perhaps expedient to leave them to their own thoughts until they come to their senses, and in the meantime not to punish them except by not administering the sacraments of the church to them, is ungodly and tends toward the destruction of the faithful, *opening up a path to the abolition of the Christian religion.*[71]

The worry, they continue, is that those consulted

> will persevere in their perversity and will soon fall away from Christianity, both they themselves and many others by their example.[72]

Here we receive two essential details. First, we learn more about why Trent resisted Erasmus's advice. The advice, if followed, encourages Christians to remain in sin. Worse, the practice would depopulate the church. This concern fits Aquinas's. Second, we now know *who* vows on behalf of infants: godparents. Aquinas may have had godparents in mind when he discussed the case of infant baptism.

This *godparent condition* raises a dilemma: either the godparent vow is necessary for church citizenship or it is not. If baptism suffices, then the godparent condition falls away. But if baptism requires a godparent vow, baptism alone cannot legitimize integralist coercion.

---

[71] As quoted in Miller 2012, pp. 16–17, emphasis added.

[72] As quoted in Miller 2012, p. 17. For further discussion, see Gerardus Maiella, "Edouard Hugon, O.P. on Baptism of Children," *Lumen Scholasticum* (blog), October 24, 2016, https://lumenscholasti cum.wordpress.com/2016/10/24/edouard-hugon-o-p-on-baptism-of-children/. I am grateful to an anonymous Twitter user for a conversation on this topic and to Timothy Wilson for maintaining the cited web page.

The first horn of the dilemma gives up on the proposal that godparental vows matter. The second horn of the dilemma raises two problems: one simple, the other complex. First, the simple problem: we degrade baptism if we make the godparent vow necessary for baptism to hold. Baptism saves us; a godparent's refusal to vow can't deprive an infant of baptism's full power.

Now for the complex problem. Suppose godparents know that baptism gives their godchild new legal liabilities. They then refuse to vow. The church must decide whether to baptize anyway. It cannot refuse to baptize; that would deprive the child of spiritual benefits. But if the church baptizes anyway, godparents have a weak incentive to swear the vow. Without the vow, the infant receives the benefits of baptism without the costs—costs that could lead to the infant's execution if the baby grows up to become a heretic. This means that, in time, godparent vows will decline, if not vanish. The church-authorized state will have less control over religion as fewer and fewer citizens fall under its religious authority. The state will decay.

The integralist might maintain that pious godparents will make the vow anyway, since it pleases God and helps them care for the infant's soul. But godparents' desire to protect their godchild from prosecution might prove overriding.

So the godparent vow does not solve the problem raised by infant baptism. Integralists must maintain that baptism suffices to license religious coercion.

The Value of Vowing

An Aquinas defender could argue that baptism need only resemble vowing. Baptism shares with vowing an underlying value that explains how both baptism and vows create enforceable obligations.[73]

Consider the reasons that promises bind. One can give a contractarian or consequentialist answer, but integralists reject the associated moral theories. Instead, they might ground vowing in our interest in forming intimate relations with others.[74] Baptism works similarly: it creates intimate relations with *God and the church*. And so, if vows bind because they enable close relationships, baptism binds too.

We do not baptize people against their will, much as we avoid forced vows. Neither baptism nor a baptismal vow can bind the will. What of infants? The

---

[73] I thank Steve Wall discussing this point with me.
[74] Habib 2022, p. 23.

infant does not refuse to vow; infants are nonwilling but not unwilling. So, if infant baptism benignly increases the infant's flourishing, it may create an enforceable obligation since it does not violate the infant's will.

One could respond that infants may have different beliefs about baptism when they reach adulthood. For instance, they may no longer believe in God, hampering their relationship with him. Baptism might no longer bind in this case. A critic could reply that our vows still bind us even if we change our beliefs. Analogously, a belief change will not dissolve our baptismal obligations. Yet a vow seems binding only when I can discover that I have made one. While we can usually recall our vows, we never recall our infant baptism. Moreover, others may hide it from the baptized person.

The analogical defense of baptism has two more problems. Imagine that someone baptizes an infant against the parents' will. The child grows up in another religious community, say a Jewish one. The baptism permits the church-authorized state to remove the child from this family and faith community. Baptism, in general, might help us form intimate relationships with other people, especially our co-religionists. But in this case, it licenses the destruction of relationships.

Promises create obligations partly because our power to bind ourselves helps us flourish. Thus vows that undermine our well-being may not bind. A vow to be someone's slave does not conduce to anyone's interests. Along the same lines, baptism benefits us, but its binding power could decay if it licenses severing us from our community. Baptism would set back our good.[75]

The analogy with vowing endures, though it no longer supports the integralist's case. The binding force of baptism collapses in cases where the integralist must affirm that baptismal obligations endure—namely, the case where baptism licenses removing a child from family and community.

Second, while baptism changes the will, it does not produce specific obligations. It unites one with God, yes. But baptism itself, by virtue of its similarity to vowing, does not fix the content of our duties. When I make a vow, I expressly swear to concrete conditions. But baptism is not like this. And so baptism will not provide one with specific obligations, such as an obligation to obey the church-authorized state. (I will say more on this matter in the section on gratitude theories.)

For all Catholics, baptism creates intimate relations with God. The integralist can rest baptism's transformative power by drawing an analogy with vows of

---

[75] One could reply that baptism overrides the good of community, and one can justify baptism's priority as a result. But typically natural law theorists hesitate to make moral decisions on the basis of consequentialist-like value trade-offs.

obedience to God. Swearing such a vow creates enforceable obligations because vows help preserve and enrich our friendship with God, a great good. The great good of divine friendship explains why vows create obligations. Since baptism also helps preserve and enrich our friendship with God, it may create enforceable obligations along the same lines. Baptism can also create enforceable obligations to God by analogy with vows of obedience.

But now we need to know whether God has deputized the state to serve as the secular arm of his church. In short, let's grant that baptism creates obligations to God. How do obligations to God explain our duty to obey the church-authorized state? Most Catholics reject that we have such a duty, so what can integralists say to them now?

I return to this last point in my discussion of gratitude and associative theories.

A Constitutive Strategy

Here's one way to salvage the vow strategy.[76] One could maintain that, in the ordinary case, a vow partly constitutes a baptism. The vow is a part of the baptism. No vow, no baptism. Emergency cases may omit vows, but emergency cases are, by definition, unusual. Compare baptisms by laypersons. Laypersons should not baptize in the ordinary case; they should defer to priests. Along related lines, baptism might not occur in the absence of vows from godparents. If so, baptism always involves a vow in the ordinary case. The vow explains how baptism authorizes religious coercion.

I have two replies. First, this "constitutive strategy" moves beyond Catholic teaching on baptism. Yes, vows center the baptismal liturgy. But I see no Catholic dogma that claims baptism fails without a vow. Such a reply requires that the integralist stray beyond Catholic dogma, which makes integralists uneasy. Their power lies in their purported fidelity to church teaching.

A second reply: this division between emergency and ordinary baptisms is too convenient and may even be ad hoc. If integralists pursue this reply, they must provide independent grounds for believing that baptism requires vows. Vows are undoubtedly advisable—they may even be strict godparent duties. But, even granting this, we cannot conclude that a failure to vow means a failure to baptize.

[76] I am grateful to Paul Billingham for this point.

Theories Set Aside: Consent, Fair Play, Natural Duties of Religion

The integralist must locate a feature of baptism that licenses integralist coercion but not forced conversion. I now adapt contemporary theories of political obligation to explore whether they can identify the feature of baptism that can resolve the baptism dilemma. The adapted theories must explain why baptism is a moral transformer.

The most familiar theory of political obligation is the consent theory. In this view, people gain political obligations when they consent to state authority, yet few expressly or even tacitly consent to political order. Integralists will grimace: they disdain consent theories of political obligation for excessive individualism. They will not appeal to these theories.

Fair play theories hold that "everyone who participates in a reasonably just, mutually beneficial cooperative practice . . . has an obligation to bear a fair share of the burdens of the practice."[77] To enjoy the benefits of cooperation, members of a society must share the burdens of maintaining it. They can share these benefits by obeying the law. When citizens obey the law, the government can better benefit everyone. This theory has similarities to gratitude theories, which I think better capture the relationship of God, the church, and the individual Christian. I defer further discussion of this point until the next section.

Finally, I set aside natural duty theories. According to these theories, we have responsibilities simply by being human beings.[78] We do nothing to acquire them; they do not attach to any social role. We owe these universal *natural duties* to everyone. The natural duty of *justice* is to follow the correct principles of justice. For our purposes, assume that these are principles of natural law. When states give form and content to natural law through positive law, they make our natural duty of justice concrete. We must submit to this shared legal order because we have no other way to act justly. And so if a state is reasonably just, we must obey its law.

While integralists, as natural law theorists, might find a natural duty view attractive, I do not expect them to use it. Justice is the province of the state, by and large, whereas obligations to the church, and so to the church-authorized state, have a different basis in duties of religion. Religion, going back to Aquinas (but as rearticulated by John Finnis), grounds a duty to seek harmony with the greater-than-human order.[79]

---

[77] Dagger 2021, sec. 4.2. Fair play obligations arise when the collaborative practice is just, however, and punishing the baptized may be unjust.

[78] Wellman 2005; Stilz 2009.

[79] Aquinas 1920, II–II, q. 81; Finnis 2011, pp. 89–90.

However, baptism could license coercion in an integralist state by specifying our natural duties of religion. I examine this proposal below.

Gratitude Theories

Baptism bestows an infinite benefit on the baptized: salvation. Obligations of gratitude mandate reciprocation under certain conditions. One case occurs when the benefactor requests aid. In some instances, gratitude requires recip-rocating benefits as the benefactor desires. In the case of baptism, Christians owe God a debt of gratitude. If Catholicism is true, God asks us to respond by obeying his church. If integralism is true, God also asks us to submit to the deputized state. Baptism will create an enforceable duty of gratitude if these conditions hold. One who refuses to obey displays ingratitude.

This argument has many steps. To clarify, I alter a typical gratitude-based case for political obligation:[80]

1. God, through the Catholic Church, benefits the baptized.
2. The baptized thus owe obligations of gratitude to God.
3. Among these are obligations to obey the church and its secular arm.
4. The baptized must thus obey the church and its secular arm.
5. Apostasy and heresy violate the obligation of gratitude to God.
6. Thus, the baptized must avoid apostasy and heresy.

If Catholicism is true, proposition 1 is true. The basic logic of gratitude grounds proposition 2. We owe duties of gratitude to those who deliberately benefit us. Proposition 3 justifies an obligation to obey canon law and accept spiritual and then temporal punishment. This premise requires rigorous defense. Proposition 4 follows from 2 and 3. Proposition 5 is true because the Catholic Church forbids apostasy and heresy; presumably, a deputized state will prohibit those acts too. Proposition 6 follows from 4 and 5.

Let's assess objections to proposition 3. The first objection criticizes secular gratitude theory on the ground that only a benefactor who makes a special ef-fort or sacrifice is owed a debt of gratitude.[81] Government officials do not meet this condition. They receive compensation for their efforts. Yet, in the integralist case, Jesus is our benefactor, and he paid the ultimate price for our sins. God made a special effort.

---

[80] Manela 2019, sec. 5.3; Walker 1988, p. 205.
[81] Simmons 1981, p. 170.

Jesus's sacrifice may not transfer to the officials of the church-authorized state, however, and they might have engaged in no special effort. So, while we owe God a debt of gratitude, we may not owe gratitude to the church-authorized state. If we already know that these agents act on God's behalf, of course, then our duty to God might transfer to state officials. But we have now assumed that integralism is correct.

A second objection to secular gratitude theories proceeds as follows: Benefactors cannot always set how one must reciprocate benefits received. As philosopher John Simmons argues, benefactors have no right to fix the required response to a gift;[82] instead, people owe a *fitting* reply. But obeying the state's law may not be the only appropriate response to God. It may even be *unfitting*.

The integralist can respond that *God* may specify a fitting response to the gift of baptism and then direct us to obey his commands on pain of punishment. But do we know that God has specified that obeying the church-authorized state is a fitting response? We would think so only if we adopt integralism. After all, few living Catholic authorities think that God has made this specification.

Integralists could try to escape my argument by postulating a proposition that renders their view internally coherent. I have identified the necessary proposition. The baptism dilemma resolves if God determines that we should express gratitude by obeying a church-authorized state. The trouble is that this supposition is ad hoc. It resolves a strict contradiction between norms of integralist justice, but we have no reason to believe it.

Moreover, we must avoid the temptation to appeal to God's will *tout court*. Appealing to God's will in this way risks accusations of divine voluntarism. God presumably determines how to reciprocate gratitude for good reasons. We decide whether God has made these determinations on the basis of whether we think he had good reason to do so. Yes, sometimes God reveals his own will and does not give a reason, but integralists seldom defend themselves by bald appeals to divine commands. That approach sounds overly Protestant.

A third objection runs as follows. For proposition 3 to hold, people need some way to tell that God directs us to submit to temporal punishments for heresy and apostasy. But some baptized children never learn of their benefactor—say, if their parents die before they grow old enough to learn of their baptism. Many will lack access to God's complex directives. They may even reject Christianity for rich and subtle reasons that non-Christian groups have formulated for two thousand years. Since the baptized cannot detect the basis for gratitude, they arguably have no liability in the first place. One could respond that the obligation

---

[82] Simmons 2008, p. 34.

holds even if one cannot tell that one has it, but duties of gratitude seem to require recognition of the benefits and the benefactor.

Objection four: debts of gratitude seldom justify coercive enforcement. If John benefits Reba, John cannot therefore force Reba to reciprocate, either himself or by proxy. Such force seems off-putting. Most people want to return benefits because of a free choice, not compulsion. God might agree. Consider 2 Corinthians 9:7: "Each of you must give as you have made up your mind, not reluctantly or under compulsion, for God loves a cheerful giver" (NRSV). Forced gratitude can damage the relationships that the gift of salvation creates.

Now our fifth and final objection: the gratitude theory may require that authorities coerce the unbaptized. Baptism licenses religious coercion at least, because it provides a good, so why not think that other beneficial practices license coercion? Suppose Reba is an unbaptized person who grows up in an integralist order, and the church gives her lifesaving food and medicine. She should be grateful, but her decision to receive these goods does not license religious coercion—gratitude over-justifies coercion in this case.

The benefits provided to the unbaptized pale in comparison to the benefits of baptism. But feeding and healing people have large absolute significance. The integralist must agree that a threshold of benefits exists that, when reached, licenses coercion. Baptism must exceed the threshold, of course, but life-preserving food and medicine cannot, as this would license coercion of the unbaptized. I am not sure how integralists can set a nonarbitrary threshold.

Let's sharpen the problem by comparing infinite goods. Recall that baptism does not guarantee salvation. One may reject it through grave sin and unbelief. So baptism bestows only an *opportunity* for salvation, and this opportunity must license religious coercion. Now compare proselytization. It provides an opportunity for salvation via the opportunity for baptism, an opportunity for salvation with an additional step in the process. But that extra step does not reduce the size or availability of the good offered. By Catholic dogma, even if one converts owing to compelled proselytization, that does not license such compulsion. Gratitude does not license such force. So I cannot see how gratitude for baptism authorizes force either.

Associative Obligations

Associative theories explain political obligations through political membership. If John is a member of the state, he has duties to obey it. Philosophers motivate associative views on analogy with closer relationships. We gain obligations by becoming parents or by becoming friends. Some of our responsibilities have no deeper explanation than belonging to a group, and we have such duties whether or not we have consented to them.

Our duties to the church might arise similarly. Baptism makes us members of the body of Christ, assigning enforceable responsibilities. Such obligations side-step the objections to consent, gratitude, and fair play. Fathers have obligations to their children even if they do not know that their children exist. Blaming fathers would be inappropriate until they learn about their children, but once they become aware, their obligations activate. Religious obligations could work similarly. And, like parental duties, the state may enforce them.

Associative theories of political obligation face various criticisms. One objection grants that our obligations to, say, our family members are associative, but claims that citizens lack the close relations that they have with family members.[83] Associative accounts of religious duty can bypass this issue. Christians have ties closer than those of family members; together, we are Christ's bride.[84]

A second objection to associative political theories points out that some political communities are wicked, and we have no obligation to obey their commands. So membership cannot ground those obligations. Religious organizations may work similarly. Some religious communities are wicked, and we have no obligation to obey their commands, valid baptism or no.

Integralists can respond that God created the church—that it is his organization, and so we must obey the church when it speaks for God. Catholics must obey canon law no matter how church leaders behave. I find this reply perverse. If a church-authorized state abuses someone, a member's obligations dissolve; the point strengthens if the church is complicit. The integralist might respond that the debts to the church remain but that the church and the state lose the right to enforce them. I say that abuse dissolves even the potential authority to enforce.

Let's assume, however, that the church remains a moral community despite its bad members. Here we can focus on a third reason to reject enforceable associative religious duties. Many theorists claim that associative obligations arise from "various subjective or will-dependent features" of persons.[85] To have an associative political obligation requires "associative attitudes." One of these attitudes involves recognizing that one is a member of the relevant organization. Since these attitudes can change, associative obligations can evaporate.[86] Secular associative theorists may accept these implications, but integralists will hesitate since baptismal status cannot change.

---

[83] Wellman 1997; Dagger 2000.

[84] Though one might object that Christians may not know that they are so related.

[85] Van der Vossen 2011b, p. 491.

[86] Van der Vossen 2011b, p. 491.

The integralist faces a dilemma: accept the associative attitudes condition or reject it. An integralist who accepts it allows that some baptized people lack associative obligations. In principle, one can receive baptism as an infant and lose the associative attitudes in adulthood.

If the integralist rejects the necessity of associative attitudes, the associative theory weakens. Imagine a child baptized in the wilderness who grows up unaware that the Catholic Church even exists. Does this child have an enforceable obligation to obey the state? The integralist must answer yes, in the absence of associative attitudes (though the integralist can stress that the state should not enforce the obligation since culpability is absent).

I find it odd that one can have an obligation one cannot discover, but the integralist may not find this odd, so here's a fourth objection. Let's grant that infant baptism creates associative obligations to obey the church. Even so, state officials and members lack the intimate bonds that hold among members of the church. So one may have associative duties to the church but not to the church-authorized state.

An integralist reply: since the baptized have obligations to the church, they should obey its agents as a holy obligation. But we can question this. Intimacy—the source of associative duties—does not transfer. Suppose Alf is Betty's brother and Betty is Charlie's stepmother. Alf does not thereby have familial intimacy with Charlie. Put another way, if Alf and Betty are great friends and Betty and Charlie are great friends, Alf and Charlie may yet be enemies. Let's now assume that Alf belongs to the church and that the church can deputize the state. It does not follow that Alf has intimate relations with the state—and so he may lack associative obligations to obey it.

A further problem for this reply is that one can fulfill associative obligations in many ways. As philosopher Bas van der Vossen puts it:

> A requirement to show special concern for fellow members of one's group or to go along with its norms is open to many different interpretations. And it is not up to government officials to determine how subjects fulfill their moral obligations. Disobeying the law, in other words, need not express disrespect to the community.[87]

The integralist response: *God* can determine how subjects fulfill their moral obligations. In that case, individual church members have no discretion in upholding their associative duties.

---

[87] Van der Vossen 2011a, p. 484.

This response only works if integralism is already true: citizens must recognize that the church may direct the state to punish them and that God has given the church this power. But suppose certain citizens agree with the vast majority of living Catholic authorities and theologians. In their view, God indeed determines how citizens should uphold their obligations. But they deny that God does so by authorizing the state to enforce church law, which in turn violates natural law.[88]

Fifth, expatriation usually involves shedding political obligations. If a citizen leaves state territory, she no longer has obligations to her government. What if states prevent their citizens from emigrating? I presume one can shed one's political obligations anyway, because one wants to expatriate. Yet integralists deny that the baptized can ever shed their religious duties. Why? Baptism places us in God's hands, and no one can change that (John 10:29). Thus, baptized citizens may always have associative obligations to the church-authorized state. Apostate emigres may retain political obligations. But I contend that associative obligations weaken even in this case. True, parents cannot escape their responsibilities to their children by skipping out of town, but apostates do not abandon a weak dependent: apostates are *all* weak relative to the church and the state that attack them.

The most fundamental problem is this. Associative theories suppose that obligations attach to social relationships and need no deeper explanation. Yet even Aquinas feels compelled to resolve the baptism dilemma because the tension is plain; associative theories, on the other hand, refuse to grapple with it. If integralists wish to convince others, they must explain the most morally counterintuitive feature of their view. An associative theory does not provide an explanation at all.

Natural Duties of Religion

As noted above, another common approach to political obligation is the natural duty of justice. Natural duties are universal—we owe them to everyone. When states specify natural law through positive law, they focus on our natural duty of justice. We must submit to this shared legal order because we have no other way to act justly. Therefore, if a state is reasonably just, we must obey its law.

The integralist could adapt a natural duty view as follows. First, set aside the natural duty of *justice*, because justice is the province of the state.[89] Turn to the

---

[88] A perfect society argument cannot help here since the Church would have only powers that respect natural law. I thank Thomas Pink, John Finnis, and Mark Murphy for their insights here.

[89] Finnis 1998, pp. 219–33.

natural duty of *religion*. Recall that the duty of religion is to seek harmony with the greater-than-human order.[90]

Catholicism teaches that one can know God's existence through reason, so one has obligations to honor and obey God as reason reveals.[91] Perhaps we best discharge this obligation by joining an organization devoted to God.

Suppose that John carries out his natural duty of religion by becoming baptized. Once John is a member of the church, the church makes his duty of religion concrete. John must then obey the church—say, by avoiding heresy and apostasy.

How does baptism enter the story? John has a natural duty of religion to join a religious organization, and if John decides to become a Christian, he becomes a member of the church through baptism.[92] Assume that John is a citizen of a just state in submission to the Catholic Church. He becomes baptized and acquires dual citizenship and dual obligations. The church gives form to his natural duty of religion, while the state provides further form by extension. John acquires enforceable religious obligations.

The natural duty approach fails to explain why baptism is a moral transformer. The first problem: John can carry out his natural duty of religion in many ways. Remember that the natural duty of religion requires that we pursue God according to reason. Yet John cannot infer the truths of revelation from reason alone. God must reveal them. Without divine revelation, then, John might discharge his natural duty by joining another theistic religion.

This point holds even if John is baptized. He might not know about his baptism, or he might think it lacks force because he rejects Christianity. In this case, baptism does not make his natural duty of religion concrete—at least not as far as John can tell.

The integralist can respond as follows: John's baptism still makes his natural duty of religion concrete, no matter what he thinks. John has inherited supernatural virtue and salvation. Period.

But then why did the integralist appeal to the natural duty of religion? This duty is reflexive.[93] One must follow religious obligation as one *understands* religion, so John must honor God as reason requires, but not yet as revelation

[90] Aquinas 1920, II–II, q. 81; Finnis 2011, pp. 89–90.
[91] Catholic Church 1997, p. 18.
[92] One could describe this process as the church acquiring *jurisdiction* over baptized citizens within the territory of the state of which these citizens were already members (see Pink 2018b). But authority resembles the idea of jurisdiction enough that speaking of jurisdiction would unnecessarily detain us.
[93] Grisez, Boyle, and Finnis 1987, p. 107.

requires.[94] Baptism discharges John's duty only if he reasonably views the baptismal act as a way of doing his duty. He could easily see things differently. The problem compounds if John's parents baptized him as an infant. In baptism, John is not choosing to do his duty; he is not choosing at all.

Here's a second problem: How does baptism make John's duty of religion concrete? If the answer is that baptism makes John a church member, then we seem to draw on the associative theory of political obligation. If the answer is the reception of benefits, then we seem to draw on the gratitude theory. If the gratitude and associative theories fail, the natural duty view then also fails— integralists may as well appeal to those other theories directly.

Consider a third problem. Natural duty theorists agree that John need obey only a reasonably just state: the state must meet some threshold of justice to ground obligations to submit to it. Similarly, the church may need to meet some moral threshold to ground obligations. Integralists must maintain that baptism creates enforceable obligations regardless of church behavior. But John does his duty only if he joins an organization that he believes helps connect him to God. At some points in church history, John may reasonably think that becoming a Christian *violates* his duty of religion, given bad Christian behavior. Judaism and Islam may appear more reasonable theistic faiths. Or John may decide not to join a theistic religion but to worship God in his own way.

I leave the reader with a final problem. A duty of justice seems intuitively enforceable, but duties of religion differ. Aquinas, as noted, thinks that forcing people to keep their religious duties is fraught—the proper execution of the obligation must come from the heart, not from threats. The difference between justice and religion may cast doubt on the integralist adaptation of the natural duty theory.

The Authorization Argument Revisited and Refuted

Here's a final strategy.[95] The integralist may assume that baptism assigns responsibilities: safe ground, since Catholics agree. Thus, even if we do not know how baptism creates obligations, we see that it does so with the certainty of faith. The case for integralist baptismal obligations thus depends upon whether the church can authorize states to help achieve its mission. Integralists need not

---

[94] Note that this reply does not require that we reject Suárez's argument that coercion can create and strengthen belief in some cases, because he too thought coercing the unbaptized was out of moral bounds (see Pink 2018a).

[95] I am grateful to Mark Murphy for raising this objection.

explain how baptism creates duties, only how the church can permit the state to enforce them.

I discussed the authorization argument in Chapter 3. I allowed it to succeed. But, as noted, authorization arguments assume two things:

1. The church has the authority to physically coerce the baptized.
2. The church can transfer that authority to the state.

We can question both claims. First, natural law may prohibit physical coercion in religious matters, period. If it does, even a *communitas perfecta* lacks the authority to use religious coercion: neither church nor state may use it. A perfect society has all the power required to pursue its mission—but it must never violate natural law.

The problem is one of the order of argument. Authorization succeeds only if we already know that natural law allows religious coercion. But if new natural lawyers are right about the good of religion, then natural law forbids religious coercion, and—again—the church cannot grant the state a power it lacks.

Second, if the church may physically coerce in some cases, why not in others? In short, why can't the church act like a normal state? Hierocracy looms. Maybe every state should be a papal state! But now we stray from integralism's two-powers thesis: papal states may be legitimate but should not be the dominant form of political rule.

Let's now grant that the church may use physical coercion. Even so, we still need to know whether it can transfer that power to the political order. Natural law may prohibit religious coercion by the state, even if the church may coerce. *Dignitatis humanae* drives this point home. Pink is correct that *DH* does not address the church's power to coerce in general; but is *DH* silent about whether the church may authorize states to coerce? It reads as though *no* state may use religious coercion since the council fathers made no exception for church-authorized states.

Worse, the arguments against religious coercion in *DH* apply to all states. Church authorization changes nothing. For instance, suppose a person must have religious freedom to develop an authentic faith. This also requires freedom from church-authorized states.

The natural reading of *DH* is that states must never use religious coercion. *DH* is silent about the power of the church, with one exception: it prohibits authorizing states using civil law to enforce church law.

I conclude that integralists provide inadequate support for the authorization argument. Perhaps authorization works. But the integralist is no closer to the desired conclusion. Why? Because we must determine whether religious coercion violates natural law before we can conclude that authorization can succeed. In short, we must already settle whether baptism functions as a moral transformer.

The Baptism Dilemma and Integralist Injustice

Integralists are inconsistent: they demand religious freedom for the unbaptized but not for the baptized. The inconsistency arises because baptism fails as a moral transformer.

Integralists of old reasoned backward. They thought allowing apostasy and heresy could destroy political stability and social unity, but they also knew they had to forbid forced baptism. So they formulated a rationale, and it proved flimsy. Contemporary integralists have not fixed the problem.

Critiques Complete

Consider integralism assessed. Integralists may defend their position with the history and symmetry arguments. But the history argument is inconclusive, and the symmetry argument establishes only the proto-integralism conclusion— showing, at best, that states should promote the supernatural good *in some manner*. So we must ask *how* states should promote the supernatural good.

I think it is clear that the transition, stability, and justice arguments outweigh the history and symmetry arguments. The transition argument tells us not to approach the ideal, even if it is stable and just. The stability and justice arguments show that the ideal is neither stable nor just. Natural law, then, prohibits integralism: integralism conflicts with our natural tendency toward disagreement and affirms contradictory norms of justice.

I invite the reader to reject integralism. You can't get there, you can't stay there, and it's unfair.

This book's second goal is to set up a framework for assessing other religious anti-liberalisms, so I will turn to them in the final chapter. Here's a preview: Confucian and Islamic "integralists" can use history and symmetry arguments, both views face transition and stability challenges, and Islamic anti-liberalism shares the justice challenge.

Confucian and Islamic Anti-Liberalisms

This book creates a framework that helps us engage religious anti-liberalisms. Catholic integralism is my focal case, but we can expand the framework to Confucian and Islamic doctrines. We can understand these doctrines as religious anti-liberalisms. They agree that a divine power authorizes political institutions to advance supernatural goods and that this power requires establishing true religion with coercion. They also oppose social liberalism. They maintain that the good life does not rest on personal autonomy.

I will not cast these doctrines as forms of integralism but will describe them as scholarship does. I will examine Islamic Democracy and the Confucian Way of the Humane Authority. I will outline the case for and against them and show that they fit the anti-liberalism framework.

Let's begin with Confucianism.

Confucianism is a cultural tradition that profoundly influences East Asia. It traces back to Kongzi (551–479 BC), known as Confucius in the West.[1] Kongzi lived during China's Eastern Zhou dynasty, a period characterized by political instability. Owing to his experience as a political official, Kongzi argued that governments must restore political order. They must respect traditional rituals and teach people virtue.[2] Kongzi's ideas influenced many Chinese thinkers, including Mengzi, Xunzi, and Zhu Xi.[3] Called Confucians (or Ruists), they argue that the best life involves the practice of virtue.

---

[1] I will use the name "Kongzi" throughout. Some of Kongzi's followers prefer "Kongzi" to "Confucius." Though some Confucians prefer to be known as Ruists to avoid the misleading impression that Kongzi was a theological innovator, the term *Ruism* is so unfamiliar to my readers that I will keep the term *Confucianism*. I am grateful to Karl Adam for discussion on this point.

[2] Van Norden 2011, pp. 17–32.

[3] Some Confucians would exclude Xunzi owing to certain heterodox positions.

All the Kingdoms of the World. Kevin Vallier, Oxford University Press. © Oxford University Press 2023. DOI: 10.1093/oso/9780197611371.003.0008

The cardinal virtues in Confucianism are humaneness (*ren*), righteousness (*yi*), ritual/propriety (*li*), wisdom (*zhi*), and faithfulness (*xin*). By acquiring these virtues, one can become a sage and live in harmony with everything—other humans, nature, and Heaven (Tian). One becomes capable of living up to Heaven's divine principles.

Confucian political thought teaches that governments must adhere to the standards of Heaven. Governments receive legitimacy when they receive Heaven's Mandate, and they have the Mandate in proportion to the virtue of political officials. Sages can claim political legitimacy and, at minimum, they have the authority to advise and criticize their rulers. Confucians, particularly neo-Confucians of the Song-Ming period, stress continuity between personal morality and political authority. Their argument is often expressed in the famous slogan "inner sageliness [leading to] outer kingliness" (*nei sheng wai wang*).[4] Without sages, who are rare, rule may pass to *junzi* ("gentlemen" or "exemplary persons").

Confucian anti-liberals reject liberalism much as Catholic integralists do. The final, spiritual end of society must inform politics, which requires the acquisition of virtue so as to live in harmony with Heaven. Thus, advocates of the Way of the Humane Authority support the establishment of a Confucian confessional state. Such a state publicly adopts and coercively establishes the Confucian religion, and it provides Confucian officials with greater political power than others have. In so doing, the Confucian state submits to Heaven.

This chapter also examines Islamic anti-liberalism. Islam is one of the three Abrahamic monotheistic faiths. It affirms the existence of God and requires absolute submission to him. Islam also teaches that God has sent a series of prophets to earth to teach people God's will and how to obey it. This line of prophets culminates in the life and teachings of Muhammad (570–632). Muhammad's followers have a simple confession: "There is no god but God, and Muhammad is his prophet."

God gave Muhammad a perfect revelation of his will, the Qur'an. As God's prophet, Muhammad lived an exemplary life—so much so that his example and teachings constitute the Sunna, the second-most-important source of revelation for Muslims.[5] The Qur'an and the Sunna form the basis for the Muslim's legal and ethical code: the *shari'ah*. The shari'ah is eternal law that issues from the divine will. According to Islam, the good life is to love God and obey the shari'ah. The shari'ah comprehensively structures social life.

---

[4] Angle 2009, p. 15.
[5] It is the second-most-important source of revelation for Sunni Muslims, at least.

Islamic Democracy teaches that government derives its authority from God and bestows God's authority through the shari'ah and the *umma* (the community of Muslims). A legitimate government observes the shari'ah and receives authorization from the umma. In this model, then, the government promotes both natural and supernatural goods: the latter include acts of individual and corporate obedience to God. Islamic states promote these goods only when they establish the shari'ah and honor the umma's will.

Islamic Democracy is democratic, but it too rejects liberalism. The final, spiritual end of society must inform politics, and the shari'ah directs all of society toward that end.

I can't review both Islam and Confucianism in detail. Instead, I will outline theological doctrines that ground their respective anti-liberalisms. I focus on contemporary representatives of both positions, beginning with the Confucian anti-liberalism of Jiang Qing (1953–). My arguments for and against integralism apply to the Way of the Humane Authority (WHA), Jiang's proposal for a constitutional order rooted in the authority of Heaven and virtuous political rule. History and symmetry may support the WHA, but transition concerns undermine it.[6] The WHA's greatest weakness is stability. Confucianism affirms an ideal of moral peace that the WHA cannot realize.

I then address Islamic Democracy, understood as the ideal regime that is both democratic but fully Islamic. I briefly address the familiar Islamic Democrats, Abu'l A'la Mawdudi (1903–1979) and Sayyid Qutb (1906–1966). But I engage another figure at length—Rached Ghannouchi (1941–), the leading Islamic Democrat. My arguments for and against integralism also apply to Islamic Democracy. History and symmetry support it. Transition and stability concerns partly undermine it. Islamic Democracy's greatest weakness is justice: it affirms equality and so struggles to rationalize second-class citizenship for non-Muslims.[7]

Confucian Anti-Liberalism

Before I discuss Confucian anti-liberalism specifically, we need to review some rudimentary Confucian theological concepts.

---

[6] I am not sure a compelling justice argument applies to the WHA.

[7] Interestingly, Jiang (2013, pp. 216–17) claims that the Iranian Islamic parliamentary system is too "biased." I thank Baldwin Wong for this point. Jiang might make a similar claim about Sunni Islamic Democracy.

Heaven

Confucian doctrine rests on the transcendent power called Heaven (Tian): "Heaven is the source of Confucian spirituality."[8] Indeed, Heaven is "the ultimate source of value for most classical Chinese thinkers."[9] All Confucian principles derive from Heaven's directives about human conduct. Confucian doctrines emerge from "observing and following the laws of Heaven and Earth."[10]

Confucians disagree about the nature of Heaven, but they agree that Heaven is "the Supreme Ultimate"—a universal moral standard.[11] Heaven's way is ethical behavior. Heaven provides the preconditions for virtuous living and gives life meaning.[12]

Disagreements about Heavenly agency run deep; there is a much wider range of approaches within Confucianism than there is in disagreements about divine agency within Christianity and Islam. Some Confucians deny Heavenly agency. Philosopher Stephen Angle contends that the great neo-Confucian Zhu Xi understood *Tian* as the "cosmos."[13] Overall, most Confucians ascribe agency to Heaven. But many do not.

Importantly, Confucians have contrasted themselves with Mohists, who "conceived of Heaven as very much like a personal God," whereas Confucians "increasingly thought of Heaven as a mere abstract higher power."[14] So some thinkers see Confucian Heaven as nonagentive.

Confucian anti-liberals may overemphasize Heaven's role in Confucian political thought and misconstrue Heaven as theistic, perhaps partly for political reasons. Christianity and Islam have enormous spiritual power and influence. A political ideology rooted in a God-like Heaven may capture some of that energy.

I cannot settle this dispute, but I don't need to. Since I critique Jiang Qing, I take on his interpretation of Heaven for purposes of argument. Of course, if Jiang misrepresents Heaven, his history argument weakens.

Jiang, with some others, thinks that Heaven is the "spiritual power and the great grandfather . . . of humans."[15] Heaven "can reward the good and punish the

---

[8] Yao 2000, p. 141.

[9] Angle 2009, p. 14.

[10] Yao 2000, p. 141.

[11] Yao 2000, p. 151.

[12] Yao 2000, p. 154.

[13] Angle 2018.

[14] Van Norden 2011, p. 8.

[15] Yao 2000, p. 85. Some scholars may be ruled out of the Ru tradition for rejecting the personal aspects of Heaven, but many traditional Confucians may find this understanding acceptable.

bad" and teach people lessons.[16] Heaven even loves people. For that reason, if we wish to imitate Heaven, we must become *ren* (humane).[17]

Most Confucians agree that the will of Heaven applies to rulers, who serve as "intermediaries between the supreme ruler above and humans below." They should model their behavior on Heaven, which produces "a rational, moral, harmonious, and unified government."[18] So long as a king possesses proper virtues, he receives the Mandate of Heaven (Tian Ming) to rule and is often referred to as the "Son of Heaven."[19] Bad behavior and poor governance deprive the king of the Mandate. He loses legitimacy.

Harmony

Kongzi lived during the Spring and Autumn Period (722–481 BC). During this time, the monarchy had lost authority, and feudal lords warred against one another. In response, Kongzi and his students advocated for a stable social order. Rulers and subjects must reach harmony to avoid chaos; politics must "bring order and peace to the world."[20] Confucians identified other essential forms of harmony, such as harmony between Heaven and humans, between humanity and nature, and between soul and body (intra-human peace).[21] For this reason, the idea of harmony "penetrates all levels and dimensions of Confucian discourses."[22]

Virtue and Merit

Confucian ethics resemble Western virtue ethics, which ground right action on the activities of the virtuous person.[23] For Confucians, the right thing to do is what the sages do. True moral norms express sagely virtue.[24] These codes fit human nature; they "are themselves natural."[25] One could argue on this basis that Confucianism also closely resembles Western theories of natural law.[26]

---

[16] Yao 2000, p. 85. With the mandate of Heaven, the state may reward and punish as well.

[17] Van Norden 2011, pp. 39–40.

[18] Yao 2000, p. 167.

[19] Yao 2000, p. 167.

[20] Yao 2000, p. 34. For an explanation of how harmony lies at the heart of early Confucianism, see El Amine (2015).

[21] Li 2015.

[22] Yao 2000, p. 173.

[23] Pace Van Norden (2007), however, we should probably not identify them with one another.

[24] This could be either because morality is what sages do or because sages follow morality.

[25] Yao 2000, p. 95.

[26] Greer and Lim 1998.

Confucianism emphasizes merit over equality. While everyone could become a sage, few sages exist. When sages exist, however, they deserve political power and should rule others to ensure that others live well. Their authority comes from their superior merit. And indeed, some Confucians think that to "aim at sagehood is to aim at political leadership," since only sages fully merit political authority.[27]

Confucian political thought is perfectionist. The state should "provide conditions for people to live the good life."[28] Political officials must also possess the Confucian virtues, and virtue should determine the conduct of state.

Confucian meritocratic values still influence China. Philosopher Daniel Bell argues that China has a leading political ideal that is "widely shared by government officials, reformers, and intellectuals, and the people at large."[29] Bell calls this ideal *vertical democratic meritocracy*. The ideal advocates "democracy at lower levels of government, with the political system becoming progressively more meritocratic at higher levels of government."[30] To supplement socialist rhetoric, the Chinese Communist Party sometimes draws on Confucian themes. Party officials often stress social harmony and filial piety, and they sponsor Confucius Institutes all over the world.[31]

Confucian theories of legitimacy are also meritocratic, in part or whole. States have authority when meritorious officials rule them, and a commendable ruler should be ethical and competent. Some Confucians mistrust democracy on meritocratic grounds.[32] Democracy provides too much power to those who lack virtue and misleads the public to believe that the people alone legitimize the state.

Accordingly, some Confucians deny that legitimacy lies with the people; political authority instead comes from Heaven. Authorized by Heaven, sages should rule on behalf of the people. Government is "partly by the people and partly by the competent people," because democratic consultation requires, at minimum, meritocratic supplementation.[33]

[27] Angle 2009, p. 179.
[28] Jiang 2013, p. 101.
[29] Bell 2015, p. xiii.
[30] Bell 2015, p. xiii.
[31] Bell 2015, p. 142.
[32] Nevertheless, some contemporary Confucians defend democracy on Confucian grounds (see Tan 2004; Kim 2016).
[33] Bai 2020, p. 79. Here I should stress that Bai does not appeal to Heaven in arguing for meritocratic governance, but WHA advocates will differ.

Legitimacy

Legitimacy comes from Heaven: Heaven bestows a mandate to rule on virtuous kings. When a king has the Mandate of Heaven, he has legitimate authority, but when he loses the Mandate, he lacks legitimate authority. The "Mandate is a necessary condition for a dynasty to continue its rule,"[34] and "the only legitimate government is the one based on its consonance with the virtue of Heaven."[35] Mengzi "emphasized that Heaven alone . . . could bestow the right to rule the empire."[36]

But when does Heaven give a king the Mandate? Early Confucians claimed that the Mandate depends on whether kings provide specific services. Most importantly, they must meet people's material needs.[37] The government should provide food, shelter, and healthcare to its subjects and should teach the people how to form familial and social relationships. A ruler must practice virtue and ensure virtuous government to deliver these goods. A political leader must also be "respectful of his ancestors, kind to the people, and wise in his judgments."[38] Otherwise, the ruler may lose the Mandate of Heaven. The Confucian classics warn rulers that preserving the Mandate is not easy.[39]

According to philosopher Joseph Chan, Confucianism requires that rulers act with care and trust.[40] Democracy, Chan thinks, can help in this task. Confucians often respond that the will of the people may not reflect the will of Heaven because the people lack virtue. At times, the will of the people can express the Mandate.[41] But since few of us reach sagehood, our collective will cannot guarantee legitimate authority. Again, many Confucians advocate for a government that is "for the people" but not "by the people," because many Confucian theorists do not trust the public to make good political decisions.[42]

Jiang Qing agrees with these points. According to Jiang, Heaven grants legitimacy and orders the universe through three proximate sources: society, earth, and Heaven itself. When a government expresses the will of Heaven in these three modes, it has authority, and the people must obey it.[43]

---

[34] Yao 2000, p. 145.

[35] Yao 2000, p. 169.

[36] Yao 2000, p. 166. I should note, though, that Mengzi himself seems to see the Mandate as reducible to the support of society. See Mencius 2005, 5A6 (book 5, part A, number 6).

[37] Bai 2014, p. 348.

[38] Van Norden 2011, p. 18.

[39] Yao 2000, p. 167.

[40] Chan 2014, p. 85.

[41] Yao 2000, p. 186.

[42] Bai 2020, pp. 32–51. See also Elstein 2010.

[43] Jiang 2013, p. 28.

Stability

Heaven, harmony, virtue/merit, and legitimacy generate an ideal of moral peace. Confucians insist that political stability must not rest on power alone and reject modus vivendi order on both practical and moral grounds. They think that power alone cannot stabilize political order and that rule by fiat requires unvirtuous governance. Kongzi and other classical thinkers worried about moral decay and chaos. They looked to the Zhou dynasty as a political ideal that preserved moral order and not an order of power.[44] Kongzi thought that the early Zhou dynasty was a golden age that future dynasties should emulate.

Kongzi made it clear that, to create harmony, rulers cannot rely on "the power of cruel and punitive laws."[45] They must focus on cultivating virtue by example. By exhibiting and promoting virtue, the king creates trust between himself and his subjects. Harmony can endure. In contrast, punishments "might stop wrongdoing only for a moment."[46] Confucians thus regard punishment as "an inferior way of government"[47] and reject rule by mere "legal or military punishments."[48] Kongzi hoped that people would "rule skillfully," setting an "ethical example" that would "inspire others to follow them willingly, without the need for force."[49]

Kongzi advanced this argument against thinkers and officials whose later followers became known as Legalists. Prominent Legalists have included Shang Yang and Han Fei.[50] Legalists defend something akin to a modus vivendi theory of rule. Law and punishment produce long-term stability because people tend to act from self-interest. This means that a ruler can produce good citizens only if the ruler uses strict laws and punishments "like lightning or thunder."[51]

In contrast, Confucians understand the social order in ethical terms. The proper way of humans arises from mutual care and trust between rulers and subjects. Harmony comes from the "reconciliation of conflict" rather than from crushing dissent.[52] Confucians adopt a doctrine of moral stability for political regimes, and peace cannot come from power alone.

---

[44] Chan 2013, p. 99. Confucians look to the Zhou dynasty as a political ideal as integralists look to Saint Louis IX.

[45] Yao 2000, p. 22.

[46] Yao 2000, p. 22.

[47] Yao 2000, p. 168.

[48] Yao 2000, p. 184.

[49] Van Norden 2011, p. 19.

[50] See Van Norden 2011, chap. 11, for a review of the thought of Han Fei, a prominent classical Legalist.

[51] Often attributed to one of Shi Huangdi's advisers.

[52] Yao 2000, p. 178.

At times, Confucians seem to say that virtuous rule is *necessary and sufficient* to establish order.[53] Once the virtuous sage rules, this ruler will establish order, and order will give rise to further virtue in the populace and the government. I will return to this point below.

Jiang Qing

Jiang Qing claims that China can solve its central problems if it becomes a Confucian state. Unlike Catholic integralists, Jiang offers a detailed account of his preferred institutional structure. His proposals have helped focus debates about the WHA, and they have also helped him attract attention and followers. He offers an alternative to liberal democracy and Chinese communism.

I won't review Jiang's biography in detail, but you may find his background intriguing. From his youth, Jiang studied political philosophy and economics and cycled through a number of ideologies before he settled on Confucianism. The events of 1989 proved pivotal in Jiang's development, as he blamed the disruption on liberal intellectuals, who tried to impose Western ideals on China at the expense of social harmony. Jiang criticizes other Confucians for focusing exclusively on self-cultivation to the detriment of politics. His "political Confucianism" would transform individuals *and* institutions.

In 2001, Jiang created a private academy in Guizhou, his home province; he continues to develop his ideas and teach his students while avoiding Chinese politics. Jiang draws on traditional Confucian teachings, but also on natural law and modern theories of constitutional design.

The Way of the Humane Authority

Like Catholic integralists, Jiang disapproves of Western-style democracy.[54] He rejects the Western view that only democratic elections legitimize state officials and argues that legitimacy has multiple sources. Democratic sovereignty has two problems: people may want immoral policies and they may want shortsighted policies. For example, democracies ignore the climate crisis because they have no incentive to care about future generations or people in other countries.

Jiang calls his alternative the Confucian Way of the Humane Authority. According to the WHA, political legitimacy derives from three sources: Heaven, earth, and humanity. Heavenly legitimacy draws on transcendent moral standards, earthly legitimacy draws from history and culture, and human

---

[53] Angle 2012, p. 24.
[54] What follows is a summary of Jiang's article outlining the WHA (Jiang 2013, pp. 27–97).

legitimacy draws on society's will. Rulers should consult the people's will, but not as the chief source of legitimacy. Jiang thinks these forms of legitimacy must exist in equilibrium, but they do not have equal influence. Heavenly legitimacy exceeds that of earth and humans.

Jiang argues that ancient sage-kings in the Xia, Shang, and Zhou dynasties practiced the WHA. But new historical circumstances demand new governmental forms. China needs a tricameral legislature that mirrors the three forms of legitimacy. The House of the People draws on the legitimacy of the popular will, the House of the Nation draws on history and culture, and the House of Ru draws legitimacy from Heaven itself.

Democratic parliamentary voting selects the members of the House of the People. The House of the Nation must choose one of Kongzi's direct descendants as its leader, but might include representatives of other religions, as well as the descendants of sages and rulers. It might also include patriots, Chinese history professors, retired officials, judges, and diplomats.[55]

Confucian scholars compose the House of Ru—the most essential house in Jiang's tricameral legislature. The leader of the House of Ru rules for fifteen to twenty years; he must be a great Confucian scholar, and other Confucian scholars must recognize him as such. Regular house members may join in two ways. They can pass exams on the Confucian classics and undergo a trial period in administration, or they can receive a recommendation from other Confucian scholars. These two methods follow Confucian norms for choosing officials: examination and recommendation.[56]

The three houses deliberate according to their internal criteria and cannot control the other houses. Bills must pass two of the three houses before becoming law. The House of Ru has a veto because it alone has sacred legitimacy. The other houses limit its power. The House of Ru might propose religious intolerance, true, but the other houses can prevent prejudice from becoming law.

An "Academy" limits the power of parliament. The idea for an Academy draws on the seventeenth-century Confucian Huang Zongxi. Jiang says little about how the Academy restrains parliament, only that it plays a supervisory role. But, according to Jiang, an Academy is superior to a bill of rights. Basing new government on rights will cause cultural decay through excessive individualism. The Academy performs many supervisory tasks, including upholding religion. Jiang does not advocate theocracy. The WHA uses indirect means to create piety and virtue. Indeed, the House of Ru intervenes in politics only rarely—its members spend most of their time studying Confucian classics.

---

[55] Jiang 2013, p. 41.
[56] Jiang 2013, p. 41.

Jiang supports a symbolic monarchy because a historical monarch can connect China to its past. A king with a "noble and ancient lineage" upholds state authority. People may see the state as legitimate if the symbolic monarch commands respect; loyalty to the state has nonrational sources and so can require a personal, psychological connection between the people and the king.

Jiang insists that the monarch has only symbolic power. But Jiang's description of the monarch's duties belies this claim because the king can mediate conflicts, name officials, and issue pardons and honors. The monarch even has great moral influence that derives from successfully addressing important problems, such as ecological crises.

Jiang is refreshingly direct. We know which institutions he supports and why.

The Framework

We can now apply the anti-liberalism framework to Jiang's WHA. Let's begin with history, symmetry, transition, and justice arguments. I place stability at the end because I want to focus on it.

History

I grant that Jiang's political theology fits Confucian and neo-Confucian doctrine because I am beyond my expertise. Many Confucians accuse Jiang of literalist interpretations of the classics.[57] However, Jiang's view is more prominent among Confucians than integralism is among Catholics: some Confucians acknowledge the deeply Confucian character of his constitutionalism. The WHA has some basis in tradition.

Symmetry

Heaven authorizes three powers to govern humankind—Heaven, earth, and society—but the House of Ru, which represents Heaven, has the most authority. So political institutions receive both sacred and secular authorization, and spiritual power has priority. Confucianism also approaches natural and supernatural goods somewhat symmetrically. States should advance natural goods, such as social harmony and a healthy ecology, and they should promote supernatural goods, such as harmony with Heaven.

---

[57] Angle (2014) and Pines (2012) argue that Jiang misreads the Confucian classics, especially in describing Tian too much like Western theism.

Advocates of the WHA can thus develop their own symmetry argument. Recall the Catholic version: the common good has two aspects, natural and supernatural. Catholic perfectionists insist that the state must promote natural goods. But then why not demand that the state promote supernatural goods?

Most Confucians agree that government should promote the goods of earth and humanity, but then why not encourage harmony with Heaven through coercive policy?[58] For example, China could mandate rigorous training in the Confucian virtues that historical Confucian thinkers recommend,[59] and it could rigorously instill Confucian ideology in schoolchildren. Both policies could conform behavior to a Heavenly standard, generating transcendent spiritual goods. If the Chinese government should promote the interests of the people and of the earth, it should promote the goods of Heaven.

Transition

Jiang knows that China will probably not move in his preferred direction. The WHA is "a high-flying political ideal, very far removed from China's current situation."[60] Jiang outlines three social conditions that China must reach to establish the WHA:

1. Confucianism must undergo a great revival in China.
2. This revival must create a new, large group of scholars. These scholars would observe Confucian beliefs and practices.
3. China must add the teachings of the Confucian masters to its constitution.

Jiang defends the feasibility of the WHA based on "historical facts." It "was implemented in history," unlike democracy. He also admits that China will reach the WHA only through "a long and slow historical process."[61] So Jiang does not propose an integration-from-within-type revolution. Yet, like Adrian Vermeule, Jiang insists that political history will deliver his ideal:

> If today we can reestablish Confucian constitutionalism and make our contribution to this task, then we will have accomplished the greatest sagely enterprise available to humanity. By participating in this great creation of history and culture, we shall attain limitless joy. How noble

[58] Jiang's writings do not appear to grapple with traditional Confucian skepticism about coercion.
[59] Angle 2009, pp. 135–60.
[60] Jiang 2013, p. 67.
[61] Jiang 2013, p. 31.

the task is; let all who are concerned for the future of China's constitution work for it together.[62]

Jiang anticipates a "miraculous reversal of history in China" and insists that "it is only a matter of time."[63]

The WHA has a considerable cultural advantage over Catholic integralism. Jiang proposes the WHA for China, which once had Confucian confessional states. The Confucian WHA is *native*. Further, Confucianism has no external power base, and so WHA advocates do not have to coordinate large and diverse institutions. We can envision the WHA in China.

Further strengthening Jiang's argument, China has never been exclusively Confucian. Most Chinese have drawn on other traditions, such as Buddhism and Taoism, even though the civil service has often been almost entirely Confucian. One might argue that Jiang's constitutional order merely returns to this ancient state of affairs.[64]

Yet transition problems manifest immediately because China exhibits enormous internal pluralism. Too many people reject Confucianism. Marxism has lost intellectual authority, true, but the Chinese people adopt many ideologies. Confucianism does not dominate contemporary China—far from it.[65] We also observe China's current non-Confucian approach to pluralism, which involves suppressing diverse groups whenever they appear to threaten public order. Suppression produces routine violations of human rights.

The Chinese government can also observe prosperous and stable democracies nearby: Japan, South Korea, Taiwan, and Singapore. These nations tempt many Confucians toward democracy and away from the WHA. Some challenge the historicity of the WHA, doubting that the Xia, Shang, and Zhou dynasties had sage-kings. They also claim that China's socialist revolution built human equality into Chinese society. Many Chinese reject inegalitarian rule.[66] On these bases, the transition costs to the rather hierarchical WHA look prohibitive.

I am unsure how transition can occur without violating Confucian values such as humaneness. At some point, WHA advocates must suppress widespread dissent. But their moral principles bar them from seizing political power through mass repression. For instance, *ren* requires not killing the innocent. We saw in Chapter 4 that Vermeule's integration from within requires massive violence.

---

[62] Jiang 2013, p. 70.

[63] Jiang 2013, p. 68.

[64] I am grateful to Karl Adam for discussion on this point.

[65] Shin 2012.

[66] Or, rather, they reject rule that is overtly inegalitarian, unlike the covert inegalitarianism of the Chinese Communist Party.

Jiang's approach would require much less, but his followers must still use considerable violence if they wish to suppress pluralism enough to create a new Confucian state.

Jiang's critics raise more transition problems. Joseph Chan argues that we should not pursue Jiang's three preconditions for the WHA. Only massive state coercion can establish them. Jiang faces a chicken-and-egg problem. The government must promote Confucianism before it can become Confucian.[67] Vermeule's integration from within faces the same difficulty. How do integralists co-opt states if the leaders of the state will demolish them first?

Justice

The WHA has a more tolerant history than Catholic integralism. For example, neo-Confucianism critiques Taoism and Buddhism, yet it sometimes draws on them. Further, neo-Confucian regimes had no engrained tendency to view other religions as threats, in contrast to historical Catholic attitudes toward Judaism. Confucians did engage in persecution when Confucianism was a state ideology, but infrequently.[68]

Jiang would preserve religious tolerance. He stresses that the three houses of government can check each other. Again, the House of Ru won't become the Iranian Guardian Council—while Ru has a permanent veto, it cannot override the other two houses to pass legislation.[69]

The justice argument falters. Confucianism does not stress lists of moral prohibitions as much as Christianity and Islam do. Islamic Democracy struggles to preserve its commitment to radical human equality because it must assign Muslims special privileges in principle (if not in practice). But the WHA rejects Islam's radical egalitarianism. Yes, anyone can become a sage, but that falls far short of egalitarian commitment. Confucians will have special political rights. However, special rights create no *internal* conflict between Confucian principles.

We can accuse the WHA of another injustice if we like. Philosopher Tongdong Bai charges the WHA with elitism.[70] The WHA restricts the prestige of rule to Confucians alone. People from "other religions and cultures" lack "a strong participatory role."[71] Jiang dismisses worries about elitism. Every society has commoners and sages, and sages have more power. The WHA assigns sages

---

[67] Chan 2013, p. 104.
[68] Kim 2018, p. 8.
[69] Jiang 2013, p. 216 (also see p. 41).
[70] Bai 2013, p. 125.
[71] Bai 2013, p. 127.

political power according to merit, and the resulting distribution of power is just.[72] Since elites are inevitable, we should ensure they have virtue and wisdom.

I find this sort of elitism problematic, because it seems to violate the idea and ideal of human equality, but I will not argue for that claim. After all, Confucianism does not reject elitism. My general point is that the WHA may not invite a justice argument.

The Moral Stability of the Way of the Humane Authority

Both Catholic integralism and the WHA fail their standards of moral stability. Like Catholic integralists, Jiang claims that the WHA promotes peace and that it creates a "balanced politics" because it unites "the three forms of legitimacy." The three forms "restrain each other" so that no single form becomes dominant. Each type of legitimacy has "its own intrinsic justification" that enables each legislature to check and balance the others.[73]

Stability comes from harmony between sources of legitimacy, Jiang explains, as the WHA "shares in heaven, earth, and the human."[74] It encompasses all but respects the integrity of each. In so doing, it preserves harmony. Jiang argues that, for the WHA,

> equilibrium is an issue not only in implementation but also in legitimization. It is not only to be used in the structure and working of political power but also to be used in determining the basic meaning and legal structure of political legitimacy itself. In the [WHA], no one form of legitimacy should be allowed to become sovereign over the others, for this will lead to political bias and failings.[75]

Stability comes about by balancing the moral forces that legitimize each branch of government. Observe continuity with Catholic integralism. Heaven authorizes different groups to perform distinct functions. The temporal and spiritual authorities have their own original power, and so they must work in harmony without domination. Since the ideal of harmony includes harmony

---

[72] Jiang 2013, p. 202. Or, at least, the WHA assigns sages more power when they exist, and may otherwise assign power to gentlemen.

[73] Jiang 2013, p. 37.

[74] Jiang 2013, p. 38.

[75] Jiang 2013, p. 29.

with Heaven and since the ideal applies to politics, politics transcends secular interests. The state must realize "the Way of heaven ensuring the life of cultural wisdom."[76]

Many Confucians criticize Jiang's approach to stability, arguing that people will naturally disagree with a regime that is based on a specific metaphysics. They claim that the WHA cannot sustain moral peace but creates disharmony instead. For instance, Daniel Bell argues that Jiang's proposals base political power on "controversial transcendent values."[77] Some see Confucianism as a secular ethic. Almost no one accepts Jiang's moral metaphysics.[78] Meanwhile, Sungmoon Kim stresses that Confucians value only one form of the good life— Confucian sagehood. This "ethical monism" creates hegemonic politics.[79] While Confucianism may accommodate moral pluralism,[80] Jiang's Confucianism cannot. His ideal rulers must suppress moral conflict, not accept it, at least within government.[81] However, by suppressing ethical conflicts, they fail to create harmony and so fall short of their standards.

Jiang can reply that he seeks hegemony only among political officials. Civil bureaucracies must become Confucian or Confucian-led. Within older Confucian states, the WHA can tolerate varied local religious practices. But pluralism in modern China is more severe. It contains several powerful and exclusivist doctrines, such as Christianity, Islam, and Marxism. Buddhist and Taoist syncretism may not threaten the Confucian state, but millions of Christians, Muslims, and Marxists may prove threatening indeed.

If the Confucian state suppresses moral conflicts successfully, it might create social harmony. But social harmony will require people to adopt and strongly internalize Confucian values, which must become so ingrained that people resist conversion to exclusivist doctrines. Not even Mao could pull this off. He took extreme measures to inculcate Marxist ideology that Confucians cannot tolerate.

Some Confucians offer grounds for excluding controversial moral doctrines from politics, including comprehensive ethical Confucianism. Mou Zongsan thought that Confucian legislators must view policies from non-Confucian perspectives.[82] Confucians must support political dialogue as a precondition for valid legislation and refuse to use power without consensus. Stephen Angle

---

[76] Jiang 2013, p. 38. Jiang also thinks that the WHA promotes stability by addressing ecological issues.

[77] Bell 2013, p. 20.

[78] Bell 2013, p. 22.

[79] Kim 2018, p. 8.

[80] See Yu 2010.

[81] Yu 2010.

[82] Angle (2012, chap. 2) reviews Mou Zongsan's ideal on this matter and argues that the ideal is a kind of "self-restriction" (see also Angle 2009, pp. 193–96).

defends this position.[83] He criticizes Jiang for rejecting it; Angle sees this as non-Confucian.[84]

Bai argues that Jiang's view is intolerant. In a pluralistic society, the majority will not embrace Confucian moral metaphysics,[85] or they will adopt it owing to "sheer oppression."[86] But Confucian ethics seeks harmony even with people who have non-Confucian perspectives. Bai thinks Jiang misses this.

To me, the central problem is not intolerance. In the WHA, people have the freedom to believe in other religions. Jiang even favors freedom of speech and association.[87] Rather, China can stabilize the WHA only with unacceptable exclusion and suppression, or only with more exclusion and suppression than a more open constitutional order. Within the WHA, not even an overwhelming political majority may remove the Confucian aspects of the constitution. Confucian political elites will have permanent political and military superiority.

Another stability problem arises from unequal treatment of non-Confucians. Indeed, Confucians dominate others' political lives, which will lead to much opposition. The inegalitarianism of the WHA will threaten harmony.

Like Catholic integralism, Jiang's WHA faces pluralism problems.[88] With Bai, we must ask "why the age of perfect harmony, in which everyone becomes a sage, is not available anymore."[89] We lack sages to settle moral disputes; even exemplary persons seem in short supply.

Bai and others have a point. Moral stability forms the heart of Confucian political thought, and Jiang does not recognize the enormous threat that pluralism poses to moral stability. Those who impose the WHA could produce conflict rather than concord.

Another stability problem is this: people disagree about which actions manifest virtue, so they will adopt different standards for identifying sages and exemplary persons. Marxists, Buddhists, Taoists, Christians, Muslims, and so forth disagree about virtue and who has it. Marxists and Confucians differ on filial piety, for example. So the House of Ru needs a public criterion for empowering virtuous sages and gentlemen. Unless the House of Rule intimates the will of Heaven, the WHA falls apart.

Worse, sages are rare. Fake, power-hungry thinkers will always have greater numbers and fewer moral scruples. Confucians have no practical strategy to

[83] Angle 2012, pp. 25–35.
[84] Angle 2012, p. 32.
[85] Bai 2013, p. 125.
[86] Bai 2013, p. 113.
[87] Bell 2013, p. 22.
[88] Bai 2013, p. 118.
[89] Bai 2013, p. 125.

keep sages in charge. If the WHA defaults to gentlemen (exemplary persons), that will reduce, but not eliminate, the problem.

Imagine a Confucian society with the WHA in place. Over time, standards that identify sages will multiply and conflict. Different religions will advocate their unique moral ideals. The selection of moral exemplars will become divisive—existing sages may reflect a society's diverse moral aspirations. We have another chicken-and-egg problem. How do we empower virtuous people to choose virtuous people? On this matter, at least, Catholic integralism has an advantage since it does not base legitimacy on virtue.

Jiang's replies parallel Catholic integralist critiques of liberalism. All societies have a "leading orthodoxy" that helps communities reach consensus and "maintain social stability and harmony."[90] Liberal societies deceive themselves about this, since they too impose their sectarian values on others. They must. If they did not, liberalism would collapse. Only substantive values can secure social stability, such that "a set of comprehensive values will not harm civility" but will produce "the exact opposite" of harm.[91] To put this another way, a stable community requires consensus on substantive values, but officials may destabilize the regime through attempts to produce consensus from pluralistic conditions.

Jiang also argues that liberals hypocritically celebrate their neutrality because of their bias against religion.[92] American liberalism is sectarian secular Protestantism.[93] Jiang adds that Confucianism preserved harmony in history, unlike Christianity. Confucianism avoids religious wars.[94]

Since liberal societies also face moral disagreement, Jiang could argue that the WHA will prove as stable as liberalism. This argument does not work. Even if we grant Jiang that liberalism relies on controversial values, he has not thereby saved the stability of the WHA. He will have established, at most, that *if moral disagreement destabilizes the WHA, it will also destabilize liberalism*. But *that* claim does not establish the WHA's stability because liberalism might also decay.

Second, the WHA requires more agreement than most other political ideals. It bases legitimacy on two highly controversial metrics: officials must (1) agree on a standard for moral exemplars and (2) agree on a measure that identifies exemplars. These determinations raise more problems than do efforts to determine whether institutions embody certain moral principles.[95] I am not alone

---

[90] Jiang 2013, p. 163.
[91] Jiang 2013, p. 164.
[92] Jiang 2013, p. 164.
[93] Jiang 2013, p. 164.
[94] Jiang 2013, pp. 169–70.
[95] The best path for Jiang is to back off to a partial Confucian perfectionism of the sort advanced by Joseph Chan.

in raising this worry. Some Confucian scholars argue that Confucian political thought suffers in the interdependence it postulates between morality and politics. Confucian political ideals become hostage to their reliance on morally exemplary sage-rulers.

Islamic Anti-Liberalism

Readers familiar with Islam can skip the first bits of this section. Here I explore Muslim doctrines about the caliphate, human nature (*fitra*), and non-Muslims (once called *dhimmi*s). These ideas help place Islamic Democracy into my framework. I focus on Sunni Islam. I must leave an analysis of Shia Islam for future work.

Allah and Muhammad

The central Muslim confession is "There is no god but God, and Muhammad is his prophet." The two chief figures in the Islamic faith are the God of Abrahamic monotheism—Allah—and Muhammad. Muhammad was the last prophet of God. Muslims believe he received a final divine revelation that addresses the meaning of life, the character of morality, and the content of the law. Islam speaks to the proper order of society in all its aspects. It is a comprehensive doctrine that governs all domains of human existence, from the individual to the polity.

The Qur'an and the Sunna

Muhammad received divine revelation from the archangel Gabriel. This revelation came together as the Qur'an, the eternal word of God. It began orally, but Muslims recorded it into a single, unalterable text.

God also reveals his will through the Sunna. The Sunna is the "good example" of the prophet, which outlines the ideal personal life for the Muslim.[96] It reveals how God engages humanity through Muhammad's example. It records what the prophet said, did, and allowed, and it elaborates the "values, norms, and laws implicit or explicit" in those activities.[97]

We know about the Sunna through the *hadith*. An individual hadith is data about something Muhammad said or did. Thousands of hadith exist, and they

[96] Shepard 2014, p. 85.
[97] Shepard 2014, p. 86.

address all aspects of Islamic religion, from Qur'anic commentary to specific legal commands. Muslims differ about which hadith are authentic.

The Shari'ah

Shari'ah law is, roughly, Islamic law.[98] But the shari'ah includes not merely the Western notion of law but a system of ethical norms that God commands us to follow. The shari'ah protects and promotes "five fundamental values: (1) life, (2) intellect, (3) reputation or dignity, (4) lineage or family, and (5) property."[99] Laws may specify these values as necessities, needs, or luxuries.[100]

Islam's fundamental values issue from the Qur'an and the Sunna, but they also derive from *qiyas*—analogical or deductive reasoning. The consensus of Muslim jurists (*ijma'*) also provides the basis of law.[101] Muslims thus have a four-source theory of law: the Qur'an, Sunna, *qiyas*, and *ijma'*.[102] They regard the corresponding legal system as Islamic civilization's outstanding achievement.[103]

Islamic Jurisprudence

God makes the shari'ah, not man. The *ulema,* and other delegated authorities, discover the shari'ah, apply it to concrete circumstances, and impose temporal punishments for violations. Muslim societies can determine sentences for themselves, with the exception of a few penalties (the *hudud*) that draw from the Qur'an and the Sunna.[104] Islamic law is not a closed system, though, because it has five different schools of law and jurisprudence. (The Sunnis have four; the Shias have one.)

The Umma

The umma is the community of Muslims—God's people and, for Sunnis, the "vicegerent" of God's authority. The umma has wide latitude in structuring government. The people may choose their leaders and their selection procedures. A *caliph* historically rules the umma. The office of caliph, the *caliphate,* began

[98] Brown 2017, p. 177.
[99] Abou El Fadl 2013, p. 13.
[100] Abou El Fadl 2013, p. 13.
[101] Abou El Fadl 2013, p. 9.
[102] Brown 2017, p. 182.
[103] Brown 2017, p. 189.
[104] These include removing thieves' hands and stoning fornicators, but Islamic regimes seldom impose these penalties (see Abou El Fadl 2013, p. 18).

with Muhammad's four successors, the "rightly guided caliphs," and existed in some form until 1924, when Kemal Atatürk, the leader of Turkey, destroyed it. Since then, Muslim political theologians have come to agree that the umma is the true caliph. Philosopher Andrew March calls this doctrine the *caliphate of man*.[105]

Dhimmis

From the beginning, Muslim societies contained non-Muslims. Some of these people—Christians and Jews—qualify as "People of the Book" (*Ahl al-Kitab*). As monotheists with some true revelation, they merit toleration. Christians and Jews constitute most *dhimmi*s: non-Muslims in Muslim-run polities who have protected status. Dhimmis may practice their faith, subject to limitations. Within Islamic law and politics, dhimmis lack the same rights as Muslims. I return to this below.

Shura (Consultation)

The idea of the caliphate of man connects with the Islamic doctrine of shura, or consultation. Shura does not require a democratic choice based on popular sovereignty. Sovereignty belongs to God. The umma has authority on loan from him and may make political decisions as it pleases, though only if the legal order rests on the shari'ah. The shari'ah binds legitimate democratic action, much as liberal rights bind legislation in liberal countries.

Shura applies to the entire umma and does not distinguish among races, nationalities, castes, or social statuses, because all Muslims merit the same treatment. But the dhimmis lack the same political rights as the umma unless the umma extends power to them. The umma must recognize basic human rights, but it has no universal obligation to assign dhimmis equal political liberties.

Divine Sovereignty

The chief duty and virtue in Islam are submission to God's will. The Muslim recognizes Allah as sovereign in all aspects of life—God determines the course of the universe and society. Yes, humans have free will. Nonetheless, all authority over humans originates in God. God loans us his authority to command, legislate, and punish.

---

[105] March 2019.

Unity of Secular and Sacred

Islamic political theology does not distinguish between church and state because all religious and political authority flows from God through the umma and the shari'ah. The umma has both sacred and secular authority. Islam supports a class of jurists, the ulema, to interpret the shari'ah, but it rejects Catholicism's sharp distinction between religious and political offices. Indeed, in this respect, Islamic political theology relates to politics in a fashion unique among world religions.[106]

Fitra

Muslims believe that God has structured human nature (*fitra*). God alone satisfies us. Since our fitra desires God, it includes an inherent desire to know and obey God's law. The fitra also includes our other natural inclinations, which God gave us. Humans tend to err on moral matters—in contrast to some forms of Christianity, though, Islam teaches that people can resist immoral behavior.

Fitra and the Shari'ah

Sayyid Qutb argues that the shari'ah fits human nature by affirming, as March puts it, "the practicality and ease of Islamic law."[107] Islamic law makes easy and mostly painless demands. According to Qutb, "God created man's nature in harmony with the universe," such that Islam unifies "all powers and stabilities" and "all desires and inclinations."[108] In doing so, Islam made humans' efforts coherent.[109] Rached Ghannouchi agrees that Islam "is the religion that reflects human nature [*fitra*] at creation, and thus expresses humanity's desires and its deepest needs."[110]

Muslims often criticize Christians for adopting an overly demanding moral code. Christian morality distorts our fitra. The shari'ah, in contrast, asks the right amount of human beings. The fit between fitra and shari'ah is critical to the Islamic political ideal because Islamic Democrats want social stability to arise from moral motivation. This commitment connects Islamic Democrats to their Catholic and Confucian cousins. None of our religious anti-liberals embraces pure legal force.

---

[106] Hamid 2016, p. 242.
[107] March 2019, p. 115.
[108] March 2019, p. 130.
[109] For explanation, see March 2019, p. 130nn 50–51.
[110] Ghannouchi 2020, p. 25 (see also p. 120).

Anti-Liberalism

Islamic law prohibits forced conversion and protects freedom of conscience to a large extent. Islamic regimes recognize many rights associated with liberalism. These include the right to private property, rights to aid, and the right to equal treatment under the law. Some governments recognize voting rights for all Muslims.

In other respects, Islamic political thought contradicts liberalism. Islamic regimes ban blasphemy and, in general, any free speech rights that approximate those found in the West. Free speech rights have, at best, a prudential basis. Further, Islamic authorities appear to be required to punish apostasy and even to treat it as a capital crime, so Muslim states can sharply limit their subjects' religious liberty.

Islamic regimes adopt perfectionism and reject liberal neutralism—non-Muslims have fewer political rights than Muslims. The liberal tradition opposes preferential treatment based on religion. Many Muslims reject liberalism for this reason.

The Caliphate of Man

The caliph once ruled the umma. His office, or *caliphate*, claims the adherence of all Muslims. As noted, Atatürk abolished the caliphate. But, according to Sunni Muslims, no human can truly abolish the caliphate, so the office must still exist and represent Muslim political unity.[111]

So who is the caliph? Islamic political theologians have converged on a new answer: the umma is the caliph. As March puts it, the office of caliph "is the collective right of all those who accept and admit God's absolute sovereignty over themselves and adopt the Divine Code, conveyed through the Prophet, as the law above all Laws and Regulations."[112] Muslims, in their status as the caliph-umma, choose political officials. The doctrine of shura no longer limits itself to mere consultation: by expressing the caliph's will, shura now justifies the umma's democratic authority. Islamic Democracy can embrace democracy, more so than the Way of the Humane Authority. Surprisingly, many Salafi Muslims have a higher view of democracy than Catholic integralists do.

[111] Brown 2017, p. 155.
[112] March 2019, p. 106. Also see Mawdudi 1955, p. 114.

Islamic Democracy

In formulating the Islamic ideal, I focus on contemporary Sunni Islamic political theology. Sunni political theologians accept a political model called *Islamic Democracy*.[113] According to this model, God confers legitimacy through divine command.[114] Islamic society creates a social environment conducive to virtue through obedience to the shari'ah—God's central commands—and thereby renders God his due.

God legitimizes a social order in two ways. First, the shari'ah summarizes God's unalterable commands, which limit how legitimate states may govern. The shari'ah limits the people's sovereignty, "which is not free to violate God's law and its moral commands."[115] Second, God deputizes the umma as his vicegerent,[116] and so the umma may make authoritative political choices. In one sense, Islamic Democracy postulates a social contract between rulers and subjects. The umma can construct a democracy so long as the shari'ah constrains legislation; the umma can choose its leaders as it wishes.

The political theologians of Islamic Democracy reject liberal democracy because it fails to discourage bad democratic outcomes. Sometimes democratic people choose evil. But if God binds the will of the umma to the shari'ah, Islamic Democracy will never legitimize bad results. In this way, sovereignty in Islam is "dual," divided between the shari'ah and the umma.[117]

March claims that the caliphate-of-man doctrine suffuses contemporary Islamic political thought and grounds Islamic Democracy.[118] I will thus treat Islamic Democracy as a political ideal.

I should stress the historical novelty of Islamic Democracy.[119] The doctrine represents the modern Islamist movement, which is enormous. But it arose with the fall of the caliphate and the associated secularization movements. Further, Islamic Democrats have often supported dictators and military coups. Islamic Democracy is anathema in Saudi Arabia since the Saudi government bans Qutbist Islamism (for opposition to monarchy).

Nonetheless, Islamic Democracy is continuous with Islamic political thought. Classical Islamic political thought defends a monarchical caliphate that derives

---

[113] March 2019, p. 10.

[114] March (2019, pp. 16–17) interprets Islamic theories of legitimacy as theories of *sovereignty*. A sovereign regime is a source of ultimate lawmaking authority. It has ultimate interpretative and adjudicative authority and supreme legitimate coercive power.

[115] March 2019, pp. 11–12; Mawdudi 1955, p. 117; Tamimi 2001, pp. 98–99.

[116] March 2019, p. 11.

[117] March 2019, p. 12.

[118] March 2019, p. 11.

[119] I am grateful to Mustafa Akyol for discussion on this point.

legitimacy from enforcing the shari'ah. Islamic Democracy arose naturally following the abolition of the monarchical caliphate.

Abu'l A'la Mawdudi and Sayyid Qutb

Two of the leading contemporary influences on Islamic Democracy are Mawdudi and Qutb. March calls them "high utopian" Islamists who reject Western governance ideals.[120]

Qutb in particular inspired Salafi jihadis that Americans often confuse with all Muslims.[121] These idiosyncratic Salafists have a rationale for taking violent actions. All sovereignty comes from God, and human authority must observe the shari'ah. If a society does not respect the shari'ah, that casts its legitimacy into doubt. Muslims may impose shari'ah law on it. In so doing, they establish a just and legitimate regime.

For Qutb and Mawdudi, jihad does not conquer and suppress. Both agree with the Qur'anic claim that there is no compulsion in matters of religion (Qur'an 2:256). They argue instead that non-Muslim regimes oppress people and that Muslim governments alone serve as forces of liberation. Islam ends exploitation, protects liberty, implements social justice, and promotes virtue. Mawdudi explains, "The Islamic political community is . . . a republic of virtue" and its "shared purposes and virtues" determine institutional design.[122]

Qutb stresses that Islam respects freedom of conscience and opposes oppression and slavery. Islam treats all Muslims as equals. And jihad creates conditions in which people can freely choose to convert.

Mawdudi and Qutb had different aims in articulating their doctrines. Mawdudi helped lay the foundation for the Pakistani constitution and sought to base Pakistan's legal system on the shari'ah, which legitimizes the constitution.

Following Qutb's imprisonment, Qutb became deeply committed to liberating Islamic nations from colonialism and leading them out of *jahiliyyah*, a state of ignorance of Islam. Jahiliyyah refers to the state of Arabian ignorance of Allah before Muhammad. Qutb renovated Islamic political thought by applying jahiliyyah to Islamic nations that fall short of the ideal.[123] His book *Milestones* defends comprehensive jihad to restore Islamic civilization to its former glory.

Qutb rejects democracy as a theory of legitimacy because democratic theory tends to place government by the people above divine sovereignty. His ideal still

---

[120] March 2019, p. 75.

[121] Brown 2017, p. 301.

[122] Mawdudi 1955, p. 187.

[123] Qutb 2020. Indeed, jahiliyyah is far more comprehensive—it is subjugation to non-Islamic culture, values, and thought. I thank Andrew March for pressing me to say more here.

bases a regime on shura. Recognized community leaders nominate candidates, and the community then chooses one of them to rule.[124]

While Qutb and Mawdudi remain influential, Islamic Democrats widely reject their justifications for religious violence. Theorists overwhelmingly view jihad as the defense of Islam.

While Mawdudi and Qutb thought their societies (Pakistan and Egypt, respectively) fell far short of the Islamic ideal, they did not believe society could become Islamic through conquest. Both men recognized that the transition to Islamic democracy occurs gradually.[125] They even backed off from imposing the hudud punishments: Mawdudi claims that a government should impose the hudud only when the government becomes fully just and adequately Islamic. So, like Jiang Qing, Mawdudi and Qutb think that religious revival must precede "integralism." The ideas of all three contrast with Vermeule's integration from within.

Rached Ghannouchi

Let's turn to a more recent figure, Rached Ghannouchi, a Tunisian politician and the leading theorist of Islamic Democracy. Ghannouchi founded Tunisia's Ennahda Party and serves as its intellectual authority. He has played a central role in promoting democratic ideals in Islam, even while in exile. He was the third speaker of Tunisia's Assembly of the Representatives of the People.

Ghannouchi adopts Islamic Democracy, but he has drawn Islamic thought away from "the polarizing ideas of Mawdudi and Qutb."[126] For Ghannouchi, Islamic political thought draws on a comprehensive metaphysic. God created and governs everything, including all knowledge and law. God distinguishes humanity from other creatures by giving us reason, will, freedom, and responsibility. He even provides a divine path for human life and deputizes humans with his authority.[127]

Ghannouchi defends the caliphate-of-man theory. He summarizes the covenant of vicegerency as the "God's Shari'a and consultation of the people."[128] Ghannouchi thus embraces the Islamic Democratic ideal.

---

[124] Sec. 8 in William E. Shepard, "Sayyid Qutb (1906–1966)," *The Internet Encyclopedia of Philosophy*, accessed December 14, 2022, https://iep.utm.edu/qutb/#H8.

[125] Mawdudi, p. 95. Qutb 2020, p. 10.

[126] Esposito and Shahin 2013, p. 3. Indeed, Ghannouchi's list parallels Mawdudi's (see March 2019, pp. 110–11, 152).

[127] See Ghannouchi 2020, p. 43.

[128] Ghannouchi 2020, p. 127. Here Ghannouchi is quoting Al-Najjar 1998.

Ghannouchi's constitutionalism consists of six principles that reconcile democratic and divine sovereignty:[129]

1. Constitutional design is open within the bounds of the shari'ah, and Muslims can use independent reasoning (*ijtihad*) to argue for particular institutional structures. No definitive Islamic texts support specific choices, and valid interpretations abound. But they all honor God's will as the Qur'an and Sunna express it.
2. Islam favors cooperation and interpretation over a (Madisonian) conflict model of politics with competing political parties. Party politics can cause serious problems.[130] We must set aside the idea of a struggle between these groups. Better is a cooperative and mutually supporting model for political and other relationships.
3. The umma must prioritize preserving moral unity above managing competition, though it need not concentrate powers in the hands of a few. The umma must structure political institutions so as to not war with itself.
4. A shura-based democracy can promote Muslim unity as a practice that renders salient Muslims' commitment to their creed. Shura also allows many interpretations of the shari'ah, limiting conflict between Muslims.
5. Shura-based democracy ensures that all offices are accountable to the people. If the head of state answers only to parliament, the leader's oath of allegiance becomes a formality—the leader is no "longer truly responsible to the people." The constitution should mandate a particular promise for each state body. Each political leader swears an oath to the umma, God, and his messenger. The leader can then "respect the people's will, and abides by mutual consultation."[131]
6. We need norms to preserve democracy other than the separation of powers. Separating power cannot stop oligarchy. A unitary approach to politics, in contrast, "remains immune to creedal conflicts and special interests" owing to "its unitary religious nature, which favors complementarity and harmony."[132]

For Ghannouchi, divine sovereignty manifests itself in three ways: (1) through a perfectionist approach to politics; (2) through a voluntarist and positivist divine law, where God is the ultimate source of law and legal authority and his commands *make* law; and (3) through authority for jurists who understand divine law.[133]

[129] March 2019, p. 185; White and Siddiqui 2013, p. 147.
[130] Ghannouchi's later political activism shows that he changed his mind on this point.
[131] Ghannouchi 2020, p. 326.
[132] March 2019, p. 186.
[133] March 2019, p. 163.

Ghannouchi thinks Islamic political theology supports a moral revolution. Islamic scholar Azzam Tamimi summarizes Ghannouchi's thought as follows. For Ghannouchi, Islam is a "comprehensive revolution against idols and despots" and aims to "emancipate man from all kinds of servitude except God."[134] The Islamic state establishes a community founded on the good and on justice. It recognizes truth and invalidates falsehood across the earth.[135]

Ghannouchi rejects violent jihad, and he accords non-Muslims and women far more rights than Mawdudi, Qutb, or their followers do. He has also demonstrated a remarkable willingness to compromise with non-Muslim Tunisians. For example, he says that Islamic regimes should decriminalize homosexuality (though they should ban same-sex marriage).[136]

We can see that the caliphate-of-man doctrine allows for a wide range of laws and policies. Despite this broad range, I contend that Islamic Democracy fits my framework.

The Framework

We can now apply the anti-liberalism framework to Islamic Democracy.

History

Here I can be brief. The Islamic Democratic ideal faces much less Muslim opposition than Catholic integralism and the Way of the Humane Authority. Indeed, Islamic Democracy might prevail among Sunni Muslim theologians (though they will of course differ on how to realize the ideal in constitutional design).

Islamic law forms the heart of Islam, a relatively youthful faith (it is 1,400 years old). So Islam has relatively well-documented records of past legal regimes. Islamic Democrats can more easily establish institutional continuity with the past than Catholic integralists or Confucian advocates of the WHA. Continuity buttresses the argument that Islamic tradition favors the Islamic Democratic ideal.

On the other hand, one might argue that the "democratic" part of the ideal is quite recent and requires development from the doctrine of shura. The development might be in error because Islam requires elites to sharply limit the will of the people.

[134] Tamimi 2001, p. 75.
[135] Ghannouchi 2020, pp. 120–21. See also March 2019, p. 184n65.
[136] I am grateful to Andrew March for discussion on this point.

Symmetry

The Islamic symmetry argument makes itself. Islamic Democrats, with most Muslims, see Islam as a unified approach to social life. Mawdudi claims that we must not separate politics and religion "into water-tight compartments," because separation invites irreconcilable conflict between distinct institutions.[137]

Qutb advocates Islam on the basis of its seamless union of all aspects of life, spiritual and ordinary: "Islam chose to unite earth and heaven in a single system." This unity arises "both in the heart of the individual and in the actuality of so-ciety." Islam recognizes "no separation of practical exertion from religious im-pulse."[138] Islam is "essentially a unity."[139] As God's vicegerent, the umma has both spiritual and temporal authority.[140] Ghannouchi agrees. Islam grounds a unified law and politics. In general, Islamic Democrats deny that Islam draws fine lines between natural and supernatural goods, nor do they teach that Allah authorizes distinct institutions to promote each class of good.

One reason for this is that Islam has a much weaker natural law tradition than Catholicism and Confucianism.[141] Catholicism and Confucianism can identify a basis for political authority in natural reason, and the state can draw its authority from its promotion of natural goods. Islam disagrees somewhat. Law originates in the divine will as opposed to the divine intellect, as with Catholic natural law. Islamic law forms through divine commands directed at all aspects of existence. These commands are eternal and immutable, but we become aware of them through revelation, not merely or even mostly by reason. So Islamic political theologians do not separate the spiritual and the natural as modes of detecting the human good.[142]

Qutb echoes the dominant tradition: Islamic theology and history provide no basis for separating Islam from society. Indeed, Qutb claims that embracing separation means embracing Christianity.[143]

The history and symmetry arguments for Islamic Democracy have power, more than parallel arguments for Catholic integralism and the Way of the Humane Authority. We can now turn to the counterarguments.

---

[137] Mawdudi 1955, p. 22.

[138] Qutb 1953, p. 26.

[139] Qutb 1953, p. 27.

[140] Qutb 1953, p. 30.

[141] Though not compared with Protestant Christianity, which has often rejected the doctrine of natural law. I thank Ben Peterson for discussion on this point. For discussion of the natural law tradi-tion within Islam, see Akyol 2022.

[142] Though, as David Johnston points out, Ghannouchi allows natural reason to figure into the umma's deliberations about which constitutional structures to adopt.

[143] Qutb 1953, p. 32.

Transition

I once thought that Islamic Democracy would avoid Catholic integralist transition difficulties. Islamic regimes better approximated the Islamic Democratic ideal than Catholic regimes. I was not wholly wrong, but I did not understand how thoroughly European powers suppressed or at least co-opted the shari'ah. Islamic Democrats think that European colonial oppression wrecked Muslim civilization. As author Shadi Hamid puts it, many Muslims have a sense of loss and long for the "organic legal and political order that flourished for centuries."[144]

Qutb, for instance, thought that most Islamic nations were Islamic in name only: "Islamic society today is not Islamic in any sense of the word."[145] The Islamic community long ago "vanished from existence." Leadership passed "to other ideologies and other nations, other concepts and other systems."[146] Modern Muslims live in jahiliyyah: "There is no Islamic state to establish Islamic law or to raise armies."[147]

If Mawdudi and Qutb are correct, non-Islamic states lack legitimacy, and one may use violent means to overthrow those regimes and establish Islam.[148] But the vast majority of Muslims have feared that Qutbists in particular can impose their doctrines only by using enormous violence, in violation of Islam. Qutb understands this fear well enough. He argues at length that early Islamic conquests did not oppress, but rescued and liberated: "The Islamic conquests, then, were not wars of aggression."[149] But whatever is true of the past, these militaristic movements create enormous civil strife today; they undermine Islam more than they support it.

Islamic nations also struggle to transition from oligarchy. As we saw in the Arab Spring, democratization movements often destabilize. One source of conflict originates in the fact that democratization movements often receive considerable support from the Muslim Brotherhood. Since the Muslim Brotherhood adopts Islamic Democracy, non-Muslims (and some Muslims) resist it when it comes to power, as the fate of Mohamed Morsi in Egypt illustrates.[150] Islamic nations have had dictators because dictators impose peace on groups that would

---

[144] Hamid 2016, p. 12.
[145] Qutb 1953, p. 262.
[146] Qutb 2020, p. 10.
[147] Brown 2017, p. 301.
[148] This is a central theme of *Milestones* (Qutb 2020).
[149] Qutb 1953, p. 198.
[150] For more on the Muslim Brotherhood, see Hamid (2016), Brown (2017), and March (2019). Morsi's case is complex: Abdul Fattah al-Sisi took advantage of mass popular protests against Morsi's regime in June 2013. A large minority wanted Morsi out of power. I thank David Johnston for discussion on this topic.

otherwise fight. Attempts to transition to Islamic Democracy may thus produce bloodshed and dictatorship.

Both Qutbist and Mawdudian radical ideal theory and Ghannouchian moderation face transition barriers.

Stability

Assume that an Islamic society establishes democracy and empowers an Islamic judiciary to sustain and interpret the shari'ah. The ideal society also contains significant religious minorities (as a near-permanent and universal feature of Muslim societies). The flaws in our fitra will create some pluralism among these groups, as will the simple indeterminacy of moral and political reasoning. With Andrew March, one can argue that ethical consensus will prove elusive.[151] The unequal treatment of non-Muslims will also create resistance, which one observes in Muslim societies with a significant Christian minority.

Islamic Democrats seek moralized stability. Qutb and others stress that the shari'ah suits our fitra.[152] Indeed, Qutb's realistic utopia rests "on his use of the claim to harmony between the shari'ah and fitra."[153] Christianity speaks to our spiritual nature, communism speaks to our material nature—but Islam combines the two, creating peace and stability.[154] Islamic political theologians reject modi vivendi. Here they align with their Catholic and Confucian cousins.

March claims that Islamic Democracy "must remain at the level of ideal theory," since even Ghannouchi's view requires unrealistic "moral consensus around religion."[155] Reaching consensus necessitates extensive coercion and "long-term subject formation."[156] Qutb's thought invites a paradox. To have a stable and just political order, we must reach a social, moral consensus, but such an order is a "prerequisite for such a moral consensus in the first place."[157]

Mawdudi faces a related challenge. He argued that Pakistan should become ideologically homogeneous, one that limits non-Muslim participation in public life. Otherwise, Mawdudi argues, genuine religious leadership cannot flourish.[158]

[151] March 2019, p. xxii.
[152] March 2019, p. 115–18. Qutb is not alone here. Hassan Al-Banna argues that "Islam's comprehensiveness makes it fit for human *fitra*." Consequently, it can influence "not only the majority of people but elites as well," and so Islam "uplifts the human soul and sanctifies universal brotherhood" (quoted in Moussalli 2013, p. 134).
[153] March 2019, p. 121.
[154] Qutb 1953, p. 45.
[155] March 2019, p. xxii.
[156] March 2019, p. xxii.
[157] March 2019, p. 146.
[158] White and Siddiqui 2013, p. 149.

Islam forms a complete system of life—"an ideology, a civilization, and a legal-political order" all at once.[159] But no Islamic society can institutionalize such a system given such societies' dramatic ethical disagreements.

When Muslim regimes transition to democracy, disagreements arise owing to the great ideological distance between Sunni Islamic Democrats and everyone else. Dissenters include secular liberals, Christians, Jews, Hindus, and Shias. Islamic theorists may embrace some repression to address pluralism, following Mawdudi and Qutb. The Salafists that followed them reject pluralism as a "good thing" and often advocate political violence.[160] Some Salafi movements (such as the Islamic State group) indicate that some younger Muslims have warmed to the political ideas of Mawdudi and the later Qutb.[161]

The other response to pluralism involves moderation. As an example, Ghannouchi allowed other Tunisian political parties to reduce the Tunisian constitution's embrace of shari'ah law.[162] The Arab Spring suggested that other Muslim societies would pursue similar compromises.

But neither Salafi movements nor the Arab Spring provided long-term stability, if they provided stability at all. Neither group grapples with pluralism effectively. March argues that pluralism creates a dilemma in Muslim polities: opposing pluralism creates violence and repression, whereas welcoming pluralism waters down Islamic Democracy. Because of pluralism, we cannot have a "fully Islamic and fully democratic" political theory, which requires eliminating "sovereignty as the organizing problem for Islam and politics."[163]

Islamic regimes have maintained considerable institutional continuity compared with Confucian and Catholic regimes. Muslim confessional states litter recent human history. Through mechanisms such as the *jizya* tax, Muslims have converted non-Muslim societies. But pluralism poses a pressing problem, one that has riven Muslim communities and made democratization more difficult.

The Injustice of Islamic Democracy: The Dhimmi Dilemma

Justice arguments identify conflicts between norms of justice internal to religious anti-liberalisms. Islamic Democracy pits egalitarian principles against the rules that subjugate non-Muslims—that is, dhimmis. Muslim regimes violate equality

---

[159] White and Siddiqui 2013, p. 145.
[160] Brown 2017, p. 339.
[161] Brown 2017, p. 338.
[162] March 2019, p. 213.
[163] March 2019, p. 154.

when they restrict the political rights of non-Muslims. Dhimmis have second-class citizenship in the Islamic Democratic ideal, yet Islamic Democrats say their ideal treats people as equals. The problem arises even in Ghannouchi's work.

Let's start by exploring the norms of equality and freedom that Islamic Democrats adopt. For Mawdudi, Islam forbids "racial, caste, or ethnic distinction" and instead distinguishes people based on whether they agree with Islam.[164] Qutb claims that systems based on "subservience" to others will fail. An Islamic order must establish equality because Islam recognizes that "all men come everywhere as equals."[165] Islam establishes justice on the basis of "absolute freedom of conscience."[166] With equality and mutual responsibility, freedom defines social justice.[167]

But let's focus on Ghannouchi, who is both more contemporary than Mawdudi and Qutb and closer to Thomas Pink and to Jiang Qing. Ghannouchi does not use the term *dhimmi*, which connotes lower *legal* status. Ghannouchi instead argues that non-Muslims have a lower level of *citizenship*, and so only a lower *political* status. For Ghannouchi, the dhimmi dilemma arises from the unequal citizenship of non-Muslims.

In *Public Freedoms in the Islamic State*, Ghannouchi defends equal freedom for all.[168] Without public freedoms, an Islamic state would fail to establish justice or "free humanity from tyranny."[169] Islam is a revolution "that uproots tyranny and subjection from God's earth and conquers for the sake of the oppressed, whether men, women, or youth."[170] The revolution is egalitarian; non-Muslims merit equal treatment.[171] Everyone deserves honor "regardless of nationality, color or creed, or any social characteristic."[172]

Non-Muslims have "equality of rights and duties."[173] Islam gives every religious community expansive religious liberty. All communities have "the right to establish places of worship and follow their own rituals,"[174] though they must respect "public opinion and the general feelings of the majority." Non-Muslims can participate in government so long as they remain in the minority; the

[164] Mawdudi 1955, p. 111.
[165] Qutb 1953, p. 30. Also see Akhavi 2013, p. 163.
[166] Qutb 1953, p. 52.
[167] Qutb 1953, p. 92.
[168] Ghannouchi 2020, p. 17.
[169] Ghannouchi 2020, p. 19.
[170] Ghannouchi 2020, p. 21.
[171] Ghannouchi 2020, p. 58.
[172] Ghannouchi 2020, p. 66.
[173] Ghannouchi 2020, p. 58.
[174] Ghannouchi 2020, p. 58.

shari'ah contains no objection to non-Muslims serving in the shura assembly in that case.[175]

But now consider the other side of the dhimmi dilemma: the rationales for subjugating non-Muslims. Mawdudi argues that Islam prescribes two types of citizenship.[176] To be in the first class, you must have "faith in Islam and the nationality of an Islamic State."[177] Mawdudi excludes dhimmis from high political office. They must "pay the jizya poll tax" and endure restrictions on public religious practice in "purely Muslim habitations." Mawdudi thought that dhimmis "are not entitled to build new places of worship," though this restriction does not apply to areas not overwhelmingly Muslim.[178] The state must prohibit dhimmi practices that prove "detrimental to the public interest."[179] Minorities may nonetheless adopt their own "personal law," since personal legal systems should not endanger the Islamic state.[180]

Dhimmis can demand protections for their (more limited) rights. They can serve in parliament if they accept the Qur'an and Sunna as the chief source of public law, but they have no right to request that Muslims throw their "ideology overboard." Muslims should not pass laws against their convictions to "appease" dhimmis.[181]

Ghannouchi defends a two-level theory of citizenship. To enjoy full public rights, such as the right to be elected to high office, non-Muslims must convert; if they refuse, Muslims cannot allow them to "create obstacles for the state's proper functioning." They must instead form parties to lobby for their rights, though they may do so only if they obey "the principles and directives of Islam."[182]

Ghannouchi excludes non-Muslims from serving as head of state. A non-Muslim president would "pose a direct threat to the identity of that state—that is, to its public order."[183] Indeed, if non-Muslims had full citizenship, the regime could destabilize. No nation can stabilize unless it has "a consensus over the fixed parameters of its creed, identity, or mission."[184] No one can reasonably ask an Islamic state to allow threats to its integrity.[185] Non-Muslims can receive citizenship only if they support the state, recognize its legitimacy, and safeguard its

---

[175] Ghannouchi 2020, p. 170.
[176] Mawdudi 1955, p. 143.
[177] Mawdudi 1955, p. 143.
[178] Mawdudi 1955, p. 183.
[179] Mawdudi 1955, p. 149.
[180] Mawdudi 1955, p. 45.
[181] Mawdudi 1955, p. 45.
[182] Ghannouchi 2020, p. 398.
[183] Ghannouchi 2020, p. 202.
[184] Ghannouchi 2020, p. 398.
[185] Ghannouchi 2020, p. 395.

public: "Non-Muslims have no other recourse but to recognize the role of Islam as the faith of the majority in organizing and orienting public life. They may not create obstacles for the state's proper functioning but may form parties that lobby for rights that are allowed under the Islamic Shari'a, like being elected to the Shura Council and seeking to redress injustices. They may also join Islamic parties.""[186]

Here Ghannouchi faces the second half of the dilemma. Non-Muslims are second-class citizens. They lack full political rights unless they change religions. The Islamic state qualifies their citizenship.[187]

Attempts to Resolve the Dhimmi Dilemma

Islam teaches that all people are equals, have liberty of conscience, and may rightly take part in politics. And yet dhimmis must endure inequality with Muslims regarding political freedoms. Can we resolve this tension?

Mawdudi answers by accusing the West of hypocrisy. Western nations treat people unequally despite their official embrace of equality as a moral standard.[188] Ghannouchi makes a similar argument.[189] But hypocritical practice of religious liberty does not undermine the argument for religious liberty. If Western nations violate their own standards, they should stop violating them.

Some claim that Islamic regimes treat non-Muslims as equals by tolerating them. But toleration and equality are not the same. As others have highlighted, mere toleration legitimizes some unequal treatment, at least de facto. Toleration does not imply relations of equality. The Qur'an teaches that people have equal dignity and worth. But, according to Islamic Democrats, dhimmis have less importance in politics.[190] And Islamic regimes still often mistreat dhimmis, which suggests that these regimes' commitment to toleration is "fragile and contingent."[191]

If dhimmis have equal political rights, Islamic states might treat them better. With more political power, dhimmis could fight harder for equal treatment and so create more stability. Ghannouchi grasps the problem. But equality does not require ignoring threats to public order. Instead, Muslims can preserve an Islamic state only if they limit the political power of non-Muslims.[192] The state

---

[186] Ghannouchi 2020, p. 398.

[187] Tamimi 2001, p. 77.

[188] Mawdudi 1955, p. 172.

[189] Ghannouchi 2020.

[190] Warren and Gilmore 2014, p. 218.

[191] El Fadl 2002, p. 13.

[192] Ghannouchi 2020, p. 202.

"allows specific exceptions to the rule of equality by distinguishing between Muslims and non-Muslims, in relation to particular conditions attached to certain high government offices required by the nature of the state and its general framework."[193]

Stability trumps equality. Ghannouchi allows violations of the Islamic principle of equality to ensure political stability. And yet Ghannouchi feels compelled to justify the inequality. For the non-Muslim,

> The non-Muslim citizen of an Islamic state has the right to preserve his religious and cultural specificities, for instance in what he eats or drinks, or in his marital life. Furthermore, he is excused from some of the duties incumbent upon Muslims, like abstaining from certain prohibitions. Nevertheless, these represent a few exceptions and do not infringe upon the principle of equality, which is the principal value observed by the Islamic state.[194]

While non-Muslims have fewer freedoms in some respects, they have more freedoms in others. The additional liberties balance the restrictions.

The balance is a false one: dhimmis should not view these liberties as compensatory. Why? God forbids those freedoms to his flock in order to make them freer than they would otherwise be. Ghannouchi defines Islamic freedom as "a trust, a responsibility, an awareness of truth, and an adherence to it, sincerity in seeking it, and a sacrifice of everything, including oneself, for its sake.[195] That's the freedom that matters. So Ghannouchi does not offer non-Muslims freedoms they ought to value by his own judgment.

Ghannouchi also thinks the restricted freedoms are few in number, so restricting them does not violate the principle of equality much. He admits that inequalities exist. Yet Ghannouchi maintains, once again, that equality is the *principal value* of an Islamic state.

Ghannouchi can respond by arguing that equality is the central value observed by a *stable* Islamic state. Stability trumps equality because, otherwise, no Islamic state can exist. Once the government stabilizes, *then* it should try to establish equality. So the state's government can violate equality, but only to ensure its survival.

If equal political rights undermine Islamic states, one might agree with Ghannouchi. In that case Islamic Democrats' hands are tied. They can, at most, support the greatest equality compatible with the state's continued existence.

---

[193] Ghannouchi 2020, p. 203.
[194] Ghannouchi 2020, p. 396.
[195] Ghannouchi 2020, p. 44.

Ghannouchi does not argue that equal political rights create instability, but any such argument must unfold as follows: (1) If non-Muslims have equal political rights, they could co-opt the state or make it less Islamic. (2) But if they have second-class citizenship, then the Islamic state is secure.

Is either claim true? Maybe. If the non-Muslim population is small, equal citizenship shouldn't affect stability much because non-Muslims cannot co-opt the state. And if non-Muslims attain high office, they must bend to the will of the Muslim majority that has greater political power. On the other hand, second-class citizenship could protect the Islamic character of the state from a high official's non-Muslim values.

However, public acknowledgment of two classes of citizenship may create problems too. Consider how non-Muslims may view their second-class status. They may regard themselves as oppressed by the Islamic state and stigmatized as inferior. Non-Muslims might respond with rebellion. Treating people unequally could create more instability than stability. It has done so in the past.

Ghannouchi insists that equality is central to Islamic Democracy, which puts the burden of proof on those who defend unequal political rights. Ghannouchi needs an argument that stability requires political disparities. We should otherwise doubt that equality and stability conflict, and so we should assign non-Muslims equal political rights. Thus, if Islamic Democracy must embrace dhimmi inequality, then Islamic Democracy is unjust—on its own terms.

These brief reflections do not refute Islamic Democracy. I have only sketched the dhimmi dilemma and discussed a few ways of resolving it. But I have said enough to show the usefulness of my framework. For example, Islamic Democrats may face a dilemma akin to the justice argument against Catholic integralism. The four other arguments apply to Islamic Democracy as well.

The Framework Vindicated

We can engage anti-liberal political theologies with five arguments. The first two arguments support anti-liberalism:

1. History arguments claim that the political theology receives the support of a religious tradition.
2. Symmetry arguments assert that, if members of these religions embrace political perfectionism about natural goods, they have good reason to press for governments to promote higher, supernatural goods.

The last three arguments run as follows:

3. Transition arguments draw our attention to the grave costs one must pay to transition to an anti-liberal regime. These include the cost of violating the tenets of one's faith.
4. Stability arguments illustrate the ideal of moral stability central to all three political theologies: all oppose modus vivendi regimes. But the forces of natural and unnatural pluralism outweigh stabilizing forces.
5. Finally, Islamic Democracy and Catholic integralism face justice dilemmas: Catholics face the baptism dilemma, while Muslims face the dhimmi dilemma. (Confucians can probably escape a similar justice dilemma.)

We thus have a framework with which to engage religious anti-liberal viewpoints. Most of my readers align with the liberal tradition (classical or egalitarian), and many have no religious affiliation. Readers may struggle to assess history arguments associated with unfamiliar faith traditions, but we can have cross-framework discussions about symmetry, transition, stability, and justice. Liberals can engage anti-liberals without presupposing liberal principles.

Epilogue

Reconciliation

We have come a long way in a short time. I have taken you on a tour of integralism's strengths and weaknesses and a short trek through Islamic Democracy and the Way of the Humane Authority. I hope my readers have each found the value they sought. But don't go yet. I want to speak to all of you: anti-liberals, postliberals, and liberals. To do so, I will introduce a new integralist strategy that can satisfy postliberals and even fit within a liberal framework. *What if all three groups could get along?* Allow me to present *integration writ small*.

Integration Writ Small

The Monastic Republic of Mount Athos, located in northern Greece, has existed for over a thousand years. Its citizens: two thousand Eastern Orthodox monks living in twenty monasteries and many supplementary *sketes*. Their purpose? *Theosis*: the transformation of man into the divine likeness.[1]

The monks maintain the practices they adopted under the Byzantine Empire. They even follow the same (Julian) calendar. They keep strict fasts, live in community, work with their hands, celebrate divine liturgies (religious services), and strive to pray without ceasing (1 Thess. 5:17). After centuries of experimentation, the monks hit upon a prayer that adorns their every breath: "Lord Jesus Christ, Son of God, have mercy on me, a sinner"—the Jesus Prayer.

Since 1990, as historically Orthodox countries have shed the yoke of communism, Athos has experienced a revival. The territory has welcomed many new monks, novices, and pilgrims. Its inhabitants have restored churches and monasteries. The Orthodox Church has recently canonized ("glorified")

---

[1] Charles River Editors 2018. Russell (2009) provides an excellent overview of the Orthodox doctrine of theosis.

All the Kingdoms of the World. Kevin Vallier, Oxford University Press. © Oxford University Press 2023. DOI: 10.1093/oso/9780197611371.003.0009

several Athonite monks, such as Saint Silouan, Saint Joseph the Hesychast, Saint Porphyrios, and Saint Paisios. Athonite religious practices stretch around the globe. Athos has but two thousand citizens, yet it influences millions.

Athos is an integralist republic, if not a Catholic one.[2] Its government attends to temporal and spiritual matters. The spiritual domain has primacy. The monks rule themselves, by and large. But they submit to a temporal power and a spiritual power. The Greek Ministry of Foreign Affairs appoints their governor, and the patriarch of Constantinople—the closest office the Orthodox have to a pope—supervises their spiritual affairs.

The Athonites succeed through integration writ small. They have no interest in capturing states. Politics makes one late for liturgy. No, the Athonites set their minds on higher things. And yet their spiritual influence exceeds that of many nations.

Imagine if the Catholic integralist movement imitated the Athonites. Integralists might create dozens of Athos-like republics, lights of the world, cities "built on a hill [that] cannot be hid" (Matt. 5:14). Entrants would agree to follow canon law or leave. In time, the new republics might convince the Vatican to govern their spiritual affairs.

These republics need not form within the United States. Libertarians have created a charter city off the coast of Honduras called Próspera. Negotiations with the national government have proved difficult. Hondurans might more readily welcome a few Catholic republics off their shores.

Small societies with freedom of exit? Sounds like *liberalism*! But call an Athonite a liberal and he might ask you to repent. Or he might return to his cell and pray for your soul. The integralist strategists say that "localist" approaches like integration writ small must fail. The liberal state will not suffer them to live.[3] But integration from within is far less probable—and far more dangerous.

Integration writ small is superior in a second respect: it avoids antagonizing other conservatives. Many conservatives, especially those who lean libertarian, support political decentralization. Integralists might ally with them, encouraging them to recognize the urgency of local political autonomy. Future microrepublics might then form a bulwark against the liberal state. But the strategists have preferred to *declare war*. They trash their right-liberal forbears and "mock

[2] Though Catholics do teach that Orthodox have valid sacraments, unlike Protestants. See Joseph Ratzinger and Tarcisio Bertone, "Congregation for the Doctrine of the Faith: Note on the Expression 'Sister Churches,'" Holy See website, June 30, 2000, https://www.vatican.va/roman_curia/congregations/cfaith/documents/rc_con_cfaith_doc_20000630_chiese-sorelle_en.html.

[3] But, according to Vermeule, the state *will* hire integralists into positions of power.

or block" anyone who returns fire. This strategy serves them poorly. It creates enemies faster than friends.

Integration writ small is superior in a third way. Integralist communities can pursue their ideal without suppressing the ideals of others. They can learn much from the Athonites, who have a millennium of spiritual experience running a holy polity. They can learn from others too. Most of all, they can learn from their own heroes and history. And, in time, as they discover their political ideal, they will have much to teach us in return.

Integration from within incites hostility toward those with different ideas. The strategists make this clear every day. They show little interest in learning from those who disagree with them. They remove challengers from their community—at great price. With every harshness, they lose the opportunity for insight. Integration writ small is *smarter* because it is *kinder*.

A fourth advantage: integration writ small might bypass my criticisms. Small integralist republics face fewer transition challenges. These republics can stabilize themselves by keeping their population small and exiling dissenters. They treat others fairly: they force no one to join, allow anyone to leave, and let others form polities of their own.[4]

If integration from within is worth a shot, so is integration writ small. Indeed, integration writ small seems far superior. The strategists missed this alternative because of their limited vision and their tendency to become mired in innumerable and pointless political conflicts. But we can take a broader view. Christians should long not for an imperium but for an *archipelago*—small societies eager to learn. This is a more excellent way (1 Cor. 12:31).

Postliberalism under Liberal Institutions

Most postliberals reject integralism and other radical religious alternatives. They know that liberalism is wrong but are unsure what to do about it. I have provided postliberals with further reasons to reject religious anti-liberalisms. So what should they do now?

Localist strategies, which favor building micro-societies with rich communal bonds, hold some promise. Indeed, postliberals such as Rod Dreher and Patrick Deneen celebrated them before they came under the influence of Viktor Orbán. However, these micro-societies need the power to become micro-polities,

---

[4] And don't forget subsidiarity. Integration writ small is localist. It fits better with subsidiarity than does integration from within.

because political institutions can bolster defenses against outside threats. Recall Mount Athos.

A prior challenge is that postliberals must locate which liberalism they want to displace. Allow me to draw a distinction. An *institutional* liberal supports constitutional rights, democratic governance, markets, and the welfare state. Liberals disagree about these institutions' relative importance, especially markets. They nonetheless agree on fundamentals. *Social* liberals view liberty and equality as paramount ethical values. They believe that the noblest lives are those we live in our own way. *We* make our lives meaningful, not any higher power.

Social liberalism drove Justice Kennedy's famous remark in *Planned Parenthood v. Casey*. He claimed, "At the heart of liberty is the right to define one's own concept of existence, of meaning, of the universe, and of the mystery of human life."[5] But an institutional liberal can reject and even denounce Justice Kennedy's claim. Indeed, social and institutional liberalism might conflict. Social liberalism could lead people to suppress nonliberal doctrines, in which case nonliberals must oppose the remains of liberal order. In essence, social liberals might disrupt peace between diverse groups. Institutional liberals could respond by limiting the power of social liberals. They could do so in the name of civic freedoms and democracy.

Why don't postliberals distinguish between social and institutional liberalism? They might think separation is infeasible, but why? Yes, social and institutional liberalism correlate to some extent. But that tells us little. Further, the correlation seems weak. Many pieces of institutional liberalism predate social liberalism by centuries—in some cases, by millennia. Yes, the whole package accompanies the spread of social liberalism. But liberal institutions can take hold in societies that largely reject social liberalism. Many East Asian democracies illustrate.

The postliberal must determine the price of displacing social liberalism. It might be as high as opposing liberal institutions, but it could just as easily require *defending* liberal institutions against social liberals. Postliberal opposition to social liberalism might preserve liberal institutions. Most postliberals do not oppose such institutions, even after some grousing. They question liberal institutions chiefly because they find social liberalism pernicious. So I invite postliberals to first determine the philosophical and empirical connections between social and institutional liberalism.

Here, at the book's end, we can see the problems that arise from abandoning liberal order. Anti-liberals face both transition and stability barriers, as well as moral costs. What is the most "cost-effective" opposition to social liberalism?

---

[5] 505 U.S. 833, 851 (1992), available at https://www.law.cornell.edu/supct/html/91-744.ZO.html.

Some integralists say that the most cost-effective strategy is to capture the state and use it to crush social liberals—liberal institutions included. But integralists place too much stock in this judgment. Other postliberals can do better. Postliberals should support an exploratory order of micro-polities in which religious groups can experiment with their ideals. Varieties of postliberals can include their ideals on the list of workable micro-political orders. Integration writ small might prove attractive to some Catholics; other Christians could create their own local orders. The meta-order would reject social liberalism as a governing ideology. It could still consist of liberal institutions. But the meta-order must allow enough federalism for postliberals to secure shared spiritual goods.

Liberalism Must Adapt

Micro-polities can improve liberal order by repairing liberalism's estrangement from religion. Yes, liberal orders protect religious freedoms, but liberal cultures can still undermine communal forms of life. Micro-polities can better resist those social currents.

Most liberals, I have found, quickly dismiss these concerns. Religious freedom should suffice for people of faith, but any further demands would be unreasonable. Yet some in the liberal tradition have supported decentralization and federalism. Here classical liberals have shone the brightest. One hopes that liberalism can adapt to accommodate religious anti-liberal groups.

Liberalism must also adapt to quash the negative aspects of anti-liberal movements. These movements could grow more powerful because they have arguments that can persuade their co-religionists, which can in time generate new political expressions. Liberals must preserve liberal institutions against these new movements while a new liberalism evolves through an inter-liberal alliance I explore below.

Some will say that liberalism is a static ideology that cannot adapt to change. Not so. To make my case, I must first explain how I understand the liberal tradition.

What Is Liberalism?

The liberal tradition stresses freedom, equality, toleration, and a harmony of interests.[6] Liberals treasure each person's freedom of choice. They celebrate

---

[6] Different liberals make different values central. Michael Freeden (2015, p. 15), one of the great historians of liberalism, claims that liberalism is an ideology with seven political concepts at

human equality and insist that people consent to join social hierarchies. Liberals embrace democracy for this reason.

Liberalism was born from attempts to formulate ideals of religious toleration. It first allowed people freedom of thought and worship, which led to the freedom of speech and of the press. Liberals recognize that free reasoning produces diverse faiths and ideologies. If we are humble and respect others as equals, we must allow others to live out their own values.

Liberalism stresses that society is not a race and that politics is not a war—not by nature, anyway. Liberals endeavor to organize our social world to reduce conflict between groups with diverse interests. We must ensure that our disagreements do not erupt into violence and we must recognize that we can help each other live better than we could live apart.

Liberals differ on many issues. Some liberals stress negative liberty—the liberty of noninterference. Others stress positive liberty—the liberty of acting on one's reason and will. Liberals disagree about equality: Should we institutionalize equal opportunity or should we go further and suppress inequalities as unjust in themselves?

Toleration is also contested: Should religiously informed political activity play a large or a small role in political life? Some claim that toleration requires that people privatize their religious commitments, whereas others argue that toleration means that people can appeal to their convictions throughout their political lives.

The harmony-of-interests doctrine also takes multiple forms. Right-liberals stress the harmony of markets; left-liberals stress the harmony of democracy. Right-liberals draw inspiration from the idea that markets create peace and prosperity for all, whereas left-liberals draw inspiration from the idea that democracy does likewise.

Liberalism, Conservatism, and Socialism

To defend liberalism, we must understand its competitors. Liberalism's critics seldom model these opposing ideological forces, and this yields a simplistic analysis. I adopt a tripartite division of the prime modern political ideologies: liberalism, conservatism, and socialism.

---

its core: "liberty, rationality, individuality, progress, sociability, the general interest, and limited and accountable power." Holmes (1993, p. 4) stresses personal security, impartiality, individual liberty, and democracy.

Compared to liberalism, conservatism is less keen on freedom, stressing its costs as much as its benefits. It supports natural hierarchies and mistrusts threats to them. Conservatives allow for toleration, but not at the expense of community cohesion. We can harmonize our interests only if we order society around a common good and virtuous living. Social order must respect traditional religious institutions and beliefs.

As noted in the Introduction, socialism tends to adopt principles of equality that limit negative freedom. Socialists often wonder whether tolerating freedom of association cloaks oppression that occurs behind closed doors. The personal is political, they often say. Socialists frequently deny that human interests can harmonize without revolution. Peace arises from displacing privilege, whether that privilege concerns race, sex, or class.

Conservatisms are adaptations to local, stable social environments and resist many (though not all) ecological developments. Conservatives can miss beneficial social changes.

Socialism is by nature disruptive. It pursues quick social change but often loses steam. Most people want continuity and well-established social mores to ease their life choices.

Liberalism stands between conservatism and socialism. It pushes for toleration and the expansion of the circle of moral concern. But it does not dismiss conservative hierarchies as unjust. Nor does it pursue revolution. Liberals prefer piecemeal reform. Liberalism welcomes discoveries but pauses to consider their merits. Liberals also embrace diversity and disagreement and stress the upsides of these phenomena.

Liberalism Has Adapted

To understand liberalism's current predicament, we must consider how it has adapted to previous challenges. In telling this story, I find it helpful to imagine political ideologies as social organisms competing for energy by using different strategies. When they find food, ideologies grow into unique political and economic institutions.

Conservatism is the homegrown organism. It suits current conditions but struggles to adapt to ecological changes. Socialism is an invader organism: it replaces competitors and reconstructs the local ecosystem. Liberalism neither submits to ecological constraints nor drains stable social forms. It adapts to stress. Conservatism is more robust during periods of low change, whereas socialism gains a foothold during rapid change. But, in the long run, the adaptive ideology fares best. That is why liberalism remains globally dominant. It is flexible.

Liberalism has adapted to social change time and again. Classical liberalism—limited-government liberalism—almost died in the early twentieth century. The forces of late-nineteenth-century socialism and continental conservatism squeezed it from the left and the right. Liberalism adapted by pursuing a symbiotic relationship with socialism. Together, they birthed progressivism.

Progressives embrace liberty, equality, toleration, and harmony. But socialism influences them too, leading them to stress robust egalitarian principles and to view private social hierarchies with grave suspicion. Progressives were once more optimistic, but today they can become discouraged about the prospects for social unity. At its zenith, the progressive hybrid resisted illiberal socialism. It sprouted into the policy programs of FDR and LBJ and won World War II, destroying fascism and making communism the global runner-up.

The progressive movement ran into difficulties, especially in preserving economic dynamism and growth, so liberalism adapted by mitosis. Some liberals forged alliances with conservatism, and together they birthed the conservatism of Reagan and Thatcher. Anglophone conservatism, often called fusionism, stresses individual liberty and downplays equality.

Fusionists were tolerant in some respects but often opposed the expansion of moral concern. Some fusionists opposed the Civil Rights Act, resisted second-wave feminism, and opposed the LGBT movement. They stressed the harmony of interests in the market but were skeptical about the prospects of democratic self-government to establish consensus.

The genius of liberalism was simultaneous mitosis and symbiosis. It combined with socialism and then with conservatism and pitted the hybrids against one another. By doing so, liberalism undergirded international political contests for half a century and whittled communism down to nothing. Until 2015, dual symbiosis made liberalism seem invulnerable.

In sum, liberalism can evolve to withstand these new religious ideologies.

But Liberalism Is Dying

Here's the trouble. The liberal symbiotes repress human impulses, from tribalism and bloodlust to other more understandable tendencies, such as fear of change. Liberalism must creatively contain these forces. To do so successfully, liberalism must continuously adopt new forms. For the mitosis strategy may have reached its end. We can see this by monitoring the symbiotes: they are dying.

Progressives resemble socialists in all respects except endorsing the planned economy. They have grown less tolerant and more skeptical that liberal societies can harmonize human interests. Meanwhile, conservatives have moved further away from liberty. They have grown hostile to freedom of movement and trade; some have grown hostile to the people who need those freedoms most. Conservatives disdain equality ever more intensely. They see toleration as illusory in societies with influential progressive movements.

We live in a world of burgeoning ideological opposition. The liberal core that smoothed out ideological conflict decays. Shorn of liberalism, Right and Left undermine reconciling institutions. Their agreement on this matter is driven partly by those who enjoy political conflict. Both sides express deep antipathy toward liberals who tell them to make peace: "We want to fight. Go away."

Liberals discredit their peacemaking intentions owing to their mild-to-moderate hostility toward religion. The liberal suspicion of established religion was baked in from the start. But the anticlericalism of continental liberalism was far from universal. The sexual revolution changed this. Communities of religious conservatives changed too slowly for the revolutionaries. Today sex and gender are the chief battlefields that lie between conservatism, liberalism, and socialism. Conservatism preserves traditional sexual mores, socialism demands that these mores collapse, and liberals are once more stuck between the two.

The First Adaptation: A Liberal Alliance

Twenty-first-century liberalism must adapt to these conditions. This section and the next describe how that might look.

First, liberals must recover an appreciation for their values. We must honor liberty, equality, toleration, and harmony all at once. Left-liberals must tolerate religion. They should recognize reasonable disagreement over sex and gender. Right-liberals must defend high-functioning democratic institutions. They must also protect immigrants.

Second, liberals must recognize how much we share: in particular, the institutions of individual and group rights, democratic governance, markets, and social safety nets. Liberals must recall their shared beliefs despite their disagreements about whether safety nets should grow and whether markets require extensive regulation.

Liberals once had the luxury of ignoring their shared commitments because liberalism formed the backdrop of Western political life. But liberalism is no longer the stage. We cannot take liberal assumptions for granted. Liberals must downplay their differences and preserve liberal democratic welfare-state capitalism.

Democratic publics seem to embrace liberal institutions. They have made peace between liberalism's two wings. We face more significant threats from anti-liberal elites in other nations, China perhaps most of all. But liberalism is also at risk in its natural home—the United States.

Third, liberals must engage in honest self-examination. Liberalism all too often functions as an ideology that marginalizes nonliberal citizens. Left-liberals dislike traditional people of faith, and right-liberals have failed to acknowledge racial and gender inequalities and protect immigrants' rights. True liberalism is radically tolerant. Liberals must be peacemakers.

Consider the struggle between the LGBT community and conservative religious communities. Liberals must take a "both-and" approach to inclusivity. We must treasure diversity in racial, sexual, and gender characteristics and in religious and political worldviews. We must apply the principle of toleration to competing political ideologies. And we must guard against liberalism's temptation toward sectarianism.

We need a self-critical and tolerant liberalism that welcomes the formation of broad political coalitions. In particular, we need a liberalism that welcomes collaboration between the liberal Right and Left. To adapt to the twenty-first century, liberals must support one another to keep liberal institutions afloat. The symbiotes are not dead yet—they could recover.

The fusionist Right requires an intellectual and spiritual renewal that reforges alliances between libertarians and traditional people of faith. Opposition to communism once united these groups. Many fusionists supported the War on Terror for similar reasons, but that did not work out well—to put it mildly. Fusionists will have to uncover a sound basis for unity.

Progressives must recover the values of the 1960s. Yes, push for social equality. But remember freedom of speech, religious liberty, and open-mindedness. The left-liberal sometimes forgets to hope for reconciliation between groups with diverse and incompatible values. Many left-liberals have turned inward, chastising themselves for their inelible bigotries. Progressives will have to move away from both their tendency to overstress the flaws in Western societies and their tendency to give in to helplessness about improving our social condition.

Left-liberalism seldom resists the anti-liberal left, and right-liberals often miss the threat of the anti-liberal right. Both sides of liberalism must reject doctrines that divide the world into *us* versus *them*. But we must, at the same time, address anti-liberals by following the example of earlier generations. We must cultivate intellectual patience and take anti-liberals seriously.

The Second Adaptation: Radical Federalism

The rebirth of religious anti-liberalisms suggests that millions of people want to live within a sacred political order. Communities of faith will demand protection from political, economic, and cultural threats. They should not have to pay the steep social prices that some religious groups pay, such as the Amish or the Haredi.

The anti-liberal has a point. Liberal orders often create a culture that threatens the integrity of religious communities. Liberal orders generate constant temptations toward secular individualism. To protect these communities as well as liberal order, liberals need a new strategy. They must tolerate religious micro-polities, such as charter cities.

The Monastic Republic of Mount Athos has enough political autonomy to flourish. If liberal orders allow varied micro-polities, faith communities could organize and protect themselves. With spiritual needs met, these micro-polities could tolerate liberal order in return.

But my strategy requires concessions.

The right-liberal must accept that markets can endanger local religious communities—say, through material temptations. Liberal orders must protect these communities from some market forces. That could involve regulation. Liberal governments may have to insulate these communities from drugs and pornography, and they may even have to protect them from the egalitarian culture of liberal elites. Liberal order must reduce economic threats. Faith communities may require protection from the need to make risky financial investments.

The left-liberal must also awaken. Elite liberal culture and the welfare state also threaten local religious communities. Left-liberals often see opposition to the sexual revolution as oppression, so they may refuse to protect communities with hierarchical forms of life. These communities may indeed contain some oppression, but left-liberals must tolerate some risk of oppression to neutralize the threat of anti-liberalisms.

How Liberalism Survives

Here, then, is how liberalism adapts. Liberals must both unite to protect liberal order and concede some political independence to nonliberal communities of faith. Consider an analogy with the early American colonists. England allowed religious communities to emigrate and form their own polities, which reduced religious conflict and allowed diversity to flourish. Today we no longer have a geographical frontier. Nevertheless, liberal states can create a new frontier. For instance (as I have mentioned), they might allow charter cities: these institutions already exist and could expand.

Anti-liberals will insist that liberal order cannot accommodate these communities because liberalism is necessarily the enemy of these communities. The anti-liberal thus pits communities of faith against liberal order. But the genius of liberal order is its capacity to adapt and avoid stasis. Liberalism once co-opted socialist insights. It then co-opted conservative insights. Now it can incorporate the wisdom of religious anti-liberals.

My book critiques anti-liberalism, but this Epilogue describes how anti-liberals can thrive. What, then, is my agenda? To resist and perhaps forestall new global religious and political conflicts. That is what it means to be a liberal: to pursue the ever-present possibility of peace.

> How very good and pleasant it is when kindred live together in unity! It is like the precious oil on the head, running down upon the beard, on the beard of Aaron, running down over the collar of his robes. It is like the dew of Hermon, which falls on the mountains of Zion. For there the LORD ordained his blessing, life forevermore. (Ps. 133 NRSV).

ACKNOWLEDGMENTS

I can hardly believe that well over one hundred people helped me with this book. The story is a long one. In some respects, I have worked on religious anti-liberalism for twenty years.

My interests reach back to 2003. I was an undergraduate at Washington University in St. Louis, a new Christian, and I was attempting to develop my political commitments in light of my new faith. I had countless discussions with many friends and philosophy graduate students and faculty at St. Louis University. Outside St. Louis, two philosophers shaped my thinking on these issues the most: Edward Feser and Roderick Long.

Starting in graduate school, my interest in Christian anti-liberalism hibernated, only to reawaken in 2017 when I reconsidered my Protestantism. That process would end with my conversion to Eastern Orthodoxy in 2019. I studied Catholic anti-liberalism as part of that process because I felt it affected the truth of Catholicism. Many people helped me think these matters through, including Tim Pawl, Sherif Girgis, Halit Yerlikan, Jayson Franklin, Rob Koons, Zac Gochenour, Christopher Fleming, Alex Salter, Matthew Baddorf, Phil Swenson, Daniel McCarthy, Jonathan Jacobs, Omar Fakhri, David-Heith-Stade, Eleonore Stump, Lara Buchak, Megan Fritts, Liz Jackson, Brandon Warmke, Craig Warmke, Terence Cuneo, Rico Vitz, Stephen Carson, Erick Ybarra, Kevin Gutzman, Jeremiah Carey, Kenny Boyce, Steve Rieske, Erik Herrmann, Jerry Walls, Fr. James Dominic Rooney, Fr. Silviu Bunta, Fr. John Konkle, Chris Tomaszweski, and so many others.

In 2018, I began to track the integralist movement and its ideas. I discussed these issues at length with Halit Yerlikan, who may have more passion for these issues than I do. I thank him for our shared denominational adventure.

During this time, I also met Thomas Pink, with whom I discussed many of these matters in detail. Tom helped me understand the key Catholic teachings, which helped me better understand Christianity itself. I thank him for sharing his time and improving my thinking.

In 2019, I started blogging about my research. I gave up blogging in 2021 as I realized social media had made it irrelevant. But for a year or so, I shared my blog posts on Twitter, which led me to interact with most of the leading integralist thinkers. These included not only Pink, but Fr. Edmund Waldstein, Fr. Thomas Crean, Adrian Vermeule, Sohrab Ahmari, Chad Pecknold, Patrick Smith, Gladden Pappin, as well as a number of others, including many anonymous Twitter accounts. I also learned much from Twitter interactions with Jordan Perkins, Jason Blakely, James Patterson, Thomas Howes, Micah Schwartzman, Anna Su, Xavier Foccroulle-Ménard, Stephanie Slade, Jacob T. Levy, Yoram Hazony, Rinku Matthew, Joe Ro, Víctor Muñiz-Fraticelli, Aaron Ross Powell, Jason Kuznicki, Eric Schliesser, Jason Byas, Greg Sargent, Shikha Sood Dalmia, Gene Callahan, Paul Crider, Rachel Ferguson, Oliver Traldi, Shal Marriott, Rick Garnett, Sam Gregg, Dylan Pahman, Bill McCormick, Bryan McGraw, John Symons, Michael Tolhurst, Adam Gurri, James Wood, Robert Bork III, Timothy Trotner, Michael Cousineau, Fr. Bill Dailey, Joshua Cohen, Joshua Reagan, Will Wilkinson, Brandon Turner, and the Byzantine Scotist. I learned a great deal from those discussions in 2019 and 2020, as I did from my extensive and ongoing conversations with John Thrasher, Ryan Muldoon, and Chad Van Schoelandt, and at BGSU, Brandon Warmke, Rishi Joshi, and Jeff Carroll.

Will Combs became an almost constant source of feedback. We have discussed many philosophical issues together, from which I learned much. I hope to learn from him for many years to come.

My inquiry became far more practical and focused in 2020 when David McBride, my future editor at Oxford University Press, decided to commission a book on the new Catholic illiberalism. David asked my friend Jacob T. Levy who should write it. Jacob recommended me. David then invited me to submit a proposal, I did, and the referees were enthusiastic. The book went under contract. In 2020 I began my research in earnest. I devoted most of my free research time to strange and obscure readings (my favorite kind). I wrote the manuscript in 2021, refined it in 2022, and finished it in 2023.

That process involved even more people, at least two hundred. I asked many people for help. They gave me readings, listened to my talks, and read the papers that became book chapters. Others read the whole book and provided extensive comments. People had so much energy to help me think through these issues, and I am grateful to them.

Those individuals include, Elizabeth Anderson, Alex Motchoulski, Joseph Porter, Chris Tollefsen, John Finnis, Peter Vanderschraaf, Peter de Marneffe, Sam Schmitt, Matthew Brown, Alfredo Watkins, Chris Eberle, Mark Murphy,

Dan Moller, Jennifer Frey, Molly McGrath, Mark Koyama, Shane Courtland, David Dagan, Liz Bruenig, Ross Douthat, Pete Wehner, Michael Sitman, Michael Wear, Geoff Kabaservice, Greg Robson, and Damon Linker.

I am enormously grateful to Michael Hollerich and David Gordon for extensive comments and detailed conversations about church history.

Dozens of people gave me comments on a particular chapter and, in some cases, radically improved it. That list includes, also in no particular order, Julian Müller, Liana Reyes, Dailbor Rohac, Paul Dragos Aligica, Scott King, Jennifer Brick Murtazashvili, Jason Canon, Shadi Hamid, Enzo Rossi, Andrew Goodhart, Peter Levine, Marisa Hart, David Montgomery, Lucian Ashworth, David McCabe, Melissa Moschella, Ryan Anderson, Greg Wolcott, Matthew Sleat, Steven Wall, James Chappel, Eric Mack, Marilie Coetsee, Ryan Davis, Charles Barzun, Matthis Kramm, Henrik Dahlquist, Paul Billingham, Nevin Climenhaga, Giles Beauchamp, Hannah Norman-Krause, Toni Alimi, Cal Ledsham, Michael Barb, Luc Bovens, Geoff Sayre-McCord, Gabe McFadden, Bruce Caldwell, Jeff Pojanowski, Robert Audi, Paul Weithman, Fred D'Agostino, Daniel Philpott, Mary Keys, Adam MacLeod, Jerry Bradley, Fr. Vince Strand, Fr. Aaron Pidel, Brad Lewis, Toby Buckle, Adam Gjesdal, Fr. Peter Ryan, Stefan McDaniel, Michael Moreland, Patrick Lee, Kyle Blanchette, Dustin Crummett, Chris Suprenant, JP Messina, Jake Monaghan, Danny Shahar, Dan Hugger, Kevin Augustyn, Tom Sandurum, Gregory Reichberg, Nick Hadsell, Fabian Wendt, Baldwin Wong, Alex Phipps, Phillip Muñoz, Andrew Koppelman, Agnes Tam, Brian Buckley, Aaron James, Austin Sarat, Julia O'Donnell, Gabriel Sanchez, Samuel Zeitlin, Sam Morkal-Williams, Joseph Gregory, Joseph Duda, Kayla Fox, Nathan Ballantyne, Tyson Cain, and Cole James. BGSU graduate students Will Lugar and Grady Stuckman went above and beyond what anyone could expect in terms of feedback.

I am also grateful to Alex Schaefer for lengthy discussions on the stability chapter. It would have far more weaknesses without his wisdom.

I asked several scholars who specialize in Islam and Confucianism for feedback on Chapter 7. I was so fortunate to receive it. I'm grateful to Stephen Angle, Joseph Chan, Tongdong Bai, Baldwin Wong, Sungmoon Kim, and Karl Adam for help with Confucian thought. I'm grateful to Mustafa Akyol, Benjamin Peterson, Usama Husan, Andrew March, David Johnston, and a few others for help with Islamic thought.

I am grateful to those who organized my book manuscript workshops, including Sherif Girgis at Notre Dame, Delaney Thull at UNC Chapel Hill and Duke University, as well as Kori Hosnell and Geoff Sayre-McCord, Kaveh Pourvand at University of Arizona and David Schmidtz for the support of the Freedom Center, Madelyn Hastings, Stewart Roberts, and Brad Jackson helped organize a manuscript workshop with the Institute for Humane Studies, Nevin

Climenhaga at Australia Catholic University, Dan Jacobson at the University of Colorado, David Corey, Matthew Anderson, and Mark Tooley at Baylor in Washington, Ben Klutsey at the Mercatus Center, and Kris Mauren at the Acton Institute.

I received invaluable support from the Snider Foundation, the Charles Koch Foundation, the Institute for Humane Studies, the Mercatus Center, the Witherspoon Institute, and the Acton Institute. Each organization helped me improve the book.

Ben Klutsey and Garrett Brown provided critical help at various points, especially in connecting me with my masterful copyeditor, Corrie Schwab. And I am grateful to Jeff Pojanowski and Rick Garnett for connecting me with Athanasius Sirilla, who helped so much with my citations.

Most importantly, I thank my wife, Alicia. Her unique combination of strength, empathy, and wisdom is uncommon for ordinary mortals. Without her support, this book would not exist.

REFERENCES

Abou El Fadl, Khaled. 2002. *The Place of Tolerance in Islam*. Boston: Beacon.

Abou El Fadl, Khaled. 2013. "The Shari'ah." In *The Oxford Handbook of Islam and Politics*, edited by John L. Esposito and Emad El-Din Shahin, 7–26. Oxford: Oxford University Press.

Achen, Christopher, and Larry Bartels. 2016. *Democracy for Realists: Why Elections Do Not Produce Responsive Government*. Princeton, NJ: Princeton University Press.

Adams, Robert Merrihew. 1999. *Finite and Infinite Goods: A Framework for Ethics*. New York: Oxford University Press.

Ahmari, Sohrab. 2019. "Against David French–ism." *First Things*, May 29, 2019.

Ahmari, Sohrab. 2021. *The Unbroken Thread: Discovering the Wisdom of Tradition in an Age of Chaos*. New York: Convergent.

Akhavi, Shahrough. 2013. "Sayyid Qutb." In *The Oxford Handbook of Islam and Politics*, edited by John L. Esposito and Emad El-Din Shahin, 159–68. Oxford: Oxford University Press.

Akyol, Mustafa. 2022. "The Liberty Divide in Islam." *Law and Liberty*, August 30, 2022. https://lawliberty.org/the-liberty-divide-in-islam.

Al-Najjar, Abd al-Majid. 1988. *The Human Vicegerency: Between Reason and the People* (Khilafat al-insan bayna al-'aql wa-l-nas). Beirut: Dar al-Gharb al-Islami.

Alcoff, Linda. 2021. "Critical Philosophy of Race." *Stanford Encyclopedia of Philosophy*. Last modified September 15, 2021. https://plato.stanford.edu/entries/critical-phil-race/.

Anderson, Elizabeth. 2010. *The Imperative of Integration*. Princeton, NJ: Princeton University Press.

Anderson, Ryan T., and Robert P. George. 2019. "The Baby and the Bathwater." *National Affairs*, Fall 2019. https://www.nationalaffairs.com/publications/detail/the-baby-and-the-bathwater.

Angle, Stephen C. 2009. *Sagehood: The Contemporary Significance of Neo-Confucian Philosophy*. Oxford: Oxford University Press.

Angle, Stephen C. 2012. *Contemporary Confucian Political Philosophy*. Malden, MA: Polity.

Angle, Stephen C. 2014. "Review of a Confucian Constitutional Order: How China's Ancient Past Can Shape Its Political Future." *Philosophy East and West* 64 (2): 502–6.

Angle, Stephen C. 2018. "*Tian* as Cosmos in Zhu Xi's Neo-Confucianism." *Dao* 17: 169–85.

Aquinas, Thomas. 1920. *The Summa Theologiæ of St. Thomas Aquinas*. Translated by the Fathers of the English Dominican Province. 2nd ed. Available at New Advent, http://www.newadvent.org/summa/index.html.

Aquinas, Thomas. 1951. *Super Evangelium S. Ioannis lectura*. Translated by Raffaele Cai OP. Rome: Marietti.

Aquinas, Thomas. 2002. *Aquinas: Political Writings*. Translated by R. W. Dyson. Cambridge: Cambridge University Press.

Aquinas, Thomas. 2014. *De regno: On Kingship*. Translated by Gerald B. Phelan. Bismarck, ND: Divine Providence.

Aquinas, Thomas. 2018. *Opera Omina*. [Complete works]. Leonine edition.

Aristotle. 2000. *The Nicomachean Ethics*. Translated by Terence Irwin. Boston: Hackett.

Aristotle. 2021. *"Alexander": On Aristotle Metaphysics 12*. Translated by Fred D. Miller Jr. Ancient Commentators on Aristotle. New York: Bloomsbury.

Augustine. 1993. *On Free Choice of the Will*. Translated by Thomas Williams. Indianapolis, IN: Hackett.

Augustine. 1998. *The City of God against the Pagans*. Translated by R. W. Dyson. New York: Cambridge University Press.

Augustine. 2009. *Confessions*. Translated by Henry Chadwick. New York: Oxford University Press.

Austin, Greta. "Canon Law in the Long Tenth Century, 900–1050." In *The Cambridge History of Medieval Canon Law*, edited by Anders Winroth and John C. Wei, 46–61. New York: Cambridge University Press, 2022.

Bai, Tongdong. 2013. "An Old Mandate for a New State: On Jiang Qing's Political Confucianism." In *A Confucian Constitutional Order: How China's Ancient Past Can Shape Its Political Future*, edited by Daniel Bell and Ruiping Fan, 113–28. Princeton, NJ: Princeton University Press.

Bai, Tongdong. 2014. "Early Confucian Political Philosophy and Its Contemporary Relevance." In *Dao Companion to Classical Confucian Philosophy*, edited by Vincent Shen, 335–61. Dordrecht: Springer.

Bai, Tongdong. 2020. *Against Political Equality*. Princeton, NJ: Princeton University Press.

Barrett, Jacob, and Gerald Gaus. 2020. "Laws, Norms, and Public Justification: The Limits of Law as an Instrument of Reform." In *Public Reason and Courts*, edited by S. A. Langvatn, M. Kumm, and W. Sadurski, 201–28. New York: Cambrige University Press.

Barry, Brian. 1990. "How Not to Defend Liberal Institutions." *British Journal of Political Science* 20: 1–14.

Basu, Kaushik. 2000. *Prelude to Political Economy*. Oxford: Oxford University Press.

Bayle, Pierre. 2005. *A Philosophical Commentary on These Words of the Gospel, Luke 14:23, "Compel Them to Come in, That My House May Be Full."* Edited by John Kilcullen and Chandran Kukathas. Natural Law and Englightenment Classics. Indianapolis, IN: Liberty Fund.

Bell, Daniel. 2013. "Introduction." In *A Confucian Constitutional Order: How China's Ancient Past Can Shape Its Political Future*, edited by Daniel Bell and Ruiping Fan, 1–26. Princeton, NJ: Princeton University Press.

Bell, Daniel. 2015. *The China Model: Political Meritocracy and the Limits of Democracy*. Princeton, NJ: Princeton University Press.

Bellarmine, Robert. 2012. *On Temporal and Spiritual Authority*. Translated by Stefania Tutino. Indianapolis, IN: Liberty Fund.

Bellarmine, Robert. 2016. *De Controversiis: On the Roman Pontiff*. Vol 2. Translated by Ryan Grant. Mediatrix Press.

Benedict XVI. 2005. "Address of His Holiness Benedict XVI to the Roman Curia Offering Them His Christmas Greetings." Holy See website, December 22, 2005. https://www.vatican.va/content/benedict-xvi/en/speeches/2005/december/documents/hf_ben_xvi_spe_200 51222_roman-curia.html.

Berman, Harold J. 1983. *Law and Revolution: The Formation of the Western Legal Tradition*. Cambridge, MA: Harvard University Press.

Bettcher, Talia. 2014. "Feminist Perspectives on Trans Issues." *Stanford Encyclopedia of Philosophy Archive*. Last modified January 8, 2014. https://plato.stanford.edu/archives/spr2014/entries/feminism-trans/#TraGenTro.

Bévenot, Maurice. 1954. "Thesis and Hypothesis." *Theological Studies* 15: 440–46.

Bicchieri, Cristina. 2006. *The Grammar of Society*. New York: Cambridge University Press.

Bicchieri, Cristina. 2016. *Norms in the Wild: How to Diagnose, Measure, and Change Social Norms*. New York: Oxford University Press.

Bjørnskov, Christian. 2006. "Determinants of Generalized Trust: A Cross-Country Comparison." *Public Choice* 130: 1–21.

Bjørnskov, Christian. 2011. "Combating Corruption: On the Interplay between Institutional Quality and Social Trust." *Journal of Law and Economics* 54: 135–59.

Boettke, Peter. 1993. *Why Perestroika Failed*. New York: Routledge.

Boniface VIII. 1296. *Clericis laicos*. Available from the Internet Medieval Sourcebook (Fordham University), https://sourcebooks.fordham.edu/source/b8-clericos.asp.

Boniface VIII. (1301) 1921. "Ausculta fili." In *Les registres de Boniface VIII: Recueil des bulles de ce pape publiées ou analysées d'après les manuscrits originaux des archives du Vatican*, edited by Georges Digard 4:327–36. Paris: E. de Boccard. Available at the Internet Archive, https://archive.org/details/AuscultaFiliDigard.

Boniface VIII. 1302. *Unam sanctam*. November 18, 1302. Available at New Advent, http://www.newadvent.org/library/docs_bo08us.htm.

Bossuet, Jacques-Benigne. 2018. *The History of the Variations of the Protestant Churches*. Farmington Hills, MI: Gale Ecco.

Bouwsma, William J. 1990. "The Venetian Interdict and the Problem of Order." In *A Usable Past: Essays in European Cultural History*, edited by William J. Bouwsma, 97–111. Berkeley: University of California Press.

Bowlin, John. 1997. "Augustine on Justifying Coercion." *Annual of the Society of Christian Ethics* 17: 49–70.

Breyer, Stephen G., Richard B. Stewart, Cass R. Sunstein, Adrian Vermeule, and Michael Herz. 2017. *Administrative Law and Regulatory Policy: Problems, Text, and Cases*. 8th ed. Philadelphia, PA: Wolters Kluwer.

Brown, Daniel. 2017. *A New Introduction to Islam*. 3rd ed. Hoboken, NJ: Wiley Blackwell.

Brungardt, John. 2020. "The Question of Catholic Integralism: An Internet Genealogy." *The Josias*, June 15, 2021. https:// thejosias.com/2020/05/29/the-question-of-catholic-integralism-an-internet-genealogy/.

Buchanan, Allen, and Alexander Motchoulski. 2022. "An Ideological Explanation of How Revolutions Occur and Why They Result in New Oppressive Orders." University of Arizona.

Buchanan, James. M. 2003. "Public Choice: Politics without Romance." *Policy* 19: 13–18.

Burke, Edmund. 2003. *Reflections on the Revolution in France*. New Haven, CT: Yale University Press.

Burns, J. H., and Thomas Izbicki, eds. 1997. *Conciliarism and Papalism*. New York: Cambridge University Press.

Calleja, Ricardo. 2020. "Imperare Aude! Dare to Command! (Part I)." *Ius & Iustitium*, October 20, 2020. https://iusetiustitium.com/imperare-aude-dare-to-command/.

Campos, Andre Santos. 2019. "Francisco Suarez's Conception of the Social Contract." *Revista portuguesa de filosofia* 75 (2): 1195–218.

Carmella, Angela. 2007. "John Courtney Murray, S.J. (1904–1967) Commentary." In *The Teaching of Modern Roman Catholicism*, edited by John Witte Jr. and Frank S. Alexander, 181–210. New York: Columbia University Press.

Carney, Timothy. 2020. *Alienated America: Why Some Places Thrive While Others Collapse*. New York: Harpers.

Casey, Conor. 2023. "Defending the Prince: Vermeule on the Political Executive, Administrative State, and Common Good." Unpublished manuscript, April 10, 2023.

Catholic Church. 1997. *Catechism of the Catholic Church: Revised in Accordance with the Official Latin Text Promulgated by Pope John Paul II*. Vatican City: Libreria Editrice Vaticana.

Cessario OP, Romanus. 2018. "Non Possumus." Review of *Kidnapped by the Vatican? The Unpublished Memoirs of Edgardo Mortara*, by Vittorio Messori. *First Things*, February 2018. https://www.firstthings.com/article/2018/02/non-possumus.

Chambers, Clare. 2008. *Sex, Culture, and Justice: The Limits of Choice*. University Park: Pennsylvania State University Press.

Chan, Joseph. 2013. "On the Legitimacy of Confucian Constitutionalism." In *A Confucian Constitutional Order: How China's Ancient Past Can Shape Its Political Future*, edited by Daniel Bell and Ruiping Fan, 99–112. Princeton, NJ: Princeton University Press.

Chan, Joseph. 2014. *Confucian Perfectionism: A Political Philosophy for Modern Times*. Princeton, NJ: Princeton University Press.

Chappel, James. 2018. *Catholic Modern: The Challenge of Totalitarianism and the Remaking of the Church*. Cambridge, MA: Harvard University Press.

Charles River Editors. 2018. *Mount Athos: The History of the Greek Mountain and the Center of Eastern Orthodox Monasticism*. Charles River Editors, CreateSpace.

Chartier, Gary. 2014. *Anarchy and Legal Order: Law and Politics for a Stateless Society*. New York: Cambridge University Press.

Clarke, Peter D. 2022. "Excommunication and Interdict." In *The Cambridge History of Medieval Canon Law*, edited by Anders Winroth and John C. Wei, 550–69. New York: Cambridge University Press.

Cohen, Robert, and Reginald Zelnik, eds. 2002. *The Free Speech Movement: Reflections on Berkeley in the 1960s*. Berkeley: University of California Press.

Colander, David, and Roland Kupers. 2014. *Complexity and the Art of Public Policy: Solving Society's Problems from the Bottom Up*. Princeton, NJ: Princeton University Press.

Coleman, Janet. 1983. "Medieval Discussions of Property: Ratio and Dominium according to John of Paris and Marsilius of Padua." *History of Political Thought* 4: 209–28.

Connelly, John. 2012. *From Enemy to Brother: The Revolution in Catholic Teaching on the Jews, 1933–1965*. Cambridge, MA: Harvard University Press.

Continetti, Matthew. 2022. *The Right: The Hundred-Year War for American Conservatism*. New York: Basic Books.

Corecco, Eugenio. *The Theology of Canon Law: A Methodological Question*. Translated by F. Turvasi. Pittsburgh, PA: Duquesne University Press, 1992.

Craycraft, Kenneth R., Jr. 1999. *The American Myth of Religious Freedom*. Washington, DC: Spence.

Crean, Thomas, and Alan Fimister. 2020. *Integralism: A Manual of Political Philosophy*. Havertown, PA: Eurospan.

Cuneo, Terence. 2005. "Can a Natural Law Theorist Justify Religious Civil Liberties?" In *Religion in the Liberal Polity*, edited by Terence Cuneo, 108–30. Notre Dame, IN: University of Notre Dame Press.

Dagger, Richard. 2000. "Membership, Fair Play, and Political Obligation." *Political Studies* 48: 104–17.

Dagger, Richard. 2021. "Political Obligation." *Stanford Encyclopedia of Philosophy*. Last modified March 15, 2021. https://plato.stanford.edu/entries/political-obligation/.

Dauphinais, Michael, Barry David, and Matthew Levering, eds. 2007. *Aquinas the Augustinian*. Washington, DC: Catholic University of America Press.

Davis, Leo Donald. 1990. *The First Seven Ecumenical Councils (325–787): Their History and Theology*. Collegeville, MN: Liturgical Press.

de Maistre, Joseph. 1994. *Considerations on France*. Translated by Richard A. Lebrun. New York: Cambridge University Press.

Deneen, Patrick. 2018. *Why Liberalism Failed*. New Haven, CT: Yale University Press.

Deneen, Patrick. 2020. "Replace the Elite." *First Things*, March 2020. https://www.firstthings.com/article/2020/03/replace-the-elite.

de Vitoria, Francisco. 1991. *Vitoria: Political Writings*. Cambridge: Cambridge University Press.

Dreher, Rod. 2021. "What Do Integralists Want?" *The American Conservative*, October 27, 2021. https://www.theamericanconservative.com/what-do-integralists-want-reactionary-catholicism/.

Duffy, Eamon. 2014. *Saints and Sinners: A History of the Popes*. New Haven, CT: Yale University Press.

Dunbar, Robin. 2022. *How Religion Evolved and Why It Endures*. New York: Oxford University Press.

Einhard and Notker the Stammerer. 1969. *Two LIves of Charlemagne*. Translated by Lewis Thorpe. London: Penguin.

El Amine, Louhna. 2015. *Classical Confucian Political Thought: A New Interpretation*. Princeton, NJ: Princeton University Press.

Elstein, David. 2010. "Why Early Confucianism Cannot Generate Democracy." *Dao* 9: 427–43.

Erasmus, Desiderius. 2008. *Paraphrase on the Gospel of Matthew*. Vol. 45. Translated by Dean Simpson. Toronto: University of Toronto Press.

Errázuriz Mackenna, Carlos José. 2009. *Justice in the Church: A Fundamental Theory of Canon Law*. Translated by Jean Gray and Michael Dunnigan. English ed. Montreal: Wilson and Lafleur.

Esposito, John L., and Emad El-Din Shahin. 2013. Introduction to *The Oxford Handbook of Islam and Politics*, edited by John L. Esposito and Emad El-Din Shahin, 1–4. Oxford: Oxford University Press.

Ferguson, Adam. 1782. *An Essay on the History of Civil Society*. London: T. Cadell.

Finke, Roger, and Rodney Stark. 2005. *The Churching of America, 1776–2005: Winners and Losers in Our Religious Economy*. New Brunswick, NJ: Rutgers University Press.

Finnis, John. 1991. *Moral Absolutes: Tradition, Revision, and Truth*. Washington, DC: Catholic University of America Press.

Finnis, John. 1998. *Aquinas: Moral, Political, and Legal Theory*. New York: Oxford University Press.

Finnis, John. 2006. "Religion and State: Some Main Issues and Sources." *American Journal of Jurisprudence* 51: 107–30.

Finnis, John. 2011. *Natural Law and Natural Rights*. New York: Oxford University Press.

Finnis, John. 2013. "Reflections and Responses." In *Reason, Morality, and Law: The Philosophy of John Finnis*, edited by John Keown and Robert P. George, 459–584. Oxford: Oxford University Press.

First Vatican Council. 1870. *Pastor aeternus: Vatican I's Dogmatic Constitution on the Church of Christ*. Available at Eternal Word Television Network, https://www.ewtn.com/catholicism/teachings/vatican-is-dogmatic-constitution-pastor-aeternus-on-the-church-of-christ-243.

Freeden, Michael. 2003. *Ideology: A Very Short Introduction*. New York: Oxford University Press.

Freeden, Michael. 2015. *Liberalism: A Very Short Introduction*. Oxford: Oxford University Press.

Fudge, Thomas. 2013. *The Trial of Jan Hus: Medieval Heresy and Criminal Procedure*. New York: Oxford University Press.

Gaus, Gerald. 2003. *Contemporary Theories of Liberalism: Public Reason as a Post-Enlightenment Project*. Minneapolis: Sage.

Gaus, Gerald. 2009. "The Moral Foundations of Liberal Neutrality." In *Debates in Contemporary Political Philosophy*, edited by Thomas Christiano and John Christman, 81–98. New York: Oxford University Press.

Gaus, Gerald. 2011. *The Order of Public Reason*. New York: Cambridge University Press.

Gaus, Gerald. 2016. *The Tyranny of the Ideal*. Princeton, NJ: Princeton University Press.

Gaus, Gerald. 2021. *The Open Society and Its Complexities*. New York: Oxford University Press.

Gaus, Gerald, Shane Courtland, and David Schmidtz. 2018. "Liberalism." *Stanford Encyclopedia of Philosophy*. Last modified January 22, 2018. https://plato.stanford.edu/entries/liberalism/.

Gaus, Gerald, and John Thrasher. 2021. *On Philosophy, Politics, and Economics*. 2nd ed. Princeton, NJ: Princeton University Press.

Gelasius I. 1868. "Famuli vestrae pietatis." In *Epistolae Romanorum pontificum*, Vol. 1, edited by Andrew Thiel, 349–58. Braunsberg, East Prussia: Eduard Peter.

George, Robert P. 1988. "Recent Criticism of Natural Law Theory." *University of Chicago Law Review* 55: 1371–429.

George, Robert P. 1995. *Making Men Moral: Civil Liberties and Public Morality*. New York: Oxford University Press.

George, Robert P. 1999. *In Defense of Natural Law*. New York: Oxford University Press.

Ghannouchi, Rached. 2020. *Public Freedoms in the Islamic State*. Translated by David Johnston. New Haven, CT: Yale University Press.

Giudice, Vitorrio Del. 1970. *Nozioni Di Diritto Canonico*. 12th ed. Milan: Giuffré. <[translator?]>

Green, David. 2013. "1242: France Burns All Known Copies of the Talmud." *Haaretz*, June 17, 2013. https://www.haaretz.com/jewish/.premium-1242-all-talmuds-in-paris-are-burned-1.5281064.

Greer, Steven, and Tiong Piow Lim. 1998. "Confucianism: Natural Law Chinese Style?" *Ratio Juris* 11 (1): 80–89.

Gregory I. 2012. *The Book of the Pastoral Rule and Selected Epistles of Pope St. Gregory I (The Great)*. Translated by Rev. James Barmby D.D. Edited by Paul A. Boer Sr. Self-published, CreateSpace.

Grimes, Marcia. 2017. "Procedural Fairness and Political Trust." In *Handbook of Political Trust*, edited by Sonja Zmerli and Tom W. G. van der Meer, 256–69. Northampton, MA: Edward Elgar.

Grisez, Germain. 1978. "Against Consequentialism." *American Journal of Jurisprudence* 23: 21–72.

Grisez, Germain. 1983. *Christian Moral Principles*. Vol. 1 of *The Way of the Lord Jesus*. Chicago: Franciscan Herald Press. Available at http://www.twotlj.org/G-1-V-1.html.

Grisez, Germain. 1992. *Living a Christian Life*. Vol. 2 of *The Way of the Lord Jesus*. Quincy, IL: Franciscan Press. Available at http://www.twotlj.org/G-2-V-2.html.

Grisez, Germain. 2008. *Clerical and Consecrated Life and Service*. Draft manuscript. Vol. 4 of *The Way of the Lord Jesus*. Available at http://www.twotlj.org/G-4-V-4.html.

Grisez, Germain, Joseph Boyle, and John Finnis. 1987. "Practical Principles, Moral Truth, and Ultimate Ends." *American Journal of Jurisprudence* 32: 99–151.

Guminski, Arnold. [2015]. "An Examination of Thomas Pink's Theory of the Doctrine Concerning Religious Freedom in *Dignitatis humanae*." Available from *Academia*, https://www.academia.edu/19523482/An_Examination_of_Thomas_Pinks_Theory_of_the_Doctrine_concerning_Religious_Freedom_in_Dignitatis_Humanae.

Guminski, Arnold, and Brian W. Harrison. 2013. *Religious Freedom: Did Vatican II Contradict Traditional Catholic Doctrine? A Debate*. South Bend, IN: St. Augustine's Press.

Haberkern, Phillip. 2017. "Martin Luther's Understanding of Earlier Reformers." *Oxford Research Encyclopedia of Religion*, March 29, 2017. Oxford: Oxford University Press. https://oxfordre.com/religion/view/10.1093/acrefore/9780199340378.001.0001/acrefore-9780199340378-e-281.

Habib, Allen. 2022. "Promises." *Stanford Encyclopedia of Philosophy*. Last modified June 17, 2022. https://plato.stanford.edu/entries/promises/.

Hale, John. 2021. "Intellectuals Confront Right-Liberalism." *Irish Rover: Upholding the Catholic Character of the University of Notre Dame*, April 28, 2021. https://irishrover.net/2021/04/intellectuals-confront-right-liberalism/.

Halperin, Morton, Joe Siegle, and Michael Weinstein. 2010. *The Democracy Advantage: How Democracies Promote Prosperity and Peace*. New York: Routledge.

Hamid, Shadi. 2016. *Islamic Exceptionalism: How the Struggle over Islam Is Reshaping the World*. New York: St. Martin's Press.

Havel, Václav. 2015. "The Power of the Powerless." In *The Power of the Powerless: Citizens against the State in Central-Eastern Europe*, edited by John Keane, 23–96. London: Routledge.

Hayek, F. A. 1945. "The Use of Knowledge in Society." *American Economic Review* 35: 519–30.

Hayek, F. A. 2007. *The Road to Serfdom*. Definitive ed. Edited by Bruce Caldwell. London: Routledge.

Hendrickson, Aldean. n.d. "The Use of Witnesses in Investigations of Matrimonial Invalidity: Their Selection and Examination, and the Evaluation of Their Testimony." Accessed December 13, 2022. Available from Academia, https://www.academia.edu/1475350.

Herrin, Judith. 2021. *The Formation of Christendom*. Princeton, NJ: Princeton University Press.

Hittinger, Russell. 1988. *A Critique of the New Natural Law Theory*. South Bend, IN: University of Notre Dame Press.

Hittinger, Russell. 2007a. "Introduction to Modern Catholicism." In *The Teachings of Modern Roman Catholicism*, edited by John Witte Jr. and Frank S. Alexander, 1–38. New York: Columbia University Press.

Hittinger, Russell. 2007b. "Pope Leo XIII (1810–1903) Commentary." In *The Teachings of Modern Roman Catholicism*, edited by John Witte Jr. and Frank S. Alexander, 39–75. New York: Columbia University Press.

Hittinger, Russell. 2008. "The Coherence of the Four Basic Principles of Catholic Social Doctrine: An Interpretation." In *Pursuing the Common Good*, edited by Margaret S. Archer and Pierpaolo Donati, vol. 14, *Pontifical Academy of St. Thomas Aquinas*, 75–123.

Hobbes, Thomas. 1994. *Leviathan*. Edited by Edwin Curley. Indianapolis, IN: Hackett.

Hohfeld, Wesley. 1919. *Fundamental Legal Conceptions*. New Haven, CT: Yale University Press.

Holmes, Stephen. 1993. *The Anatomy of Antiliberalism*. Cambridge, MA: Harvard University Press.

Hume, David. 1777. *Essays Moral, Political, Literary*. Indianapolis, IN: Liberty Fund.

Hume, David. 1978. *A Treatise of Human Nature*. Oxford: Clarendon.

Humfress, Caroline. "The Early Church." In *The Cambridge History of Medieval Canon Law*, edited by Anders Winroth and John C. Wei, 11–31. New York: Cambridge University Press, 2022.

Innocent III. 1954. "Novit ille." In *Church and State through the Centuries: A Collection of Historical Documents with Commentaries*, edited by Sidney Z. Ehler and John B. Morrall, 69. London: Burns and Oats.

Jensen, Steven J. 2015. *Knowing the Natural Law: From Precepts and Inclinations to Deriving Oughts*. Washington, DC: Catholic University of America Press.

Jiang Qing. 2013. *A Confucian Constitutional Order: How China's Ancient Past Can Shape Its Political Future*. Princeton, NJ: Princeton University Press.

John Paul II. 1995. "Address of His Holiness John Paul II: United Nations Headquarters." Holy See website, October 5, 1995. https://www.vatican.va/content/john-paul-ii/en/speeches/1995/october/documents/hf_jp-ii_spe_05101995_address-to-uno.html.

Johnson, Noel, and Mark Koyama. 2019. *Persecution and Toleration: The Long Road to Religious Freedom*. New York: Cambridge University Press.

Jone, Heribet. 1946. *Moral Theology*. Edited by Urban Adelman. Westminster, MD: The Newman Bookshop.

Jones, Andrew Willard. 2017. *Before Church and State: A Study of Social Order in the Sacramental Kingdom of St. Louis IX*. Steubenville, OH: Emmaus Academic.

Jones, Andrew Willard. 2020. "What States Can't Do." *New Polity* (blog), July 24, 2020. https://newpolity.com/blog/what-states-cant-do.

Joy, John. n.d. "The Theological Note of Integralism." Dialogos Institute. Accessed April 28, 2018. http://dialogos-institute.org/blog/wordpress/the-theological-note-of-integralism/.

Joy, John. 2017. *On the Ordinary and Extraordinary Magisterium from Joseph Kleutgen to the Second Vatican Council*. Münster: Aschendorff Verlag.

Kertzer, David. 2001. *The Popes against the Jews: The Vatican's Role in the Rise of Modern Anti-Semitism*. New York: Vintage Books.

Kertzer, David. 2015. *The Pope and Mussolini: The Secret History of Pius XI and the Rise of Fascism in Europe*. New York: Random House.

Kertzer, David. 2018. "The Doctored 'Memoir' of a Jewish Boy Kidnapped by the Vatican." *The Atlantic*, April 15, 2018. https://www.theatlantic.com/international/archive/2018/04/edgardo-mortara-doctored-memoir/554948/.

Kéry, Lotte. "Criminal Law." In *The Cambridge History of Medieval Canon Law*, edited by Anders Winroth and John C. Wei, 495–510. New York: Cambridge University Press, 2022.

Keys, Mary. 2008. *Aquinas, Aristotle, and the Promise of the Common Good*. Cambridge: Cambridge University Press.

Kim, Sungmoon. 2016. *Public Reason Confucianism*. Cambridge: Cambridge University Press.

Kim, Sungmoon. 2018. *Democracy after Virtue: Toward Pragmatic Confucian Democracy*. New York: Oxford University Press.

Kirk, Russell. 1985. *The Conservative Mind: From Burke to Eliot*. Washington, DC: Regnery.

Kukathas, Chandran. 2007. *The Liberal Archipelago*. New York: Oxford University Press.

Lamont, John R. T. 2015. "Catholic Teaching on Religion and the State." *New Blackfriars* 96: 674–98.

Lefebvre, Marcel. 1994. *They Have Uncrowned Him*. Saint Marys, KS: Angelus.

Leijonhufvud, Axel. 2007. "The Individual, the Market, and the Industrial Division of Labor." *Capitalism and Society* 2: 2. https://doi.org/10.2202/1932-0213.1025.

Lenin, V. I. 2013. *What Is to Be Done?* Manfield Centre, CT: Martino Fine Books.

Leo I. 2015. *The Letters and Sermons of Saint Leo the Great*. Translated by Philip Schaff. Grand Rapids, MI: Aeterna Press.

Leo XIII. 1885. *Immortale Dei: Encyclical of Pope Leo XIII on the Christian Constitution of States*. November 1, 1885. Available at the Holy See website, http://www.vatican.va/content/leo-xiii/en/encyclicals/documents/hf_l-xiii_enc_01111885_immortale-dei.html.

Leo XIII. 1892. "Au milieu des sollicitudes: Encyclical of Pope Leo XIII on the Church and State in France." February 16, 1892. Available at the Holy See website, https://www.vatican.va/content/leo-xiii/en/encyclicals/documents/hf_l-xiii_enc_16021892_au-milieu-des-sollicitudes.html.

Leo XIII. 1895. *Longinqua: Encyclical of Pope Leo XIII on Catholicism in the United States*. January 6, 1985. Available at the Holy See website, https://www.vatican.va/content/leo-xiii/en/encyclicals/documents/hf_l-xiii_enc_06011895_longinqua.html.

Leo XIII. 1900. *Tametsi futura prospicientibus: Encyclical of Pope Leo XIII on Jesus Christ the Redeemer*. November 1, 1900. Available at the Holy See website, http://www.vatican.va/content/leo-xiii/en/encyclicals/documents/hf_l-xiii_enc_01111900_tametsi-futura-prospicientibus.html.

Leo XIII. 2014. *The Leonine Encyclicals: 1878–1902*. McPherson, KS: Agnus Dei.

Levy, Jacob T. 2015. *Rationalism, Pluralism, and Freedom*. New York: Oxford University Press.

Levy, Jacob T. 2016. "There Is No Such Thing as Ideal Theory." *Social Philosophy and Policy* 33: 312–33.

Li, Chenyang. 2015. *The Confucian Philosophy of Harmony*. New York: Routledge.

Lisska, Anthony. 1998. *Aquinas's Theory of Natural Law: An Analytic Reconstruction*. Oxford: Clarendon.

Lloyd, S. A. 2009. *Morality in the Philosophy of Thomas Hobbes: Cases in the Law of Nature*. Cambridge: Cambridge University Press.

Locke, John. (1690) 1988. *Two Treatises of Government*. Cambridge: Cambridge University Press.

Locke, John. 2009. *A Letter Concerning Toleration: Humbly Submitted*. New York: Classic Books America.

Luther, Martin. (1520) 2016. *To the Christian Nobility of the German Nation*. Translated by James M. Estes. Minneapolis: Fortress.

MacDougald, Park. 2020. "A Catholic Debate over Liberalism." *City Journal*, Winter 2020. https://www.city-journal.org/catholic-debate-over-liberalism.

Machado, Diamantino P. 1991. *The Structure of Portuguese Society: The Failure of Fascism*. Westport, CT: Praeger.

Mancini, Mark. 2023. "Against Common-Good Constitutionalism." Unpublished manuscript, January 1, 2023.

Manela, Tony. 2019. "Gratitude." *Stanford Encyclopedia of Philosophy*. Last modified August 26, 2019. https://plato.stanford.edu/entries/gratitude/.

March, Andrew. 2019. *The Caliphate of Man: Popular Sovereignty in Modern Islamic Thought*. Cambridge, MA: Harvard University Press.

Maritain, Jacques. 2012. *Man and the State*. Washington, DC: Catholic University of America Press.

Maritain, Jacques. 2020. *The Primacy of the Spiritual: On the Things That Are Not Caesar's*. Providence, RI: Cluny Media.

Marsilius. 2005. *The Defender of the Peace*. Translated by Annabel Brett. New York: Cambridge University Press.

Martinich, A. P. 1999. *Hobbes: A Biography*. Cambridge: Cambridge University Press.

Marx, Karl, and Friedrich Engels. 2011. *Capital: A Critique of Political Economy*. Vol. 1. Translated by Samuel Moore and Edward Aveling. Mineola, NY: Dover.

Mawdudi, Abul A'la. 1955. *The Islamic Law and Constitution*. Chicago, IL: Kazi Publications.

May, Simon. 2021. "Why Strict Compliance?" In *Oxford Studies in Political Philosophy*, Vol. 7, edited by David Sobel, Peter Vallentyne, and Steven Wall, 227–64. New York: Oxford University Press.

McCabe, David. 2010. *Modus Vivendi Liberalism: Theory and Practice*. New York: Cambridge University Press.

McCord-Adams, Marilyn. 1989. *William Ockham*. South Bend, IN: University of Notre Dame Press.

McCormick, William. 2022. *The Christian Structure of Politics: On the De Regno of Thomas Aquinas*. Washington, DC: The Catholic University of America Press.

McGrath, Alister. 2020. *Iustitia Dei: A History of the Christian Doctrine of Justification*. New York: Cambridge University Press.

McNabb, Tyler Dalton. 2022. *God and Political Theory*. New York: Cambridge University Press.

Mencius. 2005. *Mencius*. Translated by D. C. Lau. London: Penguin.

Ménard, Xavier Foccroulle, and Anna Su. 2022. "Liberalism, Catholic Integralism, and the Question of Religious Freedom." *BYU Law Review* 47: 1171–219.

Messori, Vittorio. 2017. *Kidnapped by the Vatican? The Unpublished Memoirs of Edgardo Mortara*. San Francisco: Ignatius Press.

Mill, John Stuart. 1963. *Collected Works*. Edited by J. M. Robson. Toronto: Toronto University Press.

Mill, John Stuart. 1978. *On Liberty*. Edited by Elizabeth Rapaport. Indianapolis, IN: Hackett.

Miller, Clarence H., ed. 2012. *Controversies: Clarifications Concerning the Censures Published in Paris in the Name of the Parisian Faculty of Theology*. Toronto: University of Toronto Press.

Miller, Robert T. 2018. "Integralism and Catholic Doctrine." *Public Discourse*, July 15, 2018. https://www.thepublicdiscourse.com/2018/07/22105/.

Moore, G. E. 2004. *Principia Ethica*. Mineola, NY: Dover.

Moussalli, Ahmad. 2013. "Hassan Al-Banna." In *The Oxford Handbook of Islam and Politics*, edited by John L. Esposito and Emad El-Din Shahin, 129–43. Oxford: Oxford University Press.

Mueller, Dennis C. 2003. *Public Choice III*. Cambridge: Cambridge University Press.

Müller, Jan-Werner. 2003. *A Dangerous Mind: Carl Schmitt in Post-War European Thought*. New Haven, CT: Yale University Press.

Müller, Wolfgang P. 2022a. "The Reinvention of Canon Law in the High Middle Ages." In *The Cambridge History of Medieval Canon Law*, edited by Anders Winroth and John C. Wei, 79–95. New York: Cambridge University Press.

Müller, Wolfgang P. 2022b. "Procedures and Courts." In *The Cambridge History of Medieval Canon Law*, edited by Anders Winroth and John C. Wei, 327–41. New York: Cambridge University Press, 2022.

Murphy, Mark. 2001. *Natural Law and Practical Rationality*. Cambridge: Cambridge University Press.

Murphy, Mark. 2005. "The Common Good." *Review of Metaphysics* 59: 133–64.

Murphy, Mark. 2019. "The Natural Law Tradition in Ethics." *Stanford Encyclopedia of Philosophy*. Last modified May 26, 2019. http://plato.stanford.edu/entries/natural-law-ethics/.

Murray, John Courtney. 1993. *Religious Liberty: Catholic Struggles with Pluralism*. Edited by J. Leon Hooper. Louisville, KY: Westminster/John Knox.

Murray, John Courtney. 2005. *We Hold These Truths: Catholic Reflections on the American Proposition*. Lanham, MD: Rowman & Littlefield.

Nash, George H. 2022. "Conservatism and Its Current Discontents: A Survey and a Modest Proposal." *Religion and Liberty* 35, https://www.acton.org/religion-liberty/volume-35-number-1-2/conservatism-and-its-current-discontents-survey-and-modest.

Nelson, Eric. 2019. *The Theology of Liberalism: Political Philosophy and the Justice of God*. Cambridge, MA: Harvard University Press.

Newman, John Henry. 1994. *An Essay on the Development of Christian Doctrine*. South Bend, IN: University of Notre Dame Press.

Newman, John Henry. 2015. *A Letter Addressed to the Duke of Norfolk: On Occasion of Mr. Gladstone's Recent Expostulation*. New York: Aeterna Press.

Nozick, Robert. 1969. "Coercion." In *Philosophy, Science, and Method: Essays in Honor of Ernest Nagel*, edited by Sidney Morgenbesser, Patrick Suppes and Morton White, 440–72. New York: St. Martin's Press.

Nussbaum, Martha C. 2018. *The Monarchy of Fear: A Philosopher Looks at Our Political Crisis*. New York: Simon & Schuster.

Nutt, Roger, and Michael De Salvo. 2021. "The Debate over *Dignitatis Humanae* at Vatican II: The Contribution of Charles Cardinal Journet." *The Thomist: A Speculative Quarterly Review* 85: 175–226.

Nye, Joseph. 2004. *Soft Power: The Means to Success in World Politics*. New York: Hatchette.

Oakley, Francis. 2003. *The Conciliarist Tradition: Constitutionalism in the Catholic Church 1300–1870*. Oxford: Oxford University Press.

Oakley, Francis. 2010. *Empty Bottles of Gentilism: Kingship and the Divine in Late Antiquity and the Early Middle Ages (to 1050)*. New Haven, CT: Yale University Press.

Oakley, Francis. 2012. *The Mortgage of the Past: Reshaping the Ancient Political Inheritance (1050–1300)*. New Haven, CT: Yale University Press.

Ostrom, Elinor. 1990. *Governing the Commons: The Evolution of Institutions for Collective Action*. Cambridge: Cambridge University Press.

O'Sullivan, John. 2008. *The President, the Pope, and the Prime Minister: Three Who Changed the World*. Washington, DC: Regnery.

Ott, Ludwig, and Robert Fastiggi. 2018. *Fundamentals of Catholic Dogma*. Oil City, PA: Baronius.

Pabst, Adrian. 2021. *Postliberal Politics: The Coming Era of Renewal*. Cambridge: Polity.

Paldiel, Mordecai. 2006. *Churches and the Holocaust: Unholy Teaching, Good Samaritans, and Reconciliation*. Jersey City, NJ: KTAV Publishing House.

Patterson, James M. 2020. "After Republican Virtue." *Law & Liberty*, April 22, 2020. https://law liberty.org/after-republican-virtue/.

Paul VI. 1965a. *Dignitatis humanae*. Vatican City: Libreria Editrice Vaticana.

Paul VI. 1964. *Lumen Gentium: Dogmatic Constitution on the Church*. November 21, 1964. Available at the Holy See website, https://www.vatican.va/archive/hist_councils/ii_vatican_coun cil/documents/vat-ii_const_19641121_lumen-gentium_en.html

Pennington, Kenneth. 2014. "Gratian and the Jews." *Bull of Medieval Canon Law* 31: 1–15.

Perreau-Saussine, Emile. 2012. *Catholicism and Democracy: An Essay in the History of Political Thought*. Translated by Richard Rex. Princeton, NJ: Princeton University Press.

Piekalkiewicz, Jaroslaw, and Alfred Wayne Penn. 1995. *Politics of Ideocracy*. Albany: State University of New York Press.

Pines, Yuri. 2012. "Review of a Confucian Constitutional Order." *China Review International* 19 (4): 608–14.

Pink, Thomas. 2012a. "Conscience and Coercion: Vatican II's Teaching on Religious Freedom Changed Policy, Not Doctrine." *First Things*, August 2012. https://www.firstthings.com/arti cle/2012/08/conscience-and-coercion.

Pink, Thomas. 2012b. "What Is the Catholic Doctrine of Religious Liberty?" June 15, 2012. Available from Academia, https://www.academia.edu/639061/What_is_the_Catholic_do ctrine_of_religious_liberty.

Pink, Thomas. 2013a. "The Interpretation of *Dignitatis humanae*: A Reply to Martin Rhonheimer." *Nova et Vetera* 11: 77–121.

Pink, Thomas. 2013b. "The Right to Religious Liberty and the Coercion of Belief: A Note on *Dignitatis humanae*." In *Reason, Morality, and Law: The Philosophy of John Finnis*, edited by John Keown and Robert P. George, 427–42. Oxford: Oxford University Press.

Pink, Thomas. 2015a. Introduction to *Selections from Three Works: A Treatise on Laws and God the Lawgiver*, by Francisco Suárez, ix–xviii. Indianapolis, IN: Liberty Fund.

Pink, Thomas. 2015b. "Jacques Maritain and the Problem of Church and State." *The Thomist: A Speculative Quarterly Review* 79: 1–42.

Pink, Thomas. 2016. "Suárez and Bellarmine on the Church as Coercive Lawgiver." In *Legge e natura: I dibattiti teologici e giuridici fra XV e XVII secolo*, edited by Riccardo Saccenti and Cinzia Sulas, 287–332. Arricia, Italy: Aracne Editrice.

Pink, Thomas. 2017. "*Dignitatis humanae*: Continuity after Leo XIII." In *"Dignitatis humanae" Colloquium: Dialogos Institute Collection*, Vol. 1, edited by Dialogos Institute, 105–46. Self-published, CreateSpace.

Pink, Thomas. 2018a. "In Defence of Catholic Integralism." *Public Discourse*, August 12, 2018. www.thepublicdiscourse.com/2018/08/39362/.

Pink, Thomas. 2018b. "Suarez on Authority as Coercive Teacher." *Quaestio* 18: 451–86.

Pink, Thomas. 2018c. "Vatican II and the Crisis in the Theology of Baptism: Part III." *The Josias*, November 8, 2018. https://thejosias.com/2018/11/08/vatican-ii-and-crisis-in-the-theol ogy-of-baptism-part-iii/#more-3953.

Pink, Thomas. [2019]. "John Finnis's Alternative History of Trent." Available from Academia, https://www.academia.edu/37861294/John_Finniss_Alternative_History_of_Trent.

Pink, Thomas. 2020. "Integralism, Political Philosophy, and the State." *Public Discourse*, May 9, 2020. https://www.thepublicdiscourse.com/2020/05/63226/.

Pink, Thomas. 2021. "On *Dignitatis humanae*: A Reply to Thomas Storck." *The Josias*, October 28, 2021. https://www.thejosias.com/2021/10/28/on-dignitatis-humanae-a-reply-to-thomas-storck/.

Pius IX. 1864. *Quanta cura: Condemning Current Errors*. Available at Papal Encyclicals Online, https://www.papalencyclicals.net/pius09/p9quanta.htm.

Pius X. 1907. *Pascendi Dominici gregis: Encyclical of Pope Pius X on the Doctrines of the Modernists*. September 8, 1907. Available at the Holy See website, https://www.vatican.va/content/pius-x/en/encyclicals/documents/hf_p-x_enc_19070908_pascendi-dominici-gregis.html.

Pius XI. 1925. *Quas primas: Encyclical of Pope Pius XI on the Feast of Christ the King*. December 11, 1925. Available at the Holy See website, https://www.vatican.va/content/pius-xi/en/ency clicals/documents/hf_p-xi_enc_11121925_quas-primas.html.

Pius XII. 1943. *Mystici corporis Christi: Encyclical of Pope Pius XII on the Mystical Body of Christ*. June 29, 1943. Available at the Holy See website, https://www.vatican.va/content/pius-xii/ en/encyclicals/documents/hf_p-xii_enc_29061943_mystici-corporis-christi.html.

Plato. 1997. *Plato: Complete Works*. Edited by John M. Cooper. Indianapolis, IN: Hackett.

Pojanowski, Jeffrey A., and Kevin C. Walsh. 2022. "Recovering Classical Legal Constitutionalism: A Critique of Professor Vermeule's New Theory." *Notre Dame Law Review* 98: 403–63.

Popowski, Mark D. 2011. *The Rise and Fall of "Triumph": The History of a Radical Roman Catholic Magazine, 1966–1976*. Lanham, MD: Lexington Books.

Porter, Jean. 2016. *Justice as a Virtue: A Thomistic Perspective*. Grand Rapids, MI: Eerdmans.

Portmore, Douglas W. 2011. *Commonsense Consequentialism: Wherein Morality Meets Rationality*. Oxford: Oxford University Press.

Posner, Eric A., and Adrian Vermeule. 2011. *The Executive Unbound: After the Madisonian Republic*. Oxford: Oxford University Press.

Posner, Eric A., and Adrian Vermeule. 2017. "Demystifying Schmitt." In *The Oxford Handbook of Carl Schmitt*, edited by Jens Meierhenrich and Oliver Simons, 612–26. New York: Oxford University Press.

Qutb, Sayyid. 1953. *Social Justice in Islam*. Translated by John B. Hardie and Hamid Algar. Oneonta, NY: Islamic Publications International.

Qutb, Sayyid. 2020. *Milestones*. Houston, TX: Islamic Book Service.

Rady, Martyn. 2017. *The Habsburg Empire: A Very Short Introduction*. Oxford: Oxford University Press.

Ramos Ascensão, Leão. 1943. *O Integralismo lusitano*. Lisbon: Edições Gama.

Raz, Joseph. 1986. *The Morality of Freedom*. Oxford: Oxford University Press.

Real Cuesta, Javier. 1985. *El carlismo vasco, 1876–1900*. Guatemalan City: Siglo Veintiuno.

Reichberg, Gregory. 2020. "Scholastic Arguments for and against Religious Freedom." *The Thomist: A Speculative Quarterly Review* 84: 1–50.

Rémond, René. 2006. "Action Française." In *The Columbia History of Twentieth-Century French Thought*, edited by Lawrence D. Kritzman and Brian Reilly, 7–8. Translated by M. B. DeBevoise. New York: Columbia University Press.

Rennie, Kriston R. *Medieval Canon Law*. Leeds: Arc Humanities Press, 2018.

Rhonheimer, Martin. 2011. "Benedict XVI's 'Hermeneutic of Reform' and Religious Freedom." *Nova et Vetera* 9 (4): 1029–54.

Rhonheimer, Martin. 2014. "*Dignitatis humanae*—Not a Mere Question of Church Policy: A Response to Thomas Pink." *Nova et Vetera* 12: 445–70.

Roach, Christopher. 2021. "The Salazar Option: To Survive Today's Leftist Threat We Need to Be Committed to Acquiring and Using Power in the Service of Counterrevolution." *American Greatness*, August 1, 2021. https://amgreatness.com/2021/08/01/the-salazar-option/.

Rousseau, Jean-Jacques. 2018. *Rousseau: "The Social Contract" and Other Later Political Writings*. Edited by Victor Gourevitch. Cambridge Texts in the History of Political Thought. 2nd ed. New York: Cambridge University Press.

Russell, Norman. 2004. *The Doctrine of Deification in the Greek Patristic Tradition*. New York: Oxford University Press.

Russell, Norman. 2009. *Fellow Workers with God: Orthodox Thinking on Theosis*. Yonkers, NY: St. Vladimir's Seminary Press.

Ryan, John, and Moorhouse Millar. 1930. *The State and the Church*. London: Macmillan.

Salvany, Felix Sarda Y. 1993. *Liberalism Is a Sin*. Translated by Conde B. Pallen. Charlotte, NC: Tan Books.

Schatz, Klaus. 1996. *Papal Primacy: From Its Origins to the Present*. Translated by John Otto and Linda M. Maloney. Collegeville, MN: Liturgical Press.

Schelling, Thomas C. 2006. *Micromotives and Macrobehavior*. New York: W. W. Norton.

Schmitt, Carl. 1996. *Roman Catholicism and Political Form*. Translated by G. L. Lumen. Westport, CT: Greenwood.

Schmitt, Carl. 2006. *Political Theology: Four Chapters on the Concept of Sovereignty*. Translated by George Schwab. Chicago: University of Chicago.

Schmitt, Carl. 2007. *The Concept of the Political*. Exp. ed. Translated by George Schwab. Chicago: University of Chicago .

Schmitt, Carl. 2008. *Constitutional Theory*. Translated by Jeffrey Seitzer. Durham, NC: Duke University Press.

Schuessler, Jennifer. 2022. "Two Religious Conservatives and a Marxist Walk into a Journal." *New York Times*, March 22, 2022. https://www.nytimes.com/2022/03/22/arts/compact-magazine-conservatives-marxists.html.

Schumacher, John. 1962. "Integrism: A Study in XIXth Century Spanish Politico-Religious Thought." *Catholic Historical Review* 48: 343–64.

Schwartzman, Micah, and Jocelyn Wilson. 2019. "The Unreasonableness of Catholic Integralism." *San Diego Law Review* 56: 1039–68.

Shepard, William E. 2014. *Introducing Islam*. 2nd ed. New York: Routledge.

Shin, Doh Chull. 2012. *Confucianism and Democratization in East Asia*. Cambridge: Cambridge University Press.

Simmons, A. John. 1981. *Moral Principles and Political Obligations*. Princeton, NJ: Princeton University Press.

Simmons, A. John. 1994. *The Lockean Theory of Rights*. Princeton, NJ: Princeton University Press.

Simmons, A. John. 2008. "Political Obligation and Authority." In *The Blackwell Guide to Social and Political Philosophy*, edited by Robert L. Simon, 17–37. Blackwell Philosophy Guides. Malden, MA: Blackwell.

Spade, Paul Vincent, and Claude Panaccio. 2019. "William of Ockham." *Stanford Encyclopedia of Philosophy*. Last modified March 5, 2019. https://plato.stanford.edu/entries/ockham/.

Stephen, James Fitzjames. 2018. *Liberty, Equality, Fraternity*. Indianapolis, IN: Liberty Fund.

Stern, Robert. 2020. "Martin Luther." *Stanford Encyclopedia of Philosophy*. Last modified July 22, 2020. https://plato.stanford.edu/entries/luther/.

Stilz, Anna. 2009. *Liberal Loyalty: Freedom, Obligation, and the State*. Princeton, NJ: Princeton University Press.

Storck, Thomas. 2021. "Recent Discussions of Religious Liberty." *The Josias*, June 3, 2021. https://thejosias.com/2021/06/03/recent-discussions-of-religious-liberty/.

Stump, Eleonore. 2005. *Aquinas*. London: Routledge.

Stump, Eleonore. 2018. *Atonement*. Oxford Studies in Analytic Theology. Oxford: Oxford University Press.

Stump, Eleonore, and Norman Kretzmann. 1991. "Being and Goodness." In *Being and Goodness: The Concept of the Good in Metaphysics and Philosophical Theology*, edited by Scott MacDonald, 98–128. Ithaca, NY: Cornell University Press.

Suárez, Francisco. (1612) 2015. *Selections from Three Works: A Treatise on Laws and God the Lawgiver*. Edited by Thomas Pink. Indianapolis, IN: Liberty Fund.

Sullivan, Francis. 2002. *Magisterium: Teaching Authority in the Catholic Church*. Eugene, OR: Wipf and Stock.

Sweet, William. 2020. "Jacques Maritain and the Universal Declaration of Human Rights." In *Christianity and Global Law*, edited by Rafael Domingo and John Witte Jr., 158–77. Law and Religion. London: Routledge.

Tamimi, Azzam S. 2001. *Rachid Ghannouchi: A Democrat within Islamism*. Religion and Global Politics. Oxford: Oxford University Press.

Tan, Sor-hoon. 2004. *Confucian Democracy: A Deweyan Reconstruction*. Albany: State University of New York Press.

Tanner, Norman, ed. 1990. *Decrees of the Ecumenical Councils*. Washington, DC: Georgetown University Press.

Tapie, Matthew. 2018. "Spiritualis Uterus: The Question of Forced Baptism and Thomas Aquinas's Defense of Jewish Parental Rights." *Bulletin of Medieval Canon Law* 35: 289–329.

Tellenbach, Gerd. 1991. *Church, State, and Christian Society at the Time of the Investiture Contest*. Translated by R. F. Bennett. Hoboken, NJ: Blackwell.

Tetlock, Philip. 2006. *Expert Political Judgment: How Good Is It? How Can We Know?* Princeton, NJ: Princeton University Press.

Tetlock, Philip, and Daniel Gardner. 2016. *Superforecasting: The Art and Science of Prediction*. New York: Broadway Books.

Toft, Monica Duffy, Daniel Philpott, and Timothy Samuel Shah. 2011. *God's Century: Resurgent Religion and Global Politics*. New York: W. W. Norton.

Tollefsen, Christopher. 2008. "The New Natural Law Theory." *Lyceum* 10 (1): 1–18.

Tornau, Christian. 2019. "Saint Augustine." *Stanford Encyclopedia of Philosophy*. Last edited September 25, 2019. https://plato.stanford.edu/entries/augustine/.

Tosi, Justin, and Brandon Warmke. 2022. "Conservative Critiques." In *The Routledge Companion to Libertarianism*, edited by Matt Zwolinski and Benjamin Ferguson, 579–92. London: Routledge.

Thrasher, John, and Kevin Vallier. 2018. "Political Stability in the Open Society." *American Journal of Political Science* 62: 398–409.

Tullock, Gordon. 1993. *Rent Seeking*. Northhampton, MA: Edward Elgar.

Tullock, Gordon. 2005. *The Rent Seeking Society*. Vol. 5 of *The Selected Works of Gordon Tullock*. Indianapolis, IN: Liberty Fund.

Ullmann, Walter. 1981. *Gelasius I. (492–496): Das Papsttum an der Wende der Spätantike zum Mittelalter*. Stuttgart: Anton Hiersemann.

Vallier, Kevin. 2019. *Must Politics Be War?* New York: Oxford University Press.

Vallier, Kevin. 2020. *Trust in a Polarized Age*. New York: Oxford University Press.

Vallier, Kevin. 2021a. "The Fairness Argument against Catholic Integralism." *Law, Culture, and the Humanities*. Published ahead of print, October 29, 2021. https://doi.org/10.1177/174387 21211054187.

Vallier, Kevin. 2021b. "The National Conservative Movement Needs Liberalism to Save Its Soul." *The UnPopulist*, November 19, 2021. https://theunpopulist.substack.com/p/the-national-conservative-movement.

Vallier, Kevin. 2022. "Public Justification." *Stanford Encyclopedia of Philosophy*. Last modified December 2, 2022. http://plato.stanford.edu/entries/justification-public/.

van der Krogt, Christopher. 1992. "Catholic Fundamentalism or Catholic Integralism?" In *To Strive and Not to Yield: Essays in Honour of Colin Brown*, edited by James Veitch, 123–35. Wellington, New Zealand: Department of World Religions, Victoria University of Wellington.

van der Vossen, Bas. 2011a. "Associative Political Obligations." *Philosophy Compass* 6: 477–87.

van der Vossen, Bas. 2011b. "Associative Political Obligations: Their Potential." *Philosophy Compass* 6: 488–96.

Van Norden, Bryan W. 2007. *Virtue Ethics and Consequentialism in Early Chinese Philosophy*. Cambridge: Cambridge University Press.

Van Norden, Bryan W. 2011. *Introduction to Classical Chinese Philosophy*. Indianapolis, IN: Hackett.

Vere, Peter John. 1999. "A Canonical History of the Lefebvrite Schism." Master's thesis, Saint Paul University, Ontario. https://www.catholicculture.org/culture/library/view.cfm?recnum=1392.

Vermeule, Adrian. 2009. "Our Schmittian Administrative Law." *Harvard Law Review* 2009: 1095–149.

Vermeule, Adrian. 2017a. "The Ark of Tradition." Review of *Roman Catholicism and Political Form*, by Carl Schmitt. Russell Kirk Center for Cultural Renewal, November 19, 2017. https://kirkcenter.org/reviews/the-ark-of-tradition.

Vermeule, Adrian. 2017b. "The Catholic Constitution." *First Things*, August 11, 2017. https://www.firstthings.com/web-exclusives/2017/08/the-catholic-constitution.

Vermeule, Adrian. 2017c. "A Christian Strategy." *First Things*, November 2017. https://www.firstthings.com/article/2017/11/a-christian-strategy.

Vermeule, Adrian. 2017d. "Liturgy of Liberalism." *First Things*, January 2017. https://www.firstthings.com/article/2017/01/liturgy-of-liberalism.

Vermeule, Adrian. 2018a. "As Secular Liberalism Attacks the Church, Catholics Can't Afford to Be Nostalgic." *Catholic Herald*, January 5, 2018. https://catholicherald.co.uk/as-secular-liberalism-attacks-the-church-catholics-cant-afford-to-be-nostalgic/.

Vermeule, Adrian. 2018b. "Integration from Within." *American Affairs* 2 (1): 202–13.

Vermeule, Adrian. 2018c. "Liberalism's Fear." *The Josias*, May 9, 2018. https://thejosias.com/2018/05/09/liberalisms-fear/.

Vermeule, Adrian. 2018d. "Ralliement: Two Distinctions." *The Josias*, March 16, 2018. https://thejosias.com/2018/03/16/ralliement-two-distinctions/.

Vermeule, Adrian. 2019a. "All Human Conflict Is Ultimately Theological." *Church Life Journal*, July 26, 2019. https://churchlifejournal.nd.edu/articles/all-human-conflict-is-ultimately-theological.

Vermeule, Adrian. 2019b. "Liberalism and the Invisible Hand." *American Affairs* 3: 172–97.

Vermeule, Adrian. 2019c. "A Principle of Immigration Priority." *Mirror of Justice* (blog), July 20, 2019. https://mirrorofjustice.blogs.com/mirrorofjustice/2019/07/a-principle-of-immigration-priority-.html.

Vermeule, Adrian. 2020. "Beyond Originalism: The Dominant Conservative Philosophy for Interpreting the Constitution Has Served Its Purpose, and Scholars Ought to Develop a More Moral Framework." *The Atlantic*, March 31, 2020. https://www.theatlantic.com/ideas/archive/2020/03/common-good-constitutionalism/609037/.

Vermeule, Adrian. 2021. "'It Can't Happen'; or, the Poverty of Political Imagination." *Postliberal Order*, November 19, 2021. https://postliberalorder.substack.com/p/it-cant-happen-or-the-poverty-of.

Vermeule, Adrian. 2022a. *Common Good Constitutionalism*. Cambridge: Polity.

Vermeule, Adrian. 2022b. "The Instruments of the Law." *Postliberal Order*, Mary 12, 2022. https://postliberalorder.substack.com/p/the-instruments-of-the-law.

Waldron, Jeremy. 1993. *Liberal Rights: Collected Papers 1981–1991*. Cambridge: Cambridge University Press.

Waldron, Jeremy. 2010. "Locke: Toleration and the Rationality of Persecution." In *Justifying Toleration: Conceptual and Historical Perspectives*, edited by Susan Mendus, 61–86. Cambridge: Cambridge University Press.

Waldstein, Edmund. 2014. "Religious Liberty and Tradition I." *The Josias*, December 31, 2014. https://thejosias.com/2014/12/31/religious-liberty-and-tradition-i/.

Waldstein, Edmund. 2015. "The Good, the Highest Good, and the Common Good." *The Josias*, February 3, 2015. https://thejosias.com/2015/02/03/the-good-the-highest-good-and-the-common-good.

Waldstein, Edmund. 2016a. "Integralism and Gelasian Dyarchy." *The Josias*, March 3, 2016. https://thejosias.com/2016/03/03/integralism-and-gelasian-dyarchy/.

Waldstein, Edmund. 2016b. "Integralism in Three Sentences." *The Josias*, October 17, 2016. https://thejosias.com/2016/10/17/integralism-in-three-sentences/.

Waldstein, Edmund. 2018. "What Is Integralism Today?" *Church Life Journal: A Journal of the McGrath Institute for Church Life*, October 31, 2018. https://churchlifejournal.nd.edu/artic les/what-is-integralism-today/.

Walker, A. D. M. 1988. "Political Obligation and the Argument from Gratitude." *Philosophy and Public Affairs* 17 (3): 191–211.

Wall, Steven. 1998. *Liberalism, Perfectionism, and Restraint*. New York: Cambridge University Press.

Warren, David, and Christine Gilmore. 2014. "One Nation under God? Yusuf Al-Qaradawi's Changing Fiqh of Citizenship in the Light of the Islamic Legal Tradition." *Contemporary Islam* 8: 217–37.

Weaver, Richard. 2013. *Ideas Have Consequences*. Exp. ed. Chicago: University of Chicago Press.

Wellman, Christopher. 1997. "Associative Allegiances and Political Obligations." *Social Theory and Practice* 23: 181–204.

Wellman, Christopher. 2005. "Samaritanism and the Duty to Obey the Law." In *Is There a Duty to Obey the Law?*, edited by A. John Simmons and Christopher Wellman, 3–89. Cambridge: Cambridge University Press.

White, Joshua, and Niloufer Siddiqui. 2013. "Mawlana Mawdudi." In *The Oxford Handbook of Islam and Politics*, edited by John L. Esposito and Emad El-Din Shahin, 144–55. Oxford: Oxford University Press.

Winroth, Anders, and John C. Wei. "Medieval Canon Law: Introduction." In *The Cambridge History of Medieval Canon Law*, edited by John C. Wei and Anders Winroth, 1–8. New York: Cambridge, 2022.

Witcover, Jules. 2003. *Party of the People: A History of the Democrats*. New York: Random House.

Wolfe, Christopher. 2009. *Natural Law Liberalism*. New York: Cambridge University Press.

Wolterstorff, Nicholas. 2012. *Understanding Liberal Democracy*. Oxford: Oxford University Press, 2012.

Yao, Xinzhong. 2000. *An Introduction to Confucianism*. New York: Cambridge University Press.

Yu, Kam-por. 2010. "The Handling of Multiple Values in Confucian Ethics." In *Taking Confucian Ethics Seriously: Contemporary Theories and Applications*, edited by Kam-por Yu, Julia Tao, and Philip J. Ivanhoe, 27–51. Albany: State University of New York Press.

Zerofsky, Elisabeth. 2021. "How the American Right Fell in Love with Hungary." *New York Times*, October 19, 2021. https://www.nytimes.com/2021/10/19/magazine/viktor-orban-rod-dreher.html.

INDEX

For the benefit of digital users, indexed terms that span two pages (e.g., 52–53) may, on occasion, appear on only one of those pages.

Tables, figures, and boxes are indicated by *t*, *f*, and *b* following the page number